D1520467

HERMAN
DOOYEWEERD

HERMAN

DOOYEWEERD

Christian Philosopher of State and Civil Society

JONATHAN CHAPLIN

University of Notre Dame Press

Notre Dame, Indiana

Library of Congress Cataloging-in-Publication Data

Chaplin, Jonathan.
Herman Dooyeweerd : Christian philosopher of state and
civil society / Jonathan Chaplin.
    p. cm.
Includes bibliographical references (p.   ) and index.
ISBN-13: 978-0-268-02305-8 (cloth : alk. paper)
ISBN-10: 0-268-02305-0 (cloth : alk. paper)
1. Dooyeweerd, H. (Herman), 1894–1977—Political and social views.
2. State, The. 3. Civil society. 4. Political science—Philosophy.   I. Title.
JC259.D66C43   2010
320.092—dc22

2010024328

CONTENTS

Contents **vii**

ACKNOWLEDGMENTS

THE UNUSUALLY LONG GESTATION PERIOD THIS BOOK HAS undergone has meant that in writing it I have incurred more debts than I can possibly record here (or even remember). I am very grateful to Nicholas Wolterstorff, whose comments on the manuscript were most helpful in improving its flow (but who bears no responsibility for any of its remaining defects). I profited from the advice of an anonymous reviewer who rightly pressed me to try to make Dooyeweerd's thought as clear as possible to someone unfamiliar with his work. Readers in that category will be the judge of how well I have succeeded. Students at the Institute for Christian Studies, Adam Smith, Mike De Moor, and especially Murray Johnston, provided valuable assistance in the preparation of the manuscript. Chuck van Hof, senior editor at the University of Notre Dame Press, has been consistent in his encouragement and showed me far more patience than I deserved. I am also very grateful to his editorial and production colleagues at the Press for their meticulous and professional work on the text.

My work on Dooyeweerd's social and political thought began when I was a graduate student at the Institute for Christian Studies (ICS) in the early 1980s. Participating in Bernard Zylstra's reading group on the third volume of Dooyeweerd's *A New Critique of Theoretical Thought* was a remarkable privilege. There could have been no better introduction to Dooyeweerd's writings than Bernard's unique combination of meticulous, critical line-by-line analysis and wide-angled historical and cultural contextualization. He was one of only nine doctoral students supervised by Dooyeweerd himself. His untimely passing in 1986 deprived the academy of a foremost interpreter of Dooyeweerd.

Bernard's colleague Paul Marshall showed me how Dooyeweerd's political thought can not only speak insightfully to key issues in contemporary political theory but also inform and inspire responses to pressing practical issues of justice. Other ICS faculty from those years, especially Albert Wolters, Hendrik Hart, Calvin Seerveld, and George Vandervelde, were also formative in my appreciation of Dooyeweerd's philosophy and the distinctive stream of Protestant thought from which it emerged.

It was an honor to be the first holder of the Dooyeweerd Chair in Social and Political Philosophy at ICS from 2004 to 2006, a post established as a result of the vision and generosity of Magnus Verbrugge, Dooyeweerd's son-in-law. The opportunity afforded by that position was of great help in bringing the manuscript to completion. I much regret that Magnus did not live to see the book in print, but I hope his wife, Maria, and their family will receive it as a tribute to Magnus's lifelong commitment to honoring the remarkable legacy of Maria's father. I am also grateful to Maria for permission to use Magnus's portrait of Dooyeweerd on the front cover.

Over many years I have learned a great deal about Dooyeweerd's thought and its contemporary relevance from the writings of and from conversations with James Skillen (former president of the Center for Public Justice), who wrote the first doctoral thesis in English on Dooyeweerd's political thought. Conversations with John Hiemstra have been consistently instructive on the application of Dooyeweerd's ideas to public policy questions. The exemplary efforts of Gerald Vandezande (formerly of Citizens for Public Justice) to put the principle of "public justice" to practical work in the nitty-gritty of Canadian politics will always remain an inspiration. Even if he doesn't read every line of this book, I hope he at least enjoys the epilogue.

I have drawn on the work of many Dooyeweerd scholars in the Netherlands associated with the Vrije Universitieit van Amsterdam (now oddly renamed VU University Amsterdam) and the Association for Reformational Philosophy, including Bob Goudzwaard, Henk Geerstema, Henk Woldring, Govert Buijs, and Cees Klop. Sander Griffioen, especially, has not only taught me much about Dooyeweerd's social philosophy (and a bit about Chinese philosophy) but also become a valued friend and colleague. It has been a particular pleasure to explore ecumenical convergences between Neo-Calvinist and Catholic social thought with several North American scholars, especially Kenneth Grasso and Jeanne Heffernan Schindler. I remain grateful for scholarly guidance and advice in the early years of this project to John Morrell and Ernest Thorpe, my doctoral supervisors at the London School of Economics and Political Science, and to Anthony Black at Dundee University, a leading specialist on associational political theory.

Those of my former ICS graduate students on whom I inflicted Dooyeweerd's writings were more helpful to this project than they realized at the time. Formal conversations in class and less guarded ones in Einstein's pub in the basement of 229 College Street, Toronto, were, respectively, stimulating and usefully diverting. Thanks especially to Chris Bosch, Robert Brink, Peter Dale, Ken Dam, Mike De Moor, Brian Dijkema, Sam Gassanov, Sara Gerritsma, Dmytro Hys, Russ Kuykendall, Mark Miller, Peter Noteboom, Daniel Sem, Adam Smith, Shin Toyokawa, and Chris Miller, whose tragic passing in 2009 took a dear friend from many associated with ICS and cut short an extremely promising academic career.

Numerous other friends and past and present colleagues have in various ways—sometimes without knowing or even intending it— enriched my understanding of Dooyeweerd's social and political thought. I am especially grateful to Richard Russell, who first put Dooyeweerd's writings into my hands and explained their unique importance and so must shoulder some the blame for what I did with them. Alan and Elaine Storkey were early (and are continuing) role models in how to use them creatively. Thanks also to Doug Blomberg, Elaine Botha, Paul Brink, Stanley Carlson-Thies, Bruce Clemenger, Roy Clouser, Adolfo García de la Sienra, Peter Heslam, Harry Kits, Robert Joustra, David Koyzis, Keith Pavlischek, Timothy Sherratt, Gideon Strauss, Bob Sweetman, Brian Walsh, and Lambert Zuidervaart.

An unceasing barrage of affectionate teasing from my children, Paul and Lucia, has helped prevent me taking this project (indeed anything I do) too seriously. It is also an unusual delight to be able to thank two other members of my family who have played a very special role in the formation of this book. Over many years I have profited from the writings of and enjoyed many conversations with my late father-in-law, Jan D. Dengerink, who wrote the first ever book on Dooyeweerd's social thought. (I hope mine isn't the last.) He was one of Dooyeweerd's doctoral students. Most of all, I thank my wife, Adrienne Dengerink Chaplin, who understood the importance of this project from the beginning and, miraculously, still believed in it at the end. Her interests in philosophical aesthetics, music, and art have kept reminding me of dimensions of human experience not well theorized by Dooyeweerd. But much more than that, her joyful and stimulating companionship has enriched not only the writing of this book, but every step of the journey we have shared for over a quarter of a century. I dedicate this book to her.

INTRODUCTION

THIS BOOK INTRODUCES A DISTINCTIVE CHRISTIAN philosophical approach to the question of the relationship between the polity and the plural institutions of "civil society." This approach was developed by the twentieth-century Dutch Protestant thinker Herman Dooyeweerd (1894–1977), a remarkable and original philosopher and the most influential intellectual successor to the nineteenth-century Calvinist theologian and statesman, Abraham Kuyper (1837–1920). Recent years have witnessed stirrings of a revival of Kuyper's thought in North America, in particular, among social and political theorists investigating potential religious resources for a renewed appreciation of civil society.[1] The central principle of Kuyper's social thought is the "sphere sovereignty" of many distinct social institutions, each expressing a certain facet of a dynamic order of divinely created possibilities and each fitted to make a unique contribution to the realization of justice and the public good. This principle is capturing attention as an illuminating way both to designate the distinctive identities of the institutions of civil society and to frame a conception of the role of the state capable of doing justice to those identities and their interrelationships.[2]

Whereas the Kuyperian origin of this principle is becoming better known today, the sophisticated elaboration of the principle in the writings of Dooyeweerd remains insufficiently appreciated. The principal aim of this book is to remedy that situation by critically expounding Dooyeweerd's social and political thought and by exhibiting its pertinence to contemporary civil society debates. I seek to show how his work

amounts to a striking and characteristically Protestant philosophy of social pluralism and civil society, comparable in range and depth to contributions emerging from twentieth-century Catholic social thinkers such
as Jacques Maritain and Heinrich Rommen and no less capable of speaking beyond the religious community from which it arose.

Dooyeweerd's work remains largely unknown in English-speaking
social and political theory, even among those interested in its Christian
currents. There are several reasons for this state of affairs, but two stand
out. Probably the most important is that Dooyeweerd is not only a very
complex thinker but also a difficult and often obscure writer. He uses several concepts forged out of early-twentieth-century Continental philosophy, many of which are alien to those schooled in English-language
social theory, but he also coins numerous novel terms bearing distinctive
and sometimes quite idiosyncratic meanings. A second reason is that, by
comparison to Catholic thinkers like Maritain or Rommen, he adopts a
markedly "antithetical" stance toward his interlocutors (including his
coreligionists). While his strategic goal—as I explain in chapter 3—is
ultimately to promote dialogue across perspectival divides, his method is
to penetrate to and expose the deepest differences between his own
thought and that of his opponents rather than to search out existing or
potential points of convergence with a view to maximizing consensus.
He is a demanding interrogator of his putative dialogue partners.

If this book does no more than make Dooyeweerd's thought intelligible to English-language social and political theorists it will have been
worth the effort. Yet it also seeks to introduce this readership to a neglected Protestant contribution to the field. There are, of course, many
towering twentieth-century Protestant *theologians* who have written extensively on social and political theory: Reinhold Niebuhr, John Luther
Adams, Karl Barth, Dietrich Bonhoeffer, and Emil Brunner, for example.
Yet there seem remarkably few Protestant *philosophers* who have offered
much of lasting value in this area. Dooyeweerd, I will show, is among the
foremost. He left behind him an impressive canon of philosophical works
(many of which are now translated)[3] and generated a small but energetic
scholarly community that has over several generations extended, cri-
tiqued, and applied his thought in many academic fields. His work
spawned the establishment in the 1930s of a philosophical association
and a philosophical journal based in the Netherlands, both still active,

and, later, centers of sympathetic scholarly activity in several locations around the world.[4] Much of this work has been done in the areas of social, political, and legal theory.

Before beginning a detailed exposition of Dooyeewerd's writings I seek to contextualize his thought, first in relation to contemporary civil society debates (chapter 1) and then in relation to the Kuyperian movement out of which it grew (chapter 2). Chapter 1 surveys and analyzes contemporary streams of theorizing about civil society, records the recent interest in identifying the connections between Christianity and civil society, and locates civil society theorizing against the larger background of earlier schools of what I shall call "normative institutional pluralism"—a family of social and political theories seeking to overcome mainstream neglect of the many intermediate institutions standing between the state and the individual. Chapter 2 presents salient details of Dooyeweerd's biography, describes his aspirations as a philosopher, and sketches the particular historical and intellectual context in which his thought took shape. I introduce his social and political thought as a comprehensive philosophical articulation of the democratic pluralist Calvinian vision projected by Kuyper. I then offer an extended summary of the flow of the book's themes, intended to assist readers—especially those unfamiliar with Dooyeweerd's work—to navigate the sequence of complex systematic concepts unfolded in subsequent chapters.

The next two chapters present an outline of Dooyeweerd's fundamental philosophical framework, which amounts to a highly intricate, original, somewhat forbidding, and often problematic conceptual apparatus. Chapter 3 introduces his view of the relationship between religion and philosophy and the central content of his religious convictions. Three core conceptual girders of his substantive general philosophy—"modality," "individuality," "interlacement"—are presented in chapter 4.

These four opening chapters supply the necessary background for a more extended presentation of Dooyeweerd's social philosophy in chapters 5 through 7. Chapter 5 outlines the distinctive theory of historical and cultural development that serves as an essential backdrop to his substantive social philosophy. Chapter 6 examines the foundations of his complex account of multiple social structures (centering on the notion of societal "structural principles"), tests one of the most telling criticisms leveled against it, and proposes a reformulation. Chapter 7 sets forth his complex classification of particular types of social structures and their various interrelationships and brings to the fore the sense in which his social philosophy is pluralist in character.

The stage is then set for a detailed examination of his theory of the state, which occupies the next three chapters. Chapter 8 considers his account of the identity crisis of the modern state and introduces his own conception of that identity, residing in a unique combination of power and justice: power is the "foundation" of the state, yet only insofar as its "destination" is the promotion of justice. This irreducible identity determines the state's sphere sovereignty over against that of other social institutions and points to its unique role in society.

Chapter 9 characterizes at greater length his conception of the definitive nature and role of the state. It opens by introducing his broad account of "spheres of justice," which amounts to a distinctive version of legal pluralism.[5] This prepares the ground for an account of the sphere of justice typical of the state: "public justice." This central notion is elaborated in chapter 10, which offers an overview of the justice-promoting role of the state in a complex modern society and then examines his applications of public justice to four broad sectors of society: nation, family, church, and economy.

Chapter 11 returns to the contemporary discussions of civil society. I revisit three problems in civil society discourse identified in chapter 1 and consider to what extent Dooyeweerd's version of Christian pluralism might help in addressing them. His contribution, I suggest, assists us in mapping more clearly and negotiating more successfully how state and civil society may be related in ways conducive to the realization of justice and the public good. A brief epilogue notes the challenges facing an overtly religious political theory in the context of a secular and pluralistic society.

ONE

CHRISTIANITY, CIVIL SOCIETY, AND PLURALISM

THE QUESTION OF THE RELATIONSHIP BETWEEN THE polity and what are now called the institutions of "civil society" has recurred in the Western tradition at different historical junctures under widely varying circumstances, as the character and claims of diverse social and political institutions evolved—at times imperceptibly, at times convulsively.[1] Aristotle's questioning of the Platonic prioritizing of unity over diversity within a self-sufficient Athenian political community was perhaps the earliest philosophical confrontation with the problem. As classical civilization unraveled, the appearance of a historically unprecedented institution asserting a transpolitical, transcendent origin and authorization—the church—decisively redefined the problem as one of the relationship between two independently constituted and mutually limiting communities. The "doctrine of the two," as O'Donovan limpidly styles this revolutionary innovation, irrevocably recast the terms of the question.[2] The ramifications of this radical relativization of the domain of the political over against the realm of the spiritual, and as a consequence over against the zones of personal and associational liberty secured in principle by that realm, were felt throughout Western society and politics not only during the Christendom era but also well beyond it. Notwithstanding the effect of other currents moving in opposite directions—notably absolutist doctrines of sovereignty—early modern political institutions can be seen as partial consolidations of the notion that only an arrangement of plural, reciprocally accountable authorities could honor the conviction that absolute sovereignty belonged exclusively to God. Reformation political thought substantially advanced this consolidation.[3] To a significant degree, this was achieved merely by drawing out bolder constitutional conclusions from ideas and practices of law, consent, and corporate representation generated within medieval Catholicism.[4] Yet the Reformation also contributed insights of its own, appealing—in time—from a conviction of both the freedom of individual conscience and the spiritual equality of all "vocations" to the principle of the political equality of all, including rulers, under the rule of a system of law impregnated with divine justice and equity.[5]

Reformed impulses also contributed to the emergence, already under way, of the multiple differentiated institutions of modernity—notably state, church, business corporation, university, family, and voluntary association—each claiming autonomy within its own proper sphere. This process, together with the stretching of the bounds of personal liberty accompanying it, again fundamentally and irreversibly reconfigured the problem. No longer could social and political plurality be harmonized institutionally by a superior unifying ecclesial jurisdiction, or even, as Weber proposed, by a shared universe of moral norms. Each, it increasingly appeared, had to discern and follow its unique institutional requirements, making its own way in a world increasingly fashioned by the contending but ambiguously interdependent imperatives of centralizing nation-states and fragmenting commercial markets. These institutional requirements, many argued, did not fall within the purview of "theology" or even the sphere of "morality" as conventionally understood. But this argument flew in the face not only of Catholic but also of Reformed (especially Calvinist) injunctions regarding the sovereignty of God over the whole of social life, including the economic sphere, launching the still-unresolved debate over the contribution of the Reformation to the process of "secularization."[6]

In our own time, among the many processes now attendant on "globalization," one is arguably a decisive—it is perhaps too early to say irreversible—rebalancing of institutional imperatives in favor of increasingly autonomous markets and against the independent capacities of both states and the institutions of civil society. The long-standing question of the just relationship between state and civil society, then, presses upon us again today, manifesting itself in the multilateral renegotiations now under way—often conflictual and increasingly violent—between states and the diverse institutions of civil society, between the contending institutions of civil society themselves, and between nation-states, each struggling to come to grips with the institutional turbulence surging up from below and cascading down from above.

What resources might Christian political philosophy today have to assist in clarifying this perplexing and ever-shifting question? On the face of it, a tradition of political thought founded on the doctrine of the two, productive of copious theorizing on law and authority and transformed by Reformation and scholastic theories of institutional accountability, might be expected to yield resources capable of addressing it. And indeed it has. In order to provide a context for appreciating these resources, including those provided by Dooyeweerd, I briefly take stock of contemporary discussions of the concept of civil society and then make a short excursus into the history of the concept. I offer a twofold proposal regarding contemporary discussions of civil society, arguing that they need to be broadened to recognize the historical contributions of Christianity and that they can best be interpreted as a revival of interest in the problematics of a distinctive tendency in social thought that I shall call "normative institutional pluralism."

BRINGING CIVIL SOCIETY BACK IN

The concept of civil society has experienced a striking resurgence over the last twenty-five years.[7] Extensive discussions of the concept and its cousins have been generated from sources situated across the ideological spectrum and located across the globe. North American observers will no doubt be most familiar with the voices gathered in Don Eberly's *The Essential Civil Society Reader.*[8] This volume represents an important "neo-Tocquevillian" strand of civil society theorizing, indicating that a principal concern of discussions in the United States is the perceived need to shore up certain institutions rendered especially fragile by the strains typical of an advanced capitalist and individualist liberal democracy, especially families, voluntary associations, churches, and neighborhoods. These institutions are held to play the primary role in generating the vital social capital on which social cohesion, active citizenship, and political unity depend. Contributors to this American debate argue that civil society in the United States is not, as is sometimes complacently assumed in comparison with other, "closed" societies, a paradigm of good health. Individuals and institutions are, as a result, dangerously vulnerable to the predatory attentions of bureaucratic states.

The earliest wave of recent civil society theorizing, however, emerged in Eastern Europe during the 1970s and 1980s.[9] Like its practitioners in Latin America shortly afterward, East Europeans invoked the notion of civil society to refer to a sphere of autonomous and "self-limiting" popular deliberation and organization capable of operating beyond the reach of the state, defending human rights, and eventually mounting democratic resistance to (respectively) totalitarian and authoritarian regimes. Later, in Western Europe and the United States, another group of theorists championed what have been typically termed "secondary associations." These "new associationalists"—among them chastened socialists and social democrats—propose a model of a decentralized economy and polity that aspires to meet human needs by means of, rather than at the cost of, democratic participation.[10] At the same time, a quite distinctive school of radical (or "agonistic") democrats have powerfully voiced concerns for the political articulation of distinctive social and cultural identities experienced as marginalized or suppressed by liberal democracy.[11] Some of the most recent contributions to civil society discourse have been occasioned by the radical antiglobalization movement, whose advocates are working for the creation of a "global civil society," populated by, for example, community-sustaining social movements, to counter the supposedly pernicious effects of deregulated globalized markets.[12]

In the United States, as Eberly's volume shows, the debate has been mainly led by neoconservatives and communitarians. As early as the 1970s—though without using the term *civil society*—neoconservatives such as Berger and Neuhaus attacked bureaucratic "megastructures" like the state and urged a recovery of those "mediating structures" that shield individuals from their predatory power and supply a vital source of subjective meaning and social values.[13] Such urgings have often also drawn upon libertarian critiques of the inefficiency and illiberality of the public sector, leading to a desire to shift responsibility for economic coordination and welfare provision onto private organizations. Communitarians such as Etzioni warn against the rapid depletion of community-sustaining

values and counsel a range of policies aimed at empowering those neglected institutions and practices, which alone can restore such values,
though without invoking libertarian economics in support.[14]

The term *civil society* initially gained momentum in Western Europe
a generation ago, and in North America more recently, because of its
apparent capacity to pinpoint telling pressure points amid the baffling
complexity of our contemporary social and political predicaments and to
suggest novel proposals to relieve them.[15] Yet, as I have already intimated,
the cluster of problems that the term seeks to name, as well as the aspiration to theorize such problems, has a much longer history than many
contemporary commentators recognize, and a further examination of aspects of this history will help set the stage for what follows. This is especially so because, as Beem has shown, the meanings invested in current
usages depend wholly on what its protagonists want civil society to *do*.[16]
The term is not a neutral descriptor but is deployed within sharply contrasting theoretical paradigms, each with distinctive historical roots,
apart from which its usages cannot be fully understood.[17]

As civil society discourse began to reenter the currency of political
debate, historians of political thought reminded protagonists that the
term goes back at least to the eighteenth century. Before then civil society
characteristically referred to the whole of a politically organized society.
By contrast, its modern usages presuppose the formulation of a distinction between state and society, making possible the identification of a
sphere of social reality *other than the state,* though not necessarily wholly
separate from or antagonistic to it. But how was that sphere to be characterized? Ehrenberg traces two contrasting emphases emerging in parallel
during the eighteenth and nineteenth centuries:[18] an individualist account oriented especially to a notion of spontaneously harmonizing economic activity among free individuals (e.g., Ferguson and Smith, and
after them Marx and Hegel),[19] and an associationist account viewing
society as a network of associations or communities intermediate between individual and state (e.g., Montesquieu, Tocqueville). Both accounts, however, presuppose the appearance of a distinctively modern
sphere of free interindividual and interinstitutional activity "liberated"
from premodern customary, religious, and political constraints, ushering
in hitherto unavailable possibilities for new forms of social interaction
among emancipated individuals and differentiated institutions. Civil

society, then, was an integral element of the very foundations of political modernity.

Many of these originating civil society theorists were attentive to the evolving Christian assumptions, premodern and early modern, that had prepared the ground for the appearance of that modern reality and that continued, sometimes ambivalently, to operate within it. Of course, not all theorists of civil society viewed those Christian assumptions as salutary: for Marx, the role of religion in sustaining bourgeois civil society was a sign of its co-optation in capitalist exploitation; whereas for Ferguson and Tocqueville, religion furnished indispensable moral resources necessary to contain and channel the fragmenting forces unleashed by civil society. Many contemporary accounts, however, have tended to overlook the role of religious, and specifically Christian, influences in the emergence of modern civil society, and this deficiency needs to be remedied.

BRINGING CHRISTIANITY BACK INTO CIVIL SOCIETY

The role of Christianity is beginning to be registered in a few of the most recent historical excavations of the concept of civil society. Ehrenberg's comprehensive study includes a chapter devoted entirely to civil society and the Christian commonwealth. It turns out, however, that he can ultimately find in Christendom little more than a sacralized version of the classical vision of the all-inclusiveness of the polity.[20] The subordination of the secular by the ecclesial realm within a unified Christian social order meant that, in spite of pervasive tendencies toward particularism, "independent institutions or ideals that could claim loyalty apart from or in opposition to the Church did not exist in sufficient strength to generate viable centers of autonomous theory or practice." Consequently, "it was impossible to generate a theory of civil society that could stand outside the strictures of the Church."[21] Taylor is more discerning, suggesting that the medieval Christian sources of freedom enjoyed in the West "can be articulated with something like the conception of civil society."[22] The medieval insight that "society is not identical with its political organization," sharpened by the assertion of the organizational independence of the church, indicated the depth of Christendom's break with the classical heritage and gave rise to a "crucial differentiation, one of the origins of the later notion of civil society, and one of the roots of western liberalism."[23]

The emergence of the church as a rival, indeed superior, source of moral authority to the polity is also central to Banner's account of Christian antecedents to the concept of civil society. Banner calls attention to two additional notions that turned out to be equally important: the universal Christian affirmation of the natural *sociability* of human beings and the emerging principle of *subsidiarity,* calling for a vertical distribution of plural social authorities.[24] Banner's piece appears in one of two collections devoted to cross-cultural comparisons of conceptions of civil society, including treatments of such conceptions, or their close parallels, in major world religions. Their appearance testifies to a recent rediscovery in the literature of mainstream political theory of the extent to which important strands of civil society theorizing have been generated by specific religious traditions.[25] Coleman's contribution, "A Limited State and a Vibrant Society: Christianity and Civil Society,"[26] underlines Banner's contention that Christian political philosophy has indeed contained substantive theorizing on civil society. Coleman's focus is the rich and wide-ranging Catholic theory of civil society and the state founded in a family of interlocking notions, notably subsidiarity, solidarity, and the common good. These notions emerged from medieval origins, in which natural law theory and organic metaphors played a central role. They were substantially refashioned in the nineteenth and twentieth centuries and received official endorsement in the "social teaching" of Vatican II and in several papal social encyclicals since the conclusion of the council in 1965.

It bears mention that this Catholic model has been the principal inspiration for what has been the most electorally successful (if academically neglected) postwar European political movement, namely, Christian Democracy.[27] In its early years this movement typically presented itself as a genuine "third way" between capitalism and socialism, and the distinctive place it accorded to civil society was central to this strategic political objective.[28] While Christian democratic governments were equally prone to pragmatic drift as their rivals, with whom in any case they were normally in coalition, their characteristic political orientation is misconstrued if classified simply as another version of conservatism, liberalism, or social democracy.[29] The founders of the movements[30] were inspired by Jacques Maritain's vision of a "pluralistically organized body politic" in which the state would be "a topmost agency concerned only with the final supervision of the achievements of institutions born out of freedom."[31] Maritain called for recognition of "an organic heterogeneity in the very structure of civil society," which is composed "not only of individuals, but of particular societies formed by them." Thus "a pluralist body politic would allow to these societies the greatest autonomy possible and would diversify its own internal structure in keeping with what is typically required by their nature."[32] A properly formed state should accommodate itself to a plural society. It was the concern to sustain associational vitality as a counterweight to both individualism and statism that lay behind the 1931 papal social encyclical *Quadragesimo Anno,* in which Pius XI warned of a decomposition of plural social structures under the influence of individualism and issued the first official formulation of the principle of subsidiarity—or, more strictly, the "subsidiary function" of the state—which charges that it is a "grave injustice" for higher social bodies to usurp the proper functions of lower bodies wherever the latter can adequately fulfill them.[33] This language indicates that in one important Christian tradition at least, the relationship between state and civil society is not merely a matter of pragmatic institutional arrangements but is indeed a vital question of *justice.*

Stackhouse introduces parallel contributions from the Reformed tradition. In contrast to the Catholic "hierarchical-subsidiarity view," Stackhouse presents a Reformed "federal-covenantal view," first clearly articulated by the seventeenth-century jurist Johannes Althusius and represented in the modern period by Kuyper.[34] In contrast to the "organic" Catholic view, the federal-covenantal view is, Stackhouse tells us, a "pluralist" model in which many kinds of institutions are "conceived as a matrix of potentially networked associations."[35] Stackhouse rightly observes that both models are equally intent on avoiding the dangers of libertarian individualism and political totalitarianism and affirm the indispensable, noninstrumental value of institutions intermediate between state and individual. As I expound Dooyeweerd's version of the Reformed view, I shall explore this intriguing ecumenical convergence.[36] Stackhouse characterizes the two conceptions thus:

One view sees these [institutions] as comprehended by a natural
moral solidarity made effective by compassionate but magisterial
leadership that seeks to guide the whole of life to fulfill innate good
ends. The other view sees various spheres of life, each populated by
associative "artefacts," each constructed on the basis of a common
discernment of need and a calling to fulfill that need, a recognition
of a pluralism of institutions with possibly conflicting ends, and
an ongoing critical analysis of our interpretations of transcendent
principles of right that may be used to assess the presumption of
innate tendencies to virtue, magisterial leadership, and any singu-
lar view of the common good.[37]

This rendition of the federal-covenantal view does not accurately capture
all of its variants (not even Kuyper's), yet Stackhouse's account certainly
confirms the presence of a substantive Protestant theory worthy of attention. However, it omits to mention the far more sophisticated articulation of the Kuyperian notion of sphere sovereignty in Dooyeweerd. This
is, perhaps, hardly surprising considering the relative inaccessibility—
both physical and philosophical—of his writings. Yet it indicates that a
study of his distinctively Calvinian philosophical approach to the question of state and civil society is overdue. Dooyeweerd's approach displays
impressive theoretical originality and scope while remaining produc-
tively engaged with concrete problems of a mature industrial society and
an emerging pluralist democracy and welfare state, problems that continue to have salience today.

BRINGING CIVIL SOCIETY BACK INTO PLURALISM

The second feature of the history of the concept of civil society to which
I want to allude is the presence of certain historical strands of social and
political theorizing that are pertinent to current debates about civil society and associations, as well as to an interpretation of Dooyeweerd, but
that are only peripherally acknowledged in recent discussions. Such
strands are often designated as "pluralism." In adopting that designation
I need to make clear that I am not referring primarily to two other types

of theory typically described as pluralist. I do not chiefly have in mind, first, explanatory theories of power and policy making associated with the early work of Dahl and other postwar students of the empirical functioning of liberal democracy, especially its American version. Nor, second, am I alluding to contemporary theories of cultural pluralism or multiculturalism as found in the works of Taylor, Kymlicka, and many others. Rather I have in mind normative institutional pluralism (normative pluralism, for short), a family of theories advancing a central normative claim that a vital feature of any just and well-ordered society is the presence of multiple kinds of mutually distinct social institutions whose integrity and autonomy it is a primary role of the state to safeguard and support. Of course, normative institutional pluralism is bound up in numerous ways with the other two types, and I advert to these linkages occasionally.

A brief, and necessarily schematic, survey of the history and diversity of normative pluralist theories will quickly disclose their significance for contemporary civil society discourse. A remarkable flowering of normative pluralist theorizing originated in late-eighteenth- and early-nineteenth-century Europe, and the shared context of its leading contributors is instructive. All were motivated by an anxiety about two characteristic features of modernity: first, the social and economic atomization produced by industrialization and the consequent disintegration of traditional institutions such as estates, guilds, and kinship communities; and second, the political centralization characteristic of the modern nation-state, dramatically accentuated in the aftermath of the French Revolution. Their interest in plural institutions standing between state and individual thus sprang from a concern about both the isolation of individuals from the supportive bonds of precapitalist society and the exposure of these unprotected individuals to the encroachments of a dangerously overweening state.

What I am calling normative pluralism embraces a wide variety of modern theories, schools, and trends, but at least five identifiable strands had crystallized by the early twentieth century.[38] First, *liberal pluralists* such as Tocqueville and J. S. Mill were impressed especially with the significance of voluntary associations and local government as guardians of political liberty and with their moral significance as training grounds for responsible self-government or (for Mill) as conduits for self-realization.

The influence of liberal pluralism, both as theory and as practice, is evident most of all in the American tradition, and as I indicated above, it is this perspective, now translated into the language of mediating structures, secondary associations, and civil society institutions, that defines the contours of current American debates.

Second, *organicist pluralists,* influenced by romanticism and including thinkers as diverse as the benign nationalist J. G. Herder, the conservative romantic Adam Müller, and the legal historian Otto von Gierke, lamented the disintegration of traditional communities under the influence of industrial capitalism and—for some—political liberalism, and called either for their reinstatement or, as with Gierke, their replacement by new, morally and affectively meaningful organic communities.[39] Organicists urged upon the atomized individuals of the modern world the need for profound allegiances to organically conceived social wholes such as family, class, or estate, church, nation, or state.

Third, many *corporatist pluralists* were also influenced by romantic organicism and shared much of its critical diagnosis of modern industrialized society.[40] They are distinguishable, however, not primarily by the philosophical influences to which they were subject but by the characteristic institutional arrangements they prescribed. More appreciative than liberal organicists of the leading role of the state in countering the disintegrative tendencies of modernity, they proposed various schemes in which large-scale, publicly instituted industrial corporations would serve to both reconcile class antagonisms between worker and capitalist and, via corporatist parliamentary representation, integrate the interests of particular industrial or agricultural sectors into the requirements of the state as a whole. The foremost representative of this position is Hegel, whose proposal that corporations could function as mediators between the particularity of civil society and the universality of the state framed much subsequent corporatist reflection.[41]

Socialist pluralists such as Proudhon, Gurvitch, Laski, and Cole accorded decisive priority to the workers' group as the most promising new source of social identity and political power. They proposed a distinctive remedy for the atomizing effects of industrial capitalism, not through large-scale nationalization realized through centralized political democracy as advocated by their state-socialist colleagues, but rather by a radically decentralized economic system centering on autonomous producer cooperatives and, in some cases, by functional representation.

I want to suggest that the Catholic and Calvinist theories of civil society sketched above are principal contributors to what amounts to a distinctive *fifth* version of normative pluralism, *Christian pluralism*. Such theories embody novel conceptions of civil society grounded in distinctive understandings of the irreducibly diverse possibilities of created human nature.[42]

Some unifying concerns emerging from this seeming cacophony of historical voices can be summarized briefly.[43] Normative pluralists typically advance versions of the following two central claims. The first is that a healthy, just, free, and stable civil society requires a multiplicity of relatively independent and qualitatively distinct associations, communities, institutions, and other social bodies, through which individual human capacities or interests can be realized and apart from which the fabric of social unity will wear thin. But unlike Aristotelians, republicans, nationalists, or collectivists of all stripes, they deny that membership in the *polis* is either morally prior to or more ennobling than membership in other communities or associations. The second is that the principal function of the state is to actively facilitate this realization by protecting or promoting the responsible independence of, and interactions between, these bodies. Unlike bureaucratic centralizers, they deny that the state has the capacity or the competence to manage and direct the whole of society, and unlike minimal statists, they deny that just and cohesive relations between social institutions arise spontaneously apart from active political coordination and regulation.

A wide range of social institutions have attracted the attention of different normative pluralists, including educational and welfare associations, business enterprises, trade unions, political parties and pressure groups, churches, kinship and ethnic communities, and cultural, national, or territorial communities. Pluralists draw upon a variety of diagnoses in order to support the unanimous claim that the modern state has overreached and thereby incapacitated itself and needs to be refashioned in a way that respects the independent contributions of a diversity of associations, communities, and institutions that have for too long either atrophied through neglect or collapsed under the impact of direct assaults from the state or indirect corrosion from unrestrained markets. As the British associationalist Paul Hirst puts it, pluralists propose that what have been misleadingly downplayed as secondary associations should instead become the *primary* means of social governance.[44]

In the light of this overview of some important strands of modern political thought, I propose that much of what today sails under the banner of civil society theorizing can most illuminatingly be seen as the latest flowering of normative pluralism. I have noted that recent historical studies of the concept of civil society have disclosed successive and contrasting usages of the term in major phases of modern (and premodern) political thought. Such studies, I am suggesting, need to be complemented by attention to the diverse schools of normative institutional pluralism, each of which represents bodies of reflection, anticipating many of the central problematics of current civil society discourse. The revival of interest in civil society, secondary associations, and mediating structures and related notions in this contemporary discourse reveals the operation, albeit in radically altered circumstances, of instincts comparable to those that first gave birth to normative pluralist theories two centuries ago: on the one hand, an *anti-statist* instinct arising,[45] in Eastern Europe, from the trauma of totalitarianism; in Latin America and elsewhere, from the persistence of authoritarianism; and in Western Europe and North America, from the failed promises of centralized state welfare and overambitious macroeconomic management; and, on the other, a *pro-community* instinct arising in reaction to the momentous evidence of the radically atomizing tendencies of (late) modernity such as those generated by economic globalization—and of which "bowling alone" is but one Western suburban manifestation.

Both these concerns powerfully animate the social and political theorizing of Kuyper and Dooyeweerd. As with Kuyper before him, a consistent emphasis in Dooyeweerd's thought is the danger of the *totalizing* tendencies at work in modern theories of the state and the propensity of such theories to lapse into various forms of "universalism." And a recurring theme in his social thought is the *atomizing* tendencies at work in many modern theories of social institutions, their propensity to fall victim to various forms of "individualism."[46] His alternative thus occupies ground similar to that taken up by recent theorists of civil society. Dooyeweerd can be seen as elaborating a modern Calvinian version of normative pluralism containing an original philosophy of the relationships between state, civil society, and other social institutions.[47] His extensive rearticulation of the notion of sphere sovereignty renders him an outstanding representative of what I have termed Christian pluralism.

I propose to show how Dooyeweerd's Christian pluralism can contribute to a clarification of three problems that have taken shape in recent civil society discourse. The first concerns the *definition and scope of the concept* of civil society. Most civil society theorists place the so-called third sector of independent voluntary associations at the center of their definitions, contrasting these with the realms of state and market. Yet there continues to be considerable disagreement, for example, over whether the family or household should be included in civil society; whether business corporations should be included in the market and so excluded from civil society; whether only voluntary associations capable of oppositional stances toward the state, or only those inclined to supportive political postures, should be included; whether religious associations should be accorded a central or peripheral role in civil society; and so on. Significant differences of scope not only indicate contrasting ideological starting points but also point toward quite divergent prescriptions for reconstruction.

The second problem concerns the *relationship between the state and civil society.* The modern concept was born out of a desire to distinguish the realm of civil society sharply from the state and to recognize its autonomous sphere of operation, and many contemporary civil society theorists, on both left and right, proceed from an attitude of suspicion toward the intrusive or oppressive tendencies at work in the modern state. But can civil society theory generate an adequate account of the constructive role of the state in regulating and integrating civil society institutions? Can it account for what Beem calls "the necessity of politics"? If so, what model of political integration and regulation seems to follow from a robust affirmation of civil society?

The third problem concerns the *utility of civil society for social critique.* Recent theorists have entered forceful reminders that what are often classified as civil society institutions are not wholly beneficial either to the flourishing of individuals or to the functioning of liberal democracy. The pervasive presence of so-called illiberal associations seems to challenge the assumption, widespread among neo-Tocquevillian theorists, that civil society needs to be reinvigorated and compels an acknowledgment that "bad civil society" will need to be contained or marginalized. Some commentators seem naively to applaud the capacities of civil society institutions to produce social cohesion and democratic initiative. But civil libertarians, on the one hand, warn of the illegitimate constraints autonomous associations sometimes impose on their members, and theorists indebted to the Marxist tradition (such as Ehrenberg), on the other, question the transformative potentials of civil society and continue to insist on a dominant role for the state in securing economic and social justice. Dooyeweerd's potential contribution to these discussions is explored in the final chapter.

TWO

DOOYEWEERD IN CONTEXT

Calvinism, Modernity, and Pluralism

I noted in chapter 1 that Kuyper formulated the idea of sphere sovereignty in the context of a concrete political struggle for religious pluralism in the nineteenth-century Netherlands. Understanding what this struggle represented is important for appreciating the sense in which his pluralistic theory of society, and that of his intellectual successor, Dooyeweerd, could be both Calvinist and, in an important if qualified sense, modern.

Kuyper was the leading figure in a significant resurgence of Dutch Calvinism in the second half of the nineteenth century.[1] A prolific theologian and influential church leader, he was also active through much of his life as a journalist, scholar, political activist, party leader, and ultimately prime minister (1901–1905). He was also the prime mover in the founding of the Vrije Universiteit (Free University) of Amsterdam in 1880. The year before, he established the Calvinist-inspired Antirevolutionary Party (ARP), so named to indicate its repudiation of militantly secular French revolutionary liberalism rather than its hostility to progressive social reform. Kuyper regarded Calvinism not only as a theological doctrine or ecclesial movement but also, like Catholicism, as a cultural force rooted in a distinctive and comprehensive vision capable of illuminating and guiding every aspect of thought and life. His theology of culture elaborates this central theme.[2] Its starting point was the classic Calvinist conviction that God had appointed human beings as his representatives on earth and commissioned them to serve him in all aspects of their individual and corporate lives. Humankind is placed within an ordered, dynamically unfolding creation governed by a coherent framework of laws, conformity with which will lead to human fulfillment. The "scholastic" separation of life into natural and supernatural realms undermines the integrality of man's religious situation, Kuyper asserts. God's grace redeems the natural realm and restores it to its original created purpose, and hence there is no need for the institutional church to function as the privileged intermediary through which grace elevates nature. The institutional church is indispensable as the community in which true faith is nurtured, but the effects of grace permeate natural life directly through the obedient action of ordinary believers in family life, business, education, or politics, without being directly administered or sanctioned by the church.[3] Accordingly, associations founded by Kuyperian neo-Calvinists rejected at the outset the practice familiar among many Catholic associations of the time whereby ecclesial authorities directly guided or even controlled associational policy. Thus, for example, the Free University was to be free from control not only by the state but also by the church.

Kuyper's goal has been described as the "rechristianization" of Dutch culture,[4] but the term risks misconstruing his actual objectives. Insofar as he worked tirelessly to restore Christian influence in Dutch public life, he sought to move toward this goal not by claiming a privileged political status for the church or its confessions, as had his early Calvinist and Puritan forebears, but rather by instituting a constitutional and legal framework that recognized the equal rights of all existing confessional or ideological groups—Calvinist, Catholic, Liberal, Socialist—to participate in the shaping of public life. He represents a decisive shift, as Skillen puts it, from an early Calvinist notion of a "covenant of grace," in which right religion was a condition of political power, to a principled endorsement of "equitable public pluralism," a constitutional model accommodating all these ideological groups without officially disfavoring or disadvantaging any of them.[5]

Kuyper can be credited as a major contributor to the emergence of a modernized, religiously and culturally plural consociational democracy in the Netherlands.[6] Working in a strategic political alliance with his Catholic co-belligerents in a campaign for recognition from an unsympathetic political establishment dominated by Enlightenment liberalism,

Kuyper struggled to resist the confinements of what many orthodox Christians experienced as a secularizing Liberal hegemony over public life, first in education and then in journalism, politics, the trade union movement, the academy, broadcasting, and other cultural sectors.[7]

The political party he founded served in governing coalitions during much of the twentieth century, supplying several prime ministers, including, as noted, Kuyper himself for a brief—and not wholly successful—period. Kuyper not only pioneered the institutionalization of equitable public pluralism but also campaigned—fitfully and not always consistently—for the democratization of the constitution, provoking the more conservative wing of the party to break away and form a second Calvinist party, the Christian Historical Union (CHU).[8] He was also instrumental in the organization of Calvinist workers, farmers, and employers and in the introduction of the first wave of "social legislation." The term *progressive Calvinism* has been applied (not without some resistance) to the movement he inspired and led.

Kuyperian neo-Calvinism can thus be classified as a modernizing and progressive form of democratic pluralism inspired by a traditional religious perspective, thus confounding secularization theorists who remained until quite recently, as Skillen and Carlson-Thies put it, "in the grip of the Enlightenment bias that societal differentiation and political modernization go hand in hand with the decline of religious influence in social life."[9] Together with social and political Catholicism, it found itself on the one hand contending with reactionaries and conservatives and on the other seeking a different, albeit partly overlapping, package of social and political reforms from those sought by liberal and socialist parties of its day. In this project both traditions were able to draw upon and develop a rich legacy of constructive public philosophy, minimizing the extent to which they succumbed to pursuing merely sectional political goals.

> Catholics and Antirevolutionaries did not function politically as pressure groups which accepted the "secularized" setting of a liberal public order while merely demanding special Christian privileges within it. Holland witnessed the development of full-fledged Christian political parties eager to be coresponsible, with liberals and socialists, for shaping the future of the Dutch polity.[10]

It can thus be seen how Kuyperian Calvinism represented a specifically Protestant form of Christian Democracy, unique in Europe. Indeed, while many Catholic political parties hesitated to commit themselves unreservedly to democratic pluralism until after World War II, the political movement Kuyper inspired arrived at that point about half a century earlier.

There is a second sense in which Kuyperian Calvinism generated a distinctively Protestant social and political theory. Central to Christian democratic political thought, as noted earlier, is the priority it attaches to safeguarding the independence of civil society institutions. This was the strategic policy orientation by which it sought to define itself as a third way between liberal capitalism and socialist collectivism. Kuyper's core principle of sphere sovereignty played the central role in the neo-Calvinist articulation of this strategy. It was on the basis of this principle that Kuyper was able to come to a guarded, critical, but essentially positive evaluation of the differentiated institutions of the modern era and the realm of individual freedom and voluntary associations accompanying them. Such differentiated "spheres," each retaining their own "sovereignty," were interpreted in the light of the early Calvinist notion of the equality of all human vocations, and so construed as coordinately related (as "co-ordained") rather than hierarchically arranged. To be sure, Kuyper was profoundly critical of what he saw as the deep distortions of the process of differentiation brought about by "modernism," by which he meant secular humanism and its offshoots in, for example, classical liberalism and socialism. Yet crucially, he did not at all view these modernizing processes as did those traditionalist Catholics who had succumbed to romantic medieval nostalgia, namely, as inherently secularizing repudiations of divine order and its historical embodiment in organic Christian civilization. Rather, through the lens of a profoundly dynamic sense of divine revelation in creation and history, he regarded them as fruits of the progressively unfolding human historical response to the "cultural mandate," the divine command to "subdue and fill the earth" (Gen. 1). Modern differentiation was a gift of God, twisted to be sure like all such gifts but to be received with thanksgiving, redirected where necessary, and put to work to advance purposes pleasing to God.

Many of these Kuyperian motifs reappear as philosophical themes in Dooyeweerd's writings. It is important to introduce them here because

Dooyeweerd himself, working out of an assumed Kuyperian vision, often takes them for granted in his writings. The original significance of Dooyeweerd's theory of state and civil society, and its potential significance today, will come into view more clearly if we keep in mind his role as the philosophical inheritor and developer of an emancipatory, antihegemonic movement of democratic pluralism. This preliminary assessment is explored in the final chapter.

Some brief biographical remarks are in order at this point.[11] Dooyeweerd was raised in a household conversant with and supportive of a Kuyperian outlook and its many organizational expressions. He was educated in law at the Free University of Amsterdam, where he received his doctorate in 1917.[12] After a short spell as a civil servant in the Ministry of Labor, he briefly served as assistant director of the Abraham Kuyper-stichting, the research department of the Antirevolutionary Party. In 1923 he helped establish the political journal *Antirevolutionare Staatkunde,* to which he contributed for much of his career. He continued to exercise a significant, though by no means uncontested and never dominant, influence on policy debates within this party.[13] He was appointed professor of law at the Free University in 1926, presenting a substantial and original inaugural lecture titled "The Significance of the Law-Idea for Legal Theory and Legal Philosophy."[14] He held this position for the remainder of his professional life (1926–1965), enjoying growing support from within and beyond the academy but also facing some protracted and vigorous opposition, especially from certain theologians at the Free University who resented his questioning of the supremacy of theology over other disciplines and worried about the unsettling effects of his work on the Reformed church, of which most Kuyperians were members.[15] His scholarly interests were not exclusively concentrated in social or political theory. Indeed the majority of his writings fall within the fields of legal theory and systematic philosophy, his interests in the latter arising out of fundamental theoretical problems encountered as he confronted the former, as the title of his inaugural lecture suggests. He published the first edition of his magnum opus, *De Wijsbegeerte der Wetsidee* (The Philosophy of the Law-Idea), in 1935–1936. The influence of this work, as well as his earlier ones and works by several of his intellectual colleagues, in Calvinist intellectual circles was very considerable, and a new society, the Association for Calvinist Philosophy, was formed shortly after its appearance, with Dooyeweerd named as its vice-chairman.[16] In 1948 he was appointed to membership in the Dutch Royal Academy of the Sciences and served as secretary-treasurer of the Literature section from 1954 to 1964. On Dooyeweerd's seventieth birthday he was described by G. E. Langemeijer, then chairman of the Royal Academy, as "the most original philosopher that the Netherlands had ever produced, not excluding even Spinoza."[17] Dooyeweerd retired in 1965 and died in 1977.

Dooyeweerd's academic responsibilities at the Free University of Amsterdam were in the fields of legal philosophy, legal history, and legal science. In these areas his interests ranged very widely indeed, though with an emphasis on Continental, especially German, nineteenth- and early-twentieth-century legal philosophers such as Von Jhering, Kelsen, and Stammler.[18] In his systematic philosophy the range of thinkers with whom he interacted critically was equally wide-ranging and included, notably, Aristotle, Aquinas, Leibniz, Fichte, Kant, Husserl, and many of their contemporary disciples. His work in both legal theory (especially on the relationship between law and the state) and systematic philosophy (especially on the ontology of social structures) contributed decisively to his publications in social and political thought.[19]

My focus is on Dooyeweerd's mature social and political thought. The writings that will receive most attention appeared during the 1940s and 1950s. The institutional and philosophical problematics on which he was to concentrate had, however, begun to take on a clear shape already in his earliest writings of the 1920s; the essential structure of his constructive philosophy had been formulated by the mid-1930s. Since his scholarly writings span five decades it is not surprising that distinct phases in the evolution of his thought can be discerned.[20] Development is also evident in his social, legal, and political theory, and significant shifts will be noted.

From "Calvinist" to "Christian" Philosophy

Although Dooyeweerd's philosophy displays considerable originality, it was evidently shaped by its intellectual-historical context.[21] I have already outlined the confessional and social dimensions of the movement of Kuyperian neo-Calvinism in which his thought was formed. More needs to be said about the philosophical aspects of this movement, but I want to first characterize the wider intellectual context that Dooyeweerd initially sought to address.

In common with many Dutch scholars during the early decades of this century, Dooyeweerd's principal philosophical interests lay in Germany. Two contemporary German philosophical schools were significant in Dooyeweerd's development, neo-Kantianism and phenomenology.[22] When Dooyeweerd began his studies at the Free University of Amsterdam, neo-Kantianism in particular was becoming the dominant philosophical school not only in Germany[23] but also in the Netherlands. Professors at the Free University expressed sympathy with its attack on materialism and positivism, which they as Calvinists also rejected.[24] This sympathy is clear from the frequency and tenor of the references to neo-Kantians in Dooyeweerd's early publications. Critical study of these philosophers also led him to a detailed analysis of Kant's own works. While an index is of course no reliable guide to a thinker's influences, that the entry for "Kant" in the index to his magnum opus runs to thirteen pages, by far the longest, is instructive. The results of Dooyeweerd's sustained critical interaction both with Kant's philosophy and that of various nineteenth-century and early-twentieth-century neo-Kantians are evident throughout his writings. The very title of *A New Critique of Theoretical Thought*[25] echoes Kant's own *Critique of Pure Reason*. This "new critique," introduced in the next chapter, is characterized by Dooyeweerd in distinctively Kantian terminology as a "transcendental critique." Its aim is a critical investigation into the transcendental conditions of the possibility of theoretical thought.

In the second German philosophical school important in Dooyeweerd's development, phenomenology, the work of Hartmann is especially interesting (though the possible influence of Heidegger should not be discounted).[26] Originally a neo-Kantian himself, Hartmann rejected the idealism of the school, as Dooyeweerd himself had. As Wolters puts it, "This was grist for the mill of men like Dooyeweerd who were making an analogous philosophical pilgrimage."[27] Dooyeweerd's pilgrimage went further, however, and he claimed to have broken with phenomenology as decisively as he had with neo-Kantianism. Nevertheless, his basic theory of reality, the theory of "modal spheres," has on its face remarkable affinities with Hartmann's *"schichtentheorie,"* the theory of the "spheres of being."

Dooyeweerd acknowledges that he was originally "strongly under the influence" of both neo-Kantianism and phenomenology.[28] Commentators have subsequently debated how far this influence continued even after he repudiated the fundamental assumptions of both these schools.[29] It was certainly his intention to avoid synthesizing his thought with that of any thinker whose root conceptions he had rejected, even when he nonetheless expressed appreciation for aspects of their thought. Heiman's comment on Hegel can also be applied to Dooyeweerd: "he was not inclined to accept any concept which he did not formulate in his own fashion."[30]

Unlike Hegel, however, Dooyeweerd self-consciously acknowledges his primary dependence upon concepts deriving from a very localized historical movement. This was late-nineteenth-century neo-Calvinism, still vigorous in Dooyeweerd's early career. His writings can be seen as a critical development of many basic neo-Calvinist ideas. In Wolters's judgment, although the two schools of German philosophy mentioned above were the major source for Dooyeweerd's specifically philosophical conceptions, his "underlying worldview" was essentially continuous with the neo-Calvinist vision.[31] An examination of the Kantian and other philosophical influences upon Dooyeweerd's thought would be an indispensable prerequisite for a critical analysis of his ontology and epistemology; to attempt it here, however, would be a needless distraction.[32] The predominant influence of his neo-Calvinist worldview as compared to German philosophy is in any case clearly evident in his social and political thought.

In chapter 1 I noted that Kuyper's primary goal was to articulate a comprehensive Calvinist worldview capable of being implemented in the industrialized and increasingly differentiated society of nineteenth-century Europe. An effective Calvinist worldview must, he believed, match in scope and depth not only that of Catholicism but also those variants of secular Enlightenment humanism, or "modernism," that were increasingly dominating Western culture. Such a worldview would have to be rooted in the most adequate and comprehensive historic Christian confession, which for Kuyper was Calvinism.

Although Kuyper did not regard Calvinism first and foremost as an intellectual system, he was convinced it ought to generate one. The Calvinist worldview must be worked out in distinctive ethical, social, legal, political, aesthetic, and epistemological theories. A worldview or faith, whether based on divine revelation or some other focus of final allegiance, inevitably comes to expression when people engage in theoretical reflection. There is no antithesis between faith and science, but there is a radical antithesis—more overt in the highly value-oriented disciplines—between "two scientific elaborations [that] are opposed to each other, each having its own faith." There are thus two "absolute forms of science," both vigorously contesting every field of human knowledge and both presupposing a "god" of some kind as its point of departure.[33]

Such was Kuyper's vision of the scope and challenge of Calvinism. The powerful influence of Kuyper's thought is plain from Dooyeweerd's earliest publications.[34] He remained committed to its essentials throughout his life, although his articulation of the vision grew considerably in subtlety and critical sophistication as his thought matured. He came to believe early in his development that the renewal of Calvinism, indeed of Christianity as a whole, required far more sophisticated intellectual resources than those so far produced within neo-Calvinism. He devoted his life's work to generating such resources, in cooperation with several other neo-Calvinist scholars, mostly associated with the Free University of Amsterdam. Such resources were needed, he believed, to enable Christianity both to expose the radically flawed foundations of non-Christian thought and the compromised relationship with it into which Christianity had allowed itself to enter and to construct an integrated framework for Christian scholarship that could support the wider renewal of Christianity Kuyper had sought.

Although throughout his academic career Dooyeweerd belonged to the law department at the Free University, early in his development he came to the view that a Calvinist theory of law could not be adequately formulated without an underlying Calvinist systematic *philosophy*, a view implied by some of Kuyper's statements but never fully articulated. It would not be enough to apply Calvinist *theological* principles directly in the field of law, or any other science. What was needed was a philosophical framework as broad in scope as that of Aristotle, Thomas, or Hegel, one that would furnish the theoretical foundations for work not only in law, but in every special discipline, including social and political theory. As we shall see, he came to the view that philosophical presuppositions lay behind any definition of the territory of the various disciplines, including theology,[35] established the relations between them, and determined their overall theoretical directions. Christian theorizing in any discipline thus required the intermediary of a specifically Christian philosophical framework.

While Dooyeweerd acknowledged points of connection between his own attempt to formulate a specifically Christian political theory and that of other Christian contemporaries, he distinguished his enterprise from others by identifying it as part of a comprehensive task of the "inner reformation" of the sciences.[36] Audaciously, he judged that most previous attempts at Christian political theory had been built on an unstable and accommodationist "synthesis" of biblical religion with some variant of non-Christian philosophy, whether pagan Greek or modern humanist. Such a synthesis consisted of an external conjunction of internally incommensurable perspectives. His aim was to develop a systematic philosophy that was internally integrated with biblical religion and that could therefore serve as the framework for Christian scholarly work in the special sciences. The Christian religion was not to serve as a mere "decorative superstructure" over an essentially non-Christian science.[37]

Attempting to rejuvenate the medieval philosophical framework, as neo-Thomists were doing, would not do because this itself was an example of such a compromised relationship. Their "scholastic" conception of the relationship between faith and philosophy ruled out the possibility of a genuine inner reformation of philosophy. A philosophical framework rooted in Calvinism could therefore not simply adopt or merely modify scholastic concepts. In spite of this critical stance toward scholasticism, however, the contrast between the impressive legacy of Thomistic thought and the paucity of Calvinist philosophizing struck Dooyeweerd as early as 1925. In an article titled "Calvinism and Natural Law," he set forth a project of vast scope. Lamenting the fact that "the great architectonic line [of Calvinism] has not been carried through consistently," he urged the development of a "philosophical systematics" to integrate the fundamental principles of Calvinism, "encompassing the whole in the synthesis of the great governing idea." He singled out Calvinist political theory as amounting to little more than "a collection of adjacent and partially unrelated concepts, a complex of notions for the most part intuitively forged in the heat of battle and confused by foreign admixtures from the storehouses of Scholasticism and German scholarship."[38]

His major philosophical work attempting to implement this encyclopedic ambition was *De Wijsbegeerte der Wetsidee*,[39] which is literally translated as "The Philosophy of the Law-Idea" but has generally, and awkwardly, been rendered into English as "The Philosophy of the Cosmonomic Idea." *A New Critique of Theoretical Thought* is the considerably revised and extended English translation, and it contains the most detailed articulation of his mature social and political theory.

I have pointed out Dooyeweerd's initial aim to elaborate philosophically the basic assumptions of Calvinism. His early writings call explicitly for the development of a "Calvinist" philosophy. Later on, however, he abandoned this designation of his project and spoke subsequently of "Christian philosophy." The "biblical ground motive" to which he adhered was, he claimed, essentially *ecumenical* in character and could never be seen as the possession of any particular confessional movement.[40] The mature philosophy to which I turn in the next chapter was animated by this ecumenical aspiration. (Later I suggest that the implications of this aspiration for social and political philosophy were not fully recognized by him.) Even though it remained clearly recognizable as a fruit of the neo-Calvinist vision, its significance and interest, I hope to show, certainly came to transcend its specific historical and confessional origins.

A GUIDE TO THIS BOOK

In view of the great complexity and at times obscurity of Dooyeweerd's thought, an extended overview of what follows may be helpful. As noted, the purpose of this book is to expound critically Dooyeweerd's social and political theory so as to exhibit its relevance for contemporary debates about the state–civil society relationship. I present Dooyeweerd as a sophisticated and penetrating (if at times grandly flawed) Christian contributor to that stream of thought I have designated normative institutional pluralism. The principal achievement of his social pluralism is the articulation of a complex, wide-ranging, and frequently illuminating

theoretical account of multiple types of social institutions and relationships. In the final chapter I seek to demonstrate the fruitfulness of key
aspects of this account in recent debates about the components and
dynamics of civil society.

Chapters 3 and 4 outline the core philosophical concepts that are
presupposed throughout all aspects of his thought, and chapters 4
through 10 present the substance of his social and political theory. That
theory is, at bottom, an account of the basic design of social reality construed as divinely created. Accordingly, the aim of chapters 3 and 4 is to
present Dooyeweerd as a philosopher of created order. But Dooyeweerd's
goal was not simply thetical but also dialogical: he was not satisfied with
simply asserting his philosophy of created order on the basis of his Christian confession but aspired to elaborate it in a way that invited and facilitated critical dialogue across convictional divides. I therefore preface the
exposition of his philosophy of created order in chapter 3 with a brief
statement of his "transcendental critique of theoretical thought." This
amounts to an analysis of why all philosophical activity in any field always necessarily proceeds on the basis of deeper presuppositions of an
ultimately religious character. I avoid delving far into epistemology or
philosophy of religion here, but an initial grasp of this novel and ambitious methodology is important in order to make sense of his methodology in social and political theory. The chief goal of this stage in the
discussion is to explain the central idea of a "religious ground motive."
Dooyeweerd's basic claim is that the history of social and political philosophy reveals the powerful if often concealed influence of such ground
motives. Any social philosopher wishing to make an informed, critical,
and self-critical contribution to the field, he holds, should understand
what these ground motives are and how they have shaped the history of
the field. Indeed it is precisely the operation of defective ground motives
that have obstructed the development of a genuinely pluralistic social
theory, one capable of resisting the constant tendencies toward either individualism or universalism—toward reducing society to merely contingent relations between individuals or construing it as some unitary,
monistic whole.

This very brief foray into epistemology is followed by an overview of
his most fundamental religious and philosophical convictions. For reasons alluded to in chapter 3, Dooyeweerd resists referring to religious

convictions as "theological" in nature, speaking instead of "the biblical ground motive of creation, fall and redemption in Jesus Christ." But it is clear that he is operating on the basis of a very distinctly Calvinian understanding of these central Christian doctrines (he also refers to them separately as "motives"). What is striking about his account of these three "motives" is their comprehensiveness: the whole of reality is construed as created, sustained, and ordered by God; such reality is comprehensively distorted (but not at all destroyed) by the fall; and the whole of reality is swept up in God's redemptive work through history. It is therefore simply inconceivable for him that any dimension of reality—the character and activities of contemporary social institutions, for instance—could be adequately made sense of without discerning the enduring created design underlying them, the effects of human evil and violence corrupting them, and their potential for redemptive redirection (even in "the present age"). The result of this vision is not to "theologize" social realities (as the school known as Radical Orthodoxy is sometimes charged with doing),[41] nor is it to call for some political campaign to "Christianize" society but rather to articulate a bona fide philosophical method allowing such a "biblical" vision to guide theory construction in any discipline from within— resulting in what he termed the "inner reformation of the [social] sciences."

This overview of his most basic "theological" convictions is followed by a sketch of his foundational philosophical assumptions. These are fundamental matters of "ontology" (or metaphysics—another term he resisted), concerning the basic design of the (created) universe. Basic to his ontology are highly distinctive concepts regarding the dependence of created reality on God ("meaning"), the dynamic design of created being ("time"), and the universally valid structure of that design ("law"). It is the latter two that play the more formative roles in his social philosophy. Like all of reality, Dooyeweerd holds, social phenomena are "temporal." By this he does not mean that they simply undergo duration but rather that they exist and function within a complex, universally holding, temporally charged design. To make sense of the order underlying them, it is necessary not simply to gaze at their particular contemporary manifestations but also to interpret them as caught up in a larger process of historical and cultural development. Equally, and like all of reality, social phenomena are "law-ordered." The sense of law here is not that associated with positivist social science—where the search is for lawlike regularities on the model of the natural sciences—but more akin to that propounded by classical natural law theories in which concrete social entities such as families are interpreted as reflecting inner imperatives arising from created human nature.

Chapter 4 then traces Dooyeweed's more detailed elaboration of these three core notions, especially that of law. He holds that two interlocking axes of order can be discerned within all and any existing phenomena. There is both an order of irreducible dimensions of things ("modal aspects") and an order of different types of things ("individuality"). On close inspection, he argues, the concrete phenomena we bump into—rocks, trees, families, and so forth—seem to display multiple dimensions or "ways of being" that cannot be reduced to each other and that are also universally shared. To identify the precise character of individual phenomena such as social institutions we need (for purposes of theory construction) to engage in a careful analysis of their many modal dimensions, isolate those that are especially important to them, draw up a conceptual map of how all these dimensions interact in distinctive ("typical") ways in each one, and then try to map how different "types" of institutions interrelate to each other in special ways (how they are "interlinked" or "interlaced" with each other). If we go wrong at this stage, we might end up devising a theory that, for example, construes families as networks of contracts, markets as centers of personal agency, or states as telephone companies (to allude to Alasdair McIntyre's provocative description of the modern state). In other words, these seemingly technical and obscure matters of social ontology (and there are delights aplenty of this kind in that chapter and the next two) shape whether a social theory is or is not conducive to human flourishing. Societal health is affected by social ontology.

Chapter 5 picks up the theme of the temporality of social realities by expounding the rich but problematic philosophy of "cultural disclosure" that Dooyeweerd constructs out of it. Social institutions, he argues, have durable natures. Yet they necessarily surface in and are profoundly shaped by particular historical contexts. How do their durability and their historicity relate? Dooyeweerd's sweeping philosophies of history and culture are sketched in this chapter with a view to showing how they frame and inform his constructive accounts of social institutions, relationships, and processes. I show how concepts of institutional "differentiation" (comparable to Weber's notion) and societal "integration" (comparable to Hegel's) play a central role.

This chapter and the next are more overtly critical than previous ones: they are especially concerned with assessing a major objection to Dooyeweerd's account of the durability and essential stability of the normative design of social institutions. He holds that social structures (a broad term including institutions, associations, communities, even "relationships" of many kinds) are conditioned by enduring normative designs ("structural principles") that substantially condition their existence and behavior. While only appearing at particular points in history, they are nevertheless "invariant" in the specific ways they contribute to human flourishing. The account of his theory of cultural development in chapter 5 places this controversial claim in its necessary context, showing how supposedly invariant institutions nevertheless seem to be tossed around on the seas of history a fair bit, even as their members strive to retain their stable identity. Yet his insistence on the invariance claim is striking and instructive, yet problematic. Chapter 6 expounds that claim in detail, subjects it to a critical interrogation, and proposes a more plausible construction. In the course of doing so, several important new features of Dooyeweerd's social ontology are introduced, notably the central role played in a "structural principle" by the two modal aspects—in some contexts referred to as "functions"—that more than any others frame the identity of any particular social structure: the "qualifying" function and the "founding" function. The differences between these are crucial in distinguishing one structure from another, and on this basis a complex classification of "types" of structures is developed.

A recurring objection to Dooyeweerd's theory of societal structural types is that it commits something like the "essentialist" fallacy—that things in the world have preordained, unchanging essences, or fixed identities—and so ends up in a social conservatism that denies historical variation and constricts freedom. The central move I then make in reconstructing his theory is to ground it much more fully than he himself does in a thick and clearly articulated conception of human flourishing. The aim is to mute if not entirely blunt the objection that in his own account human beings sometimes seem to function as fodder for institution building rather than as the *point* of building any institution at all.

Chapter 7 completes the presentation of Dooyeweerd's social theory by spelling out in more detail his accounts of many kinds of social structures. We are introduced, first, to an entirely new and somewhat unexpected set of categories for mapping such structures: these are identified as "communities" or "interlinkages"; "organized" or "natural" communities; "differentiated" or "undifferentiated" communities; and "institutional" or "voluntary" communities. Given that we already seemed to have at hand a reasonably adequate classification system (i.e., according to type), the systematic necessity for this additional classification remains somewhat opaque. Nevertheless the insights yielded by it turn out to be quite substantial, and these insights play a central role in Dooyeweerd's crucial pluralist claims. The chapter proceeds with a fuller discussion of his view of the complex interrelationships of distinct social structures, an important but often neglected part of pluralist theory. I show that Dooyeweerd's own account stands in need of significant reconceptualization if it is to do the work he intends it to do. To that end I draw on a modified version of the Catholic principle of subsidiarity. The chapter concludes by synthesizing diverse threads in Dooyeweerd's social theory and showing how that theory, notwithstanding its defects, commands attention as a significant contribution to the pluralist social vision and an insightful source of criticism of its chief rivals, individualism and universalism. Here the distinctive notion of societal sphere sovereignty, inherited from Kuyper, comes fully into its own.

Chapters 8 through 10 then address in detail those aspects of Dooyeweerd's political theory bearing directly on his pluralist vision. Dooyeweerd spends more time analyzing the state than he does any other institution. In some respects his theory of the state stands within the main parameters of the classical (especially Augustinian) and early modern (especially Calvinist) Christian political tradition (his attempts to put clear blue water between his own thought and Thomism are not always as successful as he would have wished). Yet the details of his constructive account are distinctive and illuminating.

Chapter 8 describes and assesses his depiction of the state as characterized by specific understandings of power and law. These are termed its founding and qualifying functions, respectively. The chapter opens by tracing his critical exposure of the political theories current in his time. Such theories, he ventured, had landed themselves in an insoluble theoretical crisis on account of having embraced the fallacies of positivism and historicism, causing them to abandon the quest to identify the state's enduring structure. The chapter then expounds Dooyeweerd's lengthy treatments of how power relates to law in the state. He holds that the state's coercive power is essential to its intrinsic design (a point I later criticize), yet insists that such power must always remain subservient to the definitive normative purpose of establishing a regime of just law in society. The focus here is the state's "founding function," yet it already becomes clear at this point how this function is not mere physical force but a complex of resources needed by the state if it is to be a genuinely public institution, one able to govern effectively on behalf of its entire citizenry and not find itself in thrall to sectional interests.

The theme of justice—specifically public justice (the more precise designation of the state's qualifying function) is taken up at length in chapter 9. The first section explores Dooyeweerd's understanding of the relation between law and justice, showing how what sometimes comes across as a narrowly legal or constitutional view of the state actually conveys a thick, substantive view of the state's role. The state, he holds, is charged with establishing, through law, a just balance among numerous legitimate claims thrown up by complex, dynamic modern societies. Such diverse claims arise from the fact of a plurality of "spheres of justice," to use Walzer's term. Challenging monistic theories of law that seek to derive all legal authority from the sovereign authority of the state, Dooyeweerd espouses a distinctive pluralistic theory of law in which original lawmaking power is attributed to many different social structures. The state's task is to protect and adjudicate among these legitimate claimants and not to usurp or thwart them for its own political ends. In order to do this it must, in the first instance, correctly discern the structural identities of many social institutions (as well as honor the rights of individuals). In defining the state somewhat clinically as a "public-legal community," Dooyeweerd's larger intention is that the state (whose members are both government and citizens) discharge effective justice to persons, institutions, and (as we see in chapter 10) the larger public interest. The chapter concludes by exploring critically the distinctive sense in which Dooyeweerd's theory affirms the central commitments of constitutional democracy. In the process I propose a correction to his rather thin and hesitant conception of democratic representation.

If chapter 9 is concerned with Dooyeweerd's account of what the state essentially is (its "structure"), chapter 10 moves to explore what it properly does (its "task"). The first step is to reconstruct his rather disparate and not entirely coherent expositions of the central idea of public justice. This, he holds, is the overriding norm guiding all legitimate state activities. I show how he intends this as a dynamic vocation for a just state, involving actions of many kinds across (in principle) all sectors of society, some protective in intention, some reformist. I also convey Dooyeweerd's characteristic insistence that as the state pursues public justice it must honor the unique sphere sovereignty of other structures and not trample upon it. The second part of this chapter selects four concrete applications of the state's public justice task. It assesses in some detail Dooyeweerd's accounts (which vary in depth and extent) of the relationship between, in turn, nation, family, church, and industry (the latter serving as an especially instructive example). Here we are able more fully to test the concrete relevance of the otherwise highly abstract set of concepts making up his political philosophy. Notwithstanding the criticisms of several of these concepts leveled in earlier chapters, I conclude that the idea of public justice, suitably reformulated, can nevertheless serve as a meaningful guide through some leading public policy issues facing a complex modern society.

The final chapter picks up that finding and explores it in critical dialogue with three leading questions in contemporary debates about civil society. The first of these is simply, "What is civil society?" I suggest that light is shed on the question if we make use of Dooyeweerd's distinctive pluralist notions of, first, "irreducible institutional identity" and, second, the "correlation of communities and interlinkages." These notions direct us to correctly discern and support the full range of irreducible institutions and relationships (and here I propose a new term, *interdependencies*) necessary for a flourishing human society. They also caution us against various one-sided emphases in civil society debates as to which institutional sectors are where the real action is. The second question—"What is civil society for?"—and the third—"Can the concept of civil society generate robust social critique?"—are engaged with reference to the three models of civil society I outlined in chapter 1: the protective, the integrative, and the transformative. I show how Dooyeweerd's core notions can enable us to identify valid intuitions in each of these models while arguing that his accounts yet lack sufficient transformative bite. A short epilogue returns to the question, raised in chapter 1, of how an overtly religious social theory like Dooyeweerd's might yet enter constructively into public debates in a secular, pluralistic society.

THREE

RELIGION AND PHILOSOPHY

The Necessity of Religious Presuppositions

Dooyeweerd's conception of the relationship between religion and philosophy enters a debate reaching back even before Augustine's monu-
mental effort to transform the inheritance of classical thought in the light
of biblical religion.[1] This debate has been engaged under various head-
ings, such as the relationship between faith and reason, theology and philosophy, faith and philosophy, natural and revealed knowledge, or Christian and secular thought.[2] A characteristic feature of Dooyeweerd's
contribution to this debate is his repudiation of any approach that regards these terms as pitted against each other, in tension with each other,
referring to distinct realms of being, or as standing in a relationship of
mere complementarity. On the contrary, his project is to demonstrate the
full integrality of the relationship between—to use his terms—religion
and philosophy. Christian philosophy is not a branch or extension of
theology; nor is it a set of background constraints or guidelines within
which the quest for "rational" or "natural" or "secular" knowledge is
joined; nor is it primarily what today is typically termed "philosophy of
religion." Christian philosophy, he holds, is philosophy that takes up a
common philosophical task—a systematic theoretical investigation of
the deepest structures of reality—from the perspective of and as penetrated and guided by the Christian religion.

Van Woudenberg observes that Anselm's classic formulation of
Christian philosophy as "faith seeking understanding" can be interpreted
in two ways. The dominant approach has understood this phrase as

39

referring to the rational investigation of the contents of faith: to engage in "thinking believing," as he puts it. Dooyeweerd, he suggests, represents a second approach, the aim of which is not reflection on faith with the aid of reason but rather philosophical reflection on *reality* in the light of faith: the pursuit of "believing thinking."[3]

It is entirely consonant with this second approach that Dooyeweerd opens *NC* not by outlining the neo-Calvinist religious convictions upon which it is evidently based but rather by examining the nature of *theory*. The purpose of this examination is the construction of an elaborate argument for the dependence of *all* philosophical reflection on presuppositions of a religious character. This argument is described as a "transcendental critique of theoretical thought." It is a "new" critique in the sense that it is post-Kantian; indeed, it is presented as a radical Christian critique of Kantianism. Assessing the conceptual origins and evaluating the epistemological implications of this program lie beyond the scope of this study,[4] but since Dooyeweerd's critical analyses of social and political theorists are presented as instances of his larger transcendental critique of Western philosophy as a whole, a summary sketch is necessary.

The object of the transcendental critique is to demonstrate the necessary dependence of such thought upon ultimate religious presuppositions of a pretheoretical character—to contest what Clouser calls "the myth of religious neutrality."[5] Dooyeweerd's claim is that this presuppositional dependence is an inescapable feature of all theorizing, whether Christian or not. Clearly if he can successfully prove that philosophical theories devised by thinkers who do not share his Christian confession are themselves embedded in deeper commitments of a religious nature, then he has gone a long way to removing the standard objection that a Christian philosophy and the Christian social and political theory rooted in it rest finally upon faith and not reason and so cannot be regarded as an equal partner in the rational philosophical discourse of the Western tradition. His aim is, moreover, to vindicate the enterprise of Christian philosophy without endorsing a Thomistic formulation of the distinction between revelation and natural reason, which, he claims, cedes too much autonomy to the latter and so leaves it insufficiently transformed by religion. But this justificatory aim is only a part of his larger purpose, one that grew in importance as his thought developed, which is to establish the conditions on which genuine philosophical *communication* could occur between thinkers of radically opposed standpoints. Such communication presupposed a rigorously honest exposure of the most fundamental presuppositions underlying both one's own and one's opponents' theoretical standpoints.[6]

In *NC* Dooyeweerd proposes two distinct ways to approach this task. The "first way" to a transcendental critique was already advanced in *WdW* and is reiterated in the opening pages of *NC*.[7] The "second way" was subsequently developed to meet a major criticism of the first way, and it is clear that Dooyeweerd believes it is a more persuasive approach. His first way argues that it is in the *nature of philosophy* to be oriented to ultimate presuppositions of a religious character, since it necessarily aims to grasp the totality and integrality of reality. His second way seeks to reach the same conclusion by investigating the internal structure of *theoretical thought* itself, of which philosophy is but one manifestation. The second way avoids the objection that his case rests upon a specific and controversial conception of the nature of philosophy, the acceptance of which asks too much of thinkers with whom he wishes to enter into dialogue.[8] What is needed, Dooyeweerd comes to recognize, is an account of the *internal structure of theorizing itself,* one capable of embracing any particular conception of the philosophical task.[9] This will involve nothing less than "a critical inquiry into the universally valid conditions which alone make theoretical thought possible, and which are required by the immanent structure of this thought itself."[10] Dooyewerd's aim is to show that the most basic of these conditions is the inescapable dependence of all theorizing upon a commitment of a *religious* nature.

A *transcendental* analysis of theorizing, the quest for its conditions of possibility, is to be sharply distinguished from a *transcendent* critique. This distinction is at the heart of Dooyeweerd's claim to have produced a fully Christian philosophical framework that can distinguish itself from theology and can display as genuine a philosophical character as any non-Christian philosophies. A transcendent critique

does not really touch the inner character and the immanent structure of the theoretical attitude of thought, but confronts, for instance Christian faith with the results of modern science and with the various philosophical systems, and thus ascertains whether or not factual conflicts exist. It remains dogmatic, however, as long as it fails squarely to face the primary question whether the theoretical attitude of thought itself . . . can be independent of supratheoretical prejudices.[11]

If Christians were to rely only upon a transcendent critique of modern thought they would find themselves unable to detect whether the results of such thought bear the stamp of anti-Christian presuppositions. Moreover, such a critique is dogmatic, essentially superficial, and therefore potentially dangerous in theoretical discourse. It is "valueless to science and philosophy, because it confronts with each other two different spheres whose inner point of contact is left completely in the dark."[12]

Dooyeweerd claims, after extensive argumentation, that a thorough analysis of the internal structure of theorizing discloses the presence of a "transcendental ground Idea," which all philosophies must, whether they know it or not, assume.[13] Once it has been demonstrated that such an Idea grounds all philosophical theories, the way is clear for a distinctively Christian philosophy rooted in the Christian transcendental ground Idea to be articulated without apology within the philosophical community and for it to enter into critical dialogue with non-Christian philosophies.

As Dooyeweerd's account of the transcendental critique proceeds, however, it becomes apparent that his very formulation of these basic problems presupposes large portions of his general ontology, which in *NC* are only fully elaborated long after his transcendental critique has been completed. Thus, while the second way may avoid a controversial assumption about the nature of philosophy, it seems to end up resting upon far more momentous assumptions about the nature of the whole of reality. Critics have therefore argued that the transcendental critique does not achieve the objective Dooyeweerd has in mind, namely, to prove from an analysis of the very nature of theorizing itself that theory rests on religious assumptions.[14] It is not necessary to explore this critical response here. What is significant for the purposes of this book is not whether this transcendental proof, or some modification of it, holds or not but rather the substance of Dooyeweerd's analysis of the religious assumptions underlying social and political theories and the implications of this analysis for his own pluralist theory. To do this I need to examine at greater length his account of the manner in which religious presuppositions are supposed to condition theorizing. This brings us to his notion of a religious ground motive, the analysis of which he calls "the decisive stage" of the transcendental critique.[15]

A religious ground motive is the deepest factor underlying all intellectual activity and indeed all other forms of human activity.[16] The term has an obvious affinity with parallel terms such as *zeitgeist* or *cultural ethos* but in fact has a more precise meaning. A ground motive is a comprehensive, pretheoretical and supraindividual religious vision that profoundly shapes all aspects of the cultural period of which it is characteristic.[17] Dooyeweerd identifies four ground motives as having principally determined the direction of Western civilization since classical times.[18] The first is the Greek ground motive of "form and matter." Although only receiving formal statement in Aristotle, it shaped Greek culture from the time of the city-states, originating in an "unreconciled conflict" between a deified "formless, cyclical stream of life" emerging from the ancient nature religions and a principle of order, of harmonic form, associated with the later culture religion of the Olympian deities. This form-matter motive continued to exercise cultural dominance and profoundly conditioned the character of Greek and Roman philosophy and culture.[19]

The biblical ground motive is the second, decisively breaking with the pagan assumptions of classical Greek culture and opening up the prospects for a thoroughgoing reorientation of culture (and not only in the West). I summarize Dooyeweerd's account of this motive in the next section.

The medieval scholastic ground motive of "nature and grace" amounted to an ultimately fruitless attempt to achieve a synthesis of the biblical and Greek ground motives. Although nature was now understood by all significant Christian thinkers as divine creation, it was conceived of in ways too heavily indebted to the form-matter motive of Greek thought, while grace appeared as a "supernatural" phenomenon, a "superadded" gift, raising nature to perfection through the mediatorial role of the church.[20]

Finally, modern humanism represents a secularized ground motive of "nature and freedom" in which an unbounded desire for rational "control" over "nature" (now conceived not teleologically but mechanistically) finds itself in an irreconcilable dialectical tension with a "faith in the absolute autonomy of free personality."[21] While it was Kant who raised this motive to a level of high philosophical sophistication, the humanistic ground motive originates from the collapse of the unstable scholastic synthesis, molded modern Western culture from the time of the Renaissance through the seventeenth-century scientific revolution, the Enlightenment, and the Romantic reaction, and itself began to implode in twentieth-century nihilism.[22]

The foregoing is but a schematic outline of each, summarizing hundreds of pages of detailed exposition scattered across several texts. I later expand on relevant aspects of these ground motives. The point at issue here is the way in which such ground motives influence the philosophical enterprise. Importantly, Dooyeweerd holds that ground motives do not operate immediately on philosophical thought but give direction to such thought through certain very fundamental theoretical notions—"Ideas"—situated at the boundary between religious commitment and philosophical thought. They operate on philosophy, he tells us, "through the medium of a triad of transcendental (ground) Ideas, which correspond to and yield the answers to the three transcendental basic problems."[23] These Ideas provide the fundamental determining categories on the basis of which more detailed concept formation in philosophy takes place. Their function is to mediate the contents of the pretheoretical religious ground motive in the realm of theory. The three Ideas are in fact three components of a *single* transcendental ground-Idea, referred to earlier as a "cosmonomic idea.[24] Such an idea acts, as it were, as an epistemological or discursive transformer, changing the pretheoretical current of religious presuppositions into the different current of theory.[25]

The very idea of a ground motive evidently awakens a host of critical questions.[26] Before I outline Dooyeweerd's account of the biblical ground motive and the transcendental Ideas it generates, four deserve immediate mention. First, while ground motives are characterized as comprehensive cultural forces, Dooyeweerd's account of them concentrates very largely on their *philosophical* articulations, at decisive periods of Western intellectual transition. Contrary to his intentions, this often creates the impression that ground motives are merely crystallizations of leading theoretical debates or conflicts and leaves us with little clue as to the precise relationship between philosophy and culture.[27] Second, these accounts also suggest that Dooyeweerd has lapsed into a form of speculative ideal-ist history in which multiple concrete particulars are, after the fashion of Hegel, explained as manifestations of the progressive unfolding of some underlying comprehensive cultural idea. Third, the vast scope of intellectual history supposedly explained as driven by a particular ground motive leads Dooyeweerd open to the charge of schematism, of having constructed an interpretive grid that forces ideas and thinkers into an artificial and therefore misleading schema.

This is not the place to test these three criticisms; I briefly take up the second in chapter 5 and return to the third at various points. The fourth criticism, however, is directly germane to the theme of this chapter and would stand even if he could offer cogent replies to the first three. Dooyeweerd's account of the "necessary presuppositions of philosophy" (the subtitle of the first volume of *NC*) evokes the question whether his claim regarding philosophy's rootedness in religious presuppositions is, after all, compatible with his aim of facilitating genuine philosophical communication. His case is that the ground Idea of a Christian philosophy is incommensurable with those of what he terms "immanence philosophy," that is, philosophy whose ground Idea refers to some feature immanent within the creation order itself. As I noted, an unbridgeable radical antithesis separates the two, so that no compromise *at this level* is possible. Christian philosophy "cannot permit itself to accept within its own cadre of thought problems of immanence-philosophy which originate from the dialectic ground motives of the latter."[28] Precisely such an illegitimate compromise with immanence philosophy is seen in patristic thought and even more so in medieval scholasticism. And while the Reformation's rediscovery of an integral biblical ground motive, found in purest form in Calvin, should have generated an authentically Christian philosophical tradition, Calvin's promising initiative was derailed by subsequent Protestant synthesizers and so must be reappropriated today.[29] Such a starting point implies a continuing radical "inner reformation" of philosophical thought and a repudiation of the presuppositions of immanence philosophy (some examples are noted in due course).[30]

It is essential to note that Dooyeweerd specifically urges the rejection only of the *religious presuppositions* of immanence philosophy and the philosophical problematics to which they give rise. He does not say that the *fruits* of immanence philosophy are of no value in the elaboration of a Christian philosophy. Indeed at numerous points in his writings he affirms the value of "insights" (rather than "truths"), sometimes of a fundamentally important nature, developed by leading immanence philosophers; I note some examples later. Furthermore he acknowledges that all philosophical activity, including Christian philosophy, takes place in the context of a particular historical tradition to which he attempts to do justice and whose character conditions it decisively. Dooyeweerd claims to be able to offer, within the terms of his own philosophy, an account of how immanence philosophy is able to produce such insights in spite of the radically misconceived, "apostate," orientation of its starting point. In order to do this he appeals to a notion of indisputable "states of affairs," a notion that also explains how philosophies premised on radically opposed religious starting points can cooperate in the same philosophical task. Although a philosophy is directed by particular religious presuppositions, its task is not simply to elaborate these presuppositions but rather, in their light, to render an account of the order of reality. The structure of this reality (2 x 2 = 4, for instance) is not determined by the subjective pretheoretical standpoint of the philosopher. Such states of affairs are founded in the order of creation, and they "force themselves upon everybody." It is the task of all philosophies—wittingly or not—to give an account of them.[31] In so accounting for them, however, different philosophies will interpret them differently according to their own transcendental ground Ideas.[32] Yet while no religiously neutral interpretation of undeniable states of affairs is possible, immanence philosophy can nevertheless uncover many of them, indeed many that Christian philosophy may have overlooked or misconceived.[33] Dooyeweerd acknowledges that Christian philosophy thus has no "privileged position" in this regard.

Insights into states of affairs, from wheresoever they come, contribute to the intellectual context in which Christian philosophy is historically practiced, a context that functions as a basis for communication across philosophical schools. A Christian philosophy whose aim is the inner *reformation* of philosophy could not possibly succeed were it to attempt to sever its links with historical traditions of philosophizing, for reformation "is not creation out of nothing."[34] Dooyeweerd acknowledges not only that his own philosophy can only be understood as a product of the Kuyperian neo-Calvinist movement in the nineteenth-century Netherlands[35] but also that it is "wedded to the historical development of philosophic and scientific thought with a thousand ties." Such ties, he concedes, can be perceived even in two of his most fundamental conceptions, sphere sovereignty and the transcendental critique.[36] At the same time he still insists that this weddedness signifies no marrying of ground Ideas. While a Christian *philosophy* has learned and will continue to learn from the insights of immanence philosophy, the *religious starting point* of Christian philosophy cannot be accommodated to any other and so is not negotiable.[37] His critique of Thomist social and political thought, to which I return at various points, will prove an instructive case study of the adequacy of this view of the relationship between Christian and immanence philosophy.

The Biblical Ground Motive

Dooyeweerd's most fundamental religious convictions are encapsulated in what he terms the biblical ground motive, the motive of "creation, fall and redemption through Jesus Christ in the communion of the Holy Spirit."[38] In these words Dooyeweerd believes he has captured the essential core of biblical Christianity. Claiming to stand in the line of Augustine, Calvin, and Kuyper, Dooyeweerd identifies the theme of God as absolutely sovereign creator as the indispensable foundation of biblical religion. This is the *"creation motive."* It is "integral," embracing everything created, and "radical," penetrating to the root of reality.[39] The design of the created cosmos is determined throughout by "divine law,"[40] which structures and sustains its existence.

The creation motive grounds the biblical understanding of humanity's relationship to God. God finds his creaturely image in the human "heart," the unifying religious center or "spiritual root" of human beings. The human heart is in fact the concentration point or religious unity of the whole creation. All human life therefore is to be directed to the service of God in willing obedience to his law.[41] Dooyeweerd endorses Augustine's view that the heart or soul "is identical with our relationship to God." The term *soul* does not denote any of the particular properties of the human being but is the concentrating unity of these properties. It is the "religious focus of human existence in which all . . . diverging rays are concentrated."[42]

Humankind as image bearer of God is called to exercise dominion, under divine law, over the whole of creation.[43] This is the "Divine cultural commandment" based on Genesis 1:26–8. "God created man as *lord* of creation. The powers and potentials which God had *enclosed* within creation were to be *disclosed* by man in his service of love to God and neighbour."[44] Moreover, humankind has been created as a spiritually unified community, a "religious root community," "governed and maintained by a religious spirit that works in it as a central force." God's plan in creation is that this spirit be the Holy Spirit, whose function is to unify humans with each other and with God. That human communities can be driven by a religious ground motive is thus in itself a consequence of their created structure, although the presence of *apostate* ground motives is the result of the fall.[45]

The biblical revelation of fall and redemption can only be understood against this background of the creation motive. The *fall* is essentially a radical rupturing of humankind's religious relationship to God, a rebellion against the reign of his law, the original act of apostasy. Nothing in the original creation itself made the fall in any way inevitable. The fall is an ultimately unprovoked, unprecedented, and inexplicable human act of revolt against God and his order of creation, bearing in its train catastrophic consequence for the whole of creation. In Dooyeweerd's thought there is therefore no place for any notion like *felix culpa,* a "happy fall." The fall is an act occurring within creation, a rebellion of the creature against God's law. In the fall the three central relationships in which humanity is created—with God, with itself, and with creation—are radically distorted. In its revolt humanity no longer retains a true knowledge of God. Humans are estranged from their creator. Simultaneously they lose true self-knowledge, as an "apostate ground motive" seizes the heart. Such a ground motive "forces a man to see himself in the image of his idol,"[46] and this idolatry is at the root of all false conceptions of reality, all illegitimate "absolutizations" of one particular aspect of creation.

Human beings' relationships to the rest of creation, both humans and nature, are also profoundly disturbed. Without the unifying Spirit of God the human community breaks up into conflicting spiritual communities, each also divided within itself. And humanity's relationship to the nonhuman creation is also implicated in its spiritual rebellion against the creator. Just because the meaning and destiny of the whole creation is concentrated in humankind, so the whole creation is caught up in the damaging effects of the fall. The fall "swept with it the entire temporal world precisely because the latter finds its religious root unity only in man."[47]

The fall does not abrogate the divine order of creation as such. It does not imply "an autonomous, self-determining principle of origin opposed to the creator. . . . Sin exists only in a *false relation to God* and is therefore never independent of the creator." Echoing Augustine, Dooyeweerd holds that it is only divine law which holds a fallen creation in existence: "Without the law commanding good there could be no evil. But the same law makes it possible for the creature to exist. Without the law man would sink into nothingness; the law determines his humanity."[48] Dooyeweerd therefore rejects what he takes to be the Barthian view that the original creation ordinances have been accommodated to humanity's fallen condition and are therefore no longer knowable in their original intention. "Sin changes not the creational decrees but the direction of the human heart."[49] Nor is the central cultural commandment of Genesis 1 suspended, though since humanity's capacity to respond to it is seriously impaired, an optimistic expectation of inevitable cultural progress is necessarily ruled out.[50]

Just as the fall effects a radical rupturing of creation, *redemption* brings about a radical and comprehensive restoration of creation. When the Word became flesh, it penetrated to the religious root of human life. Redemption means "the rebirth of man and, in him, of the entire created temporal world which finds in man its center." Redemption neither abrogates nor supersedes the creation, for the redemptive Word is also the creative Word.[51] For Dooyeweerd, this does not imply a universalistic conception of salvation according to which all humans, irrespective of allegiance to Christ, would be ultimately redeemed.[52] It is precisely God's redemptive intervention culminating in Jesus Christ that introduces a radical spiritual battle, or "antithesis," within the human race between the spirit of faith and the spirit of apostasy, "an unrelenting struggle between the kingdom of God and that of darkness" that will continue until the end of time, even though it is in principle already reconciled by Christ's redemption.[53] The two poles of this antithesis are not coterminous with the communities of believers and unbelievers; the spiritual battle is waged within each human being, including Christians.

The divine upholding of the law-governed order of creation in the face of human rebellion is, in its deepest sense, an act of grace, of "common grace" since it benefits believers and unbelievers alike. Yet common grace is not a realm of divine action apart from Christ but rather operates through Christ. Common grace presupposes and rests upon Christ's creative and redemptive work and is thus an expression of his kingship.[54] The resources all human beings can use to resist the destructive forces of sin—the means to fight disease, psychological disorder, injustice, or cultural degeneration—are all "fruits of Christ's work."[55] Indeed on account of divine common grace we are shielded from experiencing what the unrestrained effects of the fall on creation would have been.[56] "Common grace curbs the effects of sin and restrains the universal demonization of fallen man, so that traces of the light of God's power, goodness, truth, righteousness and beauty still shine in culture directed toward apostasy."[57] While the reality of the fall excludes an optimistic view of culture, the presence of common grace also rules out "the radical pessimism of a modern philosophy of cultural decline" and keeps Christians from "an abandonment of culture to the power of apostasy."[58] In common grace God maintains the universal order of creation holding for all humans. Humans may violate this order, but they will reap the adverse consequences of so doing.[59] Common grace is not a qualification of the antithesis between biblical and apostate ground motives. It does not introduce an area of neutral territory within which the spiritual battle is suspended but is itself part of the battle. In common grace God upholds his law in the face of human apostasy. It is thus a manifestation of the antithesis rather than a blurring of it. It will operate until the final judgment "when the reborn creation, liberated from its participation in the sinful root of human nature, will shine with the highest perfection."[60]

It is on the basis of these fundamental religious convictions that Dooyeweerd elaborates his central philosophical categories. I noted above that he conceives of ground motives as operating on philosophy via the mediation of transcendental ground Ideas, the most fundamental of all philosophical concepts.[61] He insists on a categorical distinction between the *religious* convictions making up a ground motive on the one hand and *theoretical* concepts (for example, philosophical ones) on the other. The transcendental ground Ideas, however, are generated *immediately* out of religious convictions. This is the sense in which they are located on what I called the boundary between religion and philosophy. These Ideas are not logical derivations from such convictions but something like translations of their import into specifically philosophical categories. Three of these transcendental ideas are, he believes, the "theoretical expression of the pure biblical ground-motive:"[62] meaning, time, and law.[63] So closely intertwined are they that they amount to a single Christian transcendental ground Idea (of which only the briefest of outlines is presented at this point).[64]

FOUNDATIONAL PHILOSOPHICAL IDEAS: MEANING, TIME, LAW

Although Dooyeweerd at times uses the term *meaning* in its more familiar semantic sense—as a predicate of statements or propositions—his principal usage is cosmological. "Meaning" refers to the deepest and most comprehensive character of the cosmos, its divine origin. The following phrase sums up the conceptual foundation stone of his entire philosophy: "Meaning is the being of all that has been created."[65] Characterizing "being" in terms of "meaning" is indeed, as Van der Hoeven has observed, "radical and puzzling."[66] He suggests that Dooyeweerd's intention is both to distinguish his own philosophy from Greek and medieval metaphysical notions of being and to engage with contemporary philosophical schools such as phenomenology and existentialism in which meaning and meaninglessness were of central significance. Meaning here denotes the *radically dependent nature of created reality.* The way of being of the cosmos *is* meaning, that is, radical non-self-sufficiency. It is uniquely in its complete dependence upon and determination by God that the cosmos "means" something, is significant. Without dependence on divine law the cosmos would simply be meaningless: meaning is "the creaturely mode of being under the law."[67] "As meaning, reality points towards its Origin, the Creator, without whom the creature sinks into nothingness."[68]

Frequently Dooyeweerd refers to reality, the created cosmos, simply as "meaning" or "the realm of meaning." Thus—anticipating the next section—we can say that the phrase "totality of meaning" denotes the totality of a dependent cosmos, whereas its correlate, the "speciality of meaning," denotes the diversity of such a cosmos. The speciality of meaning is seen in the multiplicity of structures—"meaning structures" or

"structures of meaning"—in the creation order. These meaning structures are of two fundamental kinds, "modal" and "typical." Reality displays both a diversity of modes of existence, "modal aspects" or "modalities," and a diversity of individual existents, "structures of individuality,"
each of which has certain "typical" features. These notions are explained
in the next chapter.

Dooyeweerd's concept of time is no less radical and puzzling than his
concept of meaning. He claims his theory of time as a philosophical
innovation and announces it as the basis of his ontology.[69] The cosmic
order is an order of time, a temporal order; meaning is temporal meaning. All things in the world are temporal; they exist in a temporal order.
In opposition to the Platonic tradition, which elevates timelessness at the
expense of temporality, Dooyeweerd regards temporality as unambigu-
ously a good creation of God. Van der Hoeven expresses the relation between meaning and time thus: "If 'meaning' points to the uniqueness and
sameness of the creative power, in its very pervasiveness, 'time' indicates
the track or course which that power takes, throughout."[70]

Cosmic time has a "law-side" and a "subject-side."[71] The subject-side
is what we ordinarily associate with the word *time,* that is, time as "duration." The law-side is the ordering framework that establishes the diversity of reality and the coherence within this diversity, that is, time as
"order." All structures of reality, both modal aspects and concrete entities,
events, processes, and so forth, are founded in the overarching, invariant
order of cosmic time.[72] Thus, for instance, while the durations of the life
of two humans may differ, they are always subject to a common biological order that moves from birth through maturity to death. The two sides
of time are inseparable correlates.[73] Although there is no duration on the
cosmonomic side of time (time as order), there is, however, within this
time-order an "order of succession" governing the disclosure or "opening
process" of the modal aspects.[74] Wide-ranging implications for social
philosophy follow from this fundamental notion, and they are traced in
the next chapter.[75]

Dooyeweerd sees the whole of created reality as governed by a divine
order of law holding for every kind of phenomenon. Van der Hoeven
captures the relation of law to meaning and time thus: "If 'meaning' is
the most basic and most comprehensive characteristic of the 'being of all
that has been created,' and 'time' indicates the 'course' through which

meaning is disclosed, then 'law' stands for the *structuration* of that course and, as far as human beings are concerned, the *signs* to be followed in order to keep *direction*."[76] I noted earlier that Dooyeweerd's Dutch designation of his philosophy, *"de wijsbegeerte der wetsidee,"*[77] literally translates as "the philosophy of the law-idea." Infelicitously, he chose to render this in English as "the philosophy of the cosmonomic idea" in order to avoid confusion with the specifically juridical sense of the term *law.* He claims to have discovered a *"wetsidee"*—idea of cosmic law—at the base of *every* major Western philosophical system.[78]

The universal subjection of all things to divine law is the corollary of the radical biblical distinction between God and creation. Law is "the universal boundary . . . between the Being of God and the meaning of his creation."[79] Three features of this universal "law-subject" relation should be noted. First, creatureliness essentially presupposes subjection to law.[80] Creatures are subjects, subject to the divine law for their being. Law is not a frustration on creaturely existence but its existential foundation. Subjection to law is the condition for meaningful existence. Without the determination and circumscription of the law, "the subject would sink away into chaos."[81] Law establishes a stable, universal order for "subjective existence." All things are uniquely individual as concrete subjects, yet all individual things are lawfully structured. Law is the "universally valid determination and limitation of the individual subjectivity which is subject to it."[82]

Second, while law establishes the necessary framework within which subjects exist, it does not stand outside or above reality but rather underlies and permeates it. Although it is indeed trans-subjective, in the sense that it transcends and places conditioning limits upon the subject-side of reality, it can only be experienced by subjects as subjects. Dooyeweerd even goes so far as to say that without subjective existence *law* has no meaning.[83] There is an "indissoluble correlation" between the two perspectives or sides from which reality can be viewed, its law-side and its subject-side.[84]

Third, laws are "principles of temporal potentiality or possibility." They are not immediately or automatically implemented at the beginning of creation but govern temporal existence; they are actualized within time (i.e., time as duration, the subject-side of time). For example, the development of technology only gets going at a particular historical time, even though it is subject to enduring "laws" that alone make its emergence possible. One implication of this view is that "everything that has real existence has many more potentialities than are actualized."[85]

This notion raises a fundamental question regarding the relation between ontology and historicity: if there is an "indissoluble correlation" between law and subject, such that law has no meaning apart from that which is subject to it, what does this correlation actually amount to at a point in history prior to the actualization of a potential? If a law-governed principle of potentiality is nowhere actualized, then how can there be any such correlation between law and subject? Dooyeweerd's intention is to distance himself from any concept of divine law bearing the mark of a Platonic notion of real, timeless essences. How far he has succeeded is a point of great significance for his social theory, as we shall see in chapters 5 and 6.

FOUR

PLURALITY, IDENTITY, INTERRELATIONSHIP

Modality and Analogy

The problem with which I concluded the previous chapter arises from Dooyeweerd's insistence on the "unbreakable correlation" between law and subject, the claim that there can *be* no law without something existing under it. This problem surfaces starkly in the case of social structures, since Dooyeweerd also holds that they too are law-governed subjects and that the law governing them is rooted in created order. What sense could it make to claim that there is a lawful (created) order for, say, the business corporation, prior to the concrete emergence of any such entity in the modern period? Or is that what Dooyeweerd actually asserts? This problem is crucial to what I have termed his core notion of the irreducible institutional identities of social structures, since his account of their irreducibility is tied to claims about a universal order of created reality. I address this problem in the final section of chapter 6. In this chapter I explicate the detailed conceptual apparatus through which he formulates the notion of irreducible institutional identities.

I have noted that Dooyeweerd conceives of reality as a differentiated order, an order revealing a plurality or speciality of meaning. This order—cosmic time—governs subjective reality around two fundamental and interlocking axes, the modal and the individual or typical. The typical order determines the structure of the actually existing individual "things, events, and relationships" that populate the world.

55

Dooyeweerd holds that everything that exists falls into one of these three classes.[1] Henceforth I frequently abbreviate this threefold categorization as *existents*.

The notion of modal diversity is often cited as one of Dooyeweerd's most creative and productive insights, although it is not without its critics.[2] I have alluded to the parallel between this notion and that of Hartmann's theory of the levels of being. More contemporary comparisons also suggest themselves, such as Oakeshott's notion of distinct "modes of human experience" and—a closer parallel—Finnis's more complex natural law theory of the "basic forms of the human good."[3] Dooyeweerd's theory exceeds these in its range and complexity. (Klapwijk, adapting Dooyeweerd's theory to notions of emergence, refers to multiple irreducible "organizational levels.")[4] After extensive reflections on the complex structures of and relations among diverse existents in the world that are unmistakably different yet appear to share certain fundamental properties, he concluded that created order was, at the deepest level, marked by a plurality of ontologically grounded, irreducible dimensions. Created reality, he came to hold, displays a multiplicity of "modal aspects."[5] The theory of modal aspects is unusual and complex, and in negotiating its thickets it helps to keep in mind that its chief intellectual objective was to expose and critique the numerous manifestations of theoretical reductionism, which Dooyeweerd claimed to observe in many contemporary academic disciplines, including social and political theory. It was devised as a response to what he perceived as a theoretical impasse in contemporary philosophy.

In *NC* Dooyeweerd identifies fifteen modal aspects of reality: numerical, spatial, kinematic, physical, biotic, psychic, logical, historical, lingual, social, economic, aesthetic, juridical, moral or ethical, and confessional or pistical (from the Greek *pistis,* meaning "faith").[6] Cosmic time is like a "prism," through which light is refracted into the seven colors of the spectrum. Time "splits up" the fullness of meaning into a diversity of aspects of meaning.[7] Just as no single color is the origin of any of the others, so no modal aspect can be the origin of the other aspects. Just as no color can be reduced to any other, each of these modal aspects reflects the "fullness of meaning" and yet remains irreducible, "sovereign in its own sphere."[8] The modal aspects are aspects of cosmic time, and the general distinction between law-side and subject-side within cosmic time is reflected in each modal aspect. Each aspect has a law-side and a subject-side; thus he also speaks of the modal spheres as "law-spheres."[9]

There is a constant danger of confusing the modal aspects with the concrete existents *of which* they are aspects. The aspects are the ways or modes in which existents operate or "function." Whereas the modal axis of the law order determines *how* all existents function, the typical axis establishes *what* actually functions.[10] Existents "display" or "function in" all the aspects; the aspects are always aspects of existents. Aspects do not themselves function; only things, events, and relationships function. For example, things such as apples, stones, and so on *have* number; they can be counted. But numbers are not objects. For "number" as such nowhere exists; only countable things exist.[11]

The modal aspects are *mutually irreducible.* Each modal aspect is sovereign in its own domain; each possesses sphere sovereignty.[12] Dooyeweerd's use of the term *sphere sovereignty* to denote this mutual modal irreducibility is obviously potentially confusing, since he also retains the term's original Kuyperian meaning in which it denotes the qualitative distinction between and autonomy of various societal structures. There is a reason for speaking of sovereignty, however, for, as indicated, the modal aspects or spheres are spheres of *law:* "Every modal aspect of temporal reality has its proper sphere of laws, irreducible to those of other modal aspects, and in this sense it is sovereign in its own orbit."[13] Rooted in the invariant order of creation, modal boundaries cannot be ignored without damaging consequences in thought and action.

A further essential feature of the modal aspects is their *"order of succession"*[14]—a notion suggesting an affinity with the idea of the emergence of one level of reality from another found in certain versions of systems theory.[15] The modal aspects do not exist in an arbitrary juxtaposition but exhibit a sequential structure, a cumulative and increasingly complex order of "prior and posterior" from the numerical aspect through to the pistical aspect.[16] Each aspect builds on the foundation of the preceding ones and is in turn the foundation for the following ones; the "earlier" aspects "found" the "later" ones.[17]

The order of succession cannot simply be posited philosophically in an a priori fashion, but can only be discovered by rigorous empirical analysis of the structure of each aspect.[18] For instance, biological—or, to use Dooyeweerd's preferred term, *biotic*—existence can be shown to presuppose physical existence. There can be physical things that have no biological functions but no biological phenomena that lack a physical basis. The biotic aspect is thus founded upon the physical rather than the reverse. The closer a modal aspect is to the pistical (the "faith" aspect), the more complex a foundation it displays.[19]

Viewing the modal aspects from the standpoint of the foundedness of one mode upon earlier ones is to view it from the "foundational" direction. From this standpoint we begin with the numerical aspect and examine how each successive aspect is founded on those preceding it in the order of cosmic time. The cosmic order of the aspects can also be viewed from the reverse, "transcendental" direction. From this standpoint we view all the aspects, from the perspective of the faith aspect, as "directed towards the religious root of our cosmos." We view the modal spheres as refractions of cosmic time, each pointing toward the religious fullness of meaning that transcends time.[20] The notion of the transcendental direction of cosmic time is central to Dooyeweerd's theories of history and culture and is addressed in the next chapter.

Reality thus manifests a complex order of modal aspects. For Dooyeweerd to have terminated the analysis here might have given the impression that the irreducible modal aspects were self-enclosed, self-sufficient dimensions, leaving open the question of how they interact. In principle there could have been two ways of framing such interaction. He could simply have argued that the modal aspects are *externally* related to each other within a harmonious order, rather like the colors of a rainbow that appear to the eye as juxtaposed but separate streams of light. Indeed, as noted, he invokes such an image to explain how irreducible aspects are yet manifestations of a coherent order: cosmic time is like a single stream of light refracted into the several colors of the rainbow when it hits a prism. The account he gives, however, is more complex. The modal aspects are not related externally but *internally*; the coherence among them is not an ordered juxtaposition but a mutual interpenetration. His account proceeds with the notion of the internal "modal structure" of an aspect. Each modal aspect has a complex internal structure. This structure revolves around and is governed by a core that determines its irreducible character, referred to variously as the "nuclear moment," "meaning nucleus," or "meaning kernel." The nuclear moment is surrounded by a cluster of "analogies" or "analogical moments."[21] The configuration of interconnections between nuclear and analogical moments constitutes the modal structure.

I first note Dooyeweerd's proposed characterizations of the nuclear moments of the fifteen aspects and then examine the concept of an analogical moment. Correctly identifying modal kernels constitutes the principal objective of modal theory. The nuclear moments, arranged according to the order of succession beginning with the earliest aspect, are as follows:

Numerical aspect:	*discrete quantity.*[22]
Spatial aspect:	*dimensional continuous extension.*[23]
Kinematic aspect:	*movement.*[24]
Physical aspect:	*energy.*[25]
Biotic aspect:	*life.*[26]
Psychic aspect:	*feeling or emotion.*[27]
Logical aspect:	*analytical distinction.*[28]
Historical aspect:	*mastery or control.*[29]
Lingual aspect:	*symbolic signification.*[30]
Social aspect:	*intercourse.*[31]
Economic aspect:	*frugality.*[32]
Aesthetic aspect:	*harmony.*[33]
Juridical aspect:	*retribution.*[34]
Ethical aspect:	*love.*[35]
Faith aspect:	*certitude.*[36]

Although mutually irreducible, the modal spheres are *reciprocally interconnected.* This is essentially what Dooyeweerd means when he speaks of "temporal coherence," the coherence of the diverse aspects of cosmic order. The modal aspects are not hermetically sealed off from one another. On the contrary, the distinctiveness of each aspect comes to expression within the internal structure of all the others. There is an "intermodal coherence" binding them all together in a unified diversity.[37] We can thus speak not only of the sovereignty of the spheres but also of their ubiquity or "universality." Modal sphere universality is the essential correlate of modal sphere sovereignty[38] and comes to expression in the phenomena of the analogical moments or analogies, which appear at the intersection points of one modal aspect with another.[39]

As modal rather than individual (typical) phenomena, analogical moments do not "exist" as such. They are *aspects of* existents. An analogical moment is a specific instance of the intersection of two modal aspects within one of the functions of a concrete existent. Such moments are of two kinds: *retrocipations* are expressions of a particular modal aspect within an earlier aspect; *anticipations* are expressions of a particular aspect within a later one. Dooyeweerd sometimes refers to these as "retrocipatory/anticipatory moments," or as "retrocipatory/anticipatory analogies." Retrocipatory analogies are instances of the referring back of one aspect to another; anticipatory analogies, of the referring forward of one aspect to another. "Logical economy" is a case of an anticipatory analogy, in which logical analysis refers forward to the economic aspect, conforming to the norm of the frugal use of (in this case, analytical) resources.[40] Logical economy, or economy of thought, is not itself an economic phenomenon. Logical economy does not mean the logical operation of an economic system. It is a logical phenomenon in which an economic norm is present. An example of a retrocipatory analogy is "historical development." This is a historical retrocipation, a referring back of the historical aspect to the biotic aspect of which growth is characteristic.[41] Historical development is not itself an organic but a historical phenomenon, one that gives evidence of the operation within the historical aspect of an organic pattern. In the phenomenon that we call historical development we encounter an analogical sense of the concept of development. Historical development is thus an example of an "analogical concept."

The analogical sense of a concept must always be carefully distinguished from its "original" sense. The original sense is given by the nuclear moment or kernel of a modal aspect. In its original sense the concept of growth always and only applies to specifically biological phenomena such as the organic development of a plant or human body. One of the examples Dooyeweerd uses to clarify this is the organicist conception of history. A consistent organicism asserts that the historical development of a culture proceeds according to principles similar to the organic growth of a plant—that both history and plant life are, finally, instances of some larger organic process embracing them both. And it is indeed the case that historical development seems to resemble organic growth in a certain sense; we frequently speak of certain historical processes "growing out of" others, or of their "evolving," "maturing," or "dying." These, Dooyeweerd suggests, are not mere figures of speech: they can be described as metaphors, but such *linguistic* metaphors testify to the reality of *ontic* analogies to which they in fact allude (and which are not to be confused with literary analogies). The phenomena that they seek to capture are accounted for by the presence of a biotic analogy within the historical aspect. Organicism is therefore not simply wrongheaded; it is motivated by a legitimate, and potentially insightful, attempt to capture a real "state of affairs."[42] Its problem is its misconstrual of the modal structure of the historical aspect, its reduction of the original meaning—the nuclear moment—of historical phenomena to one of their analogical moments (their developmental side).

Dooyeweerd deploys this notion of sphere universality to powerful critical effect, developing from it a general account of reductionism applying not only to the natural sciences but also to all academic disciplines *(wetenschappen)*.[43] Reductionism in any discipline amounts to the conflation of the original meaning of a concept with one of its analogical meanings. Examples of what Dooyeweerd means in contemporary social science are not hard to find. The attempt to turn economics into a natural science has involved, for example, the illicit attempt to characterize causal economic relations between economic actors—households, firms, governments—in terms of mathematical regularities; or, in the case of game theory, to proceed on the assumption that individuals function economically primarily in terms of rational calculation. The attempt by sociobiologists to explain social behavior primarily in terms of evolutionary biological factors is another example. Systems theory in postwar political science amounts to a skewed attempt to account for large-scale and complex networks of interactions among political actors or institutions in terms of a conceptual apparatus originally applying within cybernetics. In each case, Dooyeweerd would not sweep such enterprises aside as worthless but expose the specific kind of reductionism involved, affirm whatever valid insights it sought to capture, and urge a multidimensional explanatory methodology appropriate to the subject matter in hand.[44]

Laws and Norms

From the account so far it might appear as if Dooyeweerd is espousing some kind of naturalistic or even deterministic conception of reality in which human existence and human agency are constrained within very tightly prescribed ontological limits. Could there be any room at all in such a theory of reality for genuine human freedom? While Dooyeweerd's language can at times suggest a constriction of freedom, his fundamental distinction between *law* and *norm* makes clear that this is not at all his intention. Within the modal order appears a crucial distinction between those modal laws that presuppose the mediation of human responsibility and those that are immediately effective irrespective of such mediation. The former are the laws of the logical and postlogical aspects, the "normative law-spheres," and are referred to as "norms," whereas the latter are technically designated simply as "laws."[45] Modal laws, such as the laws of arithmetic, physics, biology, or (problematically) emotional life,[46] "are realized in the facts without human intervention."[47] Norms, by contrast, presuppose the human capacity for intentional, imaginative deliberation, initiation, and action. Just as classical natural law theory does not imply a deterministic conception of human action but requires the mediation of free, responsible, and rational human agents, so Dooyeweerd's theory of normativity is equally premised on human free agency. What he terms "normative principles" appear in the logical and all the postlogical spheres: there are distinctive and irreducible logical, linguistic, social, economic, legal, aesthetic, ethical, and pistical norms, each requiring human agency.[48] It is also worth noting that what Dooyeweerd denotes as normative principles (or "rules of conduct" or "regulative principles") are thus much wider in scope than the field designated by the term *ethics* in contemporary philosophy and theology; it includes, unusually, norms of language, aesthetics, and even faith. What he terms "ethical norms" are merely one variety of normative rules of conduct.[49] Dooyeweerd has a more capacious notion of responsible human freedom than, for example, those who hold matters of language or aesthetic taste to be morally neutral.

The "order of succession" within the modal aspects also comes to expression in the normative aspects. Dooyeweerd constructs a series of elaborate arguments to justify his proposed order, beginning with the logical aspect and moving through the historical, lingual, social, economic, aesthetic, and ethical to the pistical. He seeks to show, for example, that social intercourse can only occur on the basis of symbolic communication in language; that juridical relationships presuppose social intercourse; that ethical norms presuppose and build upon juridical phenomena such as rights; and so on.

As I have emphasized, the norms or normative principles based in the logical and postlogical aspects can only be implemented by means of the responsible choices of active human subjects. This responsible human implementation Dooyeweerd terms "positivization."[50] Norms must be historically positivized. Indeed human history, or the process of cultural formation, proceeds essentially by means of the human positivizing of normative principles. The results of positivization will vary widely throughout history and according to different levels of cultural development. The norm of justice, for example, is a divine summons to human obedience that will call for different concrete responses in different historical situations, and, unlike physical laws, is never automatically implemented. There always exists the possibility of an errant positivization of the norm. Indeed an Augustinian-Calvinist like Dooyeweerd would expect widespread deviations from norms.[51] But while the results of the positivization of norms will be historically variable, the essential requirements of the norms are invariant and universally valid. *Norms do not change, only the human responses to them.* This controversial assertion, flying in the face of the dominant schools of social theory today, is at the center of my critical discussion of Dooyeweerd's account of social institutions in the next chapter.

INDIVIDUALITY

We have seen that Dooyeweerd conceives of reality as structured by a plurality of irreducible and mutually cohering modal aspects each possessing its own laws. These aspects are modes of the existence of things, events, and social relationships, the existents that populate the world. Modal structures and laws, however, are not sufficient to account for the existence of concrete, *individual* things, events, and social relationships.[52]

Such an account must be based on an investigation of the "structures of individuality" or "individuality structures." Individual existents in the world have an ontologically founded structure that cannot be reduced simply to modal aspects. In addition to the modal axis there is the axis of individuality around which reality is structured. Both axes condition the empirical shape to which existents conform. It is the structures of individuality that are the basis for the distinct *identity* of concrete phenomena, forming the ontic conditions for their continuing factual existence.[53]

Structures of individuality, like modal structures, have a law-side and a subject-side: divine laws govern all subjectively existing structures of individuality. The laws for these structures are, like those for modal structures, founded in the created order of cosmic time. They too are *universally valid, invariant,* and *enduring:* "they are not changeable in time, since they determine the inner nature of perishable factual things, events, and social relationships functioning within their transcendental cadre."[54]

Structures of individuality are what populate the "plastic" horizon of human experience. The infelicitous term *plastic* merely gestures to the malleability and great variety of existents. In this horizon of human experience we encounter a highly complex diversity, a diversity of types of existents, each with different durabilities and each diversified still further on account of their interlacements with other existents. It is especially these interlacements that give rise to "the inexhaustible wealth of individuality." And it is this same web of interlacements that ensures that the individual existents in the world are not arranged in a "rigid, atomistic" fashion but in a "continuous dynamic-structural coherence."[55] This will turn out to be an important idea in Dooyeweerd's social theory. Indeed I will argue that his (underdeveloped) theory of the interrelationships between social structures is just as important as his (better-known) theory of their distinct identities.

Rooted as they are in the same order of cosmic time, the structures of individuality are intimately correlated with the modal aspects.[56] Each individual thing, event, or social relationship displays all the modal aspects in its concrete behavior. The "typical total structures of individuality in principle function at the same time in all the modal spheres."[57] Thus a concrete *thing* such as a chair can be counted (its numerical aspect), has extension (its spatial aspect), is someone's property (its juridical aspect), and so on. An *event,* such as the act of purchasing the chair, exhibits spatial functioning (it occurs at a certain place), economic functioning (the price of the chair), moral functioning (the mutual trust presupposed in the exchange), and so on. A *social relationship* such as marriage involves sexuality (the psychic aspect), reproduction (the biotic aspect), communication (the lingual aspect), and mutual rights and duties (the juridical aspect). This pattern of multifunctionality is the case for every existent.[58]

Now all this would be true if the universe consisted only of billions of identical things, identical events, and identical relationships. Dooyeweerd has not yet accounted for the differences between existents. He does this in terms of the distinction between the law-side of reality and its subject-side. Every existent has both a law- and a subject-side; that is, it is a law-governed subject. Both these sides give rise to differences between it and other existents. On its law-side an existent belongs to a structural "type" or kind, whereas on its subject-side it displays a unique "subjective individuality": it is *this* thing and not *that;* it possesses properties possessed by no other existent. A structural type is a class of existents sharing in common certain law-governed properties.[59] There are, as we shall see, multiple types of existent in the world, and every existent belongs to one type rather than another. Not every property of an existent can, however, be explained in terms of its type. To attempt to do so would be to reduce an existent to its law-side. Some properties are not "typical" but irreducibly individual, unique to each particular existent. The identity of an existent "must possess its law- and subject-sides in a mutual, unbreakable correlation. . . . [I]t must be both atypically individual, and determined in conformity with its internal structural principle."[60] One existent may differ from another, therefore, both in terms of its type and in terms of its subjective ("atypical") individuality.

An example of atypical or subjective individuality might be the particular, and unrepeatable, formation of branches in an individual tree; another would be a human fingerprint. A more significant one would be the unique complex of dispositions, emotional structures, inclinations, and so on that we now tend to refer to as the character or personality of a human being. Yet another would be the distinctive ethos characterizing a certain family, ethnic group, or national culture.[61] Although none of these phenomena either do or could exist apart from law, neither can any be accounted for wholly in terms of conformity to law. An obvious possible criticism of Dooyeweerd's ontology at this point, however, is that the scope of the law-side is *so* extensive that it appears to leave insufficient room for subjective individuality, especially in the social world. This point is taken up in subsequent chapters.

Structural laws establish various types of things, events, or relationships, governed by "typical structures." Each existent belongs to a specific type, all the members of which are subject to the same typical structural laws and which therefore exhibit certain common characteristics. Each structural type also displays a series of further intratypical differentiations, an "inner articulation" that can be highly intricate. This articulation terminates at a certain point; beyond that point the differences between existents are not determined by structural laws at all but reflect the uniqueness characteristic of their subjective individuality.

The most comprehensive types of things, events, and social relationships are the "radical types" (e.g., juridically qualified social structures). Within each radical type can be distinguished a series of "genotypes," which may in turn display further genotypical differentiation. The differences between radical types and genotypes are accounted for in terms of the different configurations of modal functions within an individual existent. While each thing, event, or social relationship functions simultaneously in each modal aspect, there are always *two* aspects in particular that play an essential role in determining their discrete identity, distinguishing them from the identity of others. In each concrete structure of individuality two of the modal functions present themselves as outstandingly significant in making the thing what it is. These two functions are given with the "structural principle" of an existent, and it is this that determines its radical type and genotype.

These two functions are the "qualifying" or "leading" function and the "foundational" or "founding" function.[62] Identifying the potential candidates for these two functions is, however, only the first stage in discovering its specific identity; the next essential stage is to distinguish between the two, detecting which qualifies and which founds the thing in question. The qualifying function, on the one hand, can be seen as that function which exercises what we might call a leadership role among the various functions of an existent, directing them in a structured way toward its specific "destination."[63] The foundational function, on the other hand, furnishes the indispensable support making such a destination realizable.

A structural principle, then, is the entire constellation of modal functions of a thing, event, or social relationship, characterized by its qualifying and founding functions. All structures of individuality are governed by a certain structural principle that constitutes their identity. A structural principle is an internally coherent configuration of laws—typical laws—for a thing, event, or social relationship. A *tree,* for example, has a biotic qualifying function and a physical founding function. No purely physical or chemical analysis of a tree could disclose its essential identity.[64] A *family* is qualified by its moral function and founded biotically. Moral nurture and love ought to characterize all familial behavior, while the biotically founded blood tie provides the unique basis upon which such morally qualified behavior can take place.[65] By contrast, power and law are the two outstanding components of the *state.* They correspond to its historical foundational function and its juridical qualifying function. The state is founded upon power but is characterized or qualified as a legal community, a community of justice.[66]

Notwithstanding its deficiencies, in discussing Dooyeweerd's social theory I will suggest that the notion of a qualifying function is especially fruitful in grounding what I call the notion of irreducible institutional identity and thereby in developing a robust theory of normative social pluralism.

Interlacement

Dooyeweerd's theory of the individuality of existents is coupled with a theory of their interrelationships. Existents not only have a distinct identity determined by their internal structural principle, but they also stand in a ramifying network of relationships with others. Numerous different kinds of relationships between individuality structures are conceivable.[67] Dooyeweerd gives detailed attention to one kind, namely, "enkaptic interlacements." These are a particular kind of relationship between different individuality structures having *distinct internal structural principles*—a tree and a nest, or a state and a family.[68] Such relationships are pervasive in the social world.

The purpose of the notion of enkaptic interlacement is to explain how individuality structures cohere amid their differences.[69] Enkaptic interlacements are a necessary feature of the existence of all existents. No structure can be seen as entirely self-sufficient, or "absolutized."[70] One example from the natural world is the way in which the metabolic functions of a tree cannot exist apart from the tree's biological environment. An example from the social world might be a family business, a case of an especially intimate link between two distinct structures. The mere fact that a family and a business both function in the same modal aspects does not itself account for the special relationship between the family and the business. To account for that relationship, it is necessary to explain how the concrete functioning of the family—its "household economy," for example—impinges upon and is impinged upon by the concrete functioning of the business—its schedule of debt, for example. In this case one would investigate matters such as personal loans made from the family's bank account to the business (or vice versa) or the way in which familial loyalties or family routines are unconsciously transferred across to employer-employee relationships holding between parents and children.[71]

Dooyeweerd borrowed the term *enkapsis* from the anatomist Heidenhain who used it to denote the relationship between a living organism and its various organs, holding that the latter were not the dependent parts of the former but rather "relatively independent totalities."[72] Dooyeweerd argues, however, that the relative autonomy of such organs is not sufficient to denote them as independent individualities, since an individuality structure is only truly independent if it possesses its own qualifying function. But this is not the case with the organs of a living organism. He clarifies the notion by distinguishing it sharply from the relationship of a structural *whole* to its various *parts*.[73] Unlike the two relata in an enkaptic relationship, both a whole (or "individual totality") and its parts share the same structural principle, and the relationship between whole and parts is determined by the structural principle of the whole. A part is always and only *part of a whole*.[74]

The parts of a whole should not be confused with its various modal functions. Just like the whole within which it is found, a part functions in all the modal aspects. The part always stands in a relation of dependence upon the whole in which it plays the part assigned to it by the structural principle of the whole. A part has only a relative autonomy: the degree of this autonomy is entirely dependent upon the needs of the whole in which it participates. For example, the powers of a municipality, Dooyeweerd claims, are determined by the requirements of the (national) state.[75] This distinction between the whole-part relationship characterizing the position of a municipality or province with respect to a state, and the enkaptic relationship characterizing the bond between the state and nonpolitical bodies, will prove useful in articulating a Dooyeweerdian account of civil society.

A part cannot exist without the whole in which it operates. In an enkaptic relation, by contrast, the two relata retain their possibility of independent existence; their internal structural principles are not absorbed into one another. In spite of the external relationship obtaining between them, they maintain their sphere sovereignty.[76] In an enkaptic interlacement one individuality structure is brought within the field of functioning of another; it "performs an enkaptic function" within it. A civil marriage ceremony, for example, performs the function of enabling the state to create a framework of public law. The marriage performs an enkaptic function within the state that is not determined by its own internal structural principle.[77] Dooyeweerd speaks (misleadingly I shall suggest) of the enkaptic "binding" of the structure performing the enkaptic function, a term that will be employed frequently in connection with the relation between the state and other social structures. Binding implies a limitation on the range of independent activity of a structure, if only an external one. By being brought within the scope of civil law, a marriage is subject to certain legal limitations. But it still retains its independent character as a marriage; the sphere sovereignty of the structure that performs the enkaptic function is not thereby compromised.

Specifically, the structure performing the enkaptic function, although not absorbed by the other structure, is nevertheless *made subservient, in one respect,* to the latter.[78] What this means is that it performs a function that is not determined by its own structural principle. I propose to term this relation one of "functional subservience." It is the distinctive feature of an enkaptic interlacement.[79] In the next chapter I question whether the idea of functional subservience accurately captures the diverse ways in which such social bodies perform various functions for each other and recommend a reconceptualization of enkapsis drawing on the Catholic idea of the subsidiary function of social institutions.

This chapter has introduced five core concepts at the foundation of Dooyeweerd's comprehensive, constructive philosophical framework: modality, law, norm, individuality, and interlacement. Each plays a decisive role in the social philosophy he develops on the basis of this framework. We are now equipped to investigate that social philosophy in detail.

FIVE

A PHILOSOPHY OF CULTURAL DEVELOPMENT

DOOYEWEERD'S AMBITIOUS PROJECT TO CONSTRUCT A comprehensive philosophy of social pluralism was conceived in the 1920s and 1930s and achieved mature formulation in the 1950s. The task of envisaging a social philosophy grounded in the notion of a universal order of reality was challenging enough at that time, and subsequent developments in social theory, especially the ascendancy of social constructivism and deconstructivism, have hardly made it any easier. The complex set of questions arising from these contemporary approaches lies beyond the scope of this book. In this and the next chapter I confine myself to one fundamental issue confronting the enterprise Dooyeweerd set himself, namely, his controversial proposal that social institutions possess an "invariant structural principle." In the next chapter I consider the objection that such a notion implies a static essentialism that closes off historical and social variety. In this chapter I consider the related charge that Dooyeweerd's social theory baptizes the institutions of the modern West and so lapses into occicentrism, rendering it vulnerable to conservatism. The force of both criticisms is that an imperious ontology squeezes out historical contingency and human freedom. In the next chapter I point toward a response aiming to avoid the equal and opposite problem of a thoroughgoing social constructivism.[1]

Dooyeweerd's conception of cultural development and history has at its heart the notion of the "process of disclosure." An appreciation of these is indispensable background for an adequate treatment of the central problem just identified. In the next chapter I examine closely his general account of societal structural principles, consider a major objection, and propose a critical reformulation. I hope to show that once the notions of the opening process and of societal structural principles are properly understood, the force of the charges of essentialism, ahistoricism, and conservatism is muted though far from entirely blunted.

HUMAN NORMATIVE DISCLOSURE

Dooyeweerd's notion of cultural disclosure flows from his account of the normative modal aspects, those aspects requiring the mediation of human agency (considered in chapter 4). It is essentially an account of how human historical action uncovers ever deeper layers of cultural possibility and moral meaning through a dynamic engagement with the order of creation. It generates a rich and sweeping account of societal development and historical forward movement. To make sense of it, we must first delve a bit deeper into the theory of modal aspects.

An important feature of the normative aspects not yet considered emerges from the distinction (also noted in chapter 4) between the foundational and transcendental directions of time. The distinction in fact refers to the entire modal order, not only to the normative aspects; both prelogical and normative aspects can be viewed from the foundational and the transcendental directions of time. Viewing the order of succession of the aspects from the numerical through to the pistical, we envisage time in its "foundational direction" and conceive of each aspect as necessarily presupposing earlier ones.[2] In the "transcendental direction" of time we envisage the directedness of the aspects forward toward their "fullness of meaning." We concentrate on the fact that each aspect can come to be oriented to the other aspects that it looks forward to (or "anticipates").[3] This process occurs over time; it is a temporal process. One aspect begins to be oriented to a later one at a certain period in history. The "total structure of an aspect is . . . not given at *one* time, it calls for disclosure in time."[4]

By being oriented to later aspects, each aspect discloses dimensions of its structure that are out of view when only its foundational direction is considered. When, for example, we view the biotic aspect purely from its foundational direction, we envisage its relation only to the earlier physical, kinematic, spatial, and numerical aspects (its "retrocipations"). The relationship between the modal kernel and its retrocipations constitutes the "primary structure" of a modal aspect. This primary structure is necessarily always present. In itself it undergoes no change through history, since retrocipations by definition do not come to be oriented to later aspects.[5] When viewing an aspect such as the biotic from its transcendental direction, we conceive of its relation to later aspects. What we see when viewing an aspect from the transcendental direction of time is a process whereby it comes to be "opened up" by later aspects. It is as if the later aspect lays bare its relation to the earlier aspect, unfolding new and wider potentials hitherto hidden within the earlier one. This opening up in the transcendental direction is a dynamic, historical process into which the entirety of the cosmos is caught up.[6]

Consider an example of the opening up of one normative aspect by another. In the legal order of a primitive society the kernel of the juridical aspect ("retribution," discussed in detail later) manifests itself only in its relationship to its earlier moments.[7] What this means is that, for example, legal causality (a "physical retrocipation") is seen as sufficient ground for guilt. When, over time, the notion of personal accountability for actions comes to be accepted, however, the meaning of retribution is "deepened." A new, ethical consideration is taken into account in apportioning guilt in law. This expansion of the meaning of the juridical aspect indicates that the ethical anticipation within it has been "disclosed."[8]

The opening up of one aspect by a later one occurs throughout all aspects. Linguistic communication, for instance, is enriched as the social norm of mutual respect comes into play; juridical principles lead economic activity beyond the merely frugal allocation of scarce resources toward a realization of distributive justice; the aesthetic norm of harmony directs the historical development of culture toward a balanced evolution of its various scientific, economic, or social sectors.

The name Dooyeweerd gives to the entire process whereby later aspects disclose earlier ones is "the process of disclosure."[9] It occurs as real existents (a rock, an animal, or humans) act as agents (subjects) in time. We do not, as it were, gaze into the sky and witness the disclosure of a modal aspect; rather, as agents act concretely, we witness modal disclosure.[10] The theory of disclosure is essentially an account of the dynamic unfolding of divinely created possibilities.[11] It might be described as a philosophical outworking of the theological idea of progressive general revelation. The process of disclosure is, as one commentator puts it, nothing less than "the inner dynamic of reality."[12] And humans play the decisive role in the *normative* dimensions of the process.[13] On the one hand, the cosmic order of modal aspects is an invariant order of divinely given laws; the modal laws and norms do not change throughout history. But on the other hand, their full possibilities are only disclosed historically—which is to say, *through human initiative.* Indeed modal norms actually call forth a dynamic historical process. It is not as if historical development, occurring through human positivization, begins where divine order breaks off; rather, there is a divinely given norm for humans to engage in historical development.[14] This is how Dooyeweerd seeks to escape the charge of having erected a static, Platonic conception of a timeless order standing above historical change. At the same time, as we shall see, he hopes to have avoided the relativistic perils of historicism, according to which the historical process itself becomes the ultimately authoritative source of norms.

Humans alone, then, open up the normative dimensions of the creation order. An important implication of this is that human normative disclosure takes place at particular stages of historical development. Earlier I cited the example of the way in which the "restrictive structure" of the juridical aspect is displayed in primitive legal orders. These orders are superseded at a particular period of history, as the ethical and other analogies in the juridical aspect are disclosed. Dooyeweerd expresses this point generally—and puzzlingly—by saying that *the opening process begins in a particular modal aspect,* namely, *the historical* aspect. That is, unless history itself is set moving, historical beings cannot act so as to enrich the meaning of other (posthistorical) aspects. Thus it turns out that the opening up of the historical aspect turns out to be a necessary condition for the entire normative process of disclosure.[15] The question then arises as to how the historical aspect *itself* comes to be opened up in the first place? How, in other words, does the process of cultural disclosure actually get started? Answering this puzzle requires us to appreciate Dooyeweerd's account of "the historical" as an aspect.

For Dooyeweerd, the historical way of being of a thing is not its historicity or datedness, or simply its experience of "becoming" or "genesis,"[16] but rather its "cultural" dimension; the historical aspect is thus frequently termed the cultural aspect. The definitive core, or nuclear moment, of the cultural aspect is denoted variously as "command," "control," "mastery," "free formative power," or "the controlling manner of form giving."[17] To act culturally is to exercise the distinctively human capacity—"authority"[18]—to give shape to things, events, or relationships according to a freely chosen plan. Such shaping involves the disclosing of new possibilities from a "given material" and can issue in "endless possibilities of variation."[19] This occurs, of course, always in the context of the modal and typical orders, which make all human functioning possible and at the same time delimit its scope. Human freedom manifests itself within this delimited scope; indeed freedom is actually made possible by such orders. Involving "reflection and productive fantasy," freedom is an essential feature of cultural formation, distinguishing the latter from naturally occurring processes of formation such as the spider's construction of a web.[20]

Cultural or historical activity embraces all the ways in which humans deliberately form their environment, and all humankind is continuously engaged in it. Such formation can be exercised both over natural phenomena and over humans.[21] Humans undergo cultural formation insofar as their social existence is shaped by others. This is not a deterministic process of socialization, however, for humans remain responsible cultural actors even while being acted upon by others.[22]

We might question whether the specific term *formative power* is really adequate to characterize something so broad as the experience of human historicity. Is there not far more to humanity's being a historical creature than its capacity to intentionally form its environment? In response to this question, several of Dooyeweerd's critics have indeed proposed that history be conceived of not as a modal aspect but as a transmodal category. Seerveld, for example, has suggested that while "technical, formative control" should indeed be recognized as an irreducible modal aspect, history or "the historical" should be understood much more comprehensively as "the cultural unfolding of creation's secrets."[23] Now this is essentially what Dooyeweerd designates the "normative opening process." This comprehensive cultural task might also be identified with what Reformed theologians have termed the "cultural mandate" of Genesis 1, a notion defining the outworking of the *all-encompassing* religious vocation of humankind.[24] Surprisingly, although Dooyeweerd does relate the cultural task of humankind to this mandate, he continues to regard this task as rooted in only one of the aspects, the historical. I just noted when discussing the process of disclosure that in his view the historical aspect occupies a unique, foundational position with regard to the opening up of other modal aspects. So to suggest that a phenomenon is founded in the historical aspect implies, for him, no narrowing down but rather points to a dynamic openness. Yet it certainly seems counterintuitive to locate the mainspring of a process of comprehensive cosmic scope within just one of the aspects of cosmic time, and Seerveld's proposal is an appealing alternative. Accepting it, however, does not in itself undermine Dooyeweerd's substantive conception of history but only redescribes it within his own conceptual framework. To assess that substantive conception we must investigate his complex theory of cultural development.

Dooyeweerd's theory of cultural development introduces a powerful historical dynamism into what might otherwise have appeared as—and is often misunderstood as—an ahistorical, Platonic ontology. If Dooyeweerd's social philosophy turns out to be essentialist, this cannot be laid at the door of a static notion of history. The theory is complex and wide-ranging. The "transcendental Idea"[25] that governs it is, as McIntire puts it, "a comprehensive idea which in a sweeping way embraces the entire course of human civilizations and makes use of all the elements of his general philosophy."[26]

The historical aspect implies a momentous cultural vocation for humankind, a divine calling to bring forth new possibilities from the creation order. This cultural vocation involves the exercise of formative power. Indeed such power is "the great motor of cultural development."[27] It is a "historical calling" for which those bearing it must give account, implying no boundless exploitation of the natural or social environment but rather a "normative task and mission in the development of human civilization either to guard or mould culture further, in subjection to the principles laid down by God."[28] Humanity's cultural vocation is dynamic and progressive and "can only be accomplished in a successive cultural development of mankind in its temporal social existence."[29] Humankind is to move forward continually disclosing ever new potentials enclosed in creation.[30]

Before we consider precisely how this process of cultural disclosure takes place, a final problem with the idea of cultural disclosure must be addressed. The idea that the opening process involves the opening up of the normative anticipatory moments of the modal aspects implies that prior to such opening up the modal aspects appear in a "closed" condition. At a given point in history, therefore, the possibilities available to human beings for positivizing certain norms seem to be quite seriously circumscribed. Consider two examples. First, Dooyeweerd proposes the idea that the economic aspect comes to be ethically opened up only at a certain stage of historical development. This, however, is a counterintuitive suggestion and evokes the question why the ethical anticipation in the economic aspect comes to be closed down in the first place. Can this be part of the divine creational design? For the case could equally be made that economic activity governed by ethically closed economic norms appeared historically *later* than that which was ethically opened up.[31] In this sense capitalist industrialization, although massively boosting economic productivity, could be seen in part as representing an ethical retrogression.

The implausibility is magnified when we consider his account of the crucial role of faith in the process of cultural development. Normative disclosure, as I have said, is *founded* in the historical aspect, but it proceeds under the *guidance* of the faith aspect.[32] It turns out that it is directly through the faith aspect that religious ground motives determine the direction of normative disclosure in cultural development. Faith led by the biblical ground motive shapes culture "according to Christ," whereas faith led by nonbiblical motives shapes it according to something within creation and so is idolatrous, "apostate" faith. Following Augustine, Dooyeweerd holds that history witnesses to the irreconcilable collision between these two motives, to a continual spiritual warfare—an "antithesis"—between the City of God and the earthly city.

The question arising here is whether, if faith leads the process of cultural development, an apostate faith inevitably produces an apostate culture. If so, is wholesome normative disclosure possible at all in such a culture?[33] Dooyeweerd answers positively. The details of his account of how it occurs need not detain us.[34] The crucial point is that for faith to lead the process of normative disclosure, it must *itself* be opened up. This implies, of course, that the faith aspect must itself move historically from a closed to an opened position. But this appears flatly to contradict a fundamental element of the biblical ground motive. The opening process in the faith aspect (like that in any aspect) is rooted in the creation order. But the opening up of faith implies that it begins from a closed condition. From this emerges the implausible conclusion that the closed structure of faith is the temporal point of departure for the entire normative opening process. What Dooyeweerd means by closed faith is *apostate* faith, but apostasy is a consequence of the *fall* rather than creation. The fall thus appears to be a necessary condition for the unfolding of the good creation—an implication decisively rejected elsewhere by Dooyeweerd.

Geertsema locates the problem in Dooyeweerd's correlation of the modal order of disclosure with a *temporal* process of historical development.[35] This correlation is clearly central to the theory of the opening process. The modal opening process follows the modal order (in the transcendental direction of time), but it also follows a historical sequence. The *cosmically* later aspects are opened up *historically* later in the process of historical development than the cosmically earlier ones. Because of this Dooyeweerd must presuppose that modal aspects first appear historically in a closed condition. Historical development is then viewed as proceeding along the track of normative modal disclosure.

Yet to suggest that the lingual, social, economic, or aesthetic aspects can appear in an opened condition only when a certain point in historical development is reached implies that the failings in the cultural achievements of any particular historical period are attributable to the order of creation itself. It is surely more plausible for him to attribute these either to the current limits of accumulated human experience (e.g., people learn over time to improve economic performance or artistic craftsmanship) or to apostate faith (e.g., as humanistic faith absolutizes the individual at the expense of the social), or to a combination of both. It would certainly be more consistent with his account of the biblical ground motive for Dooyeweerd to hold, as Geertsema proposes, that the *full potential* of every modal aspect is at all times available, in principle, for concrete realization by human beings, even though not every potential will in fact be realized (for at least the two reasons cited above).[36] The fundamental idea that the process of opening up the modal aspects is necessarily tied to a determinate historical sequence is therefore deeply problematic. This does not mean, however, that the entire idea of historical disclosure itself should be repudiated, as I shall now explain.

For Dooyeweerd, cultural development is a normative calling in which humans disclose the entire realm of "normative meaning" in creation. How does it actually take place? Recall again that human beings never act, whether culturally or in any other way, upon modal aspects as such. Aspects are always *aspects of* concrete existents (things, events, and relationships). What human beings act culturally upon or within are things and relationships; events, we may say, occur as they do so. The modal process of normative disclosure takes place in and through the cultural action of human beings on these existents, whether objects or humans. To characterize cultural development solely in terms of a modal process of disclosure would therefore be to give an abstracted and partial account of it. What Dooyeweerd also clearly needs is an account of cultural development in terms of the interaction between human beings and things (the development of technology) and human beings and their social relationships. He says little about the first[37] but a great deal about the second.

INTEGRATION AND DIFFERENTIATION

Dooyeweerd's central claim concerns the manner in which social relationships emerge in the course of cultural development, and his account of this process strikes the reader as emphatically—critics would say myopically—modern. This emergence takes place by means of a twofold process: "integration" and "differentiation."[38] Human civilization is envisaged as moving from a "closed" or "primitive" to an "opened" or "differentiated" condition. In a primitive society "civilization is still enclosed between the rigid walls of small sibs, tribes, or populaces." Such groups have two principal characteristics: they are isolated from one another, and they are internally unified around a single dominant authority structure that controls all the major social functions such as family, economy, polity, and cult and maintains a rigid group tradition typically oriented to nature religions.[39] Both these characteristics must be eroded if the groups are to develop culturally.[40] When the isolation of the groups breaks down through intercourse with other groups at higher cultural levels, then the process of integration gets under way: "In the removal of rigid walls of isolation, historical development moves in the line of cultural integration."[41]

The counterpart of integration is the process of differentiation, in which the functions formerly united in one communal whole branch out and are performed by separate social structures possessing an independent existence and displaying a unique character (determined by the modal function by which they are qualified, which is typical of them).[42] For instance, patriarchal political structures crumble when political authority can no longer be derived from family authority, clearing the way for the state to emerge as an autonomous institution. The process extends to all the separate social structures we know today.

> Without the process of cultural differentiation and integration there can be no question of a free unfolding of the structures of individuality in human society. As long as culture remains in an undifferentiated condition there is no room for a state, a church, a free industrial or trade-life, free associations, a free unfolding of fine arts, a scientific community etc.[43]

This differentiation of social relationships is one striking manifestation of what, as we have seen, is a creation-wide opening process: "God has created everything according to its own inner nature; and in the temporal order of genesis and development this inner nature must freely unfold itself."[44]

The twofold process of integration and differentiation is also a process of "individualization." The individuality of persons, social structures, peoples, and nations—their unique contribution to the development of culture—is permitted to flourish. It is the process of differentiation that creates the space for this flourishing of individuality while the process of integration allows each individual person, group, or structure to make its complementary contribution to the cultural development of humanity as a whole.[45]

We may well ask whether a conception of cultural development, which (from the typical standpoint) is primarily oriented to the development of social structures or relationships, is anywhere near comprehensive enough. What, for example, of the development of economy, technology, ideas, and so forth, which have been variously identified as key factors in shaping the character of a culture? In the next two chapters, however, it will become clear that the scope of the term *social structure* or *social relationship* potentially includes within it *all* the normative social contexts in which these cultural activities are practiced. For Dooyeweerd, all human activity takes places in the framework of such social structures or relationships. Although this account is arguably not yet comprehensive enough, its focus on the development of such social entities does not imply quite such a narrow perspective as first appears.

The cultural vocation of man and the twofold process of integration and differentiation it embraces are thus normative tasks. They must not be interpreted as naturalistic processes of social evolution envisaged by, for example, Spencerians.[46] Dooyeweerd thus speaks of the historical or cultural "norms of integration, differentiation and individualization." We have access to normative criteria for evaluating actual historical developments, and these enable us to determine whether a particular change is historically "progressive" or "reactionary."[47] If such a change fosters the cultural integration of hitherto separated peoples and stimulates the differentiation and individualization of persons and societal structures (including nations), then it counts as progressive. This occurred, for example, in early modern Europe, as the state broke free from ecclesial restraints. To the extent that a particular change opposes these norms, it must be deemed reactionary. For example, it was reactionary of Christian aristocrats to attempt to restore the feudal order after the defeat of Napoleon and reactionary of the Nazis to seek to reestablish an undifferentiated German *Volk*.[48]

Differentiation and individualization must themselves proceed according to further normative principles. The norm of differentiation is not sufficient in itself to direct human cultural formation. Rather it directs us to a whole series of other norms pertaining to various structures that supply the specific content of our cultural activity. The differentiation of an independent state, for instance, involves the implementation of the normative structure of the state, determined by its structural principle. Not just any independent political (or economic, or social, etc.) unit will suffice. Similarly, the general norm of integration must not override these structural norms. We are not, for instance, to interpret it as requiring the abolition of the family and the integration of all individuals into a huge collective unit, for the family is an enduring social relationship.[49]

An important macrosocial principle now emerges. Insofar as each differentiating social sphere develops according to its own internal structural norms, the overarching pattern of a culture will display a proper balance among diverse spheres. Such a culture will thereby have honored the "principle of cultural economy," one that requires that "the historical power sphere of each differentiated cultural sphere should be limited to the boundaries set by the nature proper to each life sphere." This principle is, in fact, "nothing other than the principle of sphere sovereignty applied to the process of historical development."[50] Where this is disregarded a damaging "process of overextension in culture" is operative whereby the "extreme expansion" of the power of one sphere "retards [the] unfolding" of others in an unhealthy way.[51]

It is worth noting the contrast between Dooyeweerd's and Weber's theories of differentiation, notwithstanding obvious formal parallels. For Weber, the progressive realization of "the internal and lawful autonomy of the individual spheres" is necessarily accompanied by the secularization of the nonreligious spheres (political, economic, etc.). Such spheres mark themselves out as essentially incompatible with the imperatives of religious beliefs and ethics; the state, for example, cannot be defined, as it was in premodern societies, in terms of the pursuit of religious or moral ends but solely in terms of its possession of unique means, the "legitimate monopoly of violence."[52] For Dooyeweerd, while secularization certainly did occur in many spheres under the baleful influence of the modern humanistic ground motive, this was never a necessary feature or condition of institutional differentiation. Such differentiation is, rather, testimony to the providential unfolding of the created potentials of social order.

CRITIQUE AND CLARIFICATION

Not surprisingly, Dooyeweerd's conceptions of cultural differentiation and integration have met with many critical reactions. McIntire, for example, lays several charges against them.[53] Two are most pertinent for our purposes: Dooyeweerd wrongly evaluates past (and future) cultures in the light of norms derived from the present; and he assumes a unilinear sequence of cultural stages that historical evidence belies. I think the latter criticism certainly has merit. It is true, as noted, that Dooyeweerd acknowledges the possibility of reactionary historical tendencies, which include attempts to return to undifferentiated social forms. But these are antinormative aberrations. The movement from undifferentiated to differentiated is the lawful direction: "In all its aspects, the process of becoming [organic, emotional, and historical] develops, according to law, from an undifferentiated phase to a differentiated phase."[54] Concurring with McIntire, Griffioen points out that at this juncture Dooyeweerd betrays a clear affinity with a problematic nineteenth-century cultural evolutionism.[55]

The former criticism, however, merits more careful analysis. It is true that Dooyeweerd says relatively little on the question of the *future* normative development of modern societies, and McIntire rightly asks whether he regards differentiation as an endless process. It can certainly be said that Dooyeweerd exaggerates the relative significance of differentiation as a criterion of historical development. His account strongly suggests that the process is nearing completion, or at least that a condition of "full, differentiated disclosure" is in principle realizable.[56] Yet he gives no examples of structures in Western society that still await differentiation. He does claim, however, that newly emerging processes of *integration* (which he calls "integrating tendencies") are as yet incomplete, a point to which I return in chapters 7 and 11.

What of Dooyeweerd's evaluation of past and present cultures? We can agree with McIntire that Dooyeweerd's view of such societies is "too one-sidedly negative."[57] It overlooks both the variety of primitive societies and the fact that personal individuality was not entirely subordinated to an inclusive total community in all such societies.[58] Griffioen points to evidence uncovered since Dooyeweerd wrote that undermines the suggestion that all primitive societies are characterized by rigid nature religions in which people have no sense of transcending nature.[59] But in what sense does Dooyeweerd evaluate these cultures (whatever their precise structure) in the light of norms derived from the present, as McIntire charges? He writes that Dooyeweerd's difficulty was "trying to discern the normative 'Divine world-order' itself by looking through a slide photograph of modern European societies in the middle third of the twentieth century." His conclusion is, "What he detected as normative resembled modern European society."[60]

It is undoubtedly true to say that Dooyeweerd, having denied that norms for culture are revealed fully or directly in Scripture, faces the difficult problem of discerning them within the flux of human history. Significant hurdles need to be overcome for anyone claiming to discern from history any universal and enduring norms for cultural development.[61] Of course, unless one holds that these in principle cannot be overcome, then the difficulty McIntire identifies is not by any means peculiar to Dooyeweerd; it faces any attempt to ground normative principles in natural or created order. Yet it is not true to suggest that Dooyeweerd uses only knowledge of (a "slide photograph" of) *contemporary society* with which to discern the order of creation. He draws on a wide range of evidence from a variety of historical cultures to reach conclusions about such an order.[62] And while many features of modern European society appeared to him to reflect divine order, there were many that clearly did not. Hence the judgment that "Dooyeweerd accepted the composition of modern Western society as normative in an important sense of the word"[63] needs qualification. For example, he holds "fundamental objections" to Hegel's notion of "a centripetal direction of the entire Idea of development to the modern culture of the West."[64] Indeed he held that the secularized humanistic faith that has led the development of modern civilization has wrought extensive cultural damage, not least, for example, in the destructive political and economic individualism generated by the humanistic ideal of science as well as in its totalitarian mirror image.[65] Finally, he held that the "center and end of world-history is bound neither to the Western nor to any other civilization" but to Jesus Christ who both judges every culture and sustains whatever is good in it.[66]

A provisional answer to the specific question of whether Dooyeweerd is guilty of a modernist, occicentric bias would run as follows. First, this was evidently not his intention. Second, as I noted in chapter 4, his account of the humanistic freedom-nature motive as a declaration of the radical spiritual autonomy of humanity over against divine authority and the claims of created order generates a profound and comprehensive critique of the dominant cultural forces of modernity; he might be classed as a distinctive modernity critic.[67] Third, his accounts of particular social structures—treated in subsequent chapters—nevertheless give evidence that he was at crucial points insufficiently rigorous in tracking the damaging effects of this ground motive upon their concrete formations in the modern West. Fourth, he certainly endorsed the process of institutional differentiation lying at the foundation of modern Western societies. This was not out of any ethnocentrism but because he thought he discerned in that process the progressive disclosure of the norms of created order, even against the grain of the humanistic ground motive. It is in this sense that he can certainly be described, and would describe himself, as progressive rather than conservative. We might say, then, that he was intentionally antimodern in the second sense, intentionally modern in the fourth sense, and inadvertently modern in the third.[68]

Some of these judgments will be tested as I proceed to his accounts of particular social structures in subsequent chapters. Even if they are confirmed, however, they do not yet rebut the distinct charge that the notion at the core of his social ontology, namely, invariant structural principles—that which confers upon institutions their irreducible identities—amounts to a form of essentialism.

SIX

A PHILOSOPHY OF SOCIAL PLURALISM

THE IDENTITY OF SOCIAL STRUCTURES

I have shown how Dooyeweerd conceives of social structures as emerging out of a dynamic enterprise of human cultural formation. It has become abundantly clear that the *process* by which such structures emerge cannot be accused of being static. But can the charge be applied to the *outcome* of that process? Is what historical development throws up, in spite of all its variegated manifestations, nevertheless already ontically preprogrammed? Is Dooyeweerd's ontology of social structures still too rigidly prescriptive, too constrictive of human freedom, insufficiently attentive to historical contingency? This is the most frequent charge leveled against his social philosophy, and it requires careful analysis.

Dooyeweerd claims that social structures are rooted in the order of cosmic time. This is to assert that they are subject to the law-side of reality. All social structures are subject to lawful principles rooted in created order. While they are in every case established by human initiative, they are governed by "invariant" (or "enduring," or "constant," or "immutable"), universally valid, typical structural principles that condition, and indeed make possible, their factual existence. The principal task of a social philosophy is the critical, systematic elucidation of these social structural principles in continuous interaction with empirical data drawn from as many cultural and historical contexts as possible.[1] Patterns and regularities uncovered in social analysis testify to the presence of powerful normative inclinations operating within the concrete functioning of social structures. The human establishment of a social structure does not occur in an unconstrained, unconditioned realm of subjective choice. Institution building does not operate on an ontological tabula rasa but is in every case and at every moment a human response to—a historical positivization of—given, normative imperatives embedded in social reality.

Churches, states, business corporations, families, friendships, market exchanges, and so on, all testify to the operation of normative principles that govern their fundamental internal structure. These internal principles are the transcendental conditions, the conditions of possibility, for all societal phenomena. They continually impinge upon human societal experience with sufficient force that they can, in principle, be identified. Using the "integral empirical method,"[2] it is possible to disclose structural principles by careful philosophical analysis of "factually existing structures" and, in particular, the typical behavior patterns, persisting boundaries to possible variety, or continually recurring patterns of relationship seen within them. Structural principles are discoverable because they "urge themselves" on human experience. However damaged a particular factual structure may have become, human beings cannot alter the structural principle that makes possible its factual existence.[3]

The very notion of social structures being exemplifications of normative structural principles evokes the obvious question whether the numerous variations in forms of family (nuclear, extended, patriarchal, etc.), producer group (guild, corporation, cooperative, family business, etc.), and so on manifesting themselves throughout history and across enormously divergent cultures can really be seen as manifestations of a stable, divinely given law-order? By the end of this chapter I hope to have shown that while the apparent implausibility of this idea recedes somewhat when we explore Dooyeweerd's writings in detail, some far-reaching reformulations to his account of social structure are required if it is to remain at all convincing.

In certain fundamental respects social structures share the same ontic morphology as "things." First, they function in all the modal aspects.[4] They are structural "totalities," displaying all aspects, both normative and prenormative, in their concrete functioning. The state, for example, functions spatially in possessing territory; logically, in constituting a realm of public discourse; socially, in respecting diplomatic protocols; economically, in striving to balance its budget; aesthetically, in working for harmony among contending social groups; pistically, in confessing some view of the origin of political authority.

The mere fact of multimodal functioning does not yet inform us of the unique structural identity of the state, since all social structures do the same. Thus, second, like things, social structures are shaped by a structural principle. This embraces the whole configuration of its modal functions, characterized by its two "radical" functions, its qualifying and founding functions.

The qualifying function plays the decisive role in social structural principles just as it does for the structural principles of things. It determines the distinct identity of a social structure, both by guaranteeing the coherence of its internal structure[5] and by guiding its other functions as they each contribute in their own ways to its proper functioning. Such a function is therefore also termed the "leading function."[6]

The direction toward which the qualifying function leads is also described as its "intrinsic destination." The term indicates what is actually a second type of opening process.[7] We have seen that the modal aspects serve as guiding aspects for earlier guided ones, within a *modal* opening process or process of disclosure that continues until the faith aspect. The opening process within a concrete existent like a social structure is not modal in character but typical, one internal to a structure and proceeding under its leading function. It is the process whereby a particular social structure, such as a family, develops over time from initial formation toward maturity, approaching a complete development of its potentials. The notion, undeveloped in Dooyeweerd's social theory, will prove useful in correcting some defects in his account of the structural principle of the state in chapter 9.

The intrinsic destination *(bestemming)* of a social structure must be clearly distinguished from the "external purposes" *(doeleinden)* it may pursue.[8] Dooyeweerd consistently (perhaps obsessively) avoids applying the word *purpose (doel)* to the internal nature of a social structure. He suggests, for example, that while the intrinsic destination of a marriage is companionship, the generation of children is a purpose external to that relationship. In later chapters we see more clearly why, in relation to the voluntary association and the state, the distinction matters for him. On the face of it, however, *purpose* and *doel* often do convey what Dooyeweerd essentially intends by the term *bestemming*. To say that the "purpose of the state" is to establish a legal order seems to mean essentially what Dooyeweerd means in saying that the state has a legal destiny. Thus one commentator proposes the useful term *structural purpose* to capture Dooyeweerd's intention.[9]

Third, social structural principles, also like those of things, can be classified as belonging to certain ontic types. "Typical" structural principles hold universally for all members of a type. Types are given on the law-side of reality.[10] Within each structural type can be discerned a series of intratypical differentiations, an "inner articulation" of radical types and genotypes embracing yet further subtypes.[11]

The most basic difference between structural types is determined by their respective qualifying functions,[12] which may be any of the normative modal aspects.[13] Such types are radical types; all entities qualified with the same function belong to the same radical type.[14]

To identify genotypes within a radical type (both in things and in social structures) it is necessary to ascertain the relation between the qualifying function and the founding function. The specific character of the founding function in a social structure will make itself evident in the specific character of the qualifying function.[15] For example, the state's pursuit of justice is different from that of a church, family, business, and so on, because it is, uniquely, backed up by coercive power, as distinct from the faith power of a church, the moral power of a family, the economic power of a business, and so on.[16] Political justice cannot be recognized *as political* apart from its being based in the capacity of the state to use coercive power.

Fourth, social structures, like things, also display different "phenotypes." The differences between social structures so far discussed are all given in their structural principles, and hence on the law-side. Phenotypes (or "variability types"), by contrast, arise from enkaptic interlacements with other, differently qualified social structures.[17] Although essential for the factual existence of a social structure, such interlacements do not change its inner structural principle.[18] I say more about them when I examine Dooyeweerd's notion of social enkapsis in the next chapter.

Fifth, any differences between social structures that cannot be accounted for by their radical-, geno-, and phenotypical differences are an

expression of the unique subjective individuality of each one: of my family, with all its unrepeatable idiosyncrasies, as distinct from any other.[19]
Social structures thus share certain irreducible typical properties in
common with every other of their type but also have other irreducibly individual features. These two sides display a "mutual, unbreakable correlation." Each societal structure is "both atypically individual and determined in conformity with its internal structural principle."[20]

The persisting question evoked by the analysis so far is how much
room for subjective individuality is actually left for a social structure once
we have pinned down its radical-typical, genotypical, and phenotypical
properties. How is the boundary between typicality and individual
uniqueness to be reliably identified? I pursue this question in the next
section.

The final feature of social structural principles shared by structural
principles of things is that their qualifying functions can either be a "subject function" or an "object function." This new distinction has wide application throughout his ontology but turns out to be especially important for Dooyeweerd's analysis of social structures. He holds that the
qualifying function of a tree, for example, is its last subject function, the
latest aspect in which it "functions subjectively." The distinction between
"subjective functioning" and "objective functioning" rests upon a further
fundamental ontological category, the "subject-object" relation.[21] When
something functions subjectively, it operates as a subject or agent in one
of its modal functions: it extends in space, grows, feels, thinks, claims a
legal right, and so forth. In this kind of operation or functioning *it* is
what is doing the operating. At the same time other subjects can operate
upon it (function in relation to it) in some way. They can perceive it, use
it, develop affection for it, own it, and so on. In these cases it becomes an
object to another operating or functioning subject; it "functions objectively."

The subject-object relation is evident, in varying ways, in all existents in the world. To say that the qualifying function of a tree is its last
subject function means that it does not function subjectively in any aspect beyond the biotic. It neither feels, thinks, nor behaves in any of the
other characteristically human ways associated with the logical and postlogical spheres. Certainly the tree can evoke a certain feeling in a human

observer, it can be conceived by humans, and it can be experienced aesthetically. Here it functions objectively, that is, as an object of human subjective functioning.[22]

Some things are, by contrast, qualified by one of their object functions. For example, natural objects formed by animals, such as birds' nests, are qualified by their psychic object functions. Such objects have a "secondary character," lacking a radical type of their own, and only exist in a subject-object relation to the animals producing them.[23] There is also a further category of things whose qualifying function is a *normative* object function. A sculpture, for example, is qualified by its normative aesthetic object function,[24] whereas a chair is qualified by its normative social object function.[25] The question whether *things* have a subjective or objective qualification may be resolved relatively straightforwardly. The question whether *social relationships* (families, schools, states, etc.) are qualified by a subject or an object function—that is, are such relationships *themselves* agents, or are they, simply, linkages *between* agents (persons)?—is a matter on which Dooyeweerd has an interesting position, yet one in need of an important corrective, as we shall see.

The features of social structural principles considered so far are general features of structural principles of any kind of existent. There are, not surprisingly, additional features arising from the fundamental difference between things and social structures. I discuss two of these features here and reserve the third for the next section. The first feature captures the most fundamental difference between things and social structures, namely, that the structural principles of the latter need to be brought into existence—positivized—by human action. In *WdW* Dooyeweerd refers to social structures as having a "thing-structure,"[26] but by *NC* he rejected this usage, presumably more aware of the objection that it would imply a kind of sociological naturalism. In *NC* he presents a much clearer distinction between things and social structures, referring to things as "primary types" and social structures as "secondary types."[27] Primary types are simply given in reality; secondary types have to be brought into existence, either by animals[28] or by humans. Animal secondary types are qualified by the highest subject function found in the animal realm, the psychic function. Secondary types of the human realm, including both cultural artifacts and social relationships, only come into existence as a result of formative human action.[29] In contrast to animal secondary types, they can bear a variety of different qualifications depending upon the nature of the human act for which they act as structural conduits.[30]

The second distinctive feature of the structural principles of social structures as against those of things, flowing clearly from the first, is that their concrete instantiations are enormously varied. Here we meet the first part of an answer to whether Dooyeweerd's theory of social types unduly narrows the latitude available for institutional diversity and experimentation. Earlier I noted Dooyeweerd's proposal that all individuality structures display both invariable typicality and variable subjectivity. In the nonhuman realm this variability is accounted for by a range of factors that will not be pursued here. When we consider "secondary structures of the human realm," however, and, specifically, social structures, the range of variations seems to multiply almost exponentially, and this, of course, is the result of human freedom exercised by historical creatures. Concrete social structures are positivized in enormously varied ways by culturally formative human beings.

Griffioen's observations on social variability are useful here. He points out that Dooyeweerd offers no extensive analysis of the variability of social structures, regarding this as the specialized task of the empirical social scientist rather than the social philosopher. Yet he does point out that Dooyeweerd's approach enables us at least to distinguish between two fundamental kinds of variability, those arising from the "structural" factor of cultural disclosure and those arising from the "directional" factor of religious orientation. Griffioen's terms refer to what Dooyeweerd describes, respectively, as cultural disclosure and the formative influence of religious ground motives. As Griffioen notes, the two are inseparable: structural principles "require human form-giving . . . and it is within this 'positivizing' that direction comes to be chosen."[31]

Regarding the first, the requirement of human positivizing leads us to expect a "great cultural diversity in norm-positivizing."[32] It seems clear that we can distinguish three different manifestations of structural variability arising from cultural unfolding, and keeping them apart helps clarify what Dooyeweerd intends. The first is a question of the stage of cultural development at which a particular structure appears, that is, where on the journey from a primitive or undifferentiated to a differentiated society the structure in question is located. The structure of a family in an undifferentiated society will differ markedly from one in a differentiated society. Yet, second, within any particular cultural stage further variability can be seen. For example, within a differentiated society social structures will reveal differences determined by numerous factors, such as the state of technology. Thus, for example, an early modern state, while a genuine state, lacks the bureaucratic apparatus typical of a contemporary state.[33] There is a third kind of variability (one noted by Griffioen), namely, differences arising from local cultural characteristics, lacking any universal significance.[34] Thus, for example, the norm of social respect within families or states is positivized differently in China as compared to Germany or the United States. This kind of variation cannot be wholly accounted for by either of the first two cultural factors just noted.[35]

It can be seen that all this makes the task of distinguishing invariant typical structure from variable positive form a formidable one. When we introduce the directional factor of religious orientation, the matter is yet more complex. What this draws attention to is deviations from structural norms generated by misplaced—indeed, as Dooyeweerd would put it, "idolatrous"—religious commitments. This is not to suggest that positivizations directed by false religion will produce no legitimate cultural variations, nor is it to suggest that positivizations directed by true religion display no variability; such variability will occur because of quite legitimate structural cultural factors. But antinormative positivizations will, it seems, generate their own special forms of diversity. Much of this will be a matter of the unique subjective individuality of a particular structure where that structure bears the impact of "sin." Parental selfishness or political vanity, for example, will show up in an infinite number of ways, defying classification and straddling all cultural contexts. Yet certain deviations will be evidently conditioned by those macrocultural distortions that Dooyeweerd terms apostate ground motives. Social structures will vary according to the character of the religious ground motives dominant in their culture, since ground motives will distort people's grasp of structural principles. Thus a modern Western family is likely to show adverse individualistic traits, due to the influence of humanism, that a traditional African family would not. Or a primitive economic structure will close down the economic norm of frugality, whereas an authentically Puritan one (to beg Weber's question) will open it up.

It will be obvious that the precise relation between these two kinds of factors is often exceedingly difficult to disentangle and will inevitably be continually contested, even (sometimes especially) among adherents of the same religious convictions. For example, what I just called the adverse individualistic traits of a Western family may not always be easy to distinguish from quite legitimate traits that for Dooyeweerd arise from the normative process of individualization.[36] The unwillingness of children in Western societies to care for elderly parents or of parents to protect their unborn children might be cited as illegitimate expressions of humanistic individualism, while the freedom to choose one's spouse or one's occupation without parental consent are, arguably, cases of legitimate individualization.[37] But such lines are often very difficult to draw, and this makes Dooyeweerd's project of identifying invariant structural principles truly daunting.

In addition to these structural and directional factors producing variability in social structures, a third factor appears in Dooyeweerd's account. This is the shaping effect of what he calls (somewhat confusingly) "societal forms." He holds that these are distinct both from structural principles and factually existing structures. They are the "necessary links" between the two, intermediary principles of order that function as relatively constant bridges between the unchanging structural principles and the ephemeral factual structures. Such forms arise from enkaptic interlacements between various structures.[38] An example of a societal form is the modern Western form of marriage. The form of such a marriage is conditioned by the fact that it is solemnized by the state. Such an interlacement is not necessary for a marriage to exist, and the societal form created by it may only have a relatively stable duration. Yet as long as this arrangement for legalizing marriage exists it will condition any particular marriage in Western societies.

Is this, after all, a truly distinct factor or simply one of the abovementioned structural factors under a different guise? It would seem that societal forms can be generated either by structural or by directional factors. For example, the civil registration of marriage in a church is not attributable merely to a legitimate process of cultural development but is a result of a very specific religious viewpoint characteristic of Catholic and Anglican ecclesiology. By contrast, the special features of a family business are probably better regarded as structural in nature.

It is also instructive to note what appears to be a straightforward confusion needlessly introduced by Dooyeweerd into his idea of societal forms. He claims that they "belong to the law-side of human societal life" *and* are also "products of human formation" (and so have a "certain temporal duration," longer than that of individual structures that they condition).[39] But they cannot be both. If societal forms are on the law-side, then they collapse into structural principles. If they are products of human positivization, then they must be variations on the subject-side. The latter seems better to respect the consistency of Dooyeweerd's intentions. Yet the appearance of this problem is additional evidence of the difficulty of discerning bright lines between invariant structure and variable positive form.[40]

A Critical Reformulation

One possible way to respond to the difficulty just mentioned is to do with Dooyeweerd what Taylor does with Hegel, namely, to acknowledge that his ontological vision is dead and yet put the continuingly salient aspects of his social and political philosophy to creative use.[41] Those who conclude that Dooyeweerd's ontological framework is beyond resuscitation could nevertheless still find as much of value in the details of his social and political philosophy as Taylor finds in Hegel's. Dooyeweerd aims to provide a genuinely public philosophy, one accessible in principle to those who would not share either his religious convictions or all the foundations of his ontological framework. Part of the purpose of chapters 10 and 11 is to show how. My own attempt at a reformulation of the core principle underlying his social philosophy does not, however, proceed by setting his ontological framework aside as simply redundant. Rather I try to reach for such a reformulation from the inside, dispensing with aspects that seem inconsistent, incoherent, or obviously unsustainable while attempting to reconstruct many of the remaining elements into a more satisfactory account. I focus on a single problem—invariance—but one that has ramifications for many other aspects of his construction.

The claim that social structural principles are invariant (or immutable) is the most controversial aspect of Dooyeweerd's social philosophy. This is certainly his plain meaning. While existing social structures undergo all kinds of change, their structural principles "are not changeable in time, since they determine the inner nature of perishable factual things, events and social relationships functioning within their transcendental cadre."[42] Dooyeweerd himself does not see them as rigid constraints but rather as enabling directives, norms inclining humans toward successful social activity and warning them off blind alleys or precipices. They are not fixed directives but rather "principles of temporal potentiality or possibility," which determine the "margin of latitude or possibilities of factual structures realized in time."[43]

In probing Dooyeweerd's intentions here we can begin by asking how wide he imagines this legitimate margin of latitude to be. From the discussion at the end of the previous section it can be seen that it is at least sufficiently wide to encompass all the structural variations there discussed. Structural typicality is invariant, whereas subjective individuality (and pheno-typicality) can vary immensely. Yet how can we reliably identify which features of a social structure belong in which category? For example, is it at all plausible that the limited liability corporation, invented only in nineteenth-century Europe, could be reflective of some underlying universal structural principle? How can we avoid reading ephemeral features of concrete social structures into invariant structural principles?

I have already noted Dooyeweerd's desire to differentiate his position from any association with Platonic Ideas understood as real existents located outside of time.[44] Structural principles are not existents but principles for existents; transcendental (principles of possibility) but not transcendent (existing in a different realm). This, of course, is true of cosmic law in general. The law-side and the subject-side are two sides of one and the same created reality. Law does not transcend reality but frames it from within. There is an indissoluble correlation between law and subject. On the other hand, while Dooyeweerd insists that there can be no subject without a law to which it is subject, and that without subjective existence law "has no meaning," it seems that he does *not* specifically rule out the possibility that there can be a law without a concrete subject actually subject to it.[45] And this is understandable, since his position implies that structural laws "hold" prior to the appearance of the concrete social structures embodying them. How could it be otherwise, since at a time when (say) the state was beginning to make its first concrete appearance in human history the structural principle of the state could not do its work of guiding, inclining, or propelling human beings to form an actual state unless that structural principle already held?[46] But is there any sense at all in which structural principles can be conceived as holding in the absence of any existents subject to them? Can the notion of structural principles as "principles of possibility" be rendered intelligible?

It is, of course, clear that for Dooyeweerd structural principles are disclosed through a dynamic process of historical development in which free and responsible human initiative is fundamental. Both the modal process of disclosure and the process of cultural differentiation in which distinct social structures emerge from primitive communities to make their historical debut as independent units clearly ground structural laws fully in the dynamics of historical change in a way entirely foreign to the Platonic conception. Dooyeweerd makes this clear in answering a question he poses to himself: are the structural principles really only of "an ideal-normative character" with no relevance to explaining society "as it factually is"? The question is occasioned by the observation that the concept of distinct structural principles appears to take for granted the presence of a differentiated society in which there already exist concrete structures governed by such principles. How then can these principles explain the structures of primitive, undifferentiated societies? His answer is that the assertion of an invariant structural principle for, say, the state does not mean that states have existed in every period of historical development. The establishment of states is a historical task; at some periods in some areas there simply were no states.

However, he continues, *whenever humans establish states* they are necessarily bound by the structural principle of the state. Although states differ significantly from one another, their internal nature is not determined by changing historical circumstances. The same applies to all social structures.[47] So his affirmation that social structures have a history and that their structural principles are disclosed historically does not mute his insistence that structural principles are not themselves subject to historical change. There is dynamic historical disclosure of structural law but not ontic innovation. What is disclosed is what is already given "in principle."

The importance Dooyeweerd attaches to the invariable character of structural principles is further underlined in his specific repudiation of

what he terms "evolutionism." His interest in evolutionism is not primarily in its biological implications but in its character as a comprehensive philosophical theory of reality according to which entirely new
structural principles appear in the course of a genetic process of development. Not structural principles but only their factual realization in concrete individual existents undergo such a process (i.e., the "internal
opening process" of a structure). No new structural principles emerge in
time. History throws up immense complexity, variety, and unpredict-
ability but not ontic structural novelty. This claim is obviously at least as
controversial with respect to social structures as it is with respect to biological structures. Yet Dooyeweerd is emphatic that when specific social
structures make their factual appearance at a particular point in history
they are only actualizing what invariant structural principles grounded
in the original and abidingly valid order of creation (cosmic time) make
possible.[48]

The plausibility of this notion can be tested by considering a significant critical discussion of it by Wolterstorff.[49] Although Wolterstorff is
not a social constructivist, he is evidently uncomfortable with what he
seems to regard as the static essentialism of Dooyeweerd's social ontology
and rejects the claim that social structures are bound to invariant principles. The question of the normative design of social structures, he suggests, must be answered differently according to cultural and historical
context. Dooyeweerd's analysis suggests that certain structures necessarily perform certain distinctive functions and that to assign such functions to other structures offends against the nature of such structures and
thus will cause those functions to be performed badly. Wolterstorff denies such a universally valid correlation between particular functions
and particular structures. He notes, for example, that while Dooyeweerd
holds that the distinctive function of the state is the administration of
justice (Dooyeweerd's own formulation is more complex than this, as I
discuss in chapters 8 and 9), it has proved necessary for our modern
states to perform many other functions as well, though in other societies
it might not: "The matching up of functions . . . to institutions is not to be
done by asking what *the* State and *the* Business Enterprise ought to do,
but by considering what *our* states and *our* business enterprises ought to
do in our situation."[50] Certain functions are, he acknowledges, "regularly
performed" throughout history, and that they should be performed well

is necessary to human flourishing. But they do not necessarily have to be performed by the same institution. The criterion must be what is conducive to human flourishing, not the supposed inner nature of an institution. Granted that "an institution could scarcely be considered a state unless, among other things, it saw to the administration of justice in that society," it does not follow from this that the administration of justice must always and everywhere be the exclusive function of the state.[51]

This, however, seems to confuse two distinct claims[52]—that there are certain functions that always and everywhere must be performed by states and only states; and that no other functions than these may be performed by states. Dooyeweerd certainly advances the first claim, but he specifically rejects the second. Moreover, Wolterstorff seems virtually to have conceded the validity of the first claim after all. To say that an institution would not be a state if it did not perform the function of administering justice is in effect to acknowledge that states always and everywhere must perform the function of administering justice; that there is, after all, a universal correlation between this function and the structure we call the state.

The first claim is, I suggest, a plausible one. It means, simply, that when the function of administering (public) justice is actually being performed the institution that we have come to call a state must already be present in some form. Functions are not free-floating, waiting to be taken up by this or that institution. They cannot be performed other than by functioning institutions, for they are functions *of* institutions. Now it would not be impossible to make the further case that it is *in the very nature* of this particular function—administering public justice—that only states can perform it. I show in chapters 8 and 9 that this is exactly the case Dooyeweerd makes. Other structures may attempt to administer public justice, he acknowledges—churches or families or business corporations, for example—but they do so very badly, and the progressive thrust of history pushes state builders toward acknowledging the norm of differentiation in which the state comes into its own as *the* institution fitted precisely to administer public justice.

If he can sustain this argument—and I will suggest that, with significant qualifications and reformulations, he can—then he can at least show that *when* states make their appearance on the historical stage they must have a certain form. If so, then it will not do to say, as Wolterstorff does, that "we" can match up functions to institutions simply by asking what functions "our" states should perform, as if we could simply make an unconstrained decision on this question, customizing the state entirely to suit our local requirements. For, whatever else they do, our states, like all others, will necessarily be fitted to administer public justice and will have to go on being so fitted if they are to continue to exist *as states* rather than as some other institution—say, a large-scale extended family in which public offices are awarded by nepotism, a criminal gang in which public moneys are procured and distributed by theft and intimidation, or something like an East India Company in which coercive public authority accrues to economic power. Of course such things exist in the world today, but they testify not so much to the presence of variably structured states as to the absence of properly formed states.[53]

But this is to anticipate the argument in chapters 8 and 9. Even if such an argument could be sustained, Dooyeweerd would not have shown that the state is present *always and everywhere*. As noted earlier, however, he makes no such claim. There are many periods of history in which states are absent, for example, periods prior to the commencement of the process of differentiation, in which nothing resembling an independent state has yet emerged.[54]

I have suggested that Wolterstorff's critique of Dooyeweerd's notion that social structures (once in existence) display universal properties is not as persuasive as it first appears. Although I considered the example of only one kind of social structure, the state, this at least indicates the form that the argument might take in the case of others.[55] But to claim that social structures, *when* they make their historical appearance, display universal normative properties is not yet to claim that these normative properties are *invariant*. Invariance is not identical to universality: an invariant norm might not be universal (say, "the law of the Medes and Persians"); and a universal norm might not be invariant (say, the historically evolving principles governing usury). So although I have provisionally endorsed Dooyeweerd's claim that certain historical social structures may display universal properties (of which structural principles are one, rather complex account), I have not yet vindicated his claim that structural principles are invariant.

It should be recalled that the fundamental reason why Dooyeweerd insists on their invariance is because he conceives them as being given in the order of creation. Indeed he regards this grounding of social norms in created order as indispensable for resisting the radical assertion of human moral autonomy driving the humanistic freedom motive. It is essential to Dooyeweerd that human freedom does not generate moral norms ex nihilo but is always responsive to divine sovereignty, and for him this implies that every act of human institution building must occur within a framework of normative created order. Now this is no static order, as we have seen; it actually requires and makes possible historical human action. But such action is, in the last analysis, the unfolding of normative possibilities already implanted in creation from the beginning. Creation order is historically disclosed, but such disclosure appears to resemble more a progressive unveiling of already existing normative potentials than a generation of genuinely innovative normative (as opposed to factual) possibilities.[56] Yet critics of Dooyeweerd's line of argument defend precisely such normative innovation and regard his conception as unacceptably preempting human freedom and historical contingency.[57]

I want to suggest that a promising way to address the contrast between unveiling and innovating is through a closer examination of the resources available in Dooyeweerd's philosophical anthropology.[58] Wolterstorff's critique points in that direction, highlighting Dooyeweerd's failure to adequately elaborate its potential fruitfulness for his social philosophy. His point is that Dooyeweerd's theory of the unfolding of social structures fails to make explicit the way in which such structures are *conducive to human flourishing*. This, it seems, is the deeper basis of his emphasis that states should serve "our" needs rather than being modeled on some universal norm. Dooyeweerd's problem, as he puts it, is that he has fallen victim to a "mankind-for-the-sake-of-structures way of thinking":

> Too often he gives the impression that mankind was created to unfold social structures, rather than that social structures *have no justification* unless they serve mankind. . . . It is the *fullness of human life* that is the decisive test, not the proper realization of each sphere's inner nature.[59]

Dooyeweerd's justified reply to this way of formulating the objection would be that the content of the term *fullness of human life* cannot be determined apart from knowledge of the normative nature of the essential social spheres that frame human life. But his argument would surely be more persuasive if it were actually *shown* to arise out of some notion of what constitutes a full human life, an idea of the human good. Now Dooyeweerd certainly has a profound and complex notion of the human good. What he needs is an explicit argument that shows why, and in what historical circumstances, certain kinds of social structure are necessary if this human good is to be realized. He needs a "structures-for-the-sake-of-humankind" argument, one echoing Maritain's statement, "Man is by no means for the State. The State is for man."[60] The following is an outline of the possible structure of such an argument.[61]

My starting point is a theme discussed by Dooyeweerd in a different context (his philosophical anthropology) but which opens up a far more satisfying way to conceive of the normative design of social structures. In the previous section I examined two features possessed by social structures marking them off from things: their origin in the positivizing action of humans and their extensive malleability. The theme I am about to discuss is the third such distinctive feature.

One particular category of social structure among the medley treated at greater length in the next chapter is "organized communities." Since this category embraces a very wide variety of structures—churches, states, voluntary associations, businesses, unions, clubs, and so on—the category is highly significant for Dooyeweerd's general social philosophy. Organized communities are distinguished from "natural communities," such as marriage and family, by virtue of the fact that they require deliberate human formation and so are historically founded, whereas natural communities are founded biotically.[62] They are distinguished from what I will abbreviate here as "interlinkages"[63] by virtue of the fact that they have a continuous existence outlasting that of any of their individual members. In discussing these Dooyeweerd raises the problem of what it is that secures the *continuous internal unity* of these organized, "supra-individual" communal wholes. Any theory of the internal unity of an organized community must, he suggests, begin by taking account of our ordinary (naive) experience of organized communities as real wholes, "continuous and identical unities," which persist in spite of the change of their members. We experience such communities in some sense as agents that function subjectively in many modal aspects. For example, we know intuitively the difference between private decisions of individual ministers and decisions of "the government" and easily grasp that communities can own objects like buildings.[64]

But what is the *internal structure* of such wholes intuitively grasped in naive experience? It may appear that, precisely in virtue of its apparent possession of continuous identity, subjective functioning, and internal activity, an organized community (unlike an interlinkage) has a structure similar to that of a thing. As I noted above this was Dooyeweerd's position in *WdW,* but by the time of *NC* he had acknowledged that the philosophical term *thing* is applicable exclusively to wholes that function subjectively only in the prelogical aspects (inanimate objects, plants, animals). Communities, however, function subjectively in all modal aspects. It is true that they clearly lack bodies, but they nevertheless also function in prelogical aspects: spatially, physically, biotically, and so on. In addition, they function in all the postlogical aspects. States, for example, engage in diplomatic gestures with one another (social functioning), trade with one another (economic functioning), conclude treaties with each other (juridical functioning), and trust or mistrust each other (ethical functioning).[65] It is this postlogical *subjective* functioning that gives to organized communities a categorially different sort of internal unity than that of a thing.

This was an important and necessary correction in Dooyeweerd's understanding of social structural principles. Yet his rethinking of the thinghood of communities has not gone far enough. The suggestion that communities function subjectively in the distinctively human (postlogical) aspects seems plausible, but it is much harder to imagine what their *prelogical subjective* functioning might amount to. Once it is acknowledged that communities, lacking bodies, cannot actually be measured or weighed, for example, it is not easy to propose any other convincing examples of their *subjective* spatial or physical functioning.[66] This is apparent from Dooyeweerd's rather artificial formulations of the state's prelogical subject functions.[67] For example, despite a subtle attempt to argue that the state's territory exemplifies the subjective spatial functioning of the *state,* his argument actually implies no more than that the *piece of land* in question has subjective spatial functions (which it clearly does).[68] Certainly this piece of land has a special relationship to the state: as an object of the state's public-legal jurisdiction, territory is inherent in the very notion of the state. But this does not involve the state assuming the subjective spatial functioning of the land over which it has territorial jurisdiction.[69]

In any event, for Dooyeweerd, the internal unity of an organized community is, after all, crucially determined by its *postlogical* subjective functioning. He suggests that such unity is realized not through any mysterious invisible force but simply in and through the activity of interacting members. It consists in a "social coherence of typical human acts and typical modes of human behaviour" determined by its structural principle.[70] In elaborating what this social coherence amounts to, Dooyeweerd is rightly at pains to exclude any suggestion that a community's subjective functions (e.g., psychic, logical) are in any sense independent of the subjective functioning of its individual members. He therefore rejects organicist notions, such as that espoused by Otto von Gierke, that posit separate, supra-individual entities such as a *volksgeist,* collective consciousness, or group personality.[71] What secures the internal unity and thus the identity of an organized community is, simply, the continued, interactive, structured functioning of its members.

Two statements shed light on his meaning. The first is this: "The continual existence of the [community] is dependent on the inner act-life and the social activity of human beings by which the communal relationships must be realized."[72] The phrase "inner act-life" alludes to Dooyeweerd's conception of the human body as an "act-structure," an important but—as I remarked earlier—regrettably undeveloped notion in his philosophical anthropology. He holds that various human acts— praying, thinking, feeling, dancing, and so on—are individuality structures each qualified by various modal aspects.[73] And, as we have seen, he also holds that social structures are each so qualified: a church by the faith aspect, a state by the juridical aspect, and so on. Yet, surprisingly, he does not elaborate on the obvious link between the qualification of individual human acts and the qualification of the social structures within which these acts are performed.

The second statement sheds further light: "The internal continuity of . . . a particular communal whole . . . can be actualized only in the communal structure of the relevant functions of its members."[74] That is, when members function in a community the members' functions themselves have an irreducibly communal character, which cannot be explained at all in terms of their being the functions of discrete individuals.[75] When members pray during a church service these are acts of corporate prayer, which could not be explained if they were only an aggregation of simultaneous and contiguous individual acts of prayer. It is not that the community functions in the members, or that the members function in the community, but simply that the members function *in community*. The specific character of this communal functioning is determined by the structural principle of the community in question and not by the inner act-life of individual members, even though the continued realization of this structural principle depends upon such individual acts. Thus while communities lack the subjective personality of an individual, "this fact does not exclude that *in comparison with one another,* they have an inner subjective structural unity."[76] This unity is guaranteed by the structural principle of the community that frames the functioning of individual members.

This account of the internal unity of an organized community is a promising point of departure in addressing the question of the normative design of social structures. It not only successfully avoids the pitfalls of both (methodological and ontological) individualism and collectivism but also brings much more fully to the fore the crucial point that the normative design of social structures does not make its claims upon members from outside their own normative subjective functioning but rather rises up from within it.

More needs to be said, of course, on the process whereby individual human acts connect with the collective structural imperatives of an organized community. Dooyeweerd's undeveloped notion of the human "act-structure" coming to expression in variously qualified human acts provides a clue. He conceives of the human body as not itself an individuality-structure but an act-structure, "the field of free expression for the human spirit."[77] Yet, although the act-structure of the human body is not qualified by any particular function, particular human acts, such as praying, theorizing, feeling, or dancing, *are* indeed so qualified.[78] An aesthetically qualified act of dancing thus displays all the aspects within its own structure. And, like human acts, social relationships may also be qualified by a variety of functions.[79] Regrettably Dooyeweerd fails to elaborate upon the evidently intimate links between the notion of variously qualified human acts and that of variously qualified social relationships. What follows is a gesture toward how that may be done.

Fully developed persons have capacities, given in their created nature, to engage in a diversity of variously qualified, mutually presupposing, and equivalently valuable core activities or functions: biological survival, emotional integration, social interaction, productive labor, political participation, aesthetic and linguistic expression, religious worship, and so on. Such core functions might then be subdivided, in terms of Dooyeweerd's categories, according to radical types, genotypes, and so on.[80] Arguments could then be developed to show that, at particular historical periods, certain kinds of social structures form the necessary contexts for each of these to be adequately performed and that apart from these structures humans remain unfulfilled or are even placed at serious risk. One of these arguments could be that, once institutions have differentiated, institutions called states are essential in order to protect the interactions between other structures and to secure a public space in which citizens can pursue their various goals. The next stage would be to indicate how these social structures need to be designed in certain ways and that if this design is distorted, human fulfillment is curtailed. And part of this stage of the argument would be to demonstrate, in the manner outlined above with respect to the state, that certain functions essential for human flourishing must be performed by this and not that kind of structure.

What such a line of argument would aim to show is that the normative design of social structures emerges out of a *normative conception of the human person*. The principles of possibility Dooyeweerd speaks of would then be seen as embedded fully in human nature, viewed as principles emerging from the possibilities or potentials given with the created structure of the human person. The problematic phenomenon of "laws without subjects" is then reconceptualized, less problematically, as "undisclosed human possibilities" (or "unactualized potential"). Normative structural laws could then be reconceptualized as inescapable imperatives rooted in and guided by the deeper norm of promoting human flourishing. The term *invariant* structural law could then be dispensed with and replaced with a notion of normative imperatives grounded in and directed to this given, stable, but dynamically unfolding, created structure of the human person, with its complex arrangement of functions (capacities, potentials, needs). Structures have an enduring design only in the sense, and only to the extent, that they answer to enduring human functional capacities.[81]

I said above that certain structures form the necessary context for the realization of certain capacities, "at particular historical periods." This is an important qualification, suggesting that we need a better account than Dooyeweerd supplies of the historical development of the structures through which those given (and dynamically unfolding) capacities are realized. Dooyeweerd characterizes this in rather unilinear fashion as a process of structural differentiation, whereas Dengerink speaks, more felicitously, of a division of labor among differently qualified human activities, each of which comes to expression in a series of differentiated structures the normative structure of which answers to the normative structure of the relevant activity.[82] The created possibilities within the structure of the human person could thus be seen as presenting humans with a normative historical task. In the case of the state it would need to be shown that the establishment of a distinct institution to administer public justice was, at a particular point in historical development, necessary if certain essential human functional capacities were to be protected and fostered. If such an argument were available we would have arrived at a point close to Dooyeweerd's own intentions but by a more direct and, I think, more scenic route.

Where does this leave the charge that Dooyeweerd is guilty of "essentialism"? An initial task here is to consider whether this is something any thinker should feel guilty about. What exactly is wrong with essentialism?[83] I have attempted to detach this charge from three others often hitched to it: that Dooyeweerd's social philosophy betrays a static notion of history; that it is conservative; and that it reveals a narrowly occicentric bias. I have attempted to rebut the first by depicting institution building as occurring within a dynamic historical opening process. I have partially addressed the second by indicating in broad terms the senses in which Dooyeweerd can be said to be both modern and progressive (and I address it further in subsequent chapters). And I have replied to the third by noting that to the extent that the charge is valid (and to a degree it is) it is at least against his express intentions.

The charge of essentialism is typically advanced by those who hold that a specific way of understanding the essence or nature or identity of a group of people or an institution imposes an external definition on them, disrespecting their subjectivity and misrepresenting their real interests or potentials. Politically, essentialism risks breeding stereotyping and sustaining marginalization and oppression. Philosophically, it assumes a concept of stable ontological identities that is untenable in the light of evidence of continual social flux and variation. Dooyeweerd's theory of invariant structural principles, which is the basis for his idea of what I have called irreducible institutional identities, seems on the face of it a prime candidate. Now suppose we replace the notion of invariant typical structural principles with that of normative structures rooted in universal irreducible human functions, in the way proposed. Norms for social structures are then seen as arising out of the functional capacities of a complexly articulated human nature. It is these capacities that are the deeper sources of irreducible institutional identity, in the sense that the structural configuration of an institution is not presented as an independent imperative operating on humans from without but as a requirement recognized by humans in the course of historical experience as being necessary for particular kinds of social human flourishing.

Thus modified I think this conception can avoid the charge of *institutional* essentialism: social structures are to be responsive to irreducible human capacities as these manifest themselves in particular historical conditions. Can it also preempt the charge of what might be termed *functional* essentialism? That is, can it avoid the criticism that the very notion of multiple, universal irreducible human functions is essentialist? If we review the substance of the antiessentialist complaint as stated above, it now becomes more difficult to see how a theory that celebrates a multiplicity of human functional capacities, then affirms that these need to be deployed in structured communal ways together with other human beings, necessarily implies any of the items in that complaint. It may be that for radical libertarians the view that humans are inherently communal beings is deeply problematic. But assuming here, for the sake of argument, recognition of the necessity of communal contexts for the pursuit of human flourishing, why would the very idea of multiple functional human capacities be regarded as alienating, stereotyping, or oppressive?[84]

It is, of course, clearly possible that *particular accounts* of those capacities might turn out to be all those things. A patriarchal argument that women possess less potential for rational functioning than men would indeed be so. But these and other arguments to the effect that human capacities are unequally distributed across designated classes of people can be and have been compellingly rebutted. A more difficult case would be a view of marriage as inherently and exclusively heterosexual. I will not explore that particular case here, but I mention it in order to allude to the structure of the argument that it and many other similarly controverted cases might involve. The case of marriage involves not only an assertion about human capacities in general (in this case especially moral, sexual, and emotional capacities) but also about the design of the institution or relationship most conducive to the flourishing of such capacities. Can the sexual and emotional capacities of two persons of the same sex adequately flourish if they enter the institution we have come to call "marriage," or is that institution conducive to such flourishing only between persons of the opposite sex? This question, of course, is now being energetically joined in public debate across most Western societies.[85] The answer given to this and parallel questions about social structures, I am suggesting, will depend on particular assessments of the relationship between irreducible human functions and the conducive institutional contexts in which such functions will be performed. So framing the problem of the normative design of social institutions in this way is to propose, not that particular prescriptions flow readily from the philosophical-anthropological background it assumes, but only that such debates can fruitfully be understood as debates *about* that contested relationship.[86]

My conclusion, then, is that the charge of essentialism loses much of its force against Dooyeweerd's notion of invariant structural principles when that notion is recast in the way just outlined. An affirmation of multiple irreducible human functions and of the necessary structural forms required to channel them in ways conducive to communal human flourishing does not imply any essentialist straightjacketing of social structures. In chapter 11 I take up this point in an attempt to show that, on the contrary, a Dooyeweerdian conception of civil society can help generate a distinctive form of critical social philosophy.

SEVEN

A MEDLEY OF SOCIAL STRUCTURES

THE CONCLUSION OF THE PREVIOUS CHAPTER IS THAT the ontological notion at the foundation of Dooyeweerd's social philosophy—"invariant structural principles"—requires substantial reformulation. Yet it appears that much of the detailed construction he erects on that foundation yields fruitful insights of continuing pertinence. Here I examine that construction in detail, aiming to exhibit the nature and range of those insights and to propose further reformulations. The first section opens by recording how the notion of differently qualified social structures generates a complex set of categories under which diverse social structures can be grouped. It then proceeds to discuss at greater length a second set of categories introduced by Dooyeweerd, which further illuminates his central contentions while also generating additional problems. In the second section I examine Dooyeweerd's application of the notion of enkaptic interlacements to the realm of social structures. I conclude that although his articulation of this notion needs reframing, it has the potential to be developed into a valuable tool of analysis for a philosophy of social pluralism. In particular, it helps frame a balance, which pluralistic theories sometimes lack, between the distinctness and autonomy of social structures and their interconnectedness. In these two sections the substance of Dooyeweerd's social pluralism will come more clearly into view. The final section addresses the character of that pluralism explicitly, elaborating on the sense in which it develops directly from Kuyper's social thought and contrasting it with what Dooyeweerd took to be its principal opponents, "individualism" and "universalism." The precise senses in which Dooyeweerd's Christian pluralism can be termed modern will then also appear in sharper relief.

CATEGORIES OF SOCIAL STRUCTURE

On the basis of Dooyeweerd's notion that social structures can be distinguished according to their typical structural principles, the definitive feature of which is their qualifying function, an initial classification can be readily developed. Just as things can be grouped into various radical types according to the modal aspect in which their qualifying function is found, so social structures can be similarly grouped into a series of radical types (secondary types). Since social structures are relationships between humans they will be qualified by one of the (postlingual) normative aspects characteristic of human subjective functioning. Dooyeweerd refers to six such normative radical types, listed here with some of his own examples.

1. pistically qualified: religious communities, including churches;
2. morally qualified: marriages, families, trades unions, political parties, charitable organizations, schools;[1]
3. juridically qualified: states and international political organizations;
4. aesthetically qualified: theatres, galleries, orchestras;
5. economically qualified: business corporations, industrial organizations;
6. socially qualified: clubs, fraternities.

Within each radical type will be found a series of genotypes distinguished according to the specific structural features associated with their founding functions. Finally, yet further distinctions are possible according to the variability type of a relationship. I have noted that only radical-typical and genotypical differences are determined by the internal structural principle of a social structure. Their variability types arise instead from the numerous external enkaptic interlacements into which they enter.

It might seem that this would be more than adequate for the purposes of developing a systematic classification of social structures. Yet

Dooyeweerd does not proceed in this way, introducing instead a further classification based on a different series of distinctions, which he terms "transcendental societal categories."[2] Their purpose is to give a "systematic survey of the various structural types of societal relationships."[3] This also seems to be the purpose of the classification according to structural principle, and Dooyeweerd does not convincingly explain the precise relation between the two systems.[4]

The transcendental categories supply a general classification of social structures according to four pairs of contrasting characteristics (three of which have already been mentioned).

1. "communities" or "interlinkages";
2. "organized" or "natural" communities;
3. "differentiated" or "undifferentiated" communities;
4. "institutional" or "voluntary" communities.

Communities and Interlinkages

This is the most fundamental distinction in Dooyeweerd's account of social structures and opens up some of his most interesting insights. "Interlinkages" is a less cumbersome rendition of a term Dooyeweerd uses in *NC*, "inter-individual and inter-communal relationships."[5] The core of the difference between communities and interlinkages centers on the contrast between unity and coordination. A community is "any more or less durable societal relationship which has the character of a whole joining its members into a social unity, irrespective of the degree of intensity of the communal bond." Interlinkages, by contrast, are relationships "in which individual persons or communities function in coordination without being united into a solidary whole." The term *coordination* embraces a variety of modes of interaction varying from cooperation, as in a friendship, to competition, as in a market relationship. The norms appropriate in communities, such as marriage, must not be confused with those appropriate in interlinkages, such as market interactions. Since marriage is a community the competitive interactions characteristic of market relationships are out of place between marriage partners and would violate the ethical solidarity typical of a marriage.[6]

Surprisingly, Dooyeweerd claims that not only communities but also interlinkages have distinct structural principles. The proposal that relationships between social bodies possessing structural principles themselves have structural principles seems initially counterintuitive and risks cluttering up an already well-populated social world with too many normative principles. I propose a simplifying move shortly.

With the exception of the kinship group and the neighborhood, all communities have authority relations, but these are absent in interlinkages. Authority relations can only exist within a solidary communal whole in which different members occupy differentiated roles. In interlinkages the parties stand in coordinate relations to one another for which authority and subordination have no relevance. This is not to say that parties to interlinkages stand in relations of equality. As I indicate in chapter 9 Dooyeweerd holds that the idea of equality does apply in the field of civil law, so that insofar as interlinkages have a civil law aspect, then the parties to them are indeed equal. In other respects, however, the parties are likely to be unequal in a wide variety of ways due to differences of age, sex, wealth, class, character, occupation, or political or psychological power. But these social inequalities are not integral elements in the structural principles of interlinkages. By contrast, inequalities of position within communities are determined precisely by the structural principle of the community. "Whereas in a community all individual differences in position are in the last instance integrated into the unity of a societal whole, the inter-individual and inter-communal relationships present the picture of a non-integrated inequality and diversity in social position between the different parties."[7]

Although structurally irreducible, communities and interlinkages nevertheless presuppose one another. There is a "strict correlation" between them: wherever communities exist, interlinkages will also be found.[8] Wherever communal wholes such as families or businesses exist, there will also be relationships between such different communities (i.e., intercommunal relationships) and relationships between individual members of such communities or between members of different communities (i.e., interindividual relationships). In intercommunal relationships the two distinct communal wholes do not merge into a single whole; and in interindividual relationships the two individual persons do not form a community. From the correlation between communities and interlinkages Dooyeweerd draws the enormously important implication that the full significance of human persons can never be exhausted either in their position as member of a communal whole or in their status as discrete individuals. As I explain in the final section, this is the basis of his rejection of the twin poles individualism and universalism.

More will be said about particular kinds of community in due course, but certain general features of the character of interlinkages merit attention here. The first concerns the manner of their emergence. As described in the last chapter, one of the norms of historical development is individualization. This involves the individuation of differentiated structures but also (and intrinsically linked to it) the emancipation of individual persons from undifferentiated communal bonds. The process of individualization secures for the individual a vital sphere of private liberty outside of all institutional communal ties. In undifferentiated communal relationships, people do not meet primarily as individuals as such but only as members of different tribes or families. Their communal identity takes precedence over their separate individuality.[9] Individualization liberates the individual from the confines of "closed, primitive" structures; and it presupposes differentiation in the sense that the realization of individual liberty requires the break-up of all-encompassing undifferentiated units. Its result is that "the individual may enter into free relations with other people wherever his new contacts may carry him."[10]

In contrast to those romantic or organicist thinkers who lamented the rise of such individuality, Dooyeweerd holds that in itself individualization is a legitimate development, quite compatible with Christian social thought. Interindividual relationships can be and have often been positivized in antinormative ways (in particular, in the economic sphere), yet it has been Christianity itself that has "laid the foundation of a worldwide expansion" of such relationships.[11] The affirmation of interindividual relationships is not at all premised on the humanistic idea of the free-floating, "self-sufficient, autarkical 'individuum,'" which offers no sure guarantee of liberty. [12] It is, rather, founded in a distinctively Christian idea of personal liberty, secured in three ways: first, through the existence of a diversity of differentiated communities of which the individual is a member, providing mutually limiting bases of loyalty and power; second, through humankind's common subjection to the "central religious commandment of love," which rises above the conflicting allegiances of its temporal communal ties;[13] third, and most profoundly, by the spiritual unity of the human race, which has its transcendent basis in the supertemporal religious community of mankind (a point I explain later).

The process of individualization is complemented by an equally important process of integration. As individualization proceeds, integrating tendencies simultaneously emerge through which behavior, otherwise hopelessly fragmented, comes to be coordinated. The increase in individualization does not produce more and more self-sufficient individuals. This is because the cultural opening process of which individualization is a central part immensely increases the needs of the individual person, thus continually increasing his dependence on others and establishing the need for a complex division of labor.[14] Integration is thus a process whereby individuals' interdependence is expressed.

Dooyeweerd acknowledges here his debt to Hegel's theory of civil society. Hegel discovered a "structural law of modern society," which Dooyeweerd formulates as "the normative law of correlative differentiation and integration." As noted, such a law operates in the emergence of communities; the breakup of undifferentiated units and the branching out of differentiated ones is accompanied by the rise of integrating institutional communities. What occurs here is the transformation of one (historically redundant) form of community into a variety of other communities each of which integrates members into a structured whole. Hegel also discovered that the same law can be seen operating in the development of interindividual (and intercommunal) relationships.[15] There are processes of both differentiation and integration at work here. Differentiation is seen in the vast diversity of structural types of interindividual and intercommunal relationships of modern society, such as publicity, fashion, sporting events, the press, public traffic, public artistic performances, charitable work, diplomacy, international political relations, political communication, and missionary activity. These are all examples of normatively structured types of relationships into which individuals or communities can enter without entering into communal ties. Each has a distinct structural principle; all are historically founded, though each has a distinct qualifying function. Fashion and sport are socially qualified; charitable work, morally qualified; and so on. The individuals functioning in interindividual relationships, or the communities functioning in intercommunal relationships, are indeed interdependent, but each maintains an essentially "coordinate" status in which authority, hierarchy, or solidarity are lacking.[16]

This is the category under which Dooyeweerd treats the theme of the market. A market interaction is an economically qualified interlinkage. Engaging in acts of sale or purchase does not incorporate someone into an economic community but only consists of economic interactions between (formal) equals. By contrast, signing a labor contract with an employer does incorporate the employee into the community of the business enterprise. Although Dooyeweerd does treat at some length the nature of the business community, his views on the market are provocative but undeveloped. In chapter 10 I outline some aspects of these views and in chapter 11 suggest how they might be applied to contemporary civil society debates.

How exactly are individuals integrated by such differentiated interlinkages? What occurs here is not the absorption of interindividual or intercommunal relationships into communal ones but the extension of such relationships far beyond the boundaries of any particular community.[17] In primitive undifferentiated communities interindividual relationships are entirely conditioned by and confined within the boundaries of the community. In a differentiated society, however, such relationships are established across communal boundaries and independently of membership in particular communities. In contrast to the vertical isolation of primitive units, we see the horizontal expansion of interindividual relationships of all kinds. The sphere of validity of the norms of such relationships is in principle worldwide.[18] Previously dispersed communities (national, religious, economic, etc.) among which little contact had been established come to be integrated in the sense that the members of each enter into similar kinds of relationships (such as fashion or international trading contracts). Later I shall record the sense in which Dooyeweerd recognizes the normative validity of national cultures. At least at this point, however, he appears unconcerned about the erosion of national differences due to the internationalizing tendency in every interindividual relationship.[19]

Natural and Organized Communities

Dooyeweerd further distinguishes between those communities that have a foundational function in the historical aspect and those founded in the biotic aspect. The latter are "natural communities" and include marriage, the family, the kinship group, and some forms of neighborhoods.[20] The former are "organized communities,"[21] a category I mentioned in chapter 6 when proposing a reconceptualization of Dooyeweerd's social ontology. As I noted there this term embraces a wide variety of relationships, including states, churches, businesses, and voluntary associations of many kinds. The essential difference between natural and organized communities is that the former are "founded in nature" whereas the latter are "founded historically."[22] Natural communities exist on the basis of possibilities—specifically biological possibilities—given in nature. In contrast, organized communities are established by deliberate human shaping or "organization."[23]

Two additional differences between these two kinds of communities follow from this fundamental difference in their foundation. First, while authority relations can be found in both natural and organized communities (the exceptions being kinship and neighborhood communities), these are of very different kinds. In natural communities authority displays the character of the typical biotic foundation; for example, authority in the family is parental authority.[24] In organized communities authority is historically founded. Authority in social relationships is not all of a piece but rather should be "understood from the structural types of the different communities in which it is inherent."[25] Second, natural communities do not survive the duration of the life of their members. If a spouse dies the marriage as such ceases to exist. And if both parents die the family community as such is terminated, leaving only kinship bonds among the children. But communities having an organization are independent of the duration of their members' lives (they have a "supra-individual character"). A state remains the same state even through the gradual replacement of its entire citizenry. Organized communities owe their continuous existence to such historical organization, whereas natural communities owe theirs to their biotic foundation.

However, when we recognize the fact that natural communities also only come into existence as a result of deliberate formation, this characterization of the difference between the two types of community begins to run into trouble. Marriage takes place as a result of deliberate decisions on the part of those entering it; or, in the case of arranged marriages, on the part of the relevant family members. All marriages are, in an obvious sense, "arranged" (or "organized"); they do not occur spontaneously. What is more, starting a family by having children is also the outcome of a deliberate act.[26] While it seems clear that the family bond is unique in being universally founded in biological possibilities,[27] Dooyeweerd's general characterization of the difference between natural and organized communities is misplaced. If the intention is to signal the centrality of the family to society there are other ways to do this; and in fact Dooyeweerd himself suggests one, as I note below.

A far-reaching implication seems to follow. If we must now concede that all communities are historically founded, that all are founded in the same modal aspect, then a worrying problem arises. This state of affairs seems significantly to limit the explanatory capacity of the very notion of founding functions, in contrast to that of qualifying functions, which do indeed seem to be dispersed across several modal aspects and so helpfully account for the irreducibility of many distinct types of social structure. I noted that for Dooyeweerd founding functions display the specific character of the qualifying function of the structure in which they are found, and so analyzing them is essential to identifying the unique properties of that structure.[28] But this point is also supposed to apply the other way around: the unique nature of the founding function is also supposed to illuminate the unique nature of the qualifying function. But now the explanatory connection seems to be only one way.

There is a more serious problem, however: if we accept the view of critics who question the very idea of a historical aspect, then the definition of a social structure being historically founded obviously has to be rethought. Suppose we follow Seerveld's suggestion that what Dooyeweerd intends to capture with the idea of a historical or cultural aspect is really "technical, formative control" and then relocate "the historical" as a transmodal category. We would then be left with claiming that all communities are founded in the human capacity to form their environments. But since this seems to imply little more than that human beings establish communities, it begins to sound vacuous. Perhaps the very idea of a distinct founding function is redundant. My analysis of Dooyeweerd's account of the founding function of the state lends weight to this suspicion.

It should be noted, finally, that the foregoing does not imply that communities do not display a modal aspect that we might term technical, formative control, or, as Seerveld puts it, a "techno-formative aspect." So in explaining the diverse functions of a community we would still need to investigate the sense in which its establishment and ongoing behavior involves techno-formative activity. Indeed such an investigation could certainly prove fruitful and important, throwing up evidence of both legitimate and illegitimate exercises of formative power within diverse communities. What we would not be doing, however, is attributing special foundational status to this or any other modal function.

A different response to the problem I have identified would be to explore whether what Dooyeweerd calls the normative founding functions of organized communities can after all be located in modal aspects other than the historical, say, the psychic, social, or economic. Suppose we concluded, for example, that the state was founded in the economic aspect, as Marx famously argued. I will not pursue this possibility here but only record a suspicion that such a conclusion would be reductionistic (as it is in Marx). However, if we construed the investigation instead as a search for antinormative, distorted operations or distributions of "formative power" within a community—the power of money (economic power) or the media (psychic power) in politics, for instance—or between communities—causing a violation of the principle of cultural economy, then a potentially very valuable aid toward a social scientific hermeneutic of suspicion is suggested. I consider this possibility in chapter 11.

Differentiated and Undifferentiated Social Structures

These categories were introduced in chapter 6 in the context of a discussion of Dooyeweerd's conceptions of history and culture, but important features of them require further treatment. The distinction between differentiated and undifferentiated structures demarcates social structures in terms of the normative process of historical development, in which the "free unfolding of the structures of individuality in human society" occurs.[29] In this process each typical structure comes into its own as an independent entity, whereas in primitive societies these structural principles cannot yet freely exhibit their typical characteristics. Such typical structures appear as a result of new initiatives in human formative activity, whereby the various qualifying functions of societal relationships acquire independent realization.[30] In this way economically qualified business enterprises are organized, juridically qualified states emerge, socially qualified associations are formed, and so forth.

The primary form of social structure in a primitive society is the undifferentiated organized community, such as the patriarchal extended family, sib, clan, tribe, or guild. Dooyeweerd's account of such forms is somewhat obscure, and to the extent that it is clear, problematic. Reflection on why it is problematic will further confirm the problem with the notion of invariant structural principles. These forms are not simply so many varieties of natural institutional community, since although they appear similar to kinship groups in reality they are not biotically but historically founded.[31] Undifferentiated organized communities are "suprafunctional" units. To a greater or lesser extent they all "perform all those typical structural functions for which on a more differentiated cultural level separate organized communities are formed, with typical structures of their own."[32] Such units may therefore perform characteristically economic functions, such as agriculture or cattle raising, which in a differentiated society are performed principally by economically qualified structures; or characteristically legal functions such as settlement of disputes, which are later performed by juridically qualified structures; and so forth. The actual functions performed by any particular unit may be many and various according to circumstance.[33]

Identifying these typical functions is not the same as identifying the modal functions of undifferentiated units. Modal functions are always functions of a social structure with its own structural principle. The point about undifferentiated units is that they are interlacements of different structural principles. They are not characterized by one foundational function and one leading function, which together determine the radical type and genotype of the structure. Rather in such units "various structural principles are realized in one and the same form of organization."

What occurs is an interlacement of heterogeneous structural principles, not the interlacement of diverse (differentiated) structures each with independent qualification. The latter type of interlacement is characteristic of modern society and can assume either an intercommunal or an enkaptic form. The undifferentiated units Dooyeweerd has in mind are intracommunal interlacements, a category of relationship found uniquely in primitive societies.[34]

Such units are not simply agglomerations but possess a real internal unity, which arises from the leading role that one of the interlaced structures plays within the whole unit, and the nature of such units differs according to which structure plays this leading role. Dooyeweerd offers three examples: those in which the natural family plays the leading role, such as the patriarchal extended family, the sib, or clan, and the guild;[35] those in which the natural family is displaced by a distinct political structure, such as tribal organizations;[36] and those that are unified around cultic communities.[37] In each of these a variety of functions may be performed, but one structural function can be identified as the source of the continuing unity of the community. This is a structural, not a modal, function. It is the function of a distinct structural principle. Undifferentiated communities have no single qualifying function as such. The role played in differentiated communities by this function is played in undifferentiated communities by an entire structural principle. Such communities are therefore uniquely qualified by a structural principle rather than a modal function.[38]

This seems a highly artificial and implausible way to conceptualize the complex nature of the type of community in question.[39] If the general problem with the notion of a structural principle was that it seems to allow for "laws without subjects," the case of primitive communities seems initially to raise the prospect of "subjects without laws." Such communities, or something like them, certainly have existed. And yet there is no designated structural principle for them, because no qualifying function can apparently be identified. Dooyeweerd's response to this (to him) unacceptable implication is to suggest that the structural principles of (what are destined to become) differentiated communities are at this point in history intertwined in a single (undifferentiated) community. They are "intra-communal interlacements" and thus not "subjects without laws" but "subjects under multiple laws." That such a significant deviation from his ontology of social structures could be admitted only lends additional support to my earlier critique of it.

It also gives grounds for questioning the adequacy of Dooyeweerd's account of societal differentiation. Consider, for instance, his wish to avoid the implication that primitive communities are intrinsically anti-normative. This could have been been a plausible position for him to adopt. He could argue that such communities are simply deviations resulting from a line of cultural development led by an apostate faith (e.g., paganism, naturism, or animism). He deploys precisely such an argument with reference to a differentiated society: liberalism's atomizing erosion of communal structures and, much worse, Nazism's subsumption of all human functions within a single totalitarian community are both deviations from the norms for societal structures resulting from their respective varieties of humanistic apostasy. The reason he refrains from deploying it with reference to primitive communities is this: his idea that societal differentiation is a normative process commits him to the view that the earlier phases in the process must themselves also have been normative. If human development from infancy to adulthood is a normative process, then it cannot be said that infancy is antinormative. Similarly, primitive communities are just that, primitive. There may be cases of arrested development, or even of regression (as in Nazism), but the existence of such communities could not, on his account, be regarded in itself as aberrant.

Yet considering the largely negative tone of his accounts of primitive communities—they seriously restrict individual liberty, for example—his ascription to them of normative status is surprising. The problem he faces here is precisely parallel to that generated by his view of the role of faith in the opening process. I noted that this view presupposes that the faith aspect first appears in a closed condition but that the idea that closed faith could be seen as based in the creation order is problematic. No less problematic for him is the idea that communities that significantly inhibit personal liberty—communities that are closed in a different sense—could be based in the creation order.

It may be, of course, that liberty was not so seriously restricted in at least some so-called primitive communities and that in other ways the quality of a person's life within them was much higher than Dooyeweerd supposed. If so, then there would indeed be a case for regarding them as approximations to certain social norms. But how then, if his contorted characterization is to be rejected, should their normative structure be conceived? The alternative approach to normative social structure proposed earlier, one arising out of a conception of the complex act-structure of the human person, may offer a way forward. On the basis of this approach primitive communities—communities that appear to perform a wide array of diverse functions without being dominantly characterized (qualified) by any one of them—could be viewed as historically more or less appropriate social formations, which, potentially, allow for an adequate, even optimal exercise of human functional capacities within the possibilities provided by prevailing cultural conditions (levels of technology, methods of production, social mobility, security, communication, etc.).

Such communities would be operating normatively insofar as they realized that potential within those conditions. As conditions changed it might become clear that uniting all (or many) functions within a single community was beginning to frustrate the proper exercise of certain human capacities. It might, for instance, become evident that disputes over landholding were placing strains upon kinship relationships—strains that could be avoided if one's landlord were not also one's uncle, or one's commanding officer, or one's father. Thus a hiving off of one or more functions to a distinct structure, such as an independent enterprise, or the state, would be advantageous. As noted earlier, an argument might be mounted that such a process would, given the universal structure of human nature, have to take place at some point in historical development and that therefore differentiation should indeed be regarded as a norm rather than simply an option. But, if so, it would be a norm in the sense that it would be an imperative arising from the deeper goal of the full historical flourishing of universal human capacities. This would prevent them from being seen merely as the transposition of Western modernization to other cultures.

Of course, this legitimate structural process of cultural learning would also bear the imprint of powerful directional factors arising from contending ground motives, and—at least from the standpoint of the biblical ground motive—these could be expected to skew that structural process in distorting and damaging ways (as, for example, ancestor worship might confer excessive, sacralized authority upon tribal chiefs). The broader cultural acceptance of biblical religion could therefore, on such a view, be expected to harbor emancipatory possibilities in such circumstances.[40]

Institutional and Voluntary Communities

Whereas natural and organized communities are distinguished according to their foundation, institutional communities and voluntary communities—also called "voluntary associations"—are distinguished according to their intensity of membership. Institutional communities include both natural and organized communities, which "encompass their members to an intensive degree, continuously or at least for a considerable part of their life . . . in a way independent of their will." They include marriage, family, state, and church.[41] The degree of intensity of membership differs between institutions. For example, marriage "embraces husband and wife by a bond independent of their will . . . [and] destined to unite them for life"; the fact that even divorce may take place only under "supra-individual rules" shows that marriage can never be seen as a mere voluntary association. Equally, people are born into families and can never suspend their membership (even though families can break up). Everyone is also born into a state; and although change of citizenship is sometimes possible, states cannot be left at will.[42]

By contrast, voluntary associations are organized communities whose members can freely join or leave. Dooyeweerd departs here from the widespread practice, influenced by Tönnies, of posing a sharp distinction between "community" and "association": for him, voluntary associations are simply a particular genus of the species community.[43] This lends a distinctly "communitarian" flavor to his view of associations, which he regards not as merely collective instruments for the pursuit of self-posited ends but rather as solidary conduits for the exercise of a communal responsibility to promote some normative purpose. His analysis of this category is also of special interest to this study since it contains many of the structures now typically classified as civil society institutions. The category excludes church and state but includes all other differentiated organized communities, such as business corporations, trade unions, clubs, cultural societies, and many more. It is well-populated territory.

There is a further distinction between voluntary associations having an "associatory" *(genootschappelijk)* and an "authoritarian" *(autoritaire)* form of government. In the first, the highest authority is vested in all the membership; in the second, authority is "imposed" upon them. Now the suggestion that voluntary associations have an "authoritarian" structure is obviously counterintuitive; but all that is intended by the infelicitous translation "authoritarian" is, simply, "not governed by direct democracy," as is clear from his examples.[44] "Associatory" types include social clubs, tenants' associations, or charitable organizations, whereas "authoritarian" types include schools, business corporations, and trade unions.[45] In each of the latter cases the structural location of authority in designated offices is quite compatible with representative or participatory arrangements.

A special feature of voluntary associations requiring further treatment is their relationship to interlinkages. The general correlation, noted above, between communities and interlinkages is especially evident in the case of voluntary associations. Voluntary associations cannot be reduced to interlinkages between individuals or communities. But they do originate from or develop out of them. For example, an informal grouping consisting of a few like-minded artists may eventually assume organizational form and become a voluntary association. Differentiated communities may also enter into voluntary associative relationships, as is the case with industrial confederations, for example. These too might emerge out of informal intercommunal links of various kinds. An interlinkage becomes a voluntary association when it becomes organized, a transition that, Dooyeweerd proposes, involves newly implementing (or positivizing) a structural principle.[46]

Voluntary associations are the products of an "individualizing and rationalizing process" occurring in interindividual and intercommunal relationships. Liberated from the confining "collective patterns of thinking, volition and belief" of undifferentiated communities, individuals acquire a "relative autonomy" in their interindividual relationships. They are thus "enabled to seek for free forms of organized cooperation according to a rational plan of means and ends." Emancipated from confining communal bonds, "the individual may enter into free relations with other people wherever his contacts may carry him."[47] The relative autonomy is the individualizing process while the organized cooperation is the rationalizing process, which establishes new structures within which persons coordinate their increasingly individualized activities, replacing obsolete undifferentiated communities.[48] The vast proliferation of such voluntary structures answers to the "enormous increase and variation of human needs in the process of cultural disclosure."[49] The basic goal of voluntary associations is to meet these expanding needs. Each association is thus formed with a particular purpose in mind.

To clarify this point we should recall that Dooyeweerd always sharply distinguishes purpose from structure, insisting that enduring structural principles can never be adequately characterized merely in terms of the contingent purpose(s) that a social relationship pursues. This question appears to have taxed him considerably since the publication of *WdW*, and it was only with the appearance of *NC* that he believed he had resolved it. The problem is this: if the purposive character of voluntary associations is somehow intrinsic to their structure, how does it relate to their invariant structural principles? His answer is simply that the purpose of a voluntary association and the means used to realize it can never be identical to the internal structure of the association. Nor can it be identical even to the association's leading function, since this too is part of its structure. This is the case even where said purpose is actually specified in the relevant articles of association.[50] Purpose is what an association does; structure is what it is.

The clearest example of what Dooyeweerd intends is his surprising invocation of the case of a criminal organization. Obviously the subjective purpose of the founders cannot be attributed to its structural principle since that purpose is inherently antinormative. Yet even in such a case in order to function as a coherent organization at all, the organization must adhere to certain internal norms deriving from the structural principle of this kind of voluntary association—a labor association—such as social norms (a code of honor), juridical norms (authority relations), and so on. "This structural principle is in itself independent of the criminal purpose of the association and is not different from that of a 'lawful' industrial labor organization." The criminal purpose only gives the structural principle an illegitimate positive form.[51]

Not only does purpose condition the internal relations between members of the association, but it also shapes the external relations into which it enters. For example, a mining company, like all other businesses, exists in a product market. Market relations in general are of an interindividual and intercommunal character and are quite distinct from intracommunal relationships such as those in a voluntary association like a company. Such market relations are necessarily tied to the purpose of a company, and this is a general feature of all voluntary associations. Again, however, this does not imply that the structural principle is simply defined in terms of the purpose. Another example is the legitimate labor association, which is founded for the purpose of improving working conditions and wages. This purpose cannot be pursued without external, intercommunal relations (negotiations with employers), which may eventually be regularized in permanent negotiating machinery.

The aim of the distinction between the structure and the purposes and means of voluntary associations is clear enough, but Dooyeweerd's account of it turns out not to be as straightforward as he suggests. Consider further his example of a mining company.[52] The purpose of a mining company is to extract ore from the ground in order to sell it at a profit. The means used are the actual establishment of the company. Yet neither of these inform us of the structural principle of a mining company. Such a company belongs to the radical type of economically qualified and historically founded organized communities. The founding function in its structural principle is a "historical . . . organization of power comprising capital, management, division and coordination of labor." The leading function is "the economical administration of the organized process of production." The genotype is given by the specific object of production (i.e., ore extraction). The difficulty with this example is that both purpose and means appear, contrary to Dooyeweerd's express intention, to have crept into the definition of the structural principle. In what sense is the means any different from the "capital, management," and so on, referred to in the founding function, or the purpose different from the specific object of production that identifies the genotype? Suppose we characterize the purpose simply as profit making. This is clearly closely tied to the idea of "economical administration." The two are not identical, since the latter is also a feature of nonprofit organizations such as charities. But whether we are dealing with a difference exemplifying the general contrast between the internal structure and the external purpose of an organization is, on the face of it, questionable. The structure/purpose distinction is also fundamental to Dooyeweerd's theory of the state, and I explore its difficulties further in chapter 10.

My critical survey of Dooyeweerd's account of transcendental societal categories is now complete. Three important conclusions suggest themselves. First, I proposed that the distinction between natural and organized communities cannot be sustained in the way Dooyeweerd proposes, and I propose it be dropped. The single most important insight surviving that discussion was the unique biological foundation of the family in the marriage relationship. This insight can, however, be honored adequately by developing a fuller account of the biotic function of the family (along the lines Dooyeweerd himself proposes in the third volume of NC). For Dooyeweerd, this is also its founding function. Now I have also proposed a reason for doubting the very validity of the general idea of a founding function, at least with respect to organized communities. But perhaps it is, after all, the case that the family is unique among social structures in actually having such a function, which, in addition to and in relation to its moral qualifying function, plays a distinctive role in determining its irreducible identity. If so, then we have indeed isolated part of the unique essence of the family and so, moreover, gestured toward its foundational role in human society generally. All human communities then are organized, in the general historical sense of being established by responsible human beings. But among them the family stands out as being uniquely equipped with a (biotic) founding function.

Second, I uncovered serious difficulties with Dooyeweerd's account of undifferentiated communities. The problematic phenomenon of "subjects under multiple, interlocking laws" underlines my critique of the notion of invariant structural principles in the previous chapter and lends weight to the alternative approach to understanding premodern inclusive communities outlined there. While something like Dooyeweerd's account of differentiation seems to be plausible and necessary, his contradictory interpretation of the closed, primitive communities out of which differentiated institutions emerged needs to be replaced with one more discerning of the ways in which such premodern communities may have facilitated a degree of normative multifunctional human flourishing given prevailing social, economic, technological, and other conditions. I am proposing not that this distinction be dropped entirely but that it needs substantial rethinking in the light of the problems noted and of the new historical information about premodern communities now available.

Third, I found that the distinctions between both communities and interlinkages and institutions and voluntary associations contain useful insights. A wider appreciation can now be recorded: these two contrasts can be seen to have profound significance in understanding the general relationship between communal membership and individual freedom as conditions for human flourishing. What Dooyeweerd proposes is not simply a pragmatic balance between two competing social imperatives but a sophisticated account of the complete integrality of the norm of community and the norm of individuality. These are co-implicative; they are indeed bound together in an "indissoluble correlation." In the final section I show how Dooyeweerd puts this point to effective use in a critique of two rival social philosophies, individualism and universalism.

The same applies to the relationship between institutions and voluntary associations. As I noted, Dooyeweerd's claim that both are types of communities cuts across a widespread tendency, following Tönnies, to pit "community" against "association" as morally and affectively higher and lower forms of social relationship. Dooyeweerd will have no romanticizing of the supposed face-to-face local communities of the premodern era, nor will he accept seeing associations merely as second-best, compensatory options for societies in which true community has dissolved. Such associations presuppose the presence of differentiated interlinkages and thus constitute a vital conduit through which individual freedom comes to expression and is sustained. Equally, by insisting that voluntary associations are communities, he helps resist a characteristic liberal tendency to exaggerate their voluntaristic and instrumental character. Voluntary associations are freely entered, normative, and purposive communities.

Yet this championing of voluntary associations is also balanced by an affirmation that institutional communities are, finally, "more important," because they furnish the stable, enduring communal base that alone facilitates the free and responsible activity of individual persons. Their absence or demise would be more damaging to human life than that of other communities. Marriages and families provide indispensable moral and emotional security for their members; an "inner denaturing of intimate family life is . . . disastrous to human society in all its communal relationships."[53] States provide the public legal protection without which both persons and their communities would be vulnerable to arbitrary power and discrimination. Churches provide a communal focus for nurturing the faith life of persons. Indeed Dooyeweerd adds that, unlike any other structures, all four institutions are "founded in a special divine institution" (a problematic observation I remark on later).

ENKAPTIC SOCIAL RELATIONSHIPS

The last important category in Dooyeweerd's social philosophy requiring close attention is that of enkaptic interlacements between social structures. I outlined the general concept of an enkaptic interlacement as a general ontological phenomenon in chapter 4. Here I consider its application in the social world. I begin by expounding the main features of Dooyeweerd's account. I then note an important ambiguity in this account and introduce a significant reconceptualization of the notion, elaborated by commenting on selected examples of enkaptic interlacement that he cites and completed by using a central insight implied in the Catholic principle of subsidiarity.

Methodologically, Dooyeweerd begins his social philosophy with an analysis of the distinct identities of individual social structures and only then moves on to reflect upon their interlacements with others. In itself this is a legitimate approach. However, although individuality structures and interlacements are equally essential in explaining social reality, the latter are not accorded equal treatment. His systematic treatment of social enkapsis in *NC* is, he concedes, only an "introduction."[54] His account creates a number of difficulties but also points in potentially fruitful directions.

Numerous enkaptic interlacements between various social structures can be detected. The general cosmic principle that no individuality structure can exist apart from a variety of interlacements with other individuality structures (one manifestation of the "universal coherence of meaning") applies equally in the societal realm. Such interlacements are not mere embellishments to structures but are "a necessary requirement for the realization of the inner nature of a thing."[55] Indeed every social structure is interlaced with and therefore conditioned by many others.

As noted already, enkaptic interlacements between social structures are what give rise to phenotypical variations (or variability types) within the same genotype. The phenotype of a marriage, for example, is not determined by its internal structural principle but by its interlacements with other structures (e.g., the tribe, class, religious community, state). I also noted Dooyeweerd's proposal that interlacements give rise to distinct societal forms. These, he suggests, are relatively enduring features of certain types of social structures arising from especially intimate connections that have come to be established between it and some differently qualified structure(s) and that have acquired a certain permanence within a particular society. A societal form is the concrete structural nexus—the "real nodal point"—of an enkaptic interlacement between two social structures; the nature of the societal form is determined by the nature of the enkaptic interlacement.[56]

Dooyeweerd further distinguishes between two kinds of societal form, "genetic forms" (ontstaansvormen) and "existential forms" (bestaansvormen).[57] Genetic forms are the forms in which a structure is constituted; existential forms are the forms in which it subsists. A modern Western marriage is a structure only coming into being following a civil ceremony (or an ecclesial one, which also confers civil status, under delegated civil authority). While the internal nature of the marriage itself is created by the commitments of the partners and not by the state, the civil registration—its genetic form—is necessary for this commitment to be publicly recognized. In this way marriage, an ethically qualified structure, comes to be "interlaced" with the state at its inception. By contrast, in the case of a business run by members of the same family we witness a specific existential form—the family business—placing upon it certain constraints and affording it certain opportunities common to all such businesses.[58] These arise not out of how it was constituted (such as a partnership agreement, followed by registration under appropriate public law) but out of how it subsequently functions (e.g., the circumstances arising from overlapping loyalties).

Enkaptic interlacements between social structures can be either normative or antinormative. Just as the structural principles of individuality structures can be positivized in antinormative ways, thus distorting the concrete structure concerned, so enkaptic interlacements can distort the interlaced structures. We can certainly extend to social structures the principle that Dooyeweerd applies to things, namely, that some interlacements can be damaging to the "natural unfolding of an individual whole." Indeed he does so himself, observing that interlacements between social structures can "exert a degenerating influence upon the internal subjective [life sphere] of each of these communities when one begins to dominate the other."[59] Whether such domination occurs depends on whether each party to the interlacement respects the independence of the other, and this will be the case so long as each conforms to the norms of both structural principles (a point to which I return in chapter 11). Enkaptic interlacements are not simply ad hoc relationships between normative structures; rather the interlacements themselves must conform to the norms given in these structures. The external enkaptic interlacements of a structure are circumscribed by its internal structural principle. The internal structure actually requires the presence of the external interlacement if it is to be realized and limits the range of acceptable interlacements. But these interlacements, whether acceptable or not, do not determine the internal structure.[60]

Dooyeweerd himself recognizes that this is far from a complete account of the multiple varieties of interlacement that seem to hold among different types of social structure in a modern differentiated society. The distinction between genetic and existential forms, and the interlacements to which they give rise, seems intuitively plausible and suggestive but clearly invites much more extensive sociological investigation than Dooyeweerd was able to draw upon. But notwithstanding the obvious limitations of his account, it is important to underline the central intent of the notion of interlacement. This is to insist that, amid the labyrinthine interconnections necessarily and legitimately present in a complex society, the qualitative distinctions between different types of social structures—their sphere sovereignty or irreducible institutional identity—not be obscured. Such interconnections can only be reliably mapped and identified, and their pathologies accurately diagnosed, if the irreducible identities of the distinct structures implicated in them are recognized and respected. And to this end Dooyeweerd is especially concerned to distinguish enkaptic interlacements between structures from "whole-part" relationships existing within a single, unified social structure (e.g., the relationship between a state and its army). In a whole-part relationship the structural requirements of the whole entirely determine the functioning of the part,[61] whereas in an enkaptic interlacement the encapsulating structure respects the independent functioning of the encapsulated structure that is determined by its structural principle. The political significance of this distinction turns out to be considerable, as I show in chapters 10 and 11.

Dooyeweerd's central intent can be further highlighted by means of a clarification of the precise relationship between interlacements and interlinkages (one he seems to have overlooked). Recall that the category of interlinkage embraces both interindividual and intercommunal relationships;[62] we are here concerned only with the latter kind. Such interlinkages, he holds, have three properties. They are relationships (a) between formally equal structures, (b) between structures of any radical type, and (c) having a distinct (typical) structural principle. By contrast, interlacements (as I explain further below) (a) are characterized by a relationship of subservience of one to another (one is the encapsulating, the other the encapsulated, structure), (b) hold only between structures of different radical types, and (c) lack a distinct structural principle.

I comment on these in reverse order. First, I suggested earlier that it seems otiose to propose that interlinkages possess structural principles of their own; we can sufficiently make clear their normative implications by elaborating the normative requirements of the internal structural principles of the interlinked structures. Second, it is not clear what significance there is in insisting on the distinction between relationships holding between differently qualified social structures and those holding between similarly qualified social structures. Why can there not be enkaptic interlacements between the latter?[63] Consider a long-term commercial relationship between a large business (a textile company) and a smaller essential supplier (of fabrics, for instance), in which the supplier depends on a continued flow of orders to survive and which has therefore accommodated its business practices extensively in order to secure them. This seems to qualify as an enkaptic interlacement (an existential form), but it exists between two structures that are both economically qualified. Third—with the same example in mind—it seems that enkaptic interlacements can develop out of (intercommunal) interlinkages between

formally equal parties, rendering that distinction too less than compelling.

The most straightforward way to clear up these ambiguities seems to
be, first, to redefine intercommunal interlinkages, less restrictively than
Dooyeweerd does, as relationships between formally equal social structures each having their own structural principle *(of any type)*; and, second, to classify enkaptic interlacements as a special category of intercommunal interlinkage, characterized by *relative permanence, proximity,* and
intimacy. In chapter 11 I propose an alternative to the term *interlinkage*
in order more adequately to evoke its pregnant normative force and then
to deploy it in formulating an alternate definition of civil society.

My reconceptualization of the notion of enkaptic interlacement has
only reached its first stage. The second requires some attention to the
generally rather artificial concrete examples of such interlacements
Dooyeweed presents. Of the five types of enkapsis he distinguishes,
Dooyeweerd claims to have identified three within the social world:[64]

1. irreversible foundational enkapsis, where one structure is the indis-
    pensable precondition for another, but the reverse does not apply;[65]
2. correlative enkapsis, where two structures are mutually presup-
    posing;[66]
3. territorial enkapsis, where one structure possessing territory em-
    braces others within it without absorbing them into its own struc-
    ture.[67]

In chapter 4 I designated Dooyeweerd's view of the essence of an enkaptic
interlacement, in any realm, as functional subservience. This was my
term for his notion of the one-sided binding of the functions of one
structure by those of another. In such an interlacement one structure
avails itself of the modal functions of the other.[68] This does not involve
a conflation of structural principles or any compromise of sphere sovereignty, nor is it a comprehensive subservience of one structure to another.
Rather in an enkaptic interlacement certain functions of one structure
are in a specific respect enlisted in the service of another.

Whatever its utility in the natural world, the idea clearly runs into
difficulties when applied to the social realm. I submit that on close inspection what we see in his examples of social enkapsis is not one-sided

binding but simply social structures engaging in intercommunal relationships pursuant to their own structural principle. This emerges from a brief examination of three of his more extended examples.

First, Dooyeweerd suggests that the family is "irreversibly founded" in marriage. Now certainly a marriage retains its own structural identity even when it generates a family: it does not become part of the family whole. And obviously no family can be created without people being married, while the reverse is not true.[69] But where is the functional subservience here? Marriage might be said to be functionally subservient in the sense that it makes available its own biotic functions on behalf of the family, but that would be a rather bizarre way to describe the reproductive functions of parents. Or it might be said that the marriage makes available its psychic, social, ethical, and other functions for the subsequent nurturing of children. But this is no help either, for in making available these functions the parents are functioning as members of the *family* community. They are simply fulfilling their role as father and mother, in which case we are speaking not of an enkaptic interlacement but of an intracommunal relationship. It is true that their success at parenting depends in large part on having a stable marriage. But if we were to speak of functional subservience here we would have to say that the marriage partners are making their functions available to themselves as parents. Functional subservience seems not to be a very illuminating way to describe this state of affairs.[70]

Second, voluntary associations, Dooyeweerd suggests, are irreversibly founded in differentiated interindividual relationships. We have seen that such associations can come into existence only on the basis of previously existing free relationships between individuals (whereas interindividual relationships can exist without voluntary associations).[71] But it is again unclear why this relationship counts as enkaptic. No functional subservience is indicated by Dooyeweerd, and neither is it easy to suggest what it might be. Differentiated interindividual relationships are the condition for voluntary associations, but they do not "bind" them.[72]

Third, there is, we are told, a foundational enkaptic relation between organized institutions—state and church—and differentiated interlinkages. The historical disclosure of the latter—relationships between differentiated communities and those between free individuals—depends upon the emergence of differentiated organized institutions, since only these are able to break up the undifferentiated communities that hitherto had embraced the former. Unless differentiated institutions appear, therefore, communities and individuals cannot enjoy the freedom to enter into free relationships with other communities or individuals. An initial problem here is that it is not clear why, apart from the state, only the church is thought worthy of mention as playing a significant role in this overall process. As differentiation proceeds all kinds of independent communities emerge from an undifferentiated society, and all would seem to contribute in some sense to the breakup of primitive communities and the consequent disclosure of interlinkages.

But the main problem with this example is now familiar. It is true that there is a sense in which the state plays a decisive role here, in that only when a state emerges can there be created a system of civil law whose purpose is to protect individual liberty. Primitive and feudal legal bonds must be dissolved and a system of legal equality for all members of a territorial political community established if such legally protected interindividual relationships are to emerge.[73] For example, the contracts by which voluntary associations are established presuppose a system of common private law that can exist only where there is a state. The state, it appears, is the necessary foundation for the emergence of voluntary associations.[74]

We shall see that this is an important point for a proper grasp of the general relationship between state and civil society later on. But is there a case of functional subservience here? Dooyeweerd will say that the state binds both interindividual relationships and voluntary associations in the sense that it legally regulates their operation. This binding by the state means that the actions of the bound structures are circumscribed in the public interest. The various functions of the bound structure are thus subservient in this respect to the structural principle of the state. But again there would seem to be just as much sense in saying the reverse, that is, that it is the state which is subservient to the voluntary association or interlinkage in virtue of the fact that it performs its own legal functions on behalf of and in the interests of the latter. But what this is saying is just that the state is acting like a state. Although the state's existence is a precondition for (at least) voluntary associations, the notion of functional subservience seems to shed little light on what kind of relationship this establishes.[75]

The conclusion from this discussion is that the notion of social en-kapsis as Dooyeweerd defines it fails adequately to capture the variety and subtlety of the myriad relationships between distinct social struc-tures that might qualify as interlacements (as distinct from intercommu-nal relationships).[76] Having defined enkapsis so narrowly, Dooyeweerd has difficulty finding any convincing examples.

I think it is possible to construct a more satisfactory alternative by fusing what is valid in the idea of sphere sovereignty with a modified notion of subsidiarity, or, more correctly, the "principle of subsidiary function."[77] A subsidiary function is one performed by a higher commu-nity for a lower community when the latter requires "aid" *(subsidium)* to fulfill its own functions.

Now on the standard interpretation of this principle lower commu-nities require such aid only when they fail to perform their proper func-tions. This is a widespread but arguably too narrow a reading of the principle, which actually implies that such aid is needed by *all* persons and communities *as a matter of course,* not simply to remedy a deficiency. Just as persons cannot exist apart from communities, so lower communi-ties cannot exist apart from higher ones, especially the state. Society itself performs a subsidiary function in relation to all persons and by implica-tion all communities.[78]

But there is a significant problem with this conventional formulation of the principle. As Calvez and Perrin state this formulation "subsidiarity only looks one way"—downward.[79] This is because of the assumption of a hierarchical ordering of communities lying at the foundation of the Thomistic social philosophy in which the principle is grounded. This implies that it is only higher communities that perform subsidiary func-tions on behalf of lower ones and not the reverse. Dooyeweerd argues that this assumption betrays a universalistic social philosophy, rooted in a hierarchical scholastic metaphysics, in which lower communities are conceived as standing in a part-whole relationship to the state, thus sub-verting their internal sphere sovereignty.[80] But whether or not the accu-sation of universalism is correct (I think it is not)[81] the model of a one-way, hierarchical relationship between the state and lesser communities does seem seriously to mischaracterize the complex nature of the rela-tionships required for differentiated social structures to flourish.[82] Indeed it seems not to comport well with Pius XII's crucial but badly neglected assertion that "all social activity is of its nature subsidiary."

I propose, therefore, to reconceptualize subsidiarity as *looking both ways*. Every community, I suggest, can be seen to provide for others— perhaps every other—a distinctive kind of aid. Just by being themselves families aid the state, for example, in providing responsible and critical adults ready to assume the responsibilities of citizenship; businesses provide all manner of material necessities for families and other bodies; the state provides security and justice for all; and so on. Simply by being what it is, each social structure necessarily provides conditions in which other structures can be what they are.[83] What each structure provides is unique to its type. Each offers a qualitatively distinct kind of aid to the others, corresponding to its irreducible qualification and the unique resources it possesses.

Such a horizontalized conception of subsidiarity, with types of aid further specifiable in terms of the qualifying function of a social structure, seems to offer a more satisfactory general way to conceptualize the manner in which structures make their functions available to one another. In so doing it also broadens the definition of enkaptic interlacement to one of *mutual functional subservience*. But the term *subservience* can also be improved upon. The connotation of one structure's functions being made subordinate to those of another seems misleading. Just as it appeared wrong to suggest that subsidiarity only looks one way, so also it seems wrong to suggest that enkapsis only looks one way. A better alternative might be the Dutch word *dienstbaarheid* (or *dienstigheid*), meaning "usefulness" or "serviceability."[84] Structures are "of service" *(dienstig)* to each other, and in structurally specific ways.[85] The kinds of mutual functional serviceability I have been discussing arises out of structures being what they are as they relate in diverse ways to other structures. I draw some wider implications from these proposals for the concept of civil society in chapter 11.

PLURALISM, INDIVIDUALISM, AND UNIVERSALISM

This section aims to draw together and make more explicit several of the component parts of Dooyeweerd's social pluralism, especially his conception of sphere sovereignty and its correlate, social enkapsis. I do so by means of a comparison with what he regards as two fundamental misconceptions in the history of social philosophy, individualism and universalism, of which he proposes a novel interpretation and critique. This will prepare the way for a transition to an account of his political philosophy in chapters 8 through 11.

The Pluralist Principle: Sphere Sovereignty in Kuyper

Surprisingly, and to the consternation of students of his social thought, Dooyeweerd nowhere sets forth a detailed statement of the principle of societal sphere sovereignty. The reader has to synthesize a number of disparate passages on various topics in quite different sources. This is in part because the principle arises immediately from the categories of his social philosophy, so that, once these are understood, the intent of the principle already swings into view. A more significant reason is that during the period when he wrote, the meaning of Kuyper's initial formulation of the principle was still widely understood in the Netherlands and needed little restatement. Elaborating Kuyper's conception is thus my first task.[86]

For Kuyper, the principle of sphere sovereignty *(souvereiniteit in eigen kring)* expresses the idea that there exist a variety of distinct types of social institutions, each endowed with a divinely ordained nature and purpose and each possessing rights and responsibilities that must not be conflated with or absorbed by those of other types. I have already intimated how Dooyeweerd elaborates this central idea. But it is necessary immediately to note that in Kuyper this idea is coupled with another of which Dooyeweerd is critical, namely, an organic conception of society.[87] In Kuyper's view both sphere sovereignty and organic unity reflect a divinely created order for society. Sphere sovereignty emphasizes the diversity of this created social order, organic unity the coherence among the diverse spheres. The two ideas receive varying emphasis in different areas of his writings, but in spite of an apparent tension between them Kuyper regards them as integrally related.

The sovereignty of God issues forth in the diverse laws for each aspect of creation. By concentrating a part of his power in each creature

God endows it with its own unique nature and value. Each has been "furnished by God with an unchangeable law of its existence."[88] Human beings are also subject to such law. God has ordained various "life functions," intellectual, aesthetic, ethical, or religious, each with its own sphere of functioning in human life and each subjected to a particular "law of life" (levenswet). Social life is the arena in which human beings respond to these varying laws and ordinances. The different life functions are performed through a variety of institutions and communities, or "spheres" (kringen), each established for a particular purpose. The social spheres are readily recognizable. Dengerink has garnered the following references from Kuyper's diverse writings: household, family, town or village, province, state, church, guild, charity, university, school, art academy, trade union, factory, stock exchange, business, fishery, trade, labor, commerce, technology, agriculture, hunting.[89] Each has received a divine mandate to fulfill its own function. It is through all of them, not through any one privileged institution such as church or state, that God exercises his authority over his creatures. Divine authority over human social life is thus distributed and differentiated across a plurality of human institutions. The levenswet to which each sphere is subject both accounts for its actual appearance and defines its proper sphere of independent functioning.

Kuyper envisages these laws of life as impressing themselves upon men by an "inner necessity." This is what he means by saying that humans "do not need to organize society" as such but only to "develop the germ of organization which God himself has created in our human nature."[90] Here we encounter the organic tendency in Kuyper's thought. Each sphere emerges by an organic process, propelled forward by an inner organic life, which develops according to its law of life. The laws of life are internally operative inclinations to realize certain social configurations for the purpose of pursuing a specific activity arising from created human nature.

While Kuyper avoids the language of teleology, it seems clear that in this notion we encounter a variant of teleological social thought that Carney has identified as characteristic of several early Calvinist writers, preeminently Althusius.[91] This, I suggest, is an important early source of a distinctively Protestant stream of Christian pluralism. Carney shows how Calvinist theorists from that period gradually developed an original conception of human association. Such theorists

> conceive of associations as ways of living faithfully together within, and thus of fulfilling, various aspects of human life. Associations are the places and occasions wherein we give ourselves to the glory of God and the welfare of the neighbor. They are the purposes that arise when men acknowledge fundamental human needs and commit themselves to meeting them. Thus associations are teleologically oriented. The tela, however, are neither completely given nor completely arbitrary. They are given (or natural) in that there is a determinate structure to God's creation. They are arbitrary (or voluntary) both in their adaptation to . . . human finiteness and . . . human sinfulness. The constitution or basic structure of an association, then, is a function of the vocation that, through the combination of necessity and volition, the association serves. And rule or government of an association is to be judged by how well it contributes to this vocation. . . . [I]n this sense [most early Calvinists] were constitutionalists. . . . [T]he common character of all associations in Calvinist political literature . . . is neither individualist nor absolutist. It begins neither with the self-evident rights of individuals nor with the a priori authority of rulers. Rather it asks what is the vocation (or purpose) of any association, and how can this association be so organized as to accomplish this essential business. Authority (or rule) becomes a function of vocation.[92]

Carney goes on to describe the understanding of law and covenant arising from these ideas: "Law is the expression of an objective rightness to be discovered and affirmed about man's associational experience. . . . The general form of this objective rightness is . . . a transcendent constitutionalism."[93] The notion of covenant is framed within this cluster of ideas.[94] Covenant is "the agreement of an association, or its leaders, to conduct the life of that association in keeping with the primordial essence of all true group life, as well as with the particular expressions of this essence as adopted by the association in respect of its time and place."[95]

It is instructive to contrast what might be termed this "covenantal voluntarism" with what might be called the instrumental voluntarism characteristic of much liberal thought. The Calvinist conception is certainly voluntarist in the sense that it rejects the inherited hierarchical structures of medieval society and affirms a wide public space for associations established by consent among free and responsible individuals and set up to pursue a variety of human activities (recall the Calvinist insistence of the equality of vocations). Yet it is covenantal in the sense that it regards the activities being consented to as vocations, callings, human responses to a divine invitation to community service: the practice of a trade, religious instruction, the relief of poverty. These vocations are not themselves viewed as generated by consent: they are not created ex nihilo out of the associated sovereign wills of the consenting parties.[96]

Kuyper's pluralistic theory of social spheres then stands in an identifiable line of authentically Calvinist social theorizing. Let me elaborate that theory in more detail. The divine laws or ordinances for each sphere establish a normative order rooted in human nature within which social behavior takes place. Each sphere has a duty to conform to its *levenswet,* and this duty is the foundation for its unique right to independence from other spheres. Such a right is thus not asserted on account of any self-designated purpose (as a liberal would claim), nor is it based upon historically acquired rights (as a conservative would hold), but rather upon divine delegation. This right to the independent exercise of a sphere's divinely delegated responsibilities is the core of what Kuyper refers to as its sphere sovereignty. Each sphere is sovereign with respect to these responsibilities but not to any others. Specifically, the sphere sovereignty of an institution is located in the highest authoritative organ within it. Authority within a sphere may be graduated into several levels but must culminate in a topmost "sovereign" organ, above which is no higher authority than God himself. Such sovereignty is delegated directly by God and needs no intermediary authorization from church or state. Original, unlimited sovereignty is possessed by God alone. No earthly sphere of authority, whether ruler or people, can therefore claim inherent supremacy over others. In addition to these social spheres, there is the personal sphere of the individual human being, and this too has its own sovereignty, which is the basis for individual liberties of conscience, worship, and so on.

So far I have been emphasizing how Kuyper's conception of sphere sovereignty is an outworking of his underlying Calvinist idea of a plurality of divine laws establishing each sphere as having a distinct nature, noting only one organic reference, the idea of an inner organic life of each sphere. But like other organic thinkers Kuyper not only sees each individual social entity as having an organic character in itself but also conceives of each of them standing in organic relation to others.

The divine order does not bring into being a series of separate institutions existing alongside each other and entering into relationships with others only haphazardly or instrumentally. Rather they are bound together with organic links that derive from the original creation order. It is not so much that organic bonding is a divine ordinance, in addition to those for each distinct sphere. Rather the ordinances for these spheres themselves call for organic bonds; the concept of a law of life already suggests an organic animation of group life, as noted. In Kuyper's view God originally created humans as members of an organically united human race. The various spheres ordained by God at creation must be unfolded by means of an organic differentiation, each in harmony with the other. Human society was not intended by God to be either simple or uniform but, while being divided into different spheres each with its own nature, was formed as an "infinitely composite organism."[97] Different spheres thus enter into a multiplicity of ties with others, influencing and conditioning each other in mutual interdependence.

Each sphere appears as a part or member of a larger organic whole. Indeed every living object is an organism. Kuyper defines an organism as an entity in which the parts or members, and the relations among them, are already present embryonically before actually emerging as separate units, an entity whose determinate structure emerges gradually through a process of self-development. The powers at work in the parts display the same character by virtue of being parts of the same whole. But they operate outside the will of the whole, determined by a divine will. Such organisms are thus moral rather than merely material organisms. The larger organic whole of which different spheres are parts is the nation.[98] The life of the nation is not simply the aggregation of the life of the different spheres but a living whole whose parts are organically connected as cells to a body. In turn, nations are parts of the organic community of mankind. They are organic wholes developing on the basis of the original

creation order under divine providence and composed of diverse organically related parts. The *volksgeest* idea also appears in Kuyper's thought.
The nation displays a distinctive historical instinct that emerges out of a
complex of historical circumstances that reveals the providence of God.
Each nation forms a part of the larger community of humankind.[99]

The Pluralist Principle: Sphere Sovereignty in Dooyeweerd

The sense in which Dooyeweerd's social thought is a critical elaboration
of Kuyper's idea of sphere sovereignty can now be made clear.[100] Like
Kuyper Dooyeweerd holds that social order reflects a divinely created ordering that frames and limits human social life. The parallel in Dooyeweerd to Kuyper's "laws of life" are the internal (typical) structural
principles of social structures that establish their identity and functions.
It is these structural principles that also establish the normative responsibilities and rights—the sphere sovereignty—of each social structure. The
sphere sovereignty of a social structure arises from its irreducibly distinctive internal nature. Social structures belong to structural types that must
not—and, in an important sense, cannot—be conflated. Their structural
integrity must be acknowledged and respected. Confusing one with another, allowing one to be dominated by another, ignoring one altogether:
these are all failures to acknowledge the sphere sovereignty of a social
structure. The ontological foundation for the principle is thus the theory
of social structural principles. The sphere sovereignty or irreducible distinctiveness of a particular social structure proceeds from and is determined by the typical character of its structural principle.

Human society is thus populated by a qualitative diversity of structures, a diversity given in the order of creation. This conception is "ruled
by the Biblical Idea of divine creation of all things after their proper nature."[101] Each social kind is assigned a distinctive task within the creation
order and structured in such a way appropriate to the fulfillment of that
task. "For each human societal relationship has its own inner nature, its
own structural principle. In this multiformity and originality, temporal
human society unfolds its richness in accordance with the divine ordinances."[102]

The distinctiveness of a social structure is displayed in all its modal aspects. Each structure functions in all these aspects simultaneously, and the distinctiveness of the structural principle that groups these functions in a characteristic way is apparent in every aspect. A social structure—a family, a state, or a voluntary association—is thus "sovereign" in its social, economic, aesthetic, and legal (etc.) functioning. It has its own way of functioning in each of these aspects. It is important to emphasize this because in subsequent chapters I shall focus on one particular modal expression of sphere sovereignty, namely, the legal or juridical aspect. The focus will be on the relationship between the state and other social structures, and since the state is juridically or legally qualified the most important way in which it impinges upon other structures is through its legal function. A central theme in that discussion will thus be the contrast between the legal sphere sovereignty of the state and that of other structures. It is true, of course, that the term *sovereignty* is itself of specifically legal and political origin. As I have already intimated, Dooyeweerd's purpose might have been better served by using instead a term like *irreducible identity*.

The term *sphere sovereignty*, rather confusingly, turns out to be employed by Dooyeweerd in three distinct senses. There is, first, the narrower sense, just mentioned, of legal or juridical sphere sovereignty. This rests on a second and broader sociological meaning of which the juridical sense is merely one functional instance. Third, there is the sphere sovereignty, the mutual irreducibility, of the modal aspects. In this third sense sphere sovereignty is "a universal cosmological principle which only gets its special legal expression in the juridical aspect of reality."[103] The sociological sense grounds the juridical sense thus: "Sphere sovereignty guarantees each societal sphere an intrinsic nature and law of life. And with this guarantee it provides the basis for an original sphere of authority and competence derived not from the authority of any other sphere but from the sovereign authority of God."[104]

Juridical sphere sovereignty thus refers to an original sphere of authority and competence. Elsewhere Dooyeweerd also includes in the definition of *juridical sphere sovereignty* the distinctive rights and duties of a particular sphere. Each social structure has a special divine mandate identifying the specific purpose of its existence and defining its competence, responsibility, and rights. Different types of social structures have their own irreducible field of responsibility, which sets jurisdictional boundaries that other structures may not cross. The term *juridical sphere sovereignty* therefore denotes the ontically circumscribed orbit of legal competence and obligation pertaining to a particular social structure.

"Juridical" or "legal" sphere sovereignty is only one modal expression of sociological sphere sovereignty. Although it is the one that most occupied Dooyeweerd, examples of other modal expressions can be suggested. One would be the stricture against applying the ethical norms of one structure (e.g., the family) to another (e.g., business or the state). For employers or political leaders to expect from their employees or officials the same intensity of personal devotion appropriate between family members would be to go beyond the ethical sphere sovereignty of business and state. Or suppose a political party designed its main conference hall according to aesthetic norms more appropriate to, say, a cathedral or a pop concert. This would be to misconceive the aesthetic sphere sovereignty of the conference event in which political communication ought not to be intruded upon by distracting or manipulative images.

Social structures are each sovereign in their own spheres, each possessing an identity irreducible to others. An important corollary of this structural irreducibility is that such structures stand in a coordinate relationship to each other. None is of superior value to another in the divine plan, nor is any more "perfect" than any other (as in the scholastic conception). All are equally dignified expressions of the divine purpose for human society; we might say that all have a "divine right" to exist and flourish. To prevent their existence or obstruct the opportunity for their flourishing is thus a distortion calling for rectification. The state has a particular role here, but all structures have a duty to act so as not to place any such obstruction in the way of others. A plurality of different social structures receive their nature and purpose immediately from God, not mediately via any supposedly superior entity such as society, state, party, nation, or church. Horizontal coordination, not hierarchical subordination, is the essential implication of social sphere sovereignty.

Dooyeweerd identifies and critiques various attempts to justify such a hierarchical subordination, especially among universalist theories. Among these is the scholastic conception in which the church as a supernatural institution of grace is held to be of superior value to other temporal or natural structures. His insistent denial of such a divinely ordained hierarchy among social structures is, of course, a characteristically Protestant emphasis. The institutional church has no superior value to others, he asserts, because it is only one of the many temporal expressions of the (supratemporal) "religious root community" (or *ecclesia invisibilis*), which is the fullness of meaning of all societal structures. "In this radical religious community in Christ all temporal societal structures are equivalent to one another, just as all the different law-spheres are irreplaceable refractions of the fullness of meaning in Christ, each in its own modal structure."[105]

In the scholastic conception the relation between *civitas Dei* and *civitas terrena* is erroneously regarded as corresponding to that between the church and other "natural" structures, with the result that the latter require sanctification by means of a subordination to the church. The error lies in failing to see that the relation between *civitas Dei* and *civitas terrena* is an "irreconcilable antithesis" that cuts through every social structure—including the church—and not an "axiological hierarchy" establishing ranks among particular social structures. All factual structures suffer the effects of sin, but their structural principles are maintained by God's conserving grace. The "axiological equivalence" of social structures does not in any way vitiate their irreducible structural distinctiveness. Such structures are mutually irreplaceable and equal in rank only "in their common root: the *ecclesia invisibilis*."[106] They are axiologically equivalent but structurally differentiated.[107]

Sphere Sovereignty and Enkaptic Interlacement

The principle of sphere sovereignty presupposes the distinct and irreducible identities of social structures. Since all social structures are also interwoven with others in various kinds of enkaptic relationships, the notion of societal enkapsis is, as I have noted, an essential correlate to the principle of sphere sovereignty. My earlier discussion concentrated on particular kinds of enkaptic interlacements between structures, and I concluded that Dooyeweerd's formulation of the notion is in need of significant modification and yet still susceptible to fruitful development as a way of mapping the complex interactions between distinct structures. Enkapsis certainly provides the prospect of a more reliable map than the parallel notion of organic unity in Kuyper. There is one final element in his analysis of enkapsis—the "enkaptic structural whole"—which helps illuminate its potential yet further.

It is readily apparent that a modern differentiated society will contain a rich diversity of independently qualified social structures and countless enkaptic interlacements between them. But does "society" as such have a structure? Dooyeweerd's brief comments on this question turn out to be very illuminating. In the first place he denies that society as such is an individuality structure with a distinct structural principle. If it were, then the various structures contained within it would merely be its parts. The whole-part relation cannot be applied here: society is not a community with an internal structure of authority and various modal functions determined by a qualifying function. Thus the relationship between, for example, state and society is not an intercommunal one.

Second, he denies that society is an enkaptic structural whole. This is an especially intimate kind of relationship standing midway between a normal enkaptic interlacement and a genuine whole.[108] Unlike wholes containing parts qualified by the same structural principle, enkaptic structural wholes embrace structures with distinct structural principles within a "typically qualified form-totality" that nevertheless presents itself in ordinary experience as an individual existent.[109] The key feature of enkaptic wholes is that the complex interactions between the various distinct wholes of which they are composed are directed by one of those distinct wholes. It is the structural principle of this directing whole that qualifies the entire enkaptic whole. In an enkaptic whole the directed structures perform an enkaptic function within the whole, and the whole "avails itself of the modal functions of the lower structure and orders the latter within its own operational sphere." Yet such wholes embrace "all the interwoven structures in a real enkaptic unity without encroaching upon their inner sphere sovereignty."[110]

It will be recalled that this is exactly what occurs in the case of primitive communities, which, as noted, Dooyeweerd defines as a unique form of inter-communal interlacement qualified not by a single modal function but by the entire structural principle of the directing structure. So it is now easy to see why he would not want to define an entire society as an enkaptic structural whole. Such wholes might have existed within premodern societies, but "in a differentiated human society there is no 'highest component structure' that can qualify a supposed enkaptic structural whole of human society."[111] Although on Dooyeweerd's definition an enkaptic whole does not encroach upon the sphere sovereignty of the subordinated structures, this seems to mean that the latter do not wholly dissolve into the former. Yet they are bound up in the whole in a peculiarly intensive way, such that the degree of enkaptic functional subservience is at the limit of what is compatible with the distinct identity of the subordinated structure. For Dooyeweerd, this is evidently unacceptable as a model of the interactions between differentiated social structures. Indeed not even the state or nation can perform such a role of enkaptic direction, since it would seriously compromise the sphere sovereignty of the subordinated structures; these would be cases of either statism or nationalism. An obvious implication, strangely not drawn by Dooyeweerd, is that the notion of an enkaptic societal whole seems entirely appropriate as a factual description of totalitarian societies. What has occurred in such contexts is a striking example of what he calls "unnatural" enkaptic interlacements—interlacements so intense and involving such a degree of subordination of most structures by a dominant structure (the one-party state) as to have transformed into enkaptic wholes. It becomes clear then that preventing the numerous and complex enkaptic interlacements necessary and legitimate in any modern society from being rigidified into enkaptic wholes is an indispensable task for a free and pluralist society.[112]

A further illuminating discussion of Dooyeweerd's strongly antimonist notion of society emerges from his description of the modern city. In the city we observe

> a very complicated system of enkaptic interlacements between natural, political and ecclesiastical institutional bonds of community, inter-individual relationships of a cosmopolitan character, an immense variety of voluntary associations. . . . The only really integrating communal bond in this extremely differentiated enkaptic system of societal relationships is the political bond of municipality; but it cannot make the modern metropolis in all of its differentiated communal and inter-individual relationships into a real communal whole.[113]

The modern city is a "system of enkaptic relationships" but not a communal whole. Certainly, communal bonds do remain in the modern city; not all relationships have been dissolved into interindividual ones.[114] But *the city itself is not a community* with a single structural principle. Two comments are in order here. First, by the "integrating communal bond . . . of municipality" Dooyeweerd is referring specifically and exclusively to the city as a political structure—a *metropolis*. This political community is only one of the communities in a city. There are many others—churches, schools, businesses, and so on—as well as many interlinkages. While the municipality is the only community whose function is to integrate all other structures within its territory, this is only a political kind of integration. Other communities integrate their members in other ways. Second, Dooyeweerd's introduction of the term *system*—the city is a "system of enkaptic relationships"—at this point is unusual. Regrettably this term remains undefined. An "enkaptic system" is not an enkaptic structural whole. He does not envisage the municipality as a "highest component structure," which could qualify the city as a structural whole; and no other candidates suggest themselves.

In fact, Dooyeweerd does not need the concept of system to account for whatever order there is in the modern city.[115] The political integration secured by the municipality probably itself accounts for a good deal of the order found therein. In addition, we might point to the integrating effects of local market conditions, local customs, or local communications media (respectively, the outcomes of a multiplicity of economically, socially, and aesthetically qualified interlinkages). As I have shown, Dooyeweerd does refer to the integrating tendencies in modern society, and these are three examples occurring in the city itself. These kinds of tendencies, together with numerous enkaptic interlacements (some very complex), may be sufficient to account for the order observed in the modern city. There is no need to posit a single system that integrates all these different kinds of order.

In any event, it is clear that Dooyeweerd's implicit understanding of society is essentially similar to his understanding of the city. A significant part of the order in society can also be seen to be produced by its relevant political community, the state. Other kinds of order are also produced by national markets or customs, each of which can be explained as outcomes of economic and social interlinkages or enkaptic interlacements. There is no distinct societal system, no inclusive societal whole—not even the state—embracing other structures and relationships.

The Nature of Individualism and Universalism

Dooyeweerd presents his pluralistic social philosophy as an alternative to what he takes to be its two principal opponents in the history of Western social and political philosophy, individualism and universalism.[116] There are many strands in his critique of the various traditions of Western social and political thought, and many are only distantly related to this contrast between pluralism and individualism/universalism. But the contrast is central to an evaluation of his contribution to pluralistic thought. Clarifying it will also lend greater precision to the senses in which his position is "Protestant," "modern," and "communitarian."

Sociological individualism and sociological universalism have been present from the very beginning of social and political thought in ancient Greece, and both are in clear evidence again in the nineteenth and twentieth centuries.[117] In Dooyeweerd's view they need to be critically interpreted against the background of an analysis of the four ground motives of Western thought. As noted, he holds that ground motives wield a profound and comprehensive influence in all aspects of culture and attempts to locate and evaluate particular developments in a wide variety of cultural domains in terms of this influence. His critical analysis of the development of Western social and political theory proceeds by means of the same interpretive method. He seeks to demonstrate how the fundamental elements in each ground motive, and the tensions between these elements, come to expression in various social and political theories and how in different ways those elements indebted to pagan and humanistic ground motives radically misperceive and distort the complex and coherent order of social reality. It is these two non-Christian ground motives, and the scholastic synthesis between the biblical and the pagan ground motives, that are finally responsible for the generation of individualistic and universalistic theories and thereby for hindering the articulation of a genuinely pluralistic theory.

Theories arising out of either pagan, synthesist, or humanistic ground motives must in one way or another necessarily fail adequately to account for the pluralistic nature of social reality. They will invariably tend to produce either individualistic or universalistic theories (or dialectical combinations of the two), each of which will obscure the complex diversity of the divinely created social order. The precise character of these pagan, synthesist, or humanistic antipluralistic misconceptions will differ from one thinker to another, but all will be seen to be connected, finally, with the fundamental ground motive operative in their thought. Only the biblical ground motive has the potential to generate a vision of society that does full justice to its created diversity and avoids the pitfalls of individualism and universalism.[118]

The heart of the errors of both sociological individualism and sociological universalism is that they each misconstrue the most fundamental transcendental societal distinction, that between communities and interlinkages, and as a consequence both "must result in an elimination of societal structures of individuality."[119] Sociological individualism entails a reduction of all social structures to relationships between discrete individuals, an absolutization of interindividual relationships. It attempts to "construe society from . . . elementary interrelations between human individuals. From this standpoint the reality of communities . . . as societal unities is generally denied. The latter are considered only as fictitious unities resulting from a subjective synthesis of manifold inter-individual relations in human consciousness."[120] Denying that communities have ontic status, individualism cannot account for our ordinary experience of communities as genuine wholes. In conceiving them merely as interindividual relations, "the whole dissolves itself into a plurality of elements and its structural principle is lost sight of."[121] At the same time, however, it needs to be noted that "nothing is closer to naive experience than the reality of the unifying communal bond, at least within institutional communities; and nothing is more foreign to it than the resolving of such relationships into individuals."[122] In naive experience "the members of a community are always viewed as embraced by the unifying bond of the whole." The latter is simply experienced without reflection but always distinguished from the interindividual or intercommunal relationships, which are their correlates. This naive experience is an "irreducible datum," which individualism cannot explain.[123]

In a characteristic communitarian claim, Dooyeweerd asserts that the embeddedness of the human person in a network of communal relationships is constitutive of human personality.[124] This has important juridical implications for the discussion of his theory of the state. The recognition of the legal subjectivity of the individual person, which he terms the "civil legal personality" and which stands apart from his membership in any communal relationships, was certainly the precondition for the disappearance of restrictive feudal bonds and the emergence of individual civil rights and liberties in the modern world. Indeed individualism here played a limited role under divine providence in advancing the process of differentiation.[125] But to reduce all the communities of which the individual is a member to merely interindividual relations, as individualism does, is to forget that "the civil legal personality is only a specific component of the full legal subjectivity." Such subjectivity is equally constituted by those legal relationships arising by virtue of membership of various communities.[126]

Like sociological individualism, sociological universalism is an arbitrary theoretical fiction, an "a priori philosophical construction" imposed against the grain of ordinary experience.[127] Universalist social theories have especially ominous implications. Indeed it was Dooyeweerd's judgment (made during the 1930s and 1940s) that in the twentieth century universalism is "far more dangerous" than individualism. While he engages in sharp criticism of the destructive consequences of individualism,[128] he describes universalism as "in principle a totalitarian ideology which implies a constant threat to human personality." He warns against the superficial attraction of the organic metaphor often employed by universalistic thinkers, with its suggestion of unity and harmony, as opposed to the supposedly "mechanistic" cast of individualism.[129]

Universalism's error is the mirror image of that of individualism. If individualism results from an absolutization of interindividual relationships, then universalism follows from an absolutization of communal relationships. It claims to identify one community as an all-embracing whole encompassing all specific societal relationships as its parts. Universalist conclusions will necessarily follow if the various enkaptic interlacements between structures are misconstrued as relations between an inclusive communal whole and its parts.[130] The inclusive community fastened onto by universalism may be a particular society, nation, state, or church. Indeed if universalism consistently follows the logic of its own whole-part conception it would necessarily be led to conceive of the entire human race as a single, all-inclusive community and all lesser groups as its parts.[131] Just as individualism cannot account for the naive experience of the unity of communal wholes, so universalism is unable to account for the naive experience of the correlativity of communal with interindividual relations. Our experiences of communal and interindividual relations are "co-determined,"[132] in the sense that we can only appreciate the unique character of each simultaneously. For example, we unproblematically experience the complementarity between the intimate communal sphere of, say, the family and the numerous impersonal interindividual contacts we participate in outside this sphere. The whole-part conception of universalism, which acknowledges only communal relationships, is false to this experience of codetermination.[133]

Only the biblical view of the radical spiritual solidarity of humankind can, finally, prevent the absolutizing of either communal or interindividual relationships. It offers, not a mere middle way between two extremes, but a radical alternative.[134] Universalism may appear more Christian in that it at least recognizes the unity of humankind. However, there is no reason to suppose that communities are any less corrupted by sin than interindividual relationships. There is the further problem that "more extensive communities," those favored by universalism, show a lower level of morality than those of a more intensive character.[135]

Dooyeweerd's most fundamental reason for rejecting universalism, however, is that it seeks to locate the ultimate unity of humankind within a temporal community rather than in what he calls the supratemporal religious community of humankind that transcends all temporal societal relationships.[136] Just as he seeks to account for the ultimate unity of individual human functioning in terms of a supratemporal religious center, or "heart,"[137] so he attempts to account for the ultimate unity of humankind in terms of a supratemporal religious community: "Neither a nation, nor the [institutional] Church[,] . . . nor the State, nor an international union of whatever typical character, can be the all-inclusive totality of human social life, because mankind in its spiritual root transcends the temporal order with its diversity of social structures."[138] No temporal human community can entirely absorb an individual person. The religious solidarity of human beings is entirely different from the societal solidarity posited by universalism. Since membership in the spiritual Body of Christ is entirely independent of membership in any particular temporal communal relationships the latter can never be seen as parts of the former.[139]

This appeal to the notion of supratemporality seeks to capture the ancient Christian confession that human beings have a spiritual capacity to relate to a God who transcends time and that they do so through the mediation of Christ and his "Body," the church. But the way Dooyeweerd invokes this point seems to complicate the argument against universalism needlessly.[140] He claims that the notion of supratemporal community is necessary in order to avoid absolutizing communal (or indeed interindividual) relationships.[141] But to reject universalism it is necessary for him only to deny that the significance of the human person is exhausted by or most adequately fulfilled within any single community. Individuals do not need to belong to a transcendent community *existing outside of time* in order to avoid being swallowed up in any particular temporal community. Of course, much of the Christian tradition has held that such a community does exist. What Dooyeweerd's position implies, however, is that individuals need a transcendent source guaranteeing the plurality of temporal communities; and this is the divine will sustaining the creation order. We might add that what they also need is, first, a sphere of individual civil rights and liberties and, second, membership in and rights and responsibilities within a multiplicity of such communities or other relationships. I have explained how Dooyeweerd's affirmation of the value of the individual's "civil legal personality" satisfies the first requirement. His theory of social structural principles, with its concomitant principle of sphere sovereignty, seems amply to establish the second.

The main lines of Dooyeweerd's philosophy of social pluralism have now been drawn. Sufficient has been said to confirm his stature as a Christian pluralist of considerable originality and penetration. As I now proceed to explore his theory of the state and its role in relation to the plural institutions of society, the potential significance, as well as the limits, of his thought for the problematics of civil society debates will emerge in clearer light.

EIGHT

THE IDENTITY OF
THE STATE

Political Philosophy in Crisis

Dooyeweerd developed his political philosophy in response to what he perceived as a serious crisis in the academy and in the polity. The sense of acute cultural and political crisis was widespread in continental Europe in the 1920s and 1930s, and Dooyeweerd's analysis of it reflects the sense of urgency generated by this climate.[1] The crisis in political theory, he believed, was not principally theoretical in origin but was an acute expression of a general malaise in social thought, which in turn revealed the deeper spiritual vacuum left by the collapsing humanistic ground motive—as the title of his first major work of political theory indicates: *The Crisis in the Humanistic Theory of the State*.[2] Only a few years later Jacques Maritain was to develop a remarkably parallel analysis of the "tragedy of humanism" as the source of the cultural and political crisis.[3]

The chief characteristic of the crisis was the loss of any notion of the normative structure of the state. Periodic crises in the theory of the state arise whenever a "relativistic" standpoint undermines a belief in an enduring structure of the state.[4] It is true that political theory can be said to be in a constant state of crisis insofar as it is not attuned to the divine order for the state. But a distinction can be drawn between, on the one hand, misconceiving the content of the structural principle of the state and, on the other, denying the very notion of any enduring normative structure. While critical of fundamental features of the political thought of Plato and Aristotle, Dooyeweerd expresses guarded appreciation of their recognition of a "normative essence" of the state as the indispensable precondition for any empirical investigation of actual states. Although this essence is misconceived as "metaphysical," he appreciates that Plato and Aristotle "remained free from the prejudice of modern historicistic positivism that looks upon the body politic as a variable historical phenomenon, apart from any normative structural principle."[5] It is the denial of such a normative structure that has occasioned the periodic crises in the theory of the state, and in Dooyeweerd's view this denial had become widespread and emphatic.

Some crises can be productive insofar as they represent transitional stages leading to a new, more normative formation of political life. Perhaps unexpectedly Dooyeweerd here cites Machiavelli's notion of the state that emerged from and broke through the decaying medieval political framework. Others, however, can be highly destructive, such as the crisis precipitated by the "radical left-wing sophists" that developed in the wake of the decline of Athenian democracy. The theoretical crisis in the modern humanistic theory of the state was of an especially destructive character. Although catalyzed by the crisis in political life after World War I, the theoretical crisis could nevertheless be seen as the inevitable outcome of a long process of religious and philosophical decline.[6]

The theory of the state in Dooyeweerd's time had reached an impasse, and there was no possibility of resolving it within a humanistic framework, which allowed no room for any notion of enduring normative structures. In contrast to the political thought of Plato and Aristotle, modern political thought conceived of the state as an "absolutely variable historical phenomenon."[7] This allegation is the core of Dooyeweerd's assessment of the contemporary crisis in the theory of the state. Contemporary political thought had culminated in the development of "theories of the State without a State-idea." In the words of the German theorist Richard Schmidt, "Modern political theory emancipates itself from the speculative view; it leaves alone the metaphysical question about the idea of the State and restricts itself to the empirical world."[8]

The principal culprits are *historicism* and *positivism,* movements responsible for a general debilitation of social thought and among the most

significant examples within social thought of the central dilemma generated by the adoption of the "immanence-standpoint." This dilemma is
the unavoidable tendency of thinkers oriented to this standpoint to seek
to explain the whole of reality solely in terms of either specific modal aspects or specific typical structures. Such unbalanced concentrations on
the explanatory capacity of a particular modal aspect or typical structure
amount to the "absolutization" of this aspect or structure. Dooyeweerd
has no specific term for the absolutization of specific typical structures,
but he does have one for the absolutization of specific modal aspects:
functionalism. Functionalism seeks to construct explanations solely in
terms of particular modal functions of various phenomena, ignoring the
typical structures of individuality within which they function. Many of
the numerous competing schools of thought ("-isms") in social thought
(indeed in any science) are explained as so many absolutizations of particular modal aspects, varieties of the error of functionalism.[9] In jurisprudence, for example, the "pure" theory of law developed by Gerber and
Laband and later refined by Kelsen reduced the study of law to a "positivistic legal formalism" in which legal logic was absolutized in a functionalist manner. The vain attempt was made by thinkers in this school to
devise theories of constitutional law entirely ignoring the structural principle of the state.[10]

The divergence between the principal schools of social thought cannot be interpreted simply as the result of scientific specialization in different aspects of society. For each claims to be able to explain the whole
of society in terms of its preferred aspect. Each is ultimately an attempt to
discover the "basic denominator" by which different societal phenomena
can be compared. Since they adhere to incommensurable paradigms, no
synthesis is possible: "such absolutizations cannot be corrected by other
absolutizations."[11] Historicism in sociology results from the absolutization of the historical aspect of societal phenomena. A historicist denies
the reality of transhistorical structural principles against which the historical process can be judged and seeks to account for societal norms
in terms of their historical development alone.[12] By contrast, positivism's
claim that all phenomena must be explained in terms of a sensorially perceived causal interaction betrays an illicit absolutization of the sensitive
(psychic) aspect of human knowledge. Indeed it is a common problem of
both historicism and positivism that neither penetrates beyond the realm

of visible appearances. By attending only to the societal forms in which social relationships appear, the structural principles necessarily elude them.[13] Dominated by a natural scientific methodology and a historicist outlook, social theory began systematically to eliminate those structural principles that are the very conditions for human experience of changing social phenomena.[14]

The characteristics of historicism and positivism and their implications for political theory are distinct. Describing *historicism* as "the fatal illness of our times,"[15] Dooyeweerd writes:

> Modern historicism . . . views culture in terms of unending historical development, rejecting all the constant creational structures that make this development possible. . . . [I]t has no reliable standard for distinguishing reactionary from progressive tendencies in historical development. It faces the problems of the "new age" without principles, without criteria.[16]

The damage done by *positivism* is its attempt to sever facts from norms or "values." Positivist sociology attempts to explain societal phenomena "as pure facts, apart from any normative view starting from the order of creation." It is not that norms were ignored by such sociology. However, they were typically seen as "subjective axiological psychical or mental reflections of 'objective' factual relations in human society."[17] The implication is that a normative sociology can only be the formulation of ideal principles or values rather than the investigation of the world as it is. Such a separation of social facts and norms rules out the notion that normative structural principles are embedded in and revealed through the social facts themselves. Weber's ideal types suffer from the same positivist misconception. These are not simply another version of structural principles but merely "subjective generalizing constructions"[18] developed for the purpose of imposing a certain order on diverse sociological data. They presuppose the absence of any intrinsic order beneath such data.[19]

Positivist sociology is incapable of detecting any constant differences in nature between different societal structures because it confines its investigation purely to the "positive forms" of societal structures. But Dooyeweerd denies that it is possible to acquire insight into the underlying structural principles simply by examining the surface of these widely varying forms. For example, the Dutch East and West India Companies were economically qualified trade companies, and yet they exercised the coercive legal functions of government in their areas of operation. These were specific genetic forms of trade associations arising from their close enkaptic interlacement with the Dutch state (which authorized them to exercise legal power). A positivist sociologist would have no basis on which to claim that these were not real states since the sensorially perceivable phenomena alone suggest no such distinction.[20]

Positivism thus concurs with historicism in denying the existence of enduring normative structures for societal life but goes beyond it by illegitimately extending the natural scientific method to societal phenomena. A central feature of this method is the search for causal relationships between phenomena. In itself this is entirely legitimate so long as no attempt is made to search for causal interaction between different *modal aspects* of a phenomenon. Dooyeweerd rejects the possibility of such intermodal causality because it conflicts with the irreducibility of modal laws.[21] Instead he offers a theory of "structural causality," according to which causal interactions are always determined by the typical structures of the phenomena to be explained.[22] Only existents, never aspects, "do" anything. Positivist theorists, however, posit precisely such an intermodal causality, for instance, between the economic aspect of society and the juridical aspect of the state.[23] Saint-Simon and Comte saw the state only as a "secondary product" of society conceived as a network of economic relationships. For them "civil property gives rise to class differences and class contrasts and . . . political authority always belongs to the ruling class."[24]

The focus of attention in social science was turned away by positivism from any invariant metaphysical conception of the state and instead directed to empirical analyses of society conceived as a network of social forces of which the state was a "secondary product."[25] The fundamental shift of focus due to positivism signified a radical break with the focus of the classical liberal natural-law theory of the state as an institution of the public interest in which individual freedom and legal equality were central. Positivistic sociology was not interested in these normative ideas but in class contrasts as the "driving forces in the historical process," for "these seem to be the positive social facts."[26] Developing an argument parallel to that propounded by Leo Strauss, Dooyeweerd seeks to show that without some notion of the inherent identity of a social entity it is impossible to generalize about its empirical behavior.[27] The behavior of organs of government such as parliament or monarchy, for example, cannot be meaningfully interpreted without considering their legal competence. However, authority and competence are normative states of affairs, which presuppose the validity of social norms.[28]

The consequences of these powerful historicistic and positivistic movements were evident in a wide variety of contemporary social and political theorists, all of whom dispensed with the notion of a transhistorical structure of the state and thus lost any adequate criterion for distinguishing the state from other societal structures. For example, Weber's construction of an ideal type of state was vitiated by his failure to "penetrate behind the social forms to the internal structural principles positivized by them."[29] In his view a modern state is, from a sociological standpoint, essentially the same as a large-scale economic enterprise.[30] Modern political theory was thus no longer able to accept the idea of an "immutable structural principle of the state." The elimination of all normative evaluation became the "shibboleth" of a "scientific" political theory, and the attempt was made to form an a-normative notion of the state.[31] In the context of this crisis Dooyeweerd sets himself the task of developing a postpositivist, posthistoricist theory whose intention would be "to disclose the internal structural principle of the body politic as it is found in the divine world-order." Nothing, he believed, was more pressing than a recovery of this principle.[32] I turn now to his account of the nature of this structural principle.

POWER IN SERVICE OF JUSTICE

The Structural Principle of the State

Just as the general task of social philosophy is the investigation of the invariant structural principles underlying variable factual societal structures, so the specific task of political philosophy is the investigation of the structural principle of the state.[33] The state is a distinctive kind of societal individuality structure with a typical structural principle. The joint enterprise of political philosophy and of political science is the investigation of this particular societal structure. This implies no narrow focus on institutions, as opposed to behavior or processes. The state's structural principle can only be detected by means of critical philosophical reflection on empirical evidence of all three components of political reality. It does imply, however, that political phenomena cannot even be identified as "political" apart from a notion of the state.[34]

In terms of the transcendental societal categories, the state is a *differentiated, organized, institutional community.* I explain each of these general characteristics in due course, but it makes sense first to note the position of the state in Dooyeweerd's method of identifying structures according to their qualifying functions, that is, their typical structure. The state belongs to the radical type of *juridically qualified* and *historically founded* societal structures. There is, he suggests, only one other sort of structure within this type, namely, international political institutions such as the United Nations. These, however, lack the specific kind of coercive power that Dooyeweerd holds is characteristic only of the state and that identifies the state's genotype.

The radical functions of the state are thus its historical founding function and its juridical or legal qualifying function, which I will for convenience refer to often as "power" and "law." (Later I will make clear the sense in which law is to embody justice.) In the state we encounter a structure whose most dominant features are its possession of a particular kind of power and its character as a legal institution. These features or functions are principally what enable us to distinguish the state from other societal structures. They cannot be abstracted from its other functions. Each of the state's functions contributes to its total structural identity. The state cannot be reduced to its legal and historical functions, and to consider it only in terms of these is, in effect, to reduce it to its typicality. The state is a structural whole that functions in every modal aspect according to a structuring principle in which law plays the leading role and power the supporting role.

Dooyeweerd's most extensive account of the state, in NC, is presented as an analysis of its modal aspects, commencing with its founding and leading aspects and then continuing with its other thirteen aspects.[35] This is the same approach taken in almost all his accounts of particular societal structures (regrettably lending them an unhelpfully abstract character). From among the functions of the state the following can serve to illustrate the general point. The state has a spatial aspect, for example. Space as a modal dimension is experienced in widely different contexts. In political life it is encountered as territoriality, which establishes boundaries of political jurisdiction.[36] The physical dimension of the state is its natural configuration of land, sea, climate, and so forth, which together provide the environmental preconditions for political life.[37] The state functions socially in the various forms of social interaction between government and citizens and between different organs and levels of government. This dimension is displayed, for example, in public ceremonies or the honoring of national symbols, each of which contributes to the internal integration of political life.[38] In interstate relations the social aspect is exhibited in forms of diplomatic courtesy.[39] The aesthetic aspect is expressed in the (dis)harmony characterizing the different branches of government (the "balance of powers"), or between government and citizens.[40]

It has rightly been pointed out that Dooyeweerd's account of the various modal aspects of the state appears decidedly forced at points.[41] Certain examples of one aspect could be seen as exemplifying quite a different one: the "balance of powers" might be seen as a mechanical equilibrium, thus displaying not the aesthetic but the physical aspects. One reason for the unconvincing nature of these examples is that whereas he employs a range of empirical references to describe the two typical functions of the state, he uses very few to characterize the others.

A more serious problem arises from the idea that the state has subjective functions in all the modal aspects. As I noted in chapter 6 the problem is one arising with all organized communities. I concluded there that while the idea that communities function subjectively in the normative aspects seems plausible, it is very difficult to conceive of how they could function subjectively in the prenormative aspects. Dooyeweerd acknowledges that they do not have bodies and thus lack weight, mass, space, and so forth, but his arguments for and examples of prenormative communal subject-functions are unconvincing. I illustrated this earlier with reference to the spatial aspect of the state, concluding that the attempt to depict this as an example of the state's subjective functioning is unpersuasive. We can certainly conceive of the state functioning as a subject (or agent) socially, economically, ethically, juridically, and so on, that is, in the normative aspects. When we say, for example, that diplomatic relations have cooled between two states (an example of interstate social functioning) we are not referring to a deterioration of the quality of interpersonal relations between individual members of embassy staffs; this may well not be the case. Rather we are referring to interaction between states as functioning agents, "structural wholes," to use Dooyeweerd's term. But such agents are human communities, so that speaking of them as having agency only makes sense because we can conceive of how their human members can function in community. It is much more difficult to conceive of how humans can, communally within the state, function spatially, physically, biotically, and so on.

Yet the phenomena to which Dooyeweerd is drawing attention are indeed really significant for understanding the functioning of the state. The physical environment of the state's territory, for example, although not an example of the state's subjective functioning, is politically relevant insofar as climate, landscape, and so forth may have an impact on the political behavior of citizens, or may constrain what states can do (militarily, economically, etc.). It might be more promising to regard the state's geographic environment as a special kind of enkaptic interlacement, one giving rise to what Dooyeweerd terms phenotypical variations, such as "city-states," "rural cantons," and "continental empires."

In any event Dooyeweerd holds that each of these modal aspects of the state is indispensable for its concrete functioning. Power and law are, however, the characteristic functions. How does Dooyeweerd arrive at this conclusion? As we have seen, the process of identifying the structural principle of any societal structure can only take place on the basis of empirical investigation, "in continuous confrontation with empirical reality." It is therefore interesting that in the case of the state he employs empirical evidence not only from political history—the history of the emergence and operation of actual states—but also from intellectual history—the history of theoretical reflection on states. Intellectual history can be appealed to because, in spite of the partial grasp of and frequent distorted perceptions of the true nature of the state by earlier theories, they nevertheless reveal something about the range of possible interpretations of the state. The normative reality of political life leaves its mark upon theoretical reflection on political life. The structural principle of a particular societal structure not only delimits what can actually be experienced but also, it appears, circumscribes the activity of theorizing about this factual reality, creating a normative framework of which political thought must necessarily give an account in some fashion, whether accurately or erroneously.

Taking the entire history of Western political thought in view, its central and recurring problematics can be seen as resulting from an attempt to give an account of the structural principle of the state. It is precisely the presence of these problematics in Western political thought that Dooyeweerd takes as evidence of the fundamentally inadequate basis of much Western political thought. He claims that there has been a persistent "dialectic basic problem" at the root of Western tradition since the Greeks. A theoretical dialectic consists of an inescapable contradiction between two poles within a debate, which, given the underlying presuppositions of the debate, are both necessarily asserted. Such a dialectic is inescapable within the "immanence standpoint," which takes as its ultimate reference point something within rather than beyond the creation and which therefore necessarily generates theoretical contradictions, or "antinomies." Although manifesting itself in widely differing historical, cultural, and religious contexts, the continuing problem in political theory concerns the relationship between the two dominant features of political experience, the need for power and the demand for a legal order. This problem has traditionally been expressed in terms of the relationship between "might" and "right."[42] The problem is a dialectical one because might and right, though both essential for the political order, have been viewed as inherently in conflict. Nevertheless the very presence of the two poles in the dialectic seems to suggest that power and law—might and right—are indeed the decisive components in the state's enduring normative structure.

At times both poles of the dialectic can be seen within one theory of the state, conjoined in unstable tension. Or again, political theories may emphasize one pole to the exclusion of the other, but in doing so they call forth their polar opposite, which is then developed theoretically in a dialectically exaggerated manner.[43] A correct appreciation of the special nature of the might of the state and its right, and their complete coherence in the state's structural principle, should then be the principal concern of a normative political theory.[44] The two poles were already recognized in

Plato's theory of the state. This can be seen from his acknowledgment of two political classes within the polis, the philosophers representing the idea of justice and the warriors representing the coercive power of the state. This combination "implicitly recognizes the two peculiar structural functions that will appear to be radical-typical for the State."[45] The polar contrast between might and right has also dominated modern humanistic political theory. In its early period the absolutist and natural rights theories conflicted. The "naturalistic theory of 'staatsraison' emphasizing the 'might' pole came into conflict with the 'abstract natural-law' conception," which was concerned with providing a normative foundation for the "right" of the state. In the contemporary period the "individualistic, democratic law-State" conception, with its concern to secure a just basis for the state, has been pitted against the "universalistic, authoritarian power-State" theory, revealing again the dialectical basic problem.[46] Nevertheless, in spite of the irreconcilable tension in humanistic political theory, the persistent appearance of both components testifies to the fact that both are essential to the state's enduring structure.[47]

Dooyeweerd lays great store by these pointers in the history of political thought. Indeed, although supplemented by empirical evidence from political history, he takes them as decisive confirmation of his identification of the two radical functions of the state. This appears to imply the surprising conclusion that truth about the state is disclosed even through fundamentally erroneous characterizations of it. Dooyeweerd nowhere states the position in such stark terms, but this is not a misleading formulation of his view.[48] His position suggests a resemblance to Hegel's conception of Spirit revealing itself through and by means of dialectical contradiction, but this is only a superficial resemblance. It is, rather, closer to Wolin's position, which, although recognizing the lack of unanimity in the various political "visions" of Western theorists, nevertheless attends to a "continuity of preoccupations" and a "continual reappearance of certain problematics."[49] But there is a religious conviction underlying Dooyeweerd's appeal to the dialectics of apostate thought, namely, that the creation order in which the state is rooted cannot but leave its imprint on man's attempt to theorize the essence of the state. "Apostate political philosophy" thus serves as a conduit for general revelation. This possibility, after all, is what Dooyeweerd's notion of common grace would lead us to expect.

The Founding Function of the State

The state is a historically founded community. To describe it as such is to point to the fact that it exists by virtue of deliberate human formation rather than by virtue of possibilities given in nature. As noted in the previous chapter, this is the essence of the distinction between organized and natural communities. The state is not a natural community but an organized one. I suggested that this distinction is difficult to sustain once it is recognized that natural communities also require a foundation in human shaping and that it should be dropped as one of Dooyeweerd's transcendental societal categories. Identifying a structure as historically founded tells us very little beyond the fact that it is, like all social structures, a secondary structure established by humans. I also ventured that there is a general implausibility in the idea that most social structures have a founding function. The following discussion of the state's founding function confirms this.

To say that the state has a historical or cultural foundation is to say that it is founded in deliberate human formative activity, or formative power. Dooyeweerd also uses the term *organized power* to refer to the same phenomenon.[50] His aim is to identify the irreducible character of the organized power of the state in distinction to the power possessed by many other organized communities. While formative power as modal norm applies to all societal structures, its concrete expression in factual structures is always governed by the typical structural principle of that structure.[51]

Here we encounter an example of what Dooyeweerd calls the "typical individualization" of a modal aspect. This is the specific way in which a modal function of particular individuality structures exhibits the special, typical characteristics of that structure; the way in which the legal functioning of a business corporation, for example, presents itself not just as generalized "legality" but as economically qualified "corporate law."[52] Accordingly, the historical or cultural mode is "individualized" in typically different ways in each of the organized or historically founded communities. Formative or organized power lies at the foundation of all such communities but in typically different structural constellations. Dooyeweerd makes a similar point referring specifically to the concept of organization.[53] We can expect to find "radical" differences between church organization, business organization, and state organization.[54] Organized power always appears as the power of a corporation, church, or state, and so on, and never simply as power as such. It assumes quite different characteristics according to the structural principle of the community in which it is present. Power is thus individualized in ways specific to each organized community.[55] A key pluralist conclusion that Dooyeweerd draws here is that no community may attempt to exercise the kind of organized power uniquely characteristic of another type, since to do so entails a violation of the principle of sphere sovereignty.

The uniqueness of the power of the state must therefore be recognized if one is to avoid confusing the state with nonstate structures. The irreducible "individuality type" displayed in the state's historical foundation—what makes its power foundation different from that of all other radical and genotypes—must be identified. Dooyeweerd defines this as the "monopolistic organization of the power of the sword over a particular cultural area within territorial boundaries."[56] This is evidently a version of the familiar idea of a "territorial monopoly of coercion," the exclusive control of the police and military apparatus by a single authorized agency in a specific geographic area. It bears obvious comparison with Weber's definition of the state as "a human community that (successfully) claims the monopoly of the legitimate use of physical force within a given territory," from which, perhaps, Dooyeweerd adapted it. Weber's formulation includes the concept of legitimacy—understood as a subjective attitude—which is not explicit in Dooyeweerd's definition. A notion of legitimacy is, however, implied in his account of the state's legal qualifying function, as I shall observe.

The important difference between the two definitions, however, is that for Weber power itself assumes the role of what Dooyeweerd would term the "qualifying function." Weber goes on: "the state is a relation of men dominating men, a relation supported by means of legitimate (i.e., considered to be legitimate) violence."[57] Physical force is the single characteristic making possible that relation of domination, which is what qualifies the state and distinguishes it from other associations. For Weber this is to view the state "from a sociological point of view," that is, in terms of its "means" rather than its "ends."[58] Dooyeweerd would reject this means/end distinction since it rests upon an unsustainable bifurcation of fact and value. The coercive power of the state is not simply an empirical but also a normative phenomenon.

The central claim implied in Dooyeweerd's account of the founding function of the state is that the establishment of a monopoly of (potentially lethal) physical coercion is the indispensable precondition for the emergence and continued existence of a territorially delimited political community. Coercive monopoly is an invariant, divinely given structural feature of the organized power of the state and is thus to be distinguished from all other organized communities. It is a *conditio sine qua non* for a genuine state; this is the sense in which it performs a foundational function in the state. Yet the contrast with Weber highlights that the state's coercive power can never be an end in itself; it is only the foundation of the state, not its destination. It is intended to make possible the formation of a community of public law in which "public justice" is established.

I take up the notion of public justice in the next chapter. But it is already clear that the idea of the state as a *public* institution is itself contained in Dooyeweerd's understanding of the founding function. Every genuine body politic must according to its structural principle be a *res publica*, even though not all are "republican" in the sense of nonmonarchical.[59] The state's essentially public character has long been recognized. Skinner identifies the monopoly of power and the realization of exclusive legal sovereignty as two of the main preconditions for the emergence of the modern state. This he defines as a "form of public power separate from both the ruler and the ruled, and constituting the supreme political authority within a certain defined territory." The crucial transition was from the idea of a ruler "maintaining his state" to the "more abstract idea that there is an independent political apparatus, that of the state, which the ruler may be said to have a duty to maintain."[60] This is essentially Dooyeweerd's position (though his distinctive understanding of the term *exclusive legal sovereignty* will need careful explication). He points out that a genuine *res publica* could not arise in the undifferentiated context of medieval feudalism because political power was regarded as a private possession.

> Government power could be bought and sold: it was not a public office in the sense of a *res publica*. The sovereign lords could freely dispose of it. Once in the hands of private persons or corporations

it had become their inviolable right. Hence medieval autonomy always implied the exercise of governmental power on one's own authority, which did not even change with the rise of the political estates. In this undifferentiated condition of society, in which notably the organized guilds covered all spheres of human life, a real state could not be developed.[61]

The emergence of the state as *res publica* as opposed to *res in commercio* thus presupposed the dissolution of these undifferentiated political forms. The primary task of an emerging state was always the removal of these forms, whether tribal, gentilitial, or feudal. Whatever its specific form of government, the state "has always presented itself as a *res publica*, an institution of the public interest, in which political authority is considered a public office, not a private property."[62]

The success of the Carolingians in overcoming the feudal retrogression, which occurred in the Frankish kingdom of the eighth century and earlier, exemplifies this.[63] In this case the prospect of foreign invasion and a domestic threat in the formation of a private cavalry by powerful Frankish seigneurs were simultaneously overcome by the compulsory incorporation of these private vassals into the Frankish army. This, in Dooyeweerd's judgment, stands as a paradigm of the normative monopolization of the "power of the sword" over a territorial area.[64]

I will not here assess the accuracy of Dooyeweerd's interpretations of this historical process,[65] since what concerns us is his substantive conclusion: in all instances of the normative realization of a genuine state political power had to be brought under the exclusive jurisdiction of a single governmental agency in order that the government could render truly public service. There is thus a direct relation between the public character of the state and its foundation in a monopoly of coercion. If the state were to fulfill its divine calling as a public office, then the means of physical coercion wielded by competing power groups within a territory had to be wrested from them and transferred to a single political center that henceforth carried the monopoly of governmental power. While the mere centralization of power is certainly not a sufficient condition to guarantee the public character of the state's activities (for monopolized power might be used for private benefit), it is a necessary one. The notion of public service or public office requires the impartial promotion of the interests of all within a certain territory rather than the partial concerns of a few. This can be achieved only where a single agency exercises ultimate responsibility for the adjudication—coercive if necessary—of conflicts of interest. The *exclusivity* of this responsibility is required in order that a government can serve everyone *inclusively* within its allotted territory. A genuine state can only exist where there is no preference for the interests of persons on the basis of their membership in a specific exclusive group or community.

> Public-legal governmental authority is no longer a private source of revenue, but an office, performed in the service of the "public affairs" of a public-legal community which, with the power of the strong arm, unites everyone who is domiciled on this territory into a legal community of government and subjects, irrespective of which private societal spheres, family, class, profession, or worship community one may belong to.[66]

The public character of the state, its inclusive responsibility for all within a territory, requires that it secure a monopoly of coercive power within this territory. The prejudicial promotion of private interests by means of governmental power in an undifferentiated situation could be secured only by means of privately exercised coercive power.[67] Consequently, anybody seeking to represent the interests of all within a territory was required to match power with power and win exclusive control over the means of physical coercion. Because the state is the only societal structure that has a public character, no other structure can be founded on such a coercive monopoly.

The restriction of the state's foundational power to (organized) physical power has an important corollary. A state may require a monopoly of physical coercion, but it does not require a monopoly of other kinds of power, of which there are many, such as psychological or moral influence, rational persuasion, or economic leverage. A particular state may in fact possess a monopoly of some or all of these other kinds of power—such as by controlling the economy or the media or outlawing churches and pressure groups—but they will not be indispensable to its being a state. Indeed they will be in conflict with its nature. If a state seeks a monopoly of all these kinds of power it is exceeding its normative bounds and becoming totalitarian.

I observed earlier that for Dooyeweerd the state's power appears to be both historical and physical. In fact what we encounter here is an "analogical moment," a specific instance of the (anticipatory or retrocipatory) intersection of two modal aspects within one of the functions of a concrete structural whole. The different forms of power I referred to above represent various analogical moments in the historical aspect: the emotional power of a rousing orator; the power of lucid argument; the power of industrial capital or organized labor; the power of faith; and so on.[68] Physical power is a historical retrocipation, a reaching back of the historical mode to the physical mode. The state is able to bring about its particular kind of cultural formation because it has exclusive control of the means of physical coercion. However, although the actual instruments of military and police apparatus are physically based, it is their organized employment by the state that constitutes historical power. That is, the state is not founded in its military and police as such but in its organized control of them.[69]

Dooyeweerd anticipates the objection that although a monopoly of coercive physical power may be a necessary condition for the maintenance of the state, it is not a sufficient condition. Other forms of power are also necessary for the state, such as the "moral convictions of the people," or sufficient economic means to assert its power. State power is not merely organized coercive power; it is multifaceted. Indeed in the absence of economic, moral, faith, and other forms of power it would not be capable of forming an army at all.[70]

These kinds of power are "anticipatory forms of historical power" and lack an original economic, moral, or faith character. That is, they represent genuine forms of organized power but power based on resources or factors that themselves have different modal qualifications. Thus economic power is the specific form of power created by economically qualified activity. Economic power is not itself "economic" in the core modal sense (it is not "originally" economic). His central contention is that although all these different forms of power are found in the state, they are not equivalent in significance to the state's typical form of power, which is coercive monopoly. Indeed the other forms can only be identified as forms of political power because of their ultimate dependence on the coercive monopoly, which is the state's founding function.[71]

An example would be the economic power that the state acquires by means of taxation. Here resources, which are essentially of an economic kind, are compulsorily secured by the state on the basis of its coercive sanction. No other societal structure has this capacity to compel the way in which certain originally private economic resources are used. Thus the economic power of the state is to be understood not simply as economic power but also as political-economic power, economic power serving ends typical of the state. This internal form of state power should be distinguished from economic power external to the state, such as that possessed by an independent business corporation or a private person. Such independent economic power could indeed play an important role as a source of political-economic power, perhaps by raising the general tax yield of a state. But when such economic resources are harnessed for state purposes they cross the boundary marking off the external from the internal functioning of the state and thus "necessarily assume the internal individuality structure of the latter."[72]

The foundation of the state in organized coercive monopoly thus distinguishes it decisively from all other societal relationships. The typically ecclesiastical power of the church, for instance, is "the power of the Divine Word."[73] Although the church, like the state, possesses other kinds of power—economic, juridical, and so on—"the power of the Christian faith is the typically internally integrating form of the organized power of the Church according to the ecclesiastical structural principle."[74] A further contrast is that between the foundations of the state and the political party. While both are historically founded communities, "a political party is not founded in the power of the sword, as is the State[,] . . . . but only in that of political conviction."[75] While the qualifying function of a political party is the moral solidarity binding the members together into a communal whole, this solidarity is founded upon the compelling force of shared political conviction, a force that accounts for its continuing identity. A political party can never legitimately exercise coercive measures to bind its members to party policy.

The distinctive foundational function of the state necessarily comes to expression in the kind of authority it bears. While ecclesiastical authority, for example, is characterized as "service," that of the state is "dominion" since it is reinforced by the threat of coercive sanction.[76] Political authority is characteristically coercive authority. In contrast to authority within all nonpolitical relationships, authority in the state is "governmental authority over subjects enforced by the strong arm."[77] Apart from the state's coercive sanction, "the internal public-legal order of the State cannot display that typical juridical character which distinguishes it from all kinds of private law."[78]

It is important not to confuse the various analogical concepts in the historical aspect, distinguished above as corresponding to the different forms of power, and the different typical kinds of power such as political, ecclesiastical, and so on.[79] The different forms of power possessed by the state are all forms of typically political power. All these forms of power acquire their political character by being founded on one specific form of power, the physically based power implied in the notion of a territorial monopoly of coercion. The specific type of any form of power is determined by the structural principle of the societal structure in which it is present. One can therefore distinguish between, say, the economic power of a church and the economic power of the state. The former is one form of ecclesiastical power, the latter one form of political power. Applying Dooyeweerd's conception, we can say that the economic power of the state is ultimately based on its ability to collect taxes compulsorily from all within a territory, whereas the economic power of a church is ultimately based on its "preaching of the Divine Word," which should (among other things) evoke voluntary donations from the church's members.

Dooyeweerd's argument for the distinctiveness of the power foundation of the state rests ultimately on historical evidence, which supplements the evidence supplied in his analysis of the dialectical basic problem in political thought. He claims that "there never has existed a state whose internal structure was not, in the last analysis, based on organized armed power, at least claiming the ability to break any armed resistance on the part of private organizations within its territory." The exercise of historical power is always to be seen as a normative task. The typical historical foundation of the state is "a normative structural function, implying a task, a vocation which can be realized in a better or worse way."[80] The specific norm being referred to here is not the subservience of power to law but simply the effective achievement of a monopoly of coercive power over any challengers. This is in itself a normative question (contra

Weber). The state is not conceived as having an a-normative, merely factual power base set over against a normative juridical qualification, for
this would be to lapse back into the dialectical basic problem Dooyeweerd seeks to overcome.[81] The power foundation of the state is governed
by its own intrinsic norms. If these are not followed, if the state fails to
monopolize coercion within its area, then a genuine *res publica* cannot
be formed. The foundational function of the state, so understood, cannot
be eliminated from its normative structure but is "invariable" and "constant." It is "essential in every positive historical form in which the State
has manifested itself in the course of time."[82]

The military organization of power may in some cases have been
undermined by rival military organizations within a state's territory; or a
newly formed state may have established a coercive monopoly only in
part of its claimed area. But these contingencies are not arguments against
the idea of a universally valid foundation for the state. Even if a revolution successfully challenges this power the first task of the victorious
revolutionary government is to master the military apparatus, "either
with sanguinary or with bloodless means."[83] The importance that Dooyeweerd attaches to the indispensability of military might for the existence
of a genuine state is striking. As a foundational function it assumes pride
of place in the list of imperatives set before a state.

> Before all else the state ought to obey the historico-political norm
> to actualize and maintain the typical foundation of its legal exis-
> tence as an independent power. If the state fails to protect this
> foundation it does not deserve independence. Thus Hegel's claim
> that a nation proves its right to exist in war and that history reveals
> a "higher justice" contained a moment of truth.[84]

The above account has considered the founding function of the state
abstracted from its necessary subservience to its leading function, but a
complete account must acknowledge the "indissoluble coherence" of
these two functions. Political power must always serve the juridical leading function of the state and is never self-justifying. Contra Hegel, "historical might can never be identified with legal right"[85] (a reassuring
qualification given the troubling invocation of Hegel just cited). As a
founding function power must serve some further destination than the

mere establishment of a territorial monopoly of coercion. While attaining such a monopoly is indeed a normative task, it is so only because this is the necessary means for the state to pursue its characteristic responsibility for *justice* by means of *law*.[86]

The relation of subservience of the founding function to the leading function can be expressed by saying that political power must "anticipate" legal justice. Power is opened up in the service of legal norms in the structure of the state: "the military organization of the State displays an opened, anticipatory moment that cannot be explained in terms of merely armed control."[87] The power of the state must always remain in the service of the state's overriding responsibility for the establishment of a just legal order.[88] Otherwise it would "degenerate into an organized military gang of robbers."[89]

With this account Dooyeweerd believes he has overcome the dialectical basic problem in political philosophy by arguing for the intrinsic coherence of might and right in the state's structural principle. More is said about the nature of law and justice—the arena of the state's qualifying function—in the next chapter. Among the several critical questions evoked by Dooyeweerd's account of the state's founding function, I want to concentrate on one with implications not only for his political philosophy but also for his entire social philosophy. This is the question whether Dooyeweerd's identification of coercion as a necessary dimension of the state's structural principle is consistent with its supposed basis in the creation order. The wider issue is whether in describing social reality Dooyeweerd does not at times misconstrue his own radical distinction between phenomena that express what is given in creation and those that are a consequence of the fallenness of this creation.

Coercion and Creation

In describing the structural principle of the state and its various modal functions, Dooyeweerd is setting forth norms for political life, which are rooted in the created order of cosmic time, which in turn embraces both typical structural principles and modal aspects. He insists, however, that physical coercion is an indispensable element in the state's structural principle. He therefore enters into the long-standing Christian debate over whether the state is founded in the original creation order or rather is a remedial institution established on account of the fall.

Dooyeweerd asserts that the coercive power of the state, its "power of the sword," has indeed been instituted (or "incorporated into the world order") on account of sin. "In Holy Scripture . . . the organized power of the sword . . . is emphatically related to man's fall," he claims, citing familiar biblical passages in support.[90] The implication here is that, apart from sin, such coercion would not have been necessary. Now this leaves open the possibility that while coercion is a post-fall phenomenon, the structural principle of the state has its origin in the pre-fallen creation. But, surprisingly, this is not his position. He holds that the state itself and not just its coercive power is instituted on account of sin. There are, it turns out, two societal structures, which have been ordained after the fall: church and state. The former is an "institution of special grace"; the latter, of "common" or "preserving" grace. The state as an institution of common grace is ordained on account of sin; it thus has a "soteriological vocation"—to preserve temporal society in its differentiated condition.[91]

The state is not itself a sinful institution but is a divine gift intended to preserve a sinful society from collapse. Dooyeweerd specifically rejects what he takes to be the Thomistic conception according to which governmental authority is grounded in the original order of nature while the power of the sword is necessary only on account of sin as a provision of "relative natural law."[92] If one eliminates the territorial monopoly of coercion from the state's structural principle, then "the essential foundation of the state falls away from it," and it becomes impossible to distinguish it reliably from other societal structures. One cannot therefore hold that only the power of the sword and not the state as a whole is instituted on account of sin.[93] Not only would the power of the sword have been unnecessary without sin, but also the state itself.

What can Dooyeweerd mean by claiming that the state has been "incorporated into the world-order" after the fall? According to his reading of the biblical ground motive (as described in chapter 3), "sin changed not the original creational decrees but only the direction of the human heart." What he is now saying is that although sin has not changed the original creational decrees, God has sovereignly added further decrees (for state and church) in response to sin. These have been incorporated into the world-order by God after the fall, and as such they express, just like those establishing any other societal structure, his creative sovereignty. Yet he says further that state and church though occasioned by the fall are nevertheless *based upon* the original creation order.[94] While not original with creation, the state is nevertheless grounded in what has been originally given in creation. What this means is, regrettably, left unexplained; perhaps he has in mind simply that the post-fall decrees for state and church must, like every feature of cosmic order, be "indissolubly coherent" with the pre-fall decrees. What is implied here is the appearance of a new structural principle—one fashioned to slide without friction into the original order.[95]

This is a complex and unusual position, and it generates an obvious objection. If the state as such is necessary only on account of sin we would naturally expect its functions to be explicable only as ways to deal with the consequences of sin. On Dooyeweerd's view there would not have been any functions for a state to perform if the fall had not occurred. However, by no means all these functions, as he himself at length describes them, can be explained in this way. This is especially the case—as we shall see—with those that fall within the requirements of the "public interest," such as transport infrastructure or financial coordination. Many seem to be attributable to situations arising not from directional distortion (justice as "retribution") but from structural features arising from the cultural unfolding of original creational possibilities (justice as *tribution,* a term to be defined shortly).

There are, again, resources within Dooyeweerd's own conceptual apparatus for removing this inconsistency, in this case by making use of the distinction between the invariant structural principle of a societal structure and its variable positive forms. It would seem far more plausible for him to hold that the invariant structural principle of the state is original with creation while the need for coercion is a result of the fall. As noted in chapter 7, the positive forms of societal structures vary greatly as a result of historical development, enkaptic interlacement, and also the distorting influence of apostate ground motives. In the case of the need for governmental coercion we evidently encounter a phenomenon arising from the third of these factors. At least for an Augustinian-Calvinist like Dooyeweerd, the violent impulses that the state must coercively restrain must be viewed as one of the consequences of human apostasy and not some natural or evolutionary tendency. Coercion is an attempt to correct violations of the original order that follow from this apostasy. The state's coercive character, then, need not be seen as part of its originally given, structural principle but rather as one of its positive (existential) forms. It is, no doubt, one of the least variable positive forms of the state, for there have been few if any states that have not needed to rely upon it, and in this respect Dooyeweerd's historical conclusion seems sound. But the mere universality of a phenomenon does not in itself prove that it is original with creation, for, he holds, the effects of the fall are also universally present.

Coercion is thus not intrinsically sinful; it is a normative response to sin. Dooyeweerd could have justified its use by appealing to an originally given, pre-fall, structural principle of the state. If the state is to fulfill the duties that fall to it by virtue of its structural principle—centered in the duty to promote public justice—there will be times when it is necessary to employ coercion when its citizens themselves act unjustly. The "power of the sword" could then be seen as a legitimate requirement for the post-fall positivization of the originally given structural principle of the state. This does presuppose, of course, that the original structural principle of the state implies the right to use the ultimate sanction of physical coercion, even though employing it would have been unnecessary in the absence of sin.[96]

It will be noted that in this reconstruction I have continued to employ the notion of invariant structural principles originally given in the order of creation. But since I have criticized the concept of invariance I need to explain how such a reconstruction can survive if that concept is abandoned. Simply, my proposal that the structural norms for the state can be seen as grounded in created order only needs to be reconceptualized as a proposal that they now be seen as historically emerging imperatives arising from the needs of a creationally founded multifunctional notion of human social flourishing. Thus the sense in which the state's structural principle is original with creation is that it arises necessarily out of the imperatives of human nature as originally created (and now continually sustained) by God.[97] The state emerges historically as an independent institution at points in history when experience and circumstances combine to yield conditions conducive to its establishment. We might then suppose that, prior to the emergence of the state as a differentiated institution, the necessary function of community-wide justice is approximated in better or worse ways within other organized forms.[98]

What Dooyeweerd has evidently done in his account of the state's founding function is to read a ubiquitous factual phenomenon of the state's positive form back into its creational structural principle.[99] I am proposing instead to relocate coercive power out of that part of the normative design of state that can be attributed to its creational grounding—its structural principle—and into the category of the state's positive form, acknowledging that it is a unique example of such a form in virtue of being a universal empirical property of any actual state.

The question arising now is this: if the territorial monopoly of coercive power is not the unique individuality type of the state's power, then what is? Recall that for Dooyeweerd the coercive monopoly in the state's foundation is indispensable for distinguishing the state from other societal structures. Identifying the radical type of the state is not sufficient for this purpose. The fact that the state has a juridical leading function does indeed distinguish it from churches, schools, and businesses, but it does not distinguish it from other genotypes within the same radical type. But since there is only one other genotype within the state's radical type—"international public legal voluntary associations" such as the United Nations[100]—perhaps this can be achieved in another way. Perhaps the quest for genotypical differentiation within the radical type of juridically qualified structures is misconceived, and the very idea of founding functions is a needless complication? To pursue this I need to propose two points: first, that the UN is actually more statelike than it may appear; and second, that not only international political bodies like the UN but also the nation-state ultimately depend crucially on legitimacy more than coercive power.

For Dooyeweerd the UN is, like the state, founded in a historical organization of power but lacks the defined territory, the coercive sanction, and the compulsory governmental authority of the state.[101] In other words, the type of individuality displayed in the UN's founding function is different from that in the state's founding function. But Dooyeweerd does not suggest what this individuality type is, and it is instructive to consider why he does not. A case can be made that just as a nation-state needs coercive power in order to secure justice within its territory, so international justice can only be secured if an international coercive power is established. If so, then the UN would in Dooyeweerd's terms be under a historical vocation to acquire such power. We could regard the UN as a juridically qualified structure at a very early stage of its "internal opening process," an immature international state, analogous to emerging nation-states prior to their secure establishment of a territorial monopoly of coercion. This would then imply the need for a gradual but substantial change to the nation-state as it has been understood since the consolidation of the Westphalian system premised on a doctrine of absolute territorial sovereignty and the ushering in of a new, international structure of political integration, or perhaps several such structures.[102] An advantage of this approach is that it is more attentive to the continual historical dynamics in the evolution of structures whose task is to establish public justice, thus avoiding regarding the nation-state as sacrosanct, a historically finalized structure.[103] My suggestion, then, is to conceive of nation-states and the UN, not as different genotypes of the same radical type possessing different founding functions, but as structures of the same radical type operating at different levels of political authority and with different degrees of legal and coercive power.

What would it mean to suggest that all juridically qualified structures like states and international political authorities depend as much on legitimacy as on coercive power? It is clear that whatever formative power the UN has until now possessed has rested almost entirely on the degree to which it is acknowledged internationally as a legitimate body; hence its current relative fragility. Its power is derived from its legitimacy, which in turn is determined by the degree to which member states regard it as upholding some conception of international justice. The greater the perceived justice of its action, the more weight its resolutions and actions carry, and vice versa. A predominant dependence on legitimacy is likely to continue even if it acquired extended coercive authority.

But a case can also be made that the power of the *state* is also crucially determined by the degree to which its citizens regard it as legitimate. Where legitimacy is entirely lacking, even states with high levels of physical power at their disposal are severely crippled. Emil Brunner's judgment in this regard is pertinent.

> The justice of the State . . . increases its power, for as a rule that power is a moral rather than a physical fact. People do not normally obey the State because disobedience would be punished, but because they feel it is right to do so, quite apart, of course, from the mere force of habit. But where doubts about the justice of the State arise, its power is already undermined. . . . The State lives far more on its moral credit than is generally believed, and that means on the conviction of its lawfulness and legality.[104]

In fact Brunner then falls back on coercive monopoly as the state's *ultimate* foundation and holds that "moral credit" is only supplementary. However, his idea of moral credit points us toward a conception of political power construed as grounded in creation rather than fall, and so one in which coercion is not a necessary structural element. Even in an unfallen situation, as Dooyeweerd would recognize, the state would still need formative power. Such power would, in large part, rest upon its moral credit, on the recognition of its legitimacy by its citizens. Of course, in a fallen world its formative power must also rely on coercive sanction (as well as other forms of power), with the balance between them varying historically. But the fact of the fall does not mean a *complete* shift to reliance on coercion rather than securing moral credit. Indeed there is a powerful reason why Dooyeweerd ought to agree with this, namely, that norms based in the original creation still impinge upon human beings in spite of the fall. Fallen humans, he could argue, still retain some awareness of the need for states to be just and some willingness to obey them if they are. Just as he argues that the structural principle of the family limits what humans can do to actual families, so he could argue that the structural principle of the state at least partially reins in the excesses that make coercion necessary.

If Dooyeweerd had taken this route out of his problem, however, he would have created another: how to characterize the individuality type that I am now proposing as characteristic of the state's founding function? What type of formative power is the "recognition of legitimacy"? Once again he himself provides a clue. I already noted that he refers to a form of state power deriving from the "moral convictions of the people." What he has in mind is the power that accrues to the state from the strength of the moral principles of the citizenry—mutual respect, honesty, promise keeping, tolerance—and on which it relies for the effective performance of many of its functions. The power accruing to it from the citizenry's recognition of its authority—what Brunner calls its moral credit and what political philosophers style "subjective legitimacy"— would seem to be of the same kind, though its content is specifically political. The power of subjective legitimacy refers not to general ethical principles like promise keeping but to convictions about normative political order: the rule of law, civil rights, just distribution, and so on. In the absence of a widespread belief that the state seeks to honor such political principles the state is seriously weakened.

This is a genuine form of what Dooyeweerd terms historical (or formative) power. The power of subjective legitimacy still has to be harnessed—"organized," as Dooyeweerd puts it—by the state. So he could still hold that the state is founded in the historical aspect. I noted that coercive, physical power is a historical retrocipation (a reaching back of the historical aspect to the physical). But what form of historical power is that based in subjective legitimacy? It could, perhaps, plausibly be seen as a form of "trust," a pistical (faith) phenomenon. Subjective legitimacy as political trust would be necessary even in the absence of the need for coercion. And even though in a fallen world it must be backed up by the ultimate sanction of coercive power, it is still an indispensable foundation for the continuing stable existence of a state.

I have argued, then, that Dooyeweerd does not need to view coercive monopoly as an integral feature of the state's original structural principle but only to acknowledge its necessity as one form of formative power indispensable to the post-fall positivization of the state's creationally grounded structural principle. And I have proposed an alternative form of formative power—power drawn from subjective legitimacy— which can be seen as part of this original creational norm. As I indicated earlier, there is a larger question lurking behind this specific discussion of the state's founding function, namely, the plausibility of regarding social structures as having founding functions at all, of singling out one particular function as uniquely significant in supporting the qualifying function. It may be that whether any particular functions or properties of social structures do play such a unique role depends on the structure concerned, as I proposed in the case of the family. Dooyeweerd certainly wishes to avoid a priori constructions, but it appears that, at least in the case of the state, he has fallen victim to one.

The essential question is whether the state's historical function (whether conceived as power based in coercive monopoly or in subjective legitimacy) is uniquely significant in determining the irreducible identity of the state, and so in enabling it to secure public justice. I have conceded that it is a uniquely important dimension of the positive form of the state in a fallen world; the need for a coercive sanction is indeed universal. But I am suggesting that what Dooyeweerd should really be looking for, if he is to be consistent, is the underlying structural norm arising from creation. This is not a quest for an ideal form of the state but rather an attempt to distinguish between features of actual states that respond to the imperatives of created human nature from those that respond to deviations from that created nature. So I am formulating the question as follows: given that the state needs power of many kinds in order to advance public justice, is historical power so evidently more important than the state's other functions? Why, for example, should we not describe its spatial function (territory), or its economic function (taxation), as its founding function? Both are very obviously indispensable for a state to promote public justice, or indeed to be a state at all; empirical observation confirms that they too are always present in every state; and Dooyeweerd would agree on both counts.

As I have noted, he formulates the problem as one of discovering the type of individuality of the leading function of the state. It turns out that this is a retrocipatory type of individuality because the leading juridical function reaches back to the earlier historical founding function and cannot be accounted for apart from this retrocipatory character. But this, after all, seems questionable. We can hold that the state has a public-legal leading function without necessarily implying that this function is uniquely related to the possession of historical power. It is so related, we may admit, but then it is also related to all the other functions of the state. It is true that coercive power seems to have been a feature of all known states, but then so has economic or other forms of power. His argument that coercive power is unique, and so foundational, is not compelling; indeed it finally seems less like an argument than an assertion. The attempt to single out one function as having a privileged link to the leading function seems artificial. Here is one of several instances where Dooyeweerd has allowed the desire to maintain the systematic coherence of his overall social philosophy to take precedence over the need for sustained argument.[105] He should, it appears, have been more critical of the historical Western debate whose dialectical basic problem cued him to identify coercive power as the state's founding function.

The state, I conclude, *has no founding function.*[106] Dooyeweerd wishes to identify the founding function in order to distinguish the state as an irreducible genotype within the radical type of juridically qualified structures. But the search for such genotypical distinctiveness is unnecessary. Identifying the radical type to which the state belongs is sufficient to achieve Dooyeweerd's central objective of identifying its internal structure sufficiently clearly to be able to define its sphere sovereignty. This is by no means to suggest that his substantial account of the operation of political power is of no value. On the contrary, it contains an original and forthright statement of a crucial point—that whatever power may be necessary for the state to exist and function must be seen as being possessed exclusively in order to make possible the realization of its qualifying function, the promotion of public justice. Justice may never be allowed to become subservient to the imperatives of acquiring or wielding power, but power must always remain in the service of justice. While this clearly rules out obvious excesses such as authoritarianism or totalitarianism at home and militarism and imperialism abroad, it also implies that any exercise of coercive power, which cannot be justified as advancing the goal of public justice, is fundamentally illegitimate. This is the deeper normative dynamic behind the abstract assertion of an "indissoluble correlation between the two radical functions of the state." The potential for articulating this account into a demanding critical standard against which the activity of states must be rigorously tested will become clearer as I turn to a detailed analysis of his account of the qualifying function of the state.

NINE

THE JUST STATE

IN CHAPTER 8 I INVESTIGATED DOOYEWEERD'S ACCOUNT OF
the distinctive, irreducible identity of the state. Secured by the state's
structural principle, this identity is determined essentially by the specific
relationship between power and law. I examined how the founding function of the state is subservient to, and can only be analyzed adequately in
relation to, its leading function. The coercive power at the *foundation* of
the state exists not for its own sake but only to sustain the state in realizing its definitive normative *destination,* which is the discharge of its distinctive task of advancing public justice. The notion of public justice is
examined in detail in the next chapter. The task of the present chapter is
to penetrate further into the nature of the juridical qualifying function of
the state. In the first section the intricate and subtle relationship between
law and justice will become clear as I trace Dooyeweerd's general account
of the nature of the juridical aspect. The second section clarifies a major
pluralist conclusion emerging from this account: since every social
structure functions in the juridical aspect there are multiple spheres of
irreducible juridical or legal functioning. This is captured in the central
principle of "legal sphere sovereignty," inviting comparison and contrast
with Walzer's idea of "spheres of justice." These discussions are indispensable to a sure grasp of Dooyeweerd's account of the state's leading
function, the focus of the third section. The theme of that section is not
so much what kind of things the state *does*—that is addressed in the next
two chapters—but what kind of institution it is in order that it can do
those things. A treatment of the legal sphere sovereignty of the state then
leads into a consideration of Dooyeweerd's notions of constitutionalism
and representative democracy, the theme of the final section.

LAW AND JUSTICE

The state, Dooyeweerd holds, is a juridically qualified community. More expansively, he characterizes it as a "territorial public legal community,"[1] and each of these terms requires careful explication. Here the focus is on his account of the irreducible dimension of reality termed the legal or juridical aspect. His analyses of this aspect and of its typical individualizations are extensive, complex, and sometimes abstruse. Dooyeweerd was by profession a legal theorist. After *NC* his most substantial work was his multivolume *Encyclopaedia of Law,* the final version of which ran to over a thousand pages.[2] This includes, first, an extensive history of Western legal philosophy.[3] Then it sets forth his mature systematic legal theory, the culmination of over forty years' work developed in several books and numerous articles.[4] Only a brief indication of its outlines need be presented here.[5]

This systematic legal theory is organized as an analysis of the "modal structure of the juridical aspect." Dooyeweerd holds that this analysis yields the fundamental concepts of jurisprudence, just as a similar analysis of, say, the economic aspect would yield the basic concepts of economic theory.[6] It is beyond our purpose to explore these here,[7] but a grasp of the general nature and core of the juridical aspect is important for understanding his theory of the state as a legally qualified community.

The juridical or legal aspect is a universal, normative, and irreducible aspect of reality. First, the juridical aspect is *universally valid,* a specific instance of the general principle of *sphere universality.* Juridical or legal phenomena have no privileged relationship to the state or its judicial organs; all social structures have a juridical aspect and function juridically. I explore this seminal point in detail in the next section.

Second, law is an inherently *normative* phenomenon. The English language is an impoverished medium for rendering this typically Continental notion. The principal Dutch term for "law" is *recht.* This can also be translated as "right" or sometimes "justice," terms usually understood as normative concepts, in contrast to "law," which in modern English legal language is not (partly due the influence of legal positivism). Hence when the adjective *rechtelijk* is translated as either "legal" or "juridical" its normative connotation is lost. Dooyeweerd frequently uses these two terms to refer to the legal or juridical aspect, and to the state as qualified by this aspect. He also uses the term *juridisch* as a substitute for *rechtelijk,* and although this typically refers to positive law as such, in his usage it bears the same normative meaning as the latter.

Dooyeweerd repudiates any dualism between a normative concept of justice or right and a supposedly a-normative concept of positive law. Positive law is not a value-free datum but a normative phenomenon, governed by "normative legal principles" rooted in the juridical aspect. It is the human positivization of normative juridical principles.[8] In other words the juridical aspect has a law-side and a subject-side. On the law-side are the normative legal principles; on the subject-side are positive laws. These specify the three principal fields "legal right," "legal duty," and "legal competence."

The third feature of the juridical aspect that requires elucidation is its *irreducibility.*[9] Dooyeweerd warns of a constant danger that this aspect will be conflated with others, that its modal sphere sovereignty will be compromised. A common error is to conceive of juridical norms as ethical, where "ethics" is viewed as an inclusive science of normativity. All aspects of reality from the logical through to the pistical are normative, but the ethical aspect is only one of these aspects. The ethical aspect does not embrace all normative principles but concerns only one specific kind, those governing interpersonal relationships of love.[10] Attempting to derive juridical norms from ethical principles is thus a form of reductionism.[11] This is a weakness in the Thomistic natural law theory, which fails to honor the irreducibility of the juridical aspect by regarding law as a mere means to an ethical end, the moral perfection of man.[12] Another error is to reduce juridical norms to mere "instincts of revenge."[13] Such instincts are psychically qualified. There can indeed be "feelings of justice," but these are "psychic analogies."[14]

The juridical aspect, then, is universal, normative, and irreducible. What, however, is its distinctive content, its "nuclear moment"? Dooyeweerd suggests that this core can be denoted with the term *retribution,* which "designates the irreducible meaning-kernel of what is signified by the words δίχη, *jus, justice, recht, dritto, droit,* etc."[15] The classical formulation of justice as *suum cuique tribuere* supports this view, he holds. It was "based upon an older cosmological conception of justice whose retributive meaning cannot be doubted."[16] The purpose of retribution is "to maintain a just balance by a just reaction";[17] it "reacts against every *ultra vires*. It binds every legal power and subjective right to its limits."[18] The irreducible core of the idea is the *balancing and harmonizing of legal interests*. A normative legal order harmonizes legal interests by weighing them against each other and then reconciling them.[19] Such juridical interests will be immensely varied. They will include both public or private interests and individual or social interests. An example of a possible disharmony between public and private legal interests would be an incursion of public law into the area properly belonging to (private) civil law, a squeezing of individual rights allegedly in the "public interest."[20] An example of a disharmony between individual and social legal interests would be the imbalance between the rights of employers and employees caused by the massive expansion of industrial capitalism in the nineteenth century, calling forth the corrective development of "social law" to protect the juridical interests of workers.

As with the nuclear moment of any modal aspect, that of the juridical aspect can be elucidated further by referring to the analogical moments surrounding it,[21] contained in the above definition. "Balance" is related to the economic aspect, "harmony" to the aesthetic. These two, and the social analogy (all retrocipatory moments), receive particular attention in Dooyeweerd's account in *NC* (though "proportionality," which is related to the mathematical aspect, is also important). The nuclear moment of the aesthetic aspect is captured by the term *harmony,* a norm requiring "unity in multiplicity."[22] That of the economic aspect is denoted by *frugality,* which means "the sparing or frugal mode of administering scarce goods, implying an alternative choice of their destination with regard to the satisfaction of different human needs." The norm of frugality proscribes "an excessive or wasteful satisfaction of a particular need at the expense of other more urgent needs."[23] To forestall such excess it is necessary to establish a rank ordering of legal interests. Not all such interests can claim equal value, and in cases of conflict the lesser should yield to the greater, though not at needless cost. Such a rank ordering should be established, not according to some timeless abstract schema, but rather taking into account the particular historical circumstances in which, for example, legal claims are advanced, legal duties fulfilled, or legal competences exercised.[24] Regrettably, Dooyeweerd fails to elaborate upon these intriguing suggestions. In any event, the meaning of retribution embodies both these analogical moments in its own internal (retrocipatory) structure. The juridical aspect therefore presupposes a harmonious balancing and a frugal or nonexcessive allocation of interests: "a well-balanced harmony of a multiplicity of interests, warding off any excessive actualizing of special concerns detrimental to others."[25]

As explained, the foundedness of an aspect upon earlier ones does not vitiate its irreducible character. The juridical aspect cannot be fully explained in terms of its analogies. The terms normally denoting retribution are not drawn from economic life; "acquittance" and "mutual discharge of debt" are not essentially (originally) economic notions. While the Dutch words *vergelding* (retribution) and *vergoeding* (compensation) are indeed based upon the roots *geld* (money) and *goed* (good), both of which have an economic connotation,[26] the crucial idea of a "deserved reaction" in the notion of retribution excludes the core economic meaning of the term. It is the notion of "desert" or "due" that is specific to the core of the juridical aspect, marking it off from the economic aspect. Whereas a "price" has an essentially economic sense since it is set according to the criterion of what is frugal, desert or due suggests something *owed,* something that can legitimately be claimed as a right. Thus, for instance, the duty upon employers to pay employees their wages is not to be reduced to an economic norm; rather it is required by the *juridical* obligation to keep contracts.[27]

Dooyeweerd's discussion of these two analogies leaves a lot to be desired. As Seerveld has indicated, what he attempts to explain in terms of the aesthetic analogy can quite adequately be accounted for in terms of the economic.[28] He seems to have overlooked some suggestive clues that the juridical mode might after all be founded directly on the economic (requiring a different order of modal aspects). While recognizing that the key Dutch terms *vergelding* and *vergoeding* have economically connotative stems, he correctly denies that they have an originally economic meaning while not acknowledging that the intimate etymological connection might have some ontic basis. Characterizing the economic analogy in the juridical aspect as the "*frugal administration* of various interests" could have been more illuminating.

The aesthetic and economic analogies are intrinsically linked to the social analogy, which is "expressed in a strict correlation between *com-*

munal interests and those of inter-individual [and, presumably, intercommunal] relationships in *juridical intercourse.*"[29] I have noted the necessary correlation between these two categories of societal relationships. In this context Dooyeweerd is attempting to demonstrate how this social correlation comes to expression within the internal structure of the juridical aspect. In the process of harmonizing various interests both categories of societal relationships must be taken into account in seeking a just balance. It does, however, seem problematic to suggest that this far-reaching implication of a transcendental societal category is somehow derived from the modal structure of but one of the modal aspects—the social—especially since that aspect receives such rudimentary discussion as compared to most others.

In any event the substantive pluralist point to which he is drawing attention here is that juridical claims in a society are legitimately advanced by communities and cannot all be derived from those of individuals.[30] Societal relationships, whether communal or interindividual, can also be bearers of juridically valid interests. The fact that legal functioning consists in far more than rendering that which is due to *individuals* is a basic presupposition of the notion of juridical sphere sovereignty.

The important implications of this social analogy become evident in a discussion of Aristotle's distinction between distributive and commutative justice. These concepts are not rejected but rather situated as genuine attempts to account for real juridical states of affairs.[31] Commutative justice was Aristotle's way to account for interindividual legal relationships, distributive justice for intracommunal legal relationships. Commutative justice applies to relationships between separate individuals, whereas distributive justice applies to relationships within communities (i.e., between members of the same community). Recognizing both types of justice as responses to normative juridical states of affairs, Dooyeweerd therefore firmly rejects what he terms the individualistic trend in the early humanistic doctrine of natural law (represented by Grotius and Hobbes, for example), which effectively excluded distributive justice as a genuine form of justice. Representatives of this trend only acknowledged juridical relationships holding between private contracting individuals and denied the reality of juridical relationships holding within and between given communal structures.[32] Individualism attempted to explain away communal juridical relationships as ultimately derived from contracts between individuals. However, he insists that distributive justice must be recognized as a genuine juridical norm since it arises in the context of communal relationships that display their own sphere of juridical functioning. The state is such a juridically functioning community. Distributive justice within the state "requires a proportional distribution of public communal charges and public communal benefits, in accordance with the bearing power and merits of the subjects."[33] This distributive, communal justice should also characterize the allocation of rights and obligations within an economic enterprise, a church, a family, and so on.

Dooyeweerd's understanding of the juridical aspect can be summarized thus: its central norm requires a harmonious balance of juridical relationships among a multiplicity of particular interests, whether individual or societal (communal or interindividual or intercommunal). It calls for an integrating activity of a specific kind, one in which such special interests can fully realize their own juridical claims but nonexcessively.

More than one commentator has suggested that Dooyeweerd's choice of the term *retribution* is hardly the most appropriate for designating the nuclear moment of the juridical aspect. In one of his later articles Dooyeweerd does recognize certain difficulties with the notion of retribution, but he does not propose an alternative.[34] The evident problem is that retribution is an essentially negative concept, implying the restoration of a violated order. The idea of retribution and its related concepts of compensation or restitution[35] are intended to "maintain the juridical balance by a just *reaction*."[36] In the case of the nuclear moments of the other normative aspects Dooyeweerd posits an essentially positive concept: distinction, formation, symbolization, intercourse, frugality, harmony, certainty. Negative concepts are of course implied in these, as in any norm. Every norm implicitly calls for a restoration of what violates it (lack of clarity in the case of distinction, wastefulness in the case of frugality, etc.). But retribution seems to be a negative implication of a more basic positive norm. Indeed the words Dooyeweerd cites as traditionally having denoted the irreducible core of justice (e.g., *jus, recht, dritto, droit*) have this positive character, as does the classical formula *suum cuique tribuere*.

One promising suggestion as to how to denote this positive norm arises from this formula itself, namely, the stem of the term *retribution:*

tribution. This has been proposed by the theologian Paul Tillich,[37] who shares Dooyeweerd's concern to probe to the ontic kernal of justice.

> Tributive or proportional justice . . . appears as distributive, attributive, retributive justice, giving everything proportionally to what it deserves, positively or negatively. It is a calculating justice, measuring the power of being of all things in terms of what shall be given to them or what shall be withheld from them. I have called this form of justice tributive because it decides about the tribute a thing or person ought to receive according to his special powers of being. Attributive justice attributes to beings what they are and can claim to be. Distributive justice gives to any being the proportion of goods which is due to him; retributive justice does the same, but in negative terms, in terms of deprivation of goods or active punishment.[38]

The parallel in Dooyeweerd to Tillich's notion of special powers of being is the notion of the irreducible identity of things (secured by their structural principles). Thus we can say that the core norm of the juridical aspect renders to each existent the tribute that is its due. In the societal realm these structural principles determine the sphere sovereignty of each societal structure. The juridical aspect is thereby more evidently linked to sphere sovereignty. Sphere sovereignty supplies a material content for what ought to be rendered or "tributed" to different societal structures. A just legal order will therefore ensure that such tribute is rendered to diverse structures as is necessary for the preservation and outworking of their sphere sovereignty.

SPHERES OF JUSTICE

It is this conception of justice that provides the basis for Dooyeweerd's notion of legal or juridical sphere sovereignty. Each societal structure functions in the juridical aspect, and the sphere sovereignty of each is expressed in this aspect (as in the others). The juridical dimension of each structure therefore possesses a uniqueness and irreducibility rooted in created order. Juridical sphere sovereignty is thus grounded ultimately in divine sovereignty.[39]

The diverse juridical spheres of the different societal relationships (and of persons) erect boundaries that the state, or indeed any other structure, may not cross. The theory of juridical sphere sovereignty is intended to give account of and safeguard the distinct character of the juridical spheres of each differentiated societal structure. Each of these structures has a responsibility to see that justice is done within its internal sphere. The promotion of justice is thus by no means the sole prerogative of the *state*. Juridical norms apply in every societal structure. No structure can be governed purely according to, say, the norms of ethical love or the imperatives of efficiency. But juridical norms must be pursued in each structure in the way appropriate to its nature. The norm of (re)tribution (I shall henceforth revert to Dooyeweerd's own term) is universally valid, but the content of its demands differs according to the nature of the various societal spheres. Retribution must be individualized according to the typical nature of the societal sphere in question. We cannot know what retribution requires simply by analyzing the structure of the juridical aspect itself. This functional viewpoint must be supplemented by the typical viewpoint, the analysis of the structural principles of the various societal structures within which the juridical aspect is expressed: "A specific social reality of a merely juridical character does not exist. The 'juridical' or 'jural' is never more than a modal aspect of social reality, and this reality is given to us only in a great diversity of typical individuality structures."[40]

The content of what is to be rendered to various members of a societal relationship depends, then, on the normative structure of the relationship of which they are members. The theory of juridical sphere sovereignty seeks to take account of these different juridical domains, distinguishing the "rights, duties and competencies" of one structure from those of another. It assumes definite structural differences between the juridical norms pertaining to families, businesses, churches, schools, states, and so on. The juridical dimension of a family, for instance, expresses itself in the right relationship between parents and children, in the proper expression of parental authority, and in the various rights and duties of each member of the family. The rights belonging to a child in a family will differ from those belonging to a worker in a firm or a citizen in a state. A child cannot claim the right to vote in family decisions, nor can an employee expect as of right (nor is she likely to want) that degree of personal affection from her employer that the employer shows to his children. The "rights, duties and competencies" of a particular societal relationship are in each case determined by its structural principle.[41] The distinctive juridical spheres of the various societal structures thus supply the criteria for the material content that is to be tributed to each societal structure.[42]

Juridical sphere sovereignty defines the rights, duties, and competencies of each societal relationship. These are the three principal expressions of its "legal subjectivity" (or agency).[43] The legal *competences (competenties)* of a societal relationship are its various powers to decide authoritatively on matters falling within its sphere, and these are bounded by juridical sphere sovereignty.[44] The structural principle of marriage, for instance, determines its distinctive legal sphere, and this must be distinguished from the spheres of civil, ecclesiastical, or other typical kinds of law. Legal relations within a marriage thus reflect the character of marriage as qualified by love and founded biotically. Thus, for example, "the internal juridical rights and duties of the marriage partners in relation to each other can never, as civil rights . . . [are], be sanctioned by the compulsive legal power of the state."[45]

The violation of the legal *rights (rechten)* of one societal structure by another constitutes an interference with its juridical sphere sovereignty. For example, if the state tried to prevent parents from sending their children to the school of their choice, it would, prima facie, be overstepping the bounds of its competence and violating the rights of parents to choose what kind of education they wish for their children. Like Gierke, Dooyeweerd holds that communities are legal subjects whose rights ought to be recognized and protected by the state. Individuals also have rights, of course, but the restriction of the category of legal subjectivity to individuals is arbitrary.[46]

Communities also have legal *duties.* Married couples, for example, have a legal duty to cohabit.[47] Preventing a member of a particular structure from fulfilling his or her duties arising from membership in that structure would represent another interference with juridical sphere sovereignty. Where a trade union, solely for reasons of improving its relative power position, makes it impossible for a government to govern justly, it obstructs the legitimate pursuit of a duty falling within the juridical sphere of the state.

Dooyeweerd holds that juridical norms set limits to what actually counts as valid law—a claim closely parallel to the Thomist view that "human law" that "breaks" natural law lacks validity and is not "binding in conscience." An action overreaching the typical juridical sphere of one social relationship actually *loses its very juridical character.* This is why "the recognition of the absolute power of a particular legislator [in any juridical sphere] would irrevocably deprive his power of any juridical meaning." Violations of the boundaries of typical societal individuality structures thus invalidate the juridical claim of the violator, for the retributive core of the juridical aspect itself is "incompatible with any absolute (and consequently juridically unlimited) power of a legislator."[48]

A highly illuminating example of the theory of juridical sphere sovereignty is provided in *NC* by Dooyeweerd's extended discussion of a juridical application of the notion of enkapsis.[49] The context of his discussion is the debate within legal philosophy over whether the state ought to be recognized as the sole source of valid law—the positivist view—or whether other bodies can also create their own law. His comments here draw upon extensive earlier studies of the problem of the sources of positive law, which, as noted, he regards as the central question facing legal theory.[50]

It follows from Dooyeweerd's principle of juridical sphere sovereignty that there exists a wide diversity of types of law, the specific character of each being determined by the structure within which it appears. Thus, in addition to state law and international law, there are distinctive spheres of ecclesiastical law, family law, trade union law, corporate law, and so on. These terms refer to an original, nonderived sphere of valid positive law, not to different branches of state or public law. The laws of a trade union derive their validity from the internal normative structure of the union, not from the state.[51] In legal positivism, however, all valid law is seen as finding its source in state organs, whether the legislature, the courts, or the executive. Nonstate rules of behavior, as Austin argued, may be morally binding but lack legal validity. Dooyeweerd claims to the contrary that each societal structure can create valid law on account of its own "sovereignty."

He observes, however, that certain legal provisions may have their "formal origin" in the legal organs of a particular societal structure and yet derive their "material content" from a legal sphere within a structure of a quite different qualification. For example, an ecclesiastical regulation may *contain* rules of either a civil-legal or even public-legal nature, but this does not mean that the church has the material competence to promulgate civil or public law.[52] It only means that the church has incorporated (or encapsulated) certain civil- or public-legal provisions, themselves originally created by the state, within its own legal provisions (e.g., one determining who within an association may assume civil duties). In this sense the church is availing itself of the services of the state in performing its own juridical operations. The ecclesiastical *form* in which such civil- or public-legal provisions are found is an example of a phenotypical variation. This is its "genetic form," the form in which it was actually positivized. But the genetic form of a law does not necessarily indicate the original sphere of competence of the societal relationship materially qualified to create such a law. Thus it is only the *material competence* and not the *formal origin* that is determined by the principle of juridical sphere sovereignty. The latter is determined by the various enkaptic relationships into which these sovereign juridical spheres may enter.[53]

The internal limits of material competence are thus determined by the invariable structural principles of the various societal relationships possessing such competences, not by the structural principles of the societal relationship whose juridical organs may have incorporated provision of the former into their own legal provision.[54] Social structures exhibit a multiplicity of reciprocally irreducible spheres of legal competence, each authorized to create laws for its own structurally delimited juridical domain and for no other.[55] The question of the scope of these irreducible spheres of competence depends entirely on the internal structural principles of the relationships in view and never on the juridical genetic form in which a certain law is actually positivized.[56]

Furthermore, a particular genetic form, that is, the form in which particular legal rule (say, the articles of association of a voluntary organization) is positivized, may be an "original" source of law in one sphere of competence (e.g., the internal sphere of the association) but a "derived" source of law in another (e.g., the sphere of civil law). But however closely different sources of law may be enkaptically linked in this way, "the original spheres of competence bind and limit each other."[57] Thus law displaying the typical structure of a particular societal relationship falls within the material competence of that societal relationship and is only *formally* connected with other spheres of competence.[58]

This theory of legal sphere sovereignty amounts to a sophisticated version of legal pluralism.[59] In the next section I show how it provides the foundation for Dooyeweerd's view of the distinctive sphere of justice of the state and how it leads him to repudiate emphatically the dominant modern understanding of state sovereignty. To conclude this section, some remarks on the similarities and differences between Dooyeweerd's notion of juridical sphere sovereignty and Walzer's influential pluralistic theory of "spheres of justice" will serve to bring the distinctiveness of Dooyeweerd's position into sharper relief.

Walzer's notion of spheres of justice is not a product of legal theory but a theory of distributive justice sharing goals very similar to Dooyeweerd's principle of societal sphere sovereignty and its legal correlate. Its principal motivation is to contend against reductionist theories that seek to subordinate all spheres of social interaction to a single, universally valid principle of distributive justice. Instead Walzer proposes a theory of "complex equality" offering the prospect of equal treatment between spheres while acknowledging the validity of different distributive principles within each sphere. Each sphere is sui generis, irreducible to all others: "personal qualities and social goods have their own sphere of operation, where they work effects freely, spontaneously, and legitimately."[60] Since each sphere is governed by distinct principles of distribution appropriate to the internal imperatives of that sphere, no single distributive criterion can be universally imposed. Within spheres unequal distributions, perhaps even a monopoly, of the relevant good might be appropriate; in the political community there is rightly a monopoly of political authority in the state. But between spheres equality should be approximated: no sphere should be allowed to achieve "domination" over others by deploying its "extramural effectiveness" outside its own sphere.[61] Capitalists, for example, in the sphere of money, must be prevented from using what might be their monopoly position in that sphere to dominate other spheres, such as education, politics, or the family. "A radically laissez-faire economy would be like a totalitarian state, invading every other sphere, dominating every other distributive process."[62] Something like this principle of equality between spheres is captured in Dooyeweerd's principle of cultural economy,[63] by which the historical process of differentiation should be guided, preventing any unbalanced expansion of one sphere at the expense of others.

Walzer's maxim, "Good fences make just societies,"[64] could serve as a pithy summary of what Dooyeweerd's idea of sphere sovereignty is all about. The intent of Dooyeweerd's idea, however, can be made yet clearer by noting a significant philosophical difference between them. Walzer identifies himself as a "radical particularist," arguing that distributive principles are only valid within the particular historical cultures in which they arise. The aspiration to discern cross-cultural universal norms of distribution applying within spheres like money, politics, or the family in every culture is fundamentally misplaced. While certain key social goods may have "characteristic normative structures, reiterated across the lines . . . of time and space," yet, finally: "All distributions are just or unjust relative to the [particular] social meanings of the goods at stake, meanings which are in constant flux.[65]

This philosophical difference generates a substantial contrast in their respective estimations of the status of the political community. For Walzer the public definition of the boundaries between the spheres, and the defense of their mutual autonomy, falls to one particular sphere, the political community. This is because, by virtue of its rootedness in particular cultural communities, it is "probably the closest we can come to a world of common meanings."[66] A political community's shared cultural meanings integrate the diverse distributive principles and render them mutually comprehensible. This is why the primary good people distribute to one another is "membership" in a political community: on this everything else seems finally to depend.[67] As will be clear by now, Dooyeweerd would resist any such attribution of primacy—moral or legal—to the state. Strikingly, whereas Walzer's radically particularist communitarianism leads him to posit the primacy of the political community as the morally integrating community, Dooyeweerd's radically universalist pluralism leads him to affirm the full moral and legal equivalence of plural social spheres, of which the state is but one. Now he certainly does hold that the state performs a crucial integrating function with respect to other spheres, but this is quite compatible with a full honoring of the universally grounded sphere sovereignty of those spheres. His original and distinctive idea of "political integration" is examined in detail below; its concrete applications are displayed in the following two chapters.

The State's Sphere of Justice

The decisive difference between the juridical function of the state and the juridical functions of other societal structures is the *public* character of the state's juridical responsibilities. Every social structure exhibits a juridical domain, but only the state is qualified as a *public legal community*,[68] to use Dooyeweerd's favored designation of the nature of the state. I have already shown how the public character of the state is fundamental in Dooyeweerd's account of the founding function of the state. It is equally fundamental in his account of its leading function.

Two clarifications regarding Dooyeweerd's language are necessary before I proceed. First, it is necessary to clear up a problem remaining in Dooyeweerd's account of the state's founding function. In that discussion I noted that he conceives of the public character of the state as inseparably linked with the unique physically coercive basis of its power. But I argued earlier that coercion cannot consistently be included in the definition of the state's creational structural principle. Dooyeweerd, however, also speaks as if the state's coercive basis is also necessarily reflected in its *leading* function. Although generally defining the leading function simply as a "public-juridical" or "public-legal" *(publiekrechtelijk)* community, the assumption throughout is that the public-juridical competence of the state is distinctive because of its physically coercive base. Thus he characterizes the state in one context as a "public-juridical coercive community."[69] The authority of the state is, uniquely, "governmental authority over subjects enforced by the strong arm."[70] "Public" and "coercive" are for him inseparable elements of the structural principle. The following discussion underlines my claim that this is not a satisfactory conceptualization. The public character of the state's *juridical* aspect, I want to show, is quite sufficient to distinguish it from the juridical aspect of all other societal structures.

Second, I have already noted the importance of the distinction between the internal functioning of a structure of individuality determined by its structural principle and its external, enkaptic relationships with other structures. Bearing this distinction in mind will prove important with reference to the state because Dooyeweerd himself fails to do so consistently. We need to distinguish the internal structural functions of the state from its external enkaptic relationships with nonstate social structures. The examples of the state's functions discussed in chapter 7—spatial, physical, social, aesthetic—are all intended as examples of the state's internal functioning. I discuss its external enkaptic relationships in the next two chapters, but here the focus is on the state's internal functioning, especially in the qualifying juridical sphere.

The state, then, is a public-legal community, empowered to pursue its ends by means of the creation of a just legal order. The fact that this legal order is directed ("destined") toward the establishment of *public* justice is the essential factor in constituting the state's distinctive identity. While all structures function juridically, only the state functions public-juridically. Earlier I noted that the state's need for a coercive monopoly as its founding function derives directly from its public character. Now it will become clear how the notion "public" is also immediately related to the state's juridical qualifying function. This notion is in one sense already implicit in the definition of the juridical aspect. I summarized the requirement of the nuclear moment of this aspect earlier as a harmoniously balanced complex of juridical relationships among a multiplicity of juridical interests. This involves *justly interrelating* different individuals and communities. Interests cannot be justly interrelated where there is a plurality of different agencies doing the interrelating. A plurality of agencies for administering justice would mean a plurality of legal frameworks each aimed at balancing and harmonizing the rights and duties of the same individuals and communities—a feudal patchwork quilt of overlapping authorities. While each community would remain responsible for justice within its own sphere, only one agency could be responsible for arbitrating between different communities (and individuals). Such an agency is then a public-legal community. It and it alone is charged with establishing public-legal interrelation.[71]

In probing further what this legal interrelation (or "harmonization") involves, we encounter Dooyeweerd's strategically important idea of "political integration."[72] He claims that his conception of political integration is decisively different from that of organicist, corporatist, and scholastic conceptions. Commencing his discussion of political integration, he announces that he has arrived at "the most crucial point" in his inquiry into the state's structural principle. His aim is to give an account of the "typical integrating character" of the state's leading function. He is referring to the way in which the state integrates *government* and *subjects* into a concretely functioning public communal whole. Its unity as a communal whole, he proposes, is guaranteed by the internal integrating function of its public-juridical qualification. "The leading function in the structure of the State has proved to be a public-legal relationship uniting government, people and territory into a politico-juridical whole." Its juridically qualified structural principle "implies the unique universality and totality of the internal legal community of the State, which is not found in any other societal structure."[73] This "unique universality and totality" does not imply what he terms "universal*ism*" but refers to the territorially inclusive—"public"—scope of its legal responsibilities and powers. No other societal structure has an internal membership necessarily including all persons and communities domiciled within a specific territory. The membership of the state is a public membership: it is both open to one and all and imposed upon one and all. That which is public pertains to any and all within a specific area, whereas that which is private pertains to determinate individuals or communities.

The inclusive character of the state leads Dooyeweerd to the observation that "the traditional universalistic theory of the State as the integral totality of all other societal structures seems thus to be justified *at least with regard to the legal organization of the body politic.*"[74] This theory, however, was misconceived because it attempted to draw all juridical relationships in society within the scope of the internal communal life of the state. Employing his distinction between an external enkaptic relationship and an internal whole-part relationship, he warns that the legal spheres of nonstate societal structures can never be subsumed under the state's public-legal qualification. The universality of the state's legal sphere does not imply a whole-part relationship to these nonstate legal spheres.[75] There is no contradiction between the universality—the public embrace—of the state's juridical functioning and the juridical sphere sovereignty of the nonstate societal structures. The universal character of the state implies only its inclusive internal membership as a communal juridical whole; it does not imply that this community embraces all other differently qualified societal structures within itself. The universal public legal community of the state integrates all persons but only insofar as they are *subjects (onderdanen)*. It does not embrace them in their capacities as parents, workers, teachers, artists, and so on. A state consists only of a *politically* integrated community. The nonpolitical "offices" that its subjects will also occupy do not fall within the political community as such.[76]

This is the basis for Dooyeweerd's notion of a "people" *(volk).*[77] The public-legal integration of all citizens in a territorially delimited area is what constitutes a people. The state organizes a people within a territory into a single public-legal community, membership of which is held irrespective of family relations, church membership, beliefs, occupations, social class, or status. It thus establishes an "integrating political unity in spite of any differences or divisions which the people display in other societal relationships."[78] The state is a communal whole embracing people and government in an integrated unity. The people have no independent existence apart from the government and vice versa.[79]

Integration into a political community takes place without subsuming the multiplicity of societal structures within the state. The nature of the integration involved when citizens become a politically unified people is determined by the state's structural principle. "This is an unparalleled, unique structural principle enabling the State to organize within its territory a truly universal legal communal bond transcending all non-juridically qualified legal societal relations."[80] Such integration creates a *community of public justice* but not a religious, moral, economic, or intellectual community. It is the leading functions of other societal structures—respectively church, family, business, or academic—that create these kinds of communities. The state's ability to create a distinctive political bond does not arise from the fact that its membership will be numerically larger than any other structure. Nor is the inability of nonstate structures to create it due to their numerically inferior position. No other structure can create such a public legal bond, "*however large the number* of the members."[81] In practice the state's membership may not always exceed that of all other communities, if for instance all citizens happened to be members of the same church. "Public" does not mean numerically larger but territorially inclusive.[82]

The uniquely public character of the state comes to expression in the distinctive character of *"state law."* Dooyeweerd draws a fundamental distinction between the *public*-legal character of the state and the *private*-legal character of all other societal structures. The distinction between public law, *jus commune,* and specific or private law, *jus specificum,* is central to his analysis. It coincides with the distinction between state law and nonstate law. All state law, as the law of a *res publica,* is therefore *public law* or *jus commune,* while all nonstate law is governed by a specific, nonjuridical qualification and is thus *private law* or *jus specificum.* Within the former category he further distinguishes between *public communal law (publiek verbandsrecht)* and *private civil law (burgelijk privaatrecht).*[83] The term *private* here might mislead: what is referred to is that which is common to private relationships. Hence he sometimes refers to this kind of law as "private common law"; I refer to it as "civil law."

The term *civil law* is used by Dooyeweerd broadly in the sense in which it is used in those European legal systems fashioned under the *Code de Napoleon,* namely, to refer to the law by which the state protects the rights and liberties of persons in the civil courts. Yet by integrating the notion into his own apparatus of legal concepts he gives it a distinctive content. Whereas public communal law governs people insofar as they are members of the political community, civil law integrates people insofar as they relate to each other, within interlinkages, outside the political community.[84] Civil law establishes a framework of legal constraints whose purpose is to protect the dignity of the individual, within which individuals or communities may enter into various relationships. Such constraints are, for example, the basis for the protection of many of the familiar civil rights and liberties of modern liberal democracies (speech, association, religion, movement, etc.), which Dooyeweerd affirms.

The fundamental material legal principles on which civil law is based are those of the freedom and equality of citizens. As noted, the appearance of civil law presupposes the collapse of undifferentiated political structures, allowing the liberation of the individual person from feudal and other restrictive social bonds; civil law arrives in history simultaneously with the differentiated state. Indeed it is precisely because only the state embraces people on a basis of equality that the state alone is competent to form civil law.[85] The very idea of a *res publica* implies that the state has made all persons in its territory into its direct subjects on the basis of equality before the law.[86]

A discussion of this theme occasions Dooyeweerd's statement of the specific sense in which he endorses the notion of "human rights," in the course of which he also offers a critical appreciation of the French Revolution. Human rights are not to be seen as rooted in some hypothetical prepolitical state of nature but are the product of a concrete historical development in Western civil law.

> Only with [the] process of differentiation is room created for the recognition of the *rights of man as such,* independent of a person's membership in particular communities like kinship bonds, nation, family, or church. Civil private law is a product of this process of development. In terms of its inner nature, civil private law is based on the rights of man and cannot tolerate dependence on race or nationality. Freedom and equality in a civil-legal sense were thus clearly not just hollow slogans of the French Revolution. . . . However[,] . . . these fruits were not produced without blemish. Humanistic individualism led to overextending the civil-legal and the public-legal idea of freedom and equality. Hence it did not recognize the rights of the private nonstate *communities* in society. It respected only the free and autonomous *individual* and his counterpart, the *state,* which was founded on the treacherous, individualistic grounds of popular sovereignty and social contract.[87]

Just as individual civil rights cannot be pitted against the rights of communities, so civil law cannot be hermetically sealed off from the legal spheres of social structures. On the contrary, all these legal spheres are interlaced with—"have an enkaptic function within"—civil law.[88] This interlacement fully respects the sphere sovereignty of the internal legal spheres in question, only effecting an external integration among them.[89] An example of such external, enkaptic integration would be the recognition in civil law of "standard contracts" or "usual conditions" holding in commercial or industrial interlinkages. Such contracts or conditions are not themselves part of civil law, since the original competence to formulate them derives from the juridical sphere sovereignty of the commercial or industrial agents involved; they are examples of economically qualified legal provisions. Civil law can, however, recognize their validity by providing them with civil legal consequences (so long as they do not violate civil or public law). For instance, in most insurance contracts an insurance company will include clauses excluding certain risks. This is done on economic grounds, namely, to protect the company's profits. In itself this is not a civil-legal matter, for the contents of a contract are a matter for the parties to it. Further it is not part of the company's economic purpose to safeguard the civil-legal principles of freedom and equality; indeed such a contract will typically be unilaterally formulated by the company, leaving the client no freedom at all to determine its contents. Hence it is the specific role of civil law to protect the client against unfair agreements, and to this end it can place detailed and numerous restrictions on the terms of contracts without any suggestion of encroaching upon the economically qualified legal sphere of the company.[90]

The distinction between public and civil law corresponds to the basic transcendental distinction between communities and interlinkages: the internal communal law of the state finds its correlate in the civil law sphere of the state, which governs interlinkages.[91] This function of civil law proves significant. Dooyeweerd is seeking to show both that in protecting the civil rights of individuals against communities of which they are members the state is not interfering with the sphere sovereignty of such communities and that communal sphere sovereignty meets its limit in individual civil rights. A robust institutional pluralism is thus not incompatible with a clear recognition of individual rights. Civil law regulates communities in the same specific and limited way that it regulates interlinkages, namely, by merely enkaptically binding their legal sphere to that of the state. By means of civil law the state can require communities to respect people's civil rights. It binds them to "the principles of inter-individual justice, legal security and equity."[92] But this is as far as the state may go. It has no competence to encroach upon the *internal* legal spheres of communities (or interlinkages) since these have a distinct qualification, and so fall within *jus specificum*.[93]

Such an enkaptic integration is of an external or formal character but only in the sense that it does not trespass upon the internal *material* legal domain of communities. It does not mean that civil law *itself* is only of a formal character. All law has material content embedded in it. This material content is determined by the structural principle of the social structure that creates it. The material content of civil law is determined by the structural principle of the state. When called to adjudicate on questions pertaining to the *internal* legal sphere of a community a civil court must therefore restrict itself to the formal question of whether a particular decision or rule has been made in accordance with its own procedural norms (stipulated in its articles of association). It is only when such decisions or rules affect a person's civil rights that a civil court may employ material criteria arising from within *its* typical legal sphere.[94]

Constitutional Democracy

An important conclusion from the previous section is that, on Dooyeweerd's view, the spheres of public law and civil law are exhaustive of the state's legal competence. This conception of the limited legal competence of the state provides the basis for his formulation of the idea of a *rechtsstaat* (law-state) and his critique of all political theories that appear to harbor absolutist implications. His understanding of the law-state is the basis of his view of the appropriate constitutional structures in the state, and this in turn is the context in which he discusses the idea of democracy. I begin with his critique of "absolutism."

Without normative legal limits on the state's competence there can be no principled alternative to an absolutist "power theory" of the state. In such a theory the state's power is released from all juridical restraint. Absolutism denies the reality of intrinsic legal limits to the authority of the state, implying "an absorption of the entire juridical position of man by his position as citizen or as subject of his government."[95] It reduces the multicontextual jural functioning of the human person to a single context, his political subjection to the government. But citizenship is only one type of juridical status, standing alongside other qualitatively different juridical positions in a relationship of coordinate equality. Bodin's conception of sovereignty carries just such absolutist implications. He was legitimately reacting against an undifferentiated situation in which "every autonomous law-sphere that claimed an original sphere of competence, at the same time claimed governmental power of its own, which turned against the idea of the *res publica,* as it did not recognize any limitation by the public interest."[96] However, he vastly overextended the scope of sovereignty. Conceiving of it as essentially indivisible, no restriction on it was deemed possible, "either in power or in task or in time." Sovereignty implies the "absolute and only original competence for the creation of law within the territory of the state." No lawmaking authority was to be tolerated other than the legislature. Not only was the validity of customary law made "absolutely dependent on direct or indirect recognition by statute law." By implication the same applied to all law created by the nonpolitical societal structures within the state's territory. This lawmaking monopoly, the logical consequence of Bodin's absolutist concept of sovereignty, was deemed by him indispensable for any state.[97]

The essential feature of Bodin's doctrine was maintained in various forms for several centuries. The notion that sovereignty was a feature exclusively of the state profoundly influenced the framework within which modern political theory was developed, both in its absolutist line and in its counterpart in liberalism. However radically different in other ways from absolutism, liberalism does not deny the exclusive sovereignty of the state but only holds that it proceeds from the consent of the individual members of the state, each seen as absolute "sovereigns" in their own right. Denying that any legal communities exist in the state of nature, liberal social contract theory was driven to the conclusion that once a state was formed, only it could create valid positive law.[98] Thus, in whatever form the doctrine of sovereignty appeared, it "implied the denial of original materially and juridically defined orbits of competence of the State and the other spheres of life."[99] By implying that all other types of law were mere derivatives of state law, it violated the central principle of juridical sphere sovereignty. Sovereignty is construed as indivisible and thus universal in scope.[100]

The exaggeration of the domain of state law presupposed in the absolutist theory of sovereignty is implied in what Dooyeweerd views as the pernicious notion of *"Kompetenz-kompetenz."* This notion, familiar in early-twentieth-century German jurisprudence, means simply the competence to determine the scope of one's own competence.[101] Its implication that there is no law beyond the state to which appeal can be made amounts to a claim for a "pseudo-juridical omnipotence." The authority of the state, so conceived, violates the norms of the juridical aspect and is reduced to "juridically *unlimited political power.*" Neither the invocation of the principles of natural law nor the concept of legal self-restriction is any use since both fail to establish external positive legal constraints on the state. The problem is that the state itself has been absolutized.

Dooyeweerd's version of the idea of the *rechtsstaat* is designed to prevent such an absolutization. A genuine law-state is one in which the limits to its lawmaking competence are acknowledged as intrinsic to its very nature: "in the true idea of the law-State, the divine structural principle of the body politic limits the peculiar universality of the internal public law to a universality and sovereignty within its own sphere of competence."[102] It is political sphere sovereignty that establishes a true *rechtsstaat,* setting material limits to what the state can lawfully do. Dooyeweerd thus advances what has been called a "material idea of the law-state."[103] It is to be contrasted not with a "welfare state" or a "culture state," neither of which it necessarily excludes, but with a "power state."[104]

A *rechtsstaat,* however, is so not only in a material but also a formal sense. The latter sense refers to constitutional and procedural rules— such as the rule of law, the separation of powers, due process, administrative justice, and so on—that aim to guarantee the realization of material legal principles by preventing arbitrary government actions. These cannot guarantee a *rechtsstaat* apart from material principles, but they can make it more difficult for such principles to be transgressed. For example, an extension of the scope of delegated legislation (in itself a necessary development) might if unchecked indeed threaten material legal principles.[105]

The various material spheres of legal competence within society cannot be seen as derived from the positive law of the state or any other juridical sphere. Any formulation of law presupposes the original competence of the juridical power capable of positing it, and this power is determined and materially limited by the structural principle of the societal structure exercising it. "As an *original* jural power—not derived from any other temporal sphere of life—it may be called *sovereign.*"[106] Dooyeweerd thus understands "sovereignty" to mean not universality of scope but *originality of source.* There exists a *plurality of legal "sovereigns,"* each possessing an irreducible original competence to form law within its own sphere. "Juridical competency is essentially never absolute or exclusive. It premises a number of original orbits of competency that are in jural relations of mutual circumscription and balance."[107]

What follows from this is that an important part of the legal task of the state here is simply granting public-legal space for such orbits of competence to function freely. This may occur through a variety of legal instruments. One of these is the recognition of the "legal personality" of certain communities, such as where an association requires civil-legal status in relation to third parties and thus needs to be brought within the scope of certain statutory (civil-legal) conditions. Legal personality is not created by such recognition, nor is it derived from state law—it is not a "creation . . . out of a juridical nothing." Rather it arises from the internal nature of the community in question. Some communities—state and church—have no need for such recognition, since their legal personality is not in doubt, and some associations simply lack legal personality on account of their internal structure. On the other hand, it falls to the state as a public authority to exercise a "preventative oversight" in this regard, and this may involve denying legal personality to a certain association deemed harmful to the public interest. But whatever the precise form of recognition by the state, the state must always respect the competence of other societal relationships to create valid positive law within their own spheres.[108] Responsibility for the discharging of a community's legal sphere sovereignty falls, moreover, ultimately to the community's highest organ alone and not to the state. A church, for example, would never be able to rest if the question of the state's competence to interfere within it were to be decided by an organ of the state itself.[109]

Dooyeweerd's version of legal pluralism is both original and fruitful. I test its concrete applicability in the next two chapters. However, an important objection—one leveled against English political pluralists like Laski, Cole, and Figgis—needs to be addressed immediately. This is that the assertion of the existence of a plurality of legal sovereigns after all proves too drastic by, in effect, removing from the state the indispensable *right of legal closure.* If there is any value in the concept of political sovereignty it is surely that for a state to discharge its responsibilities—for it to be a state at all—it must be able finally to settle disputes about the boundaries of the legal competences possessed by other spheres. We may admit that each societal structure is able to govern its internal affairs on the grounds of an original legal competence, and therefore that the state is not the sole source of valid law in a society. A trade union or a church or a university can establish legal rules governing its internal activities, which have a prima facie right to be acknowledged by the state and enforced by the courts. Inevitably, however, claims to legal competence will be disputed. There may be conflicts between different societal structures. For example, a trade union may claim the competence to impose a closed shop in a particular factory, whereas the management may claim that employment policy is a matter of corporate sphere sovereignty ("the right to manage"). And there may be conflicts between one societal structure and the state over the requirements of the public interest. A trade union, for example, will claim that decisions on its internal forms of accountability fall within its own competence, whereas a government may hold that its competence to protect the public interest requires the legal imposition of secret prestrike membership ballots (as Prime Minister Thatcher's government successfully did in Britain during the 1980s). Or a university may claim that whether or not to grant tenure to faculty is a matter of academic sphere sovereignty, whereas the government may regard this as undermining accountability for the use of public money and hence damaging to the public interest.

The point here is not which side in each of these disputes has rightly interpreted the principle of sphere sovereignty but that such disputes inevitably arise and that it falls to the state finally to resolve them. The state must retain the final say in *positivizing* the public-legal boundaries of legal sphere sovereignty. This surely is an inescapable implication of *political* sphere sovereignty. Other societal structures have original legal competence, but only the state also has final legal competence to determine the *positive* public-legal boundaries of other spheres' legal competence. If this is so, however, does it imply that, against Dooyeweerd's protests, the state also has competence to determine the positive boundaries of its own competence—*Kompetenz-kompetenz?*

In the first place, if it did imply this, this would not mean that the executive branch of the government can determine its own competence, for this would be the antithesis of constitutionalism. Dooyeweerd does not develop a full-fledged constitutional theory, but his position seems to lend strong support to, if not require, the existence of a constitutional court with the power to review both executive acts and legislation. Such courts can themselves make mistakes about the boundaries of legal competence, but they often function as an effective brake on arbitrary executive power and are thus likely to be a valuable means of protecting legal sphere sovereignty (assuming, of course, that the constitution itself protects it).

But, second, the implication that the state possesses what Dooyeweerd understands to be *Kompetenz-kompetenz* does not, after all, follow. The reason is that for Dooyeweerd all positive law is subject to "normative legal principles," which receive their substantive content from the structural principle of the social structure positivizing such law. It is, finally, the structural principle of the state that places a normative legal boundary around its legal competence. There is, of course, no positive-legal, constitutional guarantee that the officers or organs of the state at any time will actually respect that boundary. But as such agents engage in the task of positivizing legal boundaries between spheres and between them and the state itself, they remain continually subject to the norma-tive legal principles given in the state's structural principle. The deter-mining of legal competences is a matter of rightly discerning such principles; and much of political debate in democratic systems will, of course, center on what they are.

This point leads us naturally into a consideration of Dooyeweerd's view of the structures of representative democracy. Although his doc-toral dissertation was on the Dutch Cabinet, he unfortunately did not continue this interest in specific issues of constitutional design. But what little he did say about such issues turns out to be instructive.

For Dooyeweerd detailed constitutional matters fall under the analy-sis of the state's *internal* juridical functioning as distinct from its external legal relations with other structures (considered in the next two chap-ters). The sphere of "public communal law," distinguished above, em-braces the following subcategories: constitutional law, administrative law, criminal law, and international law. The first, constitutional law *(staats-recht),* includes the "organizational norms" regulating the structures, competences, and interrelationships of the organs of government. The second includes the "behavioral norms" regulating the relationships be-tween these organs and subjects (and communities).[110] These, he adds, cannot be determined abstractly for all time but must be appropriate to prevailing historical circumstances.[111] The former concern the state's internal sphere of juridical functioning; the latter regulate its external (enkaptic) relations with subjects (and communities).

Dooyeweerd refers to the internal relations as the "juridical forms of organization of governmental authority," and he observes that they vary between the poles of democracy and autocracy.[112] Such constitutional forms have a "typical historical" basis, and "their character is determined by the manner in which the political power is organized; viz. either by the free initiative of the nation itself, which by suffrage and political repre-sentation . . . retains a continuous control over the government, or by an authority which has imposed a certain governmental form upon the people."[113] The basic requirement that a genuine state must be a constitutional state (a *rechtsstaat*) is indeed given in the state's structural principle. And any variable positive forms of constitution "remain absolutely determined by" the state's structural principle. Thus a positive form that founded legal competence on economic power would be ruled out, such as in modern corporatism,[114] as would one founded on functional representation, since these compromise the state's character as a *res publica*. This was the principal burden of his critique of "political pluralism."[115] But the precise form of the constitution of a *res publica* is a matter of historical circumstance.

But a troubling implication of this position arises from the question whether the state should be autocratic or democratic. It turns out that this issue cannot be settled by appealing to the state's structural principle. Democracy, it seems, is not given on the law-side but is only a positive form, the appropriateness of which depends on historical conditions rather than on conformity to a structural norm. I think this view is problematic, but before I examine it critically it is important first to record Dooyeweerd's support for many of the basic procedures and practices of a modern parliamentary democracy.

Three elements of Dooyeweerd's (disappointingly brief) treatments of these matters are worth noting. First and most fundamentally, he holds that governments should be elected by popular vote, and government policy should be subject to the agreement of a parliamentary majority.[116] Although he does not elaborate on the point, there is no question about his commitment to these twin pillars of representative democracy.

Second, he has a high appreciation for the distinctive, and, in modern political systems, indispensable role, played by political parties in the representative process.[117] They "awaken and maintain . . . public spirit," organize electors, discipline political actors, and contribute to the necessary contest of political viewpoints through which policy consensus emerges.[118] It is by serving as organized channels for the propagation of a definite set of political principles that parties make their most effective contribution to the operation of a representative process. A political party is not, essentially (i.e., according to its structural principle), a mere coalition of interests or a vehicle for securing office, nor is it a philosophical association. It is rather "an organization of the unifying power of a political conviction concerning the principles which have to guide the policy of the state."[119] In parties serving only as the mouthpiece for a single class or as an assemblage of pressure groups, the political convictions of the members are likely to be subordinated to the demands of special interests.[120] While a proper degree of party discipline is a necessary implication of defining a party as a community of shared conviction, excessive discipline stifles independent judgment and causes passivity among members. Dooyeweerd also rejects as overly pessimistic the "elitist" analyses of political sociologists such as Ostrogorski and Sorokin: at least in the Netherlands of the 1950s party members, he claimed, still played an influential role.[121] And for him that was at least in part because of their commitment to political principle over mere power seeking. A decline of or indifference to political principle makes for superficial political debate and engagement and weakens party effectiveness.[122]

Third, he acknowledges the indispensable role of "public opinion" in the governance of a state.[123] By public opinion he does not mean the shifting and ephemeral preferences registered in opinion polls but something much weightier, a "national political community of thought" that plays a vital role in establishing a sense of unity in any political community. Public opinion performs a double integrating function within a state. On the one hand, it integrates people with government by uniting them around a shared framework of political conviction oriented to some idea of public justice and rooted in national tradition. Now since governments need to justify their policies to public opinion, they must play a leading role in sustaining it: indeed they simply "cannot govern *in opposition* to a truly national conviction."[124] On the other hand, public opinion also integrates diverse and contending social and political groups among the people. Although political parties are also its "bearers," it "transcends differences of party and of interests"—even to the extent of isolating groups that "deviate from those of the leading circles."[125]

This account evokes an obvious critical rejoinder. It is telling that Dooyeweerd refers only to the leading role of influential political elites in the formation and shaping of public opinion. This overlooks the vital historical role frequently played by popular social movements on the margins of politics, some of whose stances eventually come to be adopted by members of the political elite.[126] And it also ignores the fact that such groups often take a stand precisely in radical opposition to the prevailing "national community of thought," and precisely by appealing to an interpretation of public justice (or some other principle) that that community has wrongly suppressed. This oversight is all the more remarkable in view of Dooyeweerd's location in a tradition of emancipatory political action in the nineteenth century. The neo-Calvinist movements emerging then were indeed genuinely popular, antiestablishment movements with mass memberships. Dooyeweerd does indeed acknowledge that public opinion "is by no means the infallible interpreter of the supra-subjective principles of justice"; it can, for example, be "led astray" by manipulative leaders. He is also right to observe that public opinion "does not one-sidedly arise from a politically amorphous mass with the government standing by as an interested spectator." But an adequate account of the role of public opinion, especially in a representative democracy, surely begs a much fuller acknowledgment of the necessary, and often corrective, role of organized, principled popular democratic initiatives in shaping a political community's appreciation of public justice.[127]

Dooyeweerd does not, of course, pretend to have offered anything like a complete account even of the normative principles relevant to the operation of a representative democracy. Yet the brevity of his discussions, and especially the lacuna I observed in his account of public opinion, intensifies the question noted earlier of why he does not regard democracy as a normative structural imperative for the state (an implication of its structural principle) but only a contingent historical form. Evidently, the dominant concern of his political theory is to resist the overextension of state authority rather than to explore its internal organization, to develop a critique of *absolutism* and *totalitarianism* rather than of *autocracy*. Even so, it seems incongruous to hold that the state's invariant structural principle rules out corporatism and functional representation but not autocracy. For, as he well recognizes, the internal form of organization of a state has a decisive impact upon how it actually exercises its authority. Indeed he specifically observes that democracy provides a more reliable guarantee that a state will respect material legal principles than does autocracy.[128] On the other hand, he also denies that democracy is any firm guarantee against an overextended state. What he favors is a form of constitutional democracy in which popular will is channeled through and limited by justice-embodying constitutional structures. For him it is more important to limit the state's power and authority than to ensure that its actions reflect popular will. Indeed the doctrine of *popular* sovereignty falls afoul of his general criticisms against the dominant doctrine of sovereignty itself. Sphere sovereignty rules out this doctrine since it sets limits to what the people may through government rightfully will.[129]

It is nevertheless noteworthy that in the passage quoted above Dooyeweerd simply records the two ways in which political power comes to be organized—either from below or from above—without indicating whether one might actually be preferable. He holds that the establishment of a territorial monopoly of coercion is an essential normative historical task that every state must complete. But he does not insist that the establishment of democratic structures is also such a task.[130] Now, in one sense, he is right that a genuine state cannot exist without a monopoly of coercion, while it can indeed exist, and dispense a measure of justice, without being democratic. A case could be made, however, that the participation of citizens in the political process is indeed a structural norm—not necessarily an immediate imperative, but at least a normative vocation—implied in the very idea of the state as a *public*-legal community. If the political community is indeed a community of government and citizens, established to secure public justice, then arguably this implies that citizens are *co-responsible* with government in this enterprise. If so, then the evident corollary would seem to be that there should be some institutional mechanism for allowing citizens to participate in pursuing it.

Once again we find resources in Dooyeweerd's own conceptual apparatus to warrant a conclusion he himself did not draw (and might perhaps have resisted). Consider two possibilities. First, Koekkoek, drawing on the idea of the modal opening process, proposes that democracy can be viewed as a "regulative" legal principle, a principle of "legal morality." Specifically, it is an example of the anticipatory deepening of the juridical principle of (the equal possession of) legal personality (*juridische persoonlijkheid*), under the leading of the ethical principle of human dignity (*menselijke waardigheid*). Historically, the recognition of this legal-ethical principle of human dignity led to the gradual extension of the franchise to successively wider groups of citizens, and it still implies further extensions of effective political influence by citizens today.[131] This formulation also appeals to Dooyeweerd's distinction between *concept* and *idea*. The legal-ethical principle of human dignity is an example of "legal morality," the whole of which is governed by the "idea" of justice. Such ("regulative") legal "ideas" disclose certain possibilities of a legal order only gradually and may not be operative in every legal order. They are to be distinguished from legal "concepts," which capture essential ("constitutive") features of all legal orders, including primitive ones.

This formulation, however, may seem to suggest that political orders at an early stage of their development—early modern European states, for example—can be excused, so to speak, for having deferred democratization until a later stage. Put differently, it suggests that such states were not yet under any normative historical imperative to take steps toward introducing participatory or consensual procedures into their institutions. It could be argued, however, that the form in which many such states actually emerged—varying degrees of absolute monarchy—had less to do with normative historical structural unfolding than with a glaring directional deviation from earlier, more participatory and consensual forms.[132] Earlier I drew on Geertsema's critique of the idea of the modal opening process, and this example seems to confirm that critique. If, as Geertsema argues, the full potential of every modal aspect is available at all times, then there is no reason in modal theory to wait for the anticipatory deepening of the principle of legal personality by the principle of human dignity. This is not to say there are no reasons at all to decide, at particular moments, that specific aspects of democratization (in the sense of the establishment of representative institutions) cannot proceed, or can only proceed very slowly. But these, I suggest, will more likely have to do with the process of institutional differentiation than with the modal opening process. This becomes clear from a second possible way forward.

An alternate proposal is to invoke once more the idea of the internal opening process of a social structure. An autocratic state might then be regarded as an immature, or indeed perhaps a retarded, state, one that should be encouraged to aspire to further development into a fully mature public-legal community. Of course, no specific form of popular participation could be seen as a necessary imperative deriving from the state's normative design. But, as with my earlier example of the evolution of the UN, the advantage of this second alternative is that it draws attention to the process of state building as a dynamic historical task that, in many cases, is not yet, but should be, completed. And it also enables us to evaluate the historical development of states in terms of the degree to which popular participation played a role in their emergence. This is not to suggest that every case of imposed political authority is wrong; in a fallen world there surely have been cases where such an imposition was the only way to secure a needed public-legal authority. But it does allow us to mount a critique of the legitimacy of many such impositions, such as nineteenth-century European colonialism or the military conquest of the indigenous peoples of North America.

The second significant issue arising from Dooyeweerd's comments on the internal juridical organization of the state also relates to democracy. Although democracy is not given in the state's structural principle, it is, he insists controversially, a concept of exclusively *political* application. Democratic forms of government are valid only within the state and not within other societal structures such as industry, education, or the church. To establish what we know as political democracy within these institutions would be counter to their distinctive structural principles.[133] Authority relations in each societal structure must display the character of that structure and no other, so that introducing democratic procedures into the family might be as inappropriate as modeling political relationships on the parent-child relationship. In such a case it is easy to see that the application of democratic procedures in a particular structure would be harmful to that structure's functioning. Or, within educational institutions, while student representation may be deemed legitimate, academic decisions must surely rest with academic (and not administrative) staff. And most would agree that the decisions of the church on matters of doctrine should not be made on the basis of majoritarian voting procedures. In other contexts democratic forms might be thought more appropriate. Indeed Dooyeweerd does hold that particular forms of participation in decision making *(medezeggenschap)* are legitimate in certain communities, and his commentary on their applicability in industry will prove an instructive case study in chapter 10. This will serve as a leading instance of the concrete exemplifications of his theory of the state. Before we consider them we need first to explore closely the meaning of the central norm by which they are to be guided, the norm of public justice.

TEN

AN ACTIVE, LIMITED STATE

THE MEANING OF PUBLIC JUSTICE

Dooyeweerd defines the state as a differentiated, organized, public-legal community, marked by a juridically qualified structural principle. Its public-legal leading function implies the norm of public justice, and this norm should direct the state in all its activities. The nuclear moment of the juridical aspect is characterized as retribution, meaning the harmonious balancing of different juridical interests. The state's defining responsibility—its destination—is to realize such a harmonious juridical balance in the *public* realm.

Various interlocking concepts make their appearance in Dooyeweerd's discussion of public justice.[1] In addition to juridical harmonization, the most important of these are the distinction between internal functions and external relations; the principle of sphere sovereignty; the idea of the public interest; the distinctions between "structure" and "purpose" or "task" and "typical" and "atypical" tasks. It proves to be no easy matter to clarify precisely the meaning or interrelation of these concepts. After attempting a reconstruction of these various elements I propose an important clarification that both shields Dooyeweerd from an obvious objection and opens the door to a fruitful interchange with the Catholic notion of the common good.

A first step in attempting to clarify this idea is to underline the distinction between the internal functions of the state and its external enkaptic relations. Dooyeweerd, however, sows needless confusion at this point by failing consistently to respect the distinction between the relations obtaining in the internal sphere of the state—those between government and citizens or between different branches of government—and those obtaining outside this sphere, that is, those between the state and other kinds of societal structures with different leading functions (or persons acting in nonpolitical roles). There is, for instance, a fundamental difference between the government's relationship to its citizens expressed in electoral legislation and the state's relationship to a school expressed in compulsory curricular standards. Dooyeweerd does recognize the difference between internal and external relations, but he misleadingly refers to some of the latter as its "modal aspects." In his exposition of these modal aspects,[2] he cites illustrations of both internal relations and external relations.

The state's regulation of private economic structures is also misleadingly cited as an example of the internal economic functioning of the state.[3] A correct example of internal economic functioning would rather be the state's own housekeeping activities, such as raising taxes.[4] Of course, the two have significant effects on each other—fiscal policy is one determinant of company performance—so that it is tempting to abandon the internal/external distinction entirely. Dooyeweerd's point, however, remains a sound one. In raising its own revenue, the state is requiring its citizens to fulfill the proper duties of membership in the political community. Without such revenue the state could perform no functions at all since it could not even pay its officials. By contrast, in regulating private industry, the state relates enkaptically to independent economically qualified societal structures. This is not part of the state's internal economic life. Similarly, a valid distinction can be made between a balance of payments deficit and a budget deficit. The former refers to the national accounts, the latter to the government's own accounts.

This distinction is crucial to maintaining a clear boundary between state and society, as public and private realms respectively. I have noted Dooyeweerd's rejection of both individualistic and universalistic conceptions of society and his own view that society is not a whole with its own internal structure but a network of complex enkaptic interrelationships between structures such as schools, families, unions, political parties, and so on. The state is not involved in all these enkaptic relationships, and my focus is only on those in which the state is involved.

In Dooyeweerd's view both universalism and individualism misconceive the enkaptic character of the relationships between state and other
structures. In universalistic theories societal structures are viewed as
parts, which are dependent upon the state as an all-inclusive whole. On a
consistent universalistic theory the state is in principle entitled to regulate all areas of any human activity. Aristotle, for instance, conceived of
the household as part of the political community and proposed that citizens be divided into compulsory occupational classes with the government regulating compulsory common meals.[5] Since parts lack rights
against the whole, this is to undermine the independent rights of the
family and of economically qualified structures. By contrast, individualistic theories reduce the state to an association of privately contracting
individuals. Whereas in universalism persons and structures are viewed
as subordinate to the state, in individualism the state is viewed as an instrument of individual purposes. Its raison d'être is ultimately the legal
regulation of private interindividual property relations. Thus in classical
liberal economic theory

> non-political civil society . . . was exclusively considered from the
> economical viewpoint as a system of free market relations. But
> its foundation was private civil property, whose organized mainte-
> nance and protection was viewed as the chief aim of the political
> association of individuals. The State should not interfere with this
> "civil society," unless to prevent the formation of monopolistic
> market positions, which disturb the natural economic laws.[6]

The laissez-faire principle assumed in this conception leaves no room for
a public-legal regulation of nonpolitical societal structures except insofar
as such regulation protects private property rights. Priority is thus accorded to such rights while the rights of communities are overlooked.
The public-legal regulation of the individual property rights of an entrepreneur, such as by legislation curtailing pollution, is thus seen as undue
interference with the internal sphere of the enterprise by the state. For
Dooyeweerd, however, such regulation consists not of undue interference with sphere sovereignty but rather of a legitimate enkaptic binding
of the enterprise by the state on behalf of the rights of others to enjoy a
clean environment. As such there is no violation of the internal sphere

sovereignty of the enterprise, for only its external relations with persons and structures—its public effects—are affected.

Dooyeweerd's notion of political enkapsis thus proves central to the success of his attempt to chart a genuine alternative to both individualism and universalism. With it he seeks to deny that the state has any original competence in nonpolitical structures while also affirming the competence of the state to regulate externally any nonpolitical structure insofar as its activities have public consequences. The various interests within the state's territory are to be "harmonized," but, he adds, "only insofar as they are enkaptically interwoven with the requirements of the body politic as a whole."[7] Interlacements between the state and nonpolitical structures display a unique kind of enkapsis, namely, "territorial." This is "that particular type of interlacement which is given in the unavoidable binding of the other differentiated societal relationships to the territory of the State."[8] I have already noted a general problem with the notion of enkapsis: the inadequacy of the idea of functional subservience. The same problem arises with the specific idea of territorial enkapsis. It is not at all clear why Dooyeweerd thinks that the territorial relationship between the state and other structures domiciled within it involves these other structures being functionally subservient to the state. We could equally say that the state's functions are made subservient to the other structures, which is just another way of saying that the state is being a state.

There is, however, a valid point that Dooyeweerd makes here, even though it seems not to depend on the idea of territorial enkapsis. It is that universalistic theories that regard the state as the all-embracing communal whole wrongly suppose that its territorial inclusiveness supports their position. Two facts undermine this supposition. First, members of the same family may be of different nationalities and thus not all be citizens (still less "parts") of the same state (and thus have different political rights and duties). This illustrates the general point that "the relations between the State and its citizens may cut straight across the other societal relationships." Second, international organizations such as the Catholic Church, or international interlinkages such as trading relationships or friendships, cannot be considered as parts of the state, since they transcend its territorial boundaries.[9] The point Dooyeweerd is making here parallels that concerning the state's political integration of its citizenry.

This integration is "universal" within the state's territory but does not embrace any other societal relationships into which its citizens enter. When he speaks of the "harmonization" of the different interests within the state's territory he is making essentially the same point. Integration is specifically of a public-legal kind, and this is what he is elaborating with the idea of harmonization.

A general definition of juridical harmonization was given in the previous chapter. *Public* justice is, essentially, *political* harmonization. This is one of Dooyeweerd's more expansive definitions, and it takes us to the heart of his conception of the relation between the state and (civil) society.

> The internal political activity of the State should always be guided by the idea of public social justice. It requires the harmonizing of all the interests obtaining within a national territory, insofar as they are enkaptically interwoven with the requirements of the body politic as a whole. This harmonizing process should consist of weighing all the interests against each other in a retributive sense, based on a recognition of the sphere-sovereignty of the various societal relationships.[10]

Two clarifying comments on this passage are immediately necessary. First, the translation "public *social* justice" is inexact. This phrase appears in the parallel passage in *WdW*, as "*publiek verbandsgerechtigheid,*" which should be rendered as "public *communal* justice." The related term *publiek verbandsrecht* is normally and correctly translated as "public communal law."[11] The use of the term *verband* in both cases refers to the state's character as an organized community. Second, Dooyeweerd confuses the issue again by referring to the "internal" activity of the state, whereas he is in fact referring to the state's external relations with other structures.

The definition still leaves much to be desired. What "public justice" precisely implies for the concrete activity of states is not sufficiently elaborated. This may be partly the consequence of insufficient empirical analysis of functioning states. Dooyeweerd confines his discussion of the state largely to the level of abstract modal analysis and rarely envisages it acting as a structured totality in relation to others.[12] The complex internal structure of the state, with its various organs and agencies (or "partial structures" [deelstructuren])—army, public utilities, regulatory agencies, different tiers of authority, and so on—each with its own particular character, is also largely passed by.[13]

Yet sufficient pointers are provided to allow a general outline to be drawn. In particular, his references to the relation between public justice and sphere sovereignty shed light on his meaning. In the first instance public justice involves *harmonizing the various interests that arise from the legal sphere sovereignty of various social structures*. Whereas private justice within a particular structure requires harmonizing the interests within that structure, public justice requires harmonizing—justly interrelating—all legal interests within the territory of the state.

The term *harmonizing*, however, does not quite do the work Dooyeweerd hopes it will. He stresses it for what appears to be reasons of systematic consistency, namely, because according to his arrangement of modal aspects the legal aspect is immediately founded on the aesthetic, the core of which is harmony. But as I noted, the *economic* foundation of the legal aspect might illuminate more clearly what Dooyeweerd actually has in mind here. We might more felicitously speak of a frugal or non-excessive balancing of legal interests. The state's responsibility to render justice to each legal interest could then be described, more evocatively, as preventing the excessive satisfaction of each of these interests at the expense of others. When justice is done there will be such an element of "frugal tribution." When *public* justice is done frugal tribution will be rendered to each and all within the state's territory. The legitimate juridical interests of all persons and structures within this territory will be satisfied insofar as they are rendered what is their due and insofar as the satisfaction of any such interests does not infringe those of others.[14]

The state, then, has to weigh carefully various interests against each other, ensuring that none receives more or less than its due. The criterion of what stands as a legitimate juridical interest, of what actually is a person's or a structure's due, must be determined with reference to the normative nature of the various social structures. Unlike the prevalent concept of "interest" in much contemporary empirical political theory, Dooyeweerd's concept thus has thick normative content. The phrase "juridical interest" implies a normative claim, which may or may not be currently guaranteed in positive law or otherwise secured by positive legal provisions. If it is not, then the state is under an obligation to adjust the law accordingly. The norm of public justice is thus a dynamic norm by which to guide the formation—and, of course, democratic critique—of law and public policy. Specifically, the legitimate juridical interests of a person or structure will consist of or be an implication of their various distinctive *rights, duties,* and *competences.* Where their rights are violated, their duties obstructed, or their competences removed, the state has the duty to act on their behalf. This could require, and has required, bold corrective political action across numerous fronts. For example, the abolition of legal barriers to the formation of trade unions in the nineteenth century followed the recognition that unions were fulfilling a legitimate duty in advocating for the rights of workers, pursuant to which they required the appropriate civil-legal standing.[15]

Public justice, then, requires the state to acknowledge the legitimate rights, duties, and competences of persons and structures and to create the necessary legal protection for them to realize or fulfill them. The state is not responsible for the *internal* legal domain of a social structure; it may not impose compulsory dieting on persons or families, or set prices for private industries. It lacks the competence to fulfill such internal responsibilities and is empowered only to establish legally the external, public conditions in which these can be adequately pursued. This includes ensuring that no structure overrides the legitimate sphere of another. The state is to create a network of just interrelationships between the various social structures and persons within its territory. Not only is the state to refrain from violating the sphere sovereignty of other spheres, but it is to prevent any other structure from violating such sphere sovereignty.

Ensuring public justice, however, involves more than simply legally protecting the boundaries of other spheres. It is quite clear that Dooyeweerd recognizes this, but his attempts to characterize it are undeveloped and ambiguous. The account I have presented so far might, in itself, suggest a too narrow conception of the role of the state, as if this role consisted exclusively of legally adjudicating among various rights, duties, and competences of *private* social structures and persons. But there is no doubt that Dooyeweerd envisages the state's role embracing a wide variety of activities going beyond the adjudication of private legal spheres. I noted that the essence of the idea of public justice is the just interrelating of diverse juridical interests. I have not, however, yet considered his vitally important conception of the legal status and claims of the *"public interest."*

In various places Dooyeweerd discusses at length the traditional concept of the *salus publica,* or public interest (Dutch: *publiek belang*).[16] The central emphasis in his discussion of these concepts is that the principle of the public interest must be understood as being determined and constrained by the criterion of public justice. In his view the public interest has historically proven itself a dangerously unstable political concept, employed to justify all kinds of intrusions into the rights and freedoms of persons and structures. "The slogan of the public interest was the instrument for the destruction of the most firmly established liberties *because it lacked any juridical limitation.*"[17] To prevent such abuses the principle must be firmly tethered to the structural principle of the state, apart from which it can provide no defense against an arbitrary state.[18] The public interest must be juridically circumscribed, and "can never warrant an encroachment upon the internal sphere-sovereignty of non-political societal relationships."[19] Thus circumscribed, it must be recognized as "a material legal principle of public communal law"[20] rather than a merely formal or procedural boundary, as the formalist school of legal philosophy held.

What, then, is its material content? At times his account seems sadly lacking in clarity. Consider this definition: "The *salus publica* . . . is a political integrating principle binding all the variable political maxims to a supra-arbitrary standard. It binds the entire activity of the State to the typical leading idea of public social justice in the territorial relations between government and subjects."[21] That is, the principle of the public interest binds the state to the norm of public justice. But we have just heard him claim that the public interest is *itself* supposed to be bound by the norm of public justice, in which case he seems to be caught in a straightforward circularity. Elsewhere, the public interest is described as requiring both a recognition by the state of the sphere sovereignty of other societal structures and a balancing of the burdens laid upon various societal interests as a result of state action.[22] But, as we have also seen, both are already implied in the idea of public justice, so again such remarks seem to add little of substance.

A third definition introduces the further idea of "distributive justice." The public interest has both a positive and a negative sense. Its positive sense implies the idea of distributive justice, which "requires a proportional distribution of public communal charges and public communal benefits in accordance with the bearing power and merits of the subjects."[23] The negative sense prevents public law from becoming subservient to specific group interests and the state from exceeding its sphere of competence.[24]

The idea of distributive justice does seem to introduce a new element. It refers to the distribution of benefits and burdens arising from "public communal law," that is, from law that determines the rights and duties of people in their capacity as members of the political community—taxation, military service, political participation, and so on. The sense of public justice discussed above referred principally to the task of (retributively) balancing those juridical interests arising from membership in communities and relationships other than the state (i.e., private communities and persons), such as the rights of trade unions against those of employers. On the other hand, distributive justice so defined can be seen simply as the application of public justice to the internal functioning of the state, and if so, then it clarifies the meaning of public justice but does not introduce a substantive new public-legal principle.

Dooyeweerd does, however, clearly imply an independent and substantive meaning for principle of the public interest in his occasional concrete illustrations. Referring to the state's responsibility for public health, he says that the government must "weigh the various private legal interests carefully against each other, *and against 'the public interest,'* in a retributive sense."[25] And he envisages the state's construction of a railway embankment as being justified in "the public interest" (while adding that if private property is damaged in the process, its owners should be compensated).[26] A third example is of a particular industry legitimately being operated by the state, even at a loss, if "the public interest" required it.[27] These examples appear to imply that "the public" *is itself a bearer of a distinct interest,* amounting to more than just the balancing of private interests (and also more than the internal public-legal interests of members of the political community). This is an essential claim for him to make in order to sustain the coherence of his notion of public justice.

What exactly does he mean by "the public interest"? On the one hand, it is clear that he does not mean by it what classical liberalism means. He points out that the term should not be interpreted in the quantitative sense of the aggregation of private interests, for this would reduce the task of the state to the maximizing of the sum of private interests.[28] On the other hand, he equally repudiates any universalistic understanding of "the public," according to which it is seen as an individual totality with its own internal structure (generally he uses the term *public* not as a noun but as an adjective).

The most obvious route to grasping his meaning is to interpret "the public" in the light of his references to the state as a *res publica*. The idea of the public interest, I noted, is for him historically linked to the emergence of the state as a differentiated public community and the corresponding disappearance of undifferentiated communities, which restrict the freedom of the individual person. The public is, then, the arena in which the free citizenry of a political community exist independently from any other community. As a member of a particular family, church, or other body, a person does not function in the public arena, but insofar as her activities go beyond any of these particular communities or relationships (and are not part of the sphere of personal freedom), then she does.[29] The public is not a body of specific persons but a *realm* or space into which anyone may enter in certain capacities and circumstances. This realm, Dooyeweerd rightly observes, stands in need of public-legal protection and in this sense may be said to have its own juridical interests. These are neither—as individualism would have it—reducible to an aggregate of private interests nor even to a just balancing of private interests, and nor are they—as universalism would have it—the interests of a supposed social structure called "the public." The public interest is the interest of the public realm, a realm in which all persons and structures necessarily participate but which by no means exhausts the entirety of the interests of such persons or structures.[30]

This clarification of Dooyeweerd's meaning helps exhibit the full scope of the idea of the public interest as a discrete but integral element in the "retributive harmonizing of legal interests." Thus, in Dooyeweerd's own example above, promoting public health clearly involves a greater range of state action than can be comprehended simply in terms of justly interrelating the health interests of private individuals or organizations.

An immunization program, for instance, is intended not only to protect individuals qua individuals against disease but also to protect public space against the spread of infections. It is exactly that category of state action that goes beyond the adjudication of *private* interests to which the term *public interest* primarily refers.[31] This will be confirmed as I explore a related concept, the "task" of the state.

THE TASK OF THE STATE

Dooyeweerd distinguishes between the enduring *structure* of the state and the variable *task* of the state. The structure determines what the state essentially is; the task concerns rather the variable purposes and goals—not to be confused with its modal functions[32]—that it may pursue in conformity with its essential structure. These purposes cannot be *derived* from its structural principle but rather are determined by the changing demands of historical circumstances. The principles of public justice and public interest are implied in the enduring structural principle of the state, circumscribing its competence. But the task of the state—its concrete realization of these principles by means of policy and legislation—cannot be given a universally valid circumscription. While the principle of the public interest is indeed universally valid, its "positive contents" depend upon "an intricate complex of variable socio-cultural conditions."[33] The universally valid circumscription of the competence of the state places a boundary around the scope of its task, whatever the contents of this task may be.[34] The state's competence is given by its public-legally qualified structure, but its task is not.

> Externally the task of the State cannot be delimited in a universally valid way, because the body politic, as a real organized community, functions in all the aspects of temporal reality. . . . [I]t is impossible even to exclude the State from the spheres of morality and faith. . . . [It] may promote the interests of science and fine arts, education, public health, trade, agriculture and industry, popular morality. . . . But every governmental interference with the life of the nation is subject to the inner . . . law of the body politic, implied in its structural principle. This . . . delimits the State's task of integration

according to the political criterion of the "public interest," bound to the sphere-sovereignty of the individuality structures of human society.[35]

The distinction between structure and task underlies Dooyeweerd's critique of "theories of the purposes of the State."[36] Such theories err because they confuse the enduring structure of the state with its variable task or purposes. Classical liberal natural law theory, for example, is guilty of conceiving of the purposes of the state as strictly confined to the "organized protection of the 'innate absolute human rights' of all the citizens to freedom, property and life."[37] Such purposes can never define the state's task in a universally valid way. While the "intrinsic destination" (the qualifying function) is an "essential factor of the internal structure" of a thing, its "external teleological relations, on the contrary, can only concern its reference to other beings. . . . Such *ends* lie outside the internal structure of the actual thing."[38] In the case of any organized community the leading function "should not be misinterpreted as the end or ends that human beings try to reach in this relationship by means of their organized endeavours," a point especially important in the case of the state.[39]

The two must not be confused because internal structure is the *condicio sine qua non* for external purpose.

> The question what concrete subjective purposes a body politic has to realize at different times and in different places presupposes the internal structure of the State as such. . . . A State cannot serve any "purposes" if it does not *exist as such*. And it can have no real existence except within the cadre of its *internal structural principle* determining its essential character.[40]

The task and purposes of the state, as historically variable phenomena, can never in themselves define the invariable structure of the state. Whatever the state may have to do in concrete terms, the boundary of its competence remains unchanged, and this is given by the norm of public justice.

I already noted that a problem with the structure/purpose distinction is that what Dooyeweerd describes as structure (indeed the very word *destination*) sometimes seems very close to what normally is understood as purpose. However, it is possible to distinguish between the essential or defining purpose of a structure (what Clouser terms its "structural purpose")—that which makes it what it is and which it always necessarily pursues—and the varying particular activities in which it engages in pursuit of the defining purpose. What Dooyeweerd here has in mind is clearly the latter. Thus public justice could be described as the defining purpose of the state, while supporting public health or providing roads could be seen as particular applications of it. And the word *task* seems as good as any other (*role*, for instance) in capturing such diverse and varying particular applications.

Thus the distinction between structure and task seems plausible enough. There is a valid distinction between a political norm intended to guide the state and the concrete activities involved in applying the norm. The norm might be seen as of universal application, whereas many particular activities could not be so seen.

A particular problem arises, however, because Dooyeweerd seems in two places to suggest that certain aspects of the state's task (some of the "positive contents" of the public interest) fall *outside its competence*. The suggestion appears in his discussion of yet another distinction, that between the "typical" and the "atypical" functions of the state.[41] In this distinction we see Dooyeweerd once again attempting to come to grips with aspects of the state's role that seem not to be obviously embraced under public justice. Referring to the public juridical qualification of the state, he writes:

> This internal criterion for the delimiting of the task of the government can only be of service *insofar as this task falls within the internal sphere of the state community.* But the difficulty is precisely that the state also necessarily performs functions in human society, which indeed fall outside its original sphere of competence as a public legal community, but which cannot be separated from its task.[42]

He cites here the example of the purchase of goods (such as, perhaps, government property) necessary in the state's internal sphere of political

economy *(staatshuishouding)*. In engaging in such activities, he continues, "the state no longer moves within its original internal sphere of competence" but acts as an economic agent alongside economically qualified
structures. Hence it may not apply its governmental authority here: it
must, for example, pay the market rate.[43] In entering into such economic
or other relationships, it must respect the sphere sovereignty of the social
structures to which it is relating. There is, then, a distinction between
typical and *atypical* sides of the task of the state: "the state's task also
covers spheres which fall outside the typical nature of the state."[44]

Atypical tasks thus seem to fall outside the state's competence. If
we interpret this to mean, oddly, that the state's task includes things for
which it has no competence, then A. C. de Ruiter's conclusion seems indeed correct.

> The meaning of the distinction is that, while the typical tasks can
> be subjected to the (internal) delimiting criterion for governmen-
> tal competence, the others cannot. . . . [E]xclusively reserving the
> delimiting norms for the government to the internal or typical
> functions of the state substantially decreases the worth of these
> norms.[45]

De Ruiter rightly indicates here that Dooyeweerd implies that there are
no structural norms for the state's atypical tasks. And yet throughout *NC*
he is emphatic that *all* activities comprising the task of the state ought
to be guided by the public juridical qualification of the state.[46] But if
atypical functions fall outside the state's competence, by what criterion
can such functions be normatively defined, and thus limited?

We may first raise the question of whether Dooyeweerd needs to
make the concession he appears to be making. Consider the above example, the purchase of property for government use. It is hard to see in
what sense this act falls outside the state's original sphere of competence.
The fact that the state pays the going rate for a property, respecting the
sphere sovereignty of economic structures and relationships (the property market, in this case), rather than confiscating or compulsorily purchasing it, does not imply that it is acting beyond its sphere of competence but simply that it is respecting the competence of other structures.

It is surely within the state's competence to acquire those resources needed for it to fulfill its own administrative functions.

This, however, seems a poor example of what Dooyeweerd probably intends. A better one would be the operation of a nationalized industry, which, as noted, Dooyeweerd did not in principle rule out. This may legitimately be done not to facilitate the state's internal functioning (not, for example, to raise revenue—which is, of course, sometimes the actual reason) but with a view to the public interest. Here too the state must respect economic sphere sovereignty if the industry is to function properly. But it is not essential to the nature of the state that it operate any nationalized industries. The question is whether, on his theory, the state is after all competent to nationalize an industry, build a university, operate a postal service, run hospitals, sponsor the arts, and so on. Can these kinds of activities be seen as required by the norm of public justice, as examples of the just balancing of juridical interests? Which rights, or other juridical interests, are involved in the operation of postal services, or the building of roads, or the funding of theatres?

It is certainly true that if the government does any of these things it must do so in a manner that treats the juridical interests of the relevant persons or structures equitably. It should not, arguably, dole out huge subsidies to opera companies while starving community theatres of funds or bail out loss-making car companies while driving efficient farmers out of business. And it is also clear that the government must act in a manner that respects the sphere sovereignty of the parties involved. It must not, for instance, tie the funding of the arts or education to any test of political correctness. The norms of public justice and the principle of sphere sovereignty here seem plausibly clear criteria that government action must, once undertaken, satisfy. But it is not clear that the kinds of activity in question are themselves actually *required* by the norm of public justice, that a government steering itself exclusively by public justice would be *obliged* to undertake them. The provision of a public postal service may be in the public interest, but it is not easy to see how private juridical interests would be unjustly unbalanced in its absence.

So we reach a conclusion similar to that reached when probing the meaning of the public interest: many things rightly done by the state cannot be conceived of as cases of the just balancing of the private juridical interests of persons and communities. The notion of atypical tasks of the state seems to be introduced by Dooyeweerd as a way to capture what we have now seen are essentially public-interest-protecting activities. But the term *atypicality* proves misleading, as it implies that the state can sometimes go beyond its own competence. We can see that Dooyeweerd's problem here is that he has not sufficiently drawn out the implications of his own passing recognitions that the public interest has an independent, substantive meaning not derivable from or reducible to adjudicating among the private juridical interests of persons and social structures.[47]

I have shown, then, that public justice is for Dooyeweerd *the* definitive political norm of the state, arising directly from its public-legal qualifying function. I noted his vitally important (if undeveloped) recognition that it is necessary to appeal to a substantive idea of the public interest (or some alternative) to justify central aspects of the state's legitimate task and that the meaning of the public interest cannot itself be derived from that of public justice but carries its own independent material content. The public realm is itself a bearer of legitimate juridical interests. It brings with it claims of its own that need to be balanced *alongside* those of persons and structures. The juridical claims of the public interest can neither be *reduced* to a complex of interests attaching to private persons and structures nor automatically or surreptitiously *take precedence* over them. This formulation makes the best sense out of the key quotation cited earlier, where Dooyeweerd acknowledges that government must "weigh . . . various private legal interests carefully against each other, *and against the 'public interest,'*" in a retributive sense.

In the remainder of this chapter I examine a selection of Dooyeweerd's specific applications of public justice. In these, both the central intent of and the difficulties with his understanding of the competence and task of the state are brought into sharper focus. The first step in each case is to trace how Dooyeweerd identifies the irreducible identity of the structure in question. Public justice cannot be done to particular structures unless the sphere of their legitimate rights, duties, and competences—their legal sphere sovereignty—is correctly discerned. Of course, the exact content of such spheres was already widely disputed in Dooyeweerd's time, and he himself engages in such disputation, especially in the case of the church and industry (today the nature of the family is at the center of the storm). The general ideas of sphere sovereignty and public justice do not themselves resolve those debates, but they do, I suggest, frame them in an illuminating if not necessarily conclusive way. As I proceed, I point out in each case aspects of Dooyeweerd's accounts of these structures that invite critique. Of the four examples I consider, the second, third, and fourth are instances of the state's relating to particular communities possessing their own structural principles: family, church, and industry. I begin, however, by exploring an important and instructive exception: the nation.

State and Nation

The passages in *NC* where Dooyeweerd discusses the concept of the nation are among the denser and more obscure in his account of the state. Before examining these, however, it is worth turning to his more popular account in *Roots of Western Culture,* which on its face has a quite different accent. That accent no doubt derives from the audience he was addressing through what were originally short articles, published from 1948 to 1951, in a popular postwar journal he himself edited for a period of time. The context was the debate about Dutch postwar reconstruction, and Dooyeweerd found himself responding to an increasingly influential view, represented by the Dutch National Movement, that prewar religious distinctions (Calvinist, Catholic, Humanist) should be set aside in favor of developing a national consensus to guide the process of reconstruction. In the course of responding to this view, Dooyeweerd had occasion to reflect on the meaning of the Dutch nation, and these reflections appear, at first sight, to express a familiar and widely held *cultural* definition of nation.

We have seen that for Dooyeweerd the process of differentiation is accompanied by a process of individualization, of both social structures and persons. It is also witnessed in the emergence of distinct national cultures, in a process of "national individualization": "'National' consists of the *individuality* of a people characterized by a common historical experience and a disclosed community of culture."[48] A national culture is not a community with its own structural principle,[49] although the historical clarification of such a culture over time is indeed a normative task. Particular national cultures may, of course, contain antinormative traits, yet, notwithstanding this caution, Dooyeweerd still asserts: "The norm for the formation of a nation consists in a *type* of cultural individuality which *ought* to be realized with increasing purity as the *special calling* of a people."[50] He then presents a self-congratulatory description of the *Dutch* national type, insisting that one of its essential features is a "spiritual earnestness" that resists pragmatism and nurtures a "principled orientation" in different sectors of society. He is referring here to what has been termed the system of "pillarization" *(verzuiling)* in Dutch society, and the point of this line of thought is to argue that the Dutch National Movement's proposal to abandon prewar "principled orientations" is actually in conflict with the Dutch national character.[51] The invocation of this distinctively cultural definition of the nation is perhaps understandable as a useful rhetorical move in such a context. It stands in tension, however, with his more extended, technical account in *NC*.

Dooyeweerd's basic position in *NC* is itself quite clear, but making sense of its detailed ramifications involves a degree of imaginative reconstruction. The issue arises as he (laboriously) works his way through a series of examples of the "modal aspects of the state," and his discussion of the nation falls under his treatment of the state's moral aspect. Here we find again an example of his tendency to confuse the internal functioning of the state and its external enkaptic interlacements. He is clear, however, that the state does indeed function internally, and subjectively, in the moral sphere.[52]

In the previous chapter I introduced his notion of a "people" *(volk)* as constituted by the public-legal integration of all citizens in a territorially delimited area. The state organizes a people within a territory into a single public-legal community, membership of which is held irrespective of family relations, church membership, beliefs, occupations, social class, or status. A people has no independent existence apart from the government and vice versa.[53] In fact, the Dutch term *volk* can be translated either as "people" or as "nation," and Dooyeweerd typically uses these terms as synonyms. This indicates the most obvious apparent contrast between his account of the nation in *Roots* and that in *NC*, in which nation is defined as a political rather than cultural or ethnic reality. "A real nation never lacks a political organization," Dooyeweerd writes.[54] No nation exists prior to the process of the formation of a state, and for this process to get under way a condition of societal differentiation must obtain.

> A nation is not a natural community. . . . It is the result of a political
> formation which presupposes the differentiation and integration
> of human society. The typical character of a nationality has always
> been formed in the struggle for its internal political integration
> and for its international legal acknowledgement as an independent
> political unity.[55]

While in *Roots* the nation was described as the product merely of culturally formative activity, here such activity is specified as political in
character.

Before elaborating on this definition an initial conceptual ambiguity
needs to be dealt with. Dooyeweerd suggests that state and nation *have
the same radical type*.[56] This is a misleading formulation, since it suggests
that nations are social structures with their own structural principles but
distinct from the state; elsewhere he denies this. Compounding the confusion is his tendency to refer to the nation as displaying genotypical
characteristics.[57] Recall that genotypes are a further structural differentiation within a radical type and are also given on the law-side of reality.
The implication, then, is that there is a category—a radical type—of social structures having the same juridical qualifying function and including states, international political bodies, and nations. This is evidently
not what he intends. But while Dooyeweerd's account *excludes* certain
candidates for the genotypical characteristics of a nation, it does not actually *include* any characteristics that are not simply those of a state. I
think we can consistently read him here as meaning that "nationality" is
simply a unique property (or cluster of properties) of that radical type
of social structure we call the state. Like the various parts of the state—
organs or tiers of government—nationality bears the mark of the state's
juridical qualification since it is only generated in the very process of
state formation.

In any event one of his principal aims in claiming that the nation is
essentially political is to counter a central stream of nationalist theory—
already encountered in the previous section—deriving from romanticism and furthered by the Historical school, according to which the

nation is a prepolitical, natural community embracing all other social structures as its parts. He observes that this view derived originally from Herder who conceived of the nation as "a 'natural organism' with an entelechy of its own, a vital purposive force, in sharp contrast to the artificial organization of the state."[58] Such a view "elevated the subjective individuality of a national character to a norm of its historical development," but in fact this could only be attempted artificially by means of "idealistic construction."[59] This "irrationalistic, universalistic" view is a form of biological reductionism, elsewhere termed "organicism." Dooyeweerd identifies the problem with it thus:

> In what sense can we speak of a national science, national fine art, a national industrial life, a national Church, etc? Does this really mean that there exists an all-inclusive national community which as such is independent of any organization? If so, why has nobody succeeded in discovering any tenable criterion of such an all-embracing national whole?[60]

This version of universalism commits a characteristic error: it misconstrues the relationships existing between the nation and the various structures comprising these different spheres of social life as *parts* of the nation, whereas in fact they are complex *enkaptic* interlacements.[61] Again, we need to clarify that Dooyeweerd is not suggesting that such interlacements exist between those structures and the nation construed as an entity distinct to the state. He can only be referring to interlacements between those structures and the *state*. And his point is sound: contrary to organicist universalist theories, the relationship is not that of a part to a whole.

But is the notion of "national spirit" *(volksgeest)* or "national character" seized upon by such theories entirely false? Not so, Dooyeweerd implies. Here the two accounts begin to seem less contrasting. Indeed he pays tribute to Herder as the first to discover the phenomenon of "national individuality" and identifies this—as he did in *Roots*—as one of the individualizing tendencies associated with modern differentiation.[62] But now he characterizes national individuality as an example of a *phenotypical variation* found in states.[63] Such variations, as we have seen, typically arise from enkaptic interlacements between structures. It seems, then, that he regards the interlacements referred to above—between the state and scientific, artistic, industrial, religious institutions, and so forth—as lending to the state certain distinctive features. Although his language is both cryptic and elliptical at this point, he seems to be referring to the way in which particular artistic or religious traditions, or particular forms of economic life, as sustained by particular social structures like arts associations or museums, churches, corporations or market structures, and so on, leave their distinctive signature on *political* life. This is not an original insight, but it is important for Dooyeweerd to have recognized it (though identifying such factors as arising from enkaptic interlacements is original). Nor is it wholly convergent with his definition of nation in *Roots,* though we can now begin to see how the two accounts might begin to be harmonized.

Dooyeweerd also identifies other forms of cultural influence on the state (which cannot, contrary to his implication, be classified as *inter-structural* interlacements). These include a common language, religion, or ethnic origin. At one point he suggests there can exist enkaptic inter-lacements between family and social class, yet the latter is also not a distinct social structure with a structural principle. This alerts us to an important categorial lacuna in Dooyeweerd's social theory, namely, his inability adequately to identify social phenomena that are neither individuality structures nor interlacements (nor interlinkages) between them (even complex ones, like a city or a whole society). For example, linguistic communities, ethnic communities, or social classes are palpably important realities in social life standing in need of explanation and analysis, but his social theory seems to offer us meager resources to that end.

In any event his main point here is to deny that features such as shared language, religion, or ethnicity are *essential* structural (genotypical) features of the national state. And again, this point seems eminently sound. As he puts it:

> [A] nation is a people (and not merely a group of persons of the same nationality within a foreign country) which has become conscious of its internal political solidarity irrespective of its . . . ethnic [or other] differences. The present Dutch nation was not born

before the common political trial of the Napoleonic rule melted together the different provinces, which formerly could never conquer
their particularism.[64]

At this point another important question arises. This political conception of nationality might appear to leave little room for the recognition of national or other cultural *minorities* within a state, or even to rule
out the very idea of a multination state. Indeed the Austro-Hungarian
Empire is cited as evidence of the "inner weakness of a pluri-national
state." The state's task of realizing a public-legal political integration is a
question of survival: "It is possible that initially a state embraces different
nations. But if it does not succeed in integrating this difference into a
higher national unity, it contains in itself the germ of political dissolution."[65] It seems that the requirement to establish national political integration takes priority over the protection of particular cultural communities.[66]

One important, and salutary, implication of this priority is that the
status of citizenship can never be made dependent on the membership of
any nonpolitical affiliation, including a cultural or ethnic one. But citizenship is not merely a matter of legal integration. Because the state,
through its national citizenry, functions in all modal aspects, this integration will come to expression in other ways. For example, the psychic
function of the state is manifested in the sentiment of national solidarity,
which emerges from political integration: "The political feeling of national solidarity is a social feeling that . . . binds government, country and
nation together."[67] Such national feeling should shore up citizens' commitment to the norm of public justice.[68] Political integration also comes
to expression in the moral aspect in the form of patriotism, or "love of
country." Such love is not to be reduced to love of a particular ethnic, linguistic, or religious group. Indeed it shows its true character either in the
struggle for an independent state where a political community is already
emerging or in the defense of the state against foreign domination.[69]

Yet, after all, Dooyeweerd is clear that the process of national integration need not rule out the continued cohabitation of different culturally defined communities within the same state.[70] Multination states are
possible, it seems, *so long as a higher political unity holds them together.*[71]
The stance of the state toward such communities is exactly the same as

in relation to any other social structure: to promote public justice.[72] The state should treat the various cultural groups under its jurisdiction equitably, resisting the skewing of law or policy in favor of one or another national group. Thus in the case of multilingual states such as Belgium, which Dooyeweerd cites, the state must integrate different linguistic communities under this norm.

> When the nation has more than one language spoken within its territory, public justice requires the government to strive after peace between these languages. When in its internal policy a government tries to enforce a lingual integration by oppressing one of the competing languages, a particular national group will be tyrannized. Then the government exceeds the limits of its office.[73]

The wider—and now familiar—point at stake here is that the political integration of a nation must never compromise the legitimate independence of nonpolitical social structures. So, for example, when the state promotes a national culture by financing national museums or requiring national history to be part of a school curriculum, it must do so subject to recognition of the "sphere sovereignty of the non-political cultural circles." Such circles must be left sufficiently free to perform their own distinctive (nonpolitical) integrating role in society.[74] Equally, loyalty to the nation—"patriotic feeling" or "love of country"—is never to intrude upon the many other loyalties citizens will rightfully harbor toward the multiple nonpolitical social structures of which they are members and to which they have duties. Love of country is no higher than any other kind of love. Other social structures, like family or church, can and should generate feelings of love on the part of their members, and each structurally specific expression of love is equivalent to all others. While we can love our country, this is entirely compatible with loving other communities, and the former should never be allowed to dominate the latter.[75]

To conclude this assessment of Dooyeweerd's account of the nation, it is necessary to confront his less appealing discussion of state and race. This occurs where he considers the internal biotic functioning of the state (whereas, again, the issue is one of the external relationship between the state and a particular social group). A legitimate claim he makes is that over time a state's people comes to form a special bond with their land, and due to the "biotic coherence of the successive generations,"[76] this bond leaves its mark on them: "The state's population is internally [sic] interwoven with the national soil, and in the long run a bio-psychic type may be formed. This type is not a mere product of nature but the result of formation in a particular political vital area."[77] This point seems to be simply another instance of his general conception of political integration. The phenomenon is not a necessary feature of all states. Nor is it to be conceived "naturalistically": "it is not the 'blood' that creates the nation and the state, but the very opposite."[78] Dooyeweerd emphatically repudiates any form of racial political theory and attacks the "criminal" application of such a theory in Hitler's "inhuman anti-semitic policy."[79]

Yet he also accepts uncritically the contemporary views of theorists such as Sorokin who, he claims, have demonstrated that there are "considerable differences" between races.[80] He then cites the example of South Africa, remarking that there "the ruling white race is confronted with a majority of primitive ethnic groups of black race, mixed race, etc." Notwithstanding the veiled warning concluding the following passage, it is obviously disconcerting to record the absence of any trenchant critique of apartheid in these lines.

> It is difficult to see how in the near future a real national political unity could arise in which all of these different racial groups are integrated. And here again it appears that the natural law ideas of freedom and equality of men cannot be realized without an adequate historical political basis. Such a basis is certainly not present as long as a majority of black people are still in a condition of primitive culture. At the same time it must be established that the condition of such a body politic in which the majority of the people are placed under the guardianship of a white minority and are not really integrated with the latter into a national unity, is extremely precarious.[81]

State and Family

The family (gezin) is one of three natural institutional communities, alongside marriage and kinship or cognate family (familie). All three are founded biotically and qualified morally, and all are found at every period of human history. By "family" Dooyeweerd means the nuclear family—the immediate community of parents and their (minor) children.[82] It is "an institutional moral community of love between parents and their children under age, structurally based upon biotic ties of blood relationship." The biotic blood tie provides a most intimate basis for the moral community of familial love, lending to it "a degree of moral intensity which cannot be matched by any other moral relation" except marriage. Familial love between parents and children is a unique kind of love that cannot be explained simply as love in its general modal sense. It implies reciprocal moral responsibilities and duties of a very particular kind.[83]

Ambiguity is created, however, as Dooyeweerd attempts to explain more precisely the relation between biotic foundation and moral qualification. On the one hand, he claims that in the absence of a biotic foundation there can be no genuinely parental love. But then he saves himself from this obviously unwarranted statement by acknowledging that in the case of foster children such love can be "transferred" to the child;[84] the same, of course, must apply even more clearly to adopted children. Indeed he quite rightly states that parental love ought not to be conceived naturalistically as the outcome of biological causation, since "a biotic complex of factors as such can have no moral effects."[85] Nor should it be regarded as a mere instinctive feeling of sympathy, although this is certainly one of its aspects; and it may be added that such feelings are just as intense in the case of adopted children. Familial love, both that of parents and that of children, cannot be reduced to any of its natural (prelogical) functions but is of a normative character. It is this love, not the biotic blood tie in itself, that establishes the identity and internal unity of the family.[86]

I suggested in chapter 7 that Dooyeweerd's general distinction between natural and organized communities could not be sustained because the organized establishment of natural communities seems as important in their origin as that of what he terms "organized" communities. But I allowed an exception in the case of the family, acknowledging that it does seem to have something like a founding function, in view of its unique, universal foundation in parental procreation. This is not in conflict with a recognition that families depend essentially on moral bonds of love and not necessarily on blood ties. For it can be seen that the examples of foster and adopted children are always regarded as corrective—we might say redemptive—remedies in cases where biological parents either have died or cannot care for their offspring.

A family, like all social relationships, functions in all the modal aspects.[87] It has a social sphere shown in parental respect; a psychic sphere of feeling; a spatial sphere displayed in the reality of the "home"; a legal sphere of rights, duties, and competences; a cultural aspect seen in parental education; and so on. Its functioning in each of these aspects is to proceed under the guidance of its moral leading function. The experience of "home," for instance, cannot be understood as a purely spatial phenomenon; it only has meaning as a domain of moral love. The cultural aspect of the family is seen in the formative influence that parents exercise over children during their early years. This is a unique kind of formation, different from that provided by the school. The molding of character required during the early stages of a child's development can only be provided in the intimate sphere of the family. The state is simply incapable of assuming this responsibility, even though it may be compelled in emergencies to take children into care. It certainly may not compel parents to send their children to state nurseries. Parental nurture decisively conditions the future life of the child and cannot be replaced. Indeed the health of the family has repercussions for other relationships of a communal character. Family life offers an experience of communal solidarity that uniquely prepares children for participating in other communities. "A decline . . . of intimate family life is therefore disastrous to human society in all of its communal relationships."[88]

The role of the state in relation to the family comes to the fore when we consider the legal relationships within a family. These include the competence of parents to direct behavior, the rights of the child to physical and emotional care, and so on, and they cannot be reduced to those within any other social relationship. In the church, for example, legal relationships are to be governed by the church's character as a community of faith, whereas in the state they are to be directed by the state's public-legal structure. Legal relationships in the family are to serve the typical moral bonds that make the family what it is.[89] Thus the authority of parents is "bound to a specific destination: the upbringing of the child under the guidance of parental love."[90]

Accordingly, civil law rightly gives formal recognition to the authority of parents over children. But it also rightly limits this authority by defending the civil rights of the child to adequate provision of food, necessary medical care, and so forth. Where parents are guilty of sustained neglect of these responsibilities, the state is quite within its bounds to remove a child from the custody of its parents.[91] No violation of the sphere sovereignty of the parents would here be involved, for in this case the state is merely fulfilling its own specific responsibilities. Indeed, in such a case, the structure of the family would in effect already have disintegrated. This general principle holds good not only in the area of civil law but also in that of public communal state law. To the civil law justification of such state intervention Dooyeweerd sometimes adds a second, public interest argument, which is that family life plays such a pivotal role in society that it must be protected in the interests of the nation as a whole.[92] Yet, the state's civil-legal competence is limited by the nature of the family: "Civil law cannot give positive rules for the internal family structure of these competencies and duties. . . . Civil justice has to be concerned with external, abstract standards."[93] The state may, for instance, enforce compulsory education and military service on account of the fact that both are essential to its own internal functioning; the first, "because a modern citizenry requires a certain level of elementary education"; the second, "because the authority to regulate [military] service flows immediately out of the inner nature of the state."[94]

The competence of the state—both civil-legal and public-legal—thus finds its limit in the internal communal life of the family. It is important to stress that parental duties are by no means exhausted in meeting such external, abstract standards: "a man who carries out his civil-legal duty of providing sustenance of life has not yet really fulfilled these obligations in the sense of the internal family law."[95] The child has a right to sustenance, but it also has a right to love that implies far more than such minimum requirements. But it is precisely here that the state finds its limit: no state can force a parent to love its child.

A contemporary question evoked by this analysis is whether the state should allow same-sex couples to adopt children. Of course, it is hardly surprising that Dooyeweerd, writing in the 1950s, did not raise the question of whether same-sex couples could legally qualify as parents and so be entitled to foster or adopt children, and as far as I am aware he did not express himself on this question at any later stage. I raise it here merely to illustrate further the kind of question that his framework seems to pose. Given Dooyeweerd's premises, those who would question same-sex adoption would need (among other things) to mount an argument to the effect that sexual and gender complementarity between parents is sufficiently distinctive and important a component in enabling the specific quality of parental moral nurture to come to expression and to be received by children as to warrant public-legal preference. That is to say, the question of the public-legal status of such adoption would not be answered in terms of the moral acceptability of same-sex relationships per se; nor would it be conclusively settled by citing particular instances of successful (for children) same-sex adoptions. It would need to be addressed in terms of the public interest in safeguarding the norm of heterosexual parenting as in the overriding interests of children.

The inevitability and escalating intensity of such debates today indicates another vitally important point about Dooyeweerd's notion of sphere sovereignty, namely, that deeply divergent interpretations of the identity of particular social structures can only be expected to make their presence powerfully felt in political debates in a religiously and morally plural society. The role of the state in a Dooyeweerdian analysis is to reach public-legal resolutions of these debates insofar as they impinge upon the public (civil) rights and duties of particular structures, or more broadly on the public interest. Some religious and moral communities will inescapably find themselves at odds in attempting to discern the structural identities that a just state should respect, and how. This makes Dooyeweerd's view of the relationship between state and *church* of special interest.

State and Church

I have noted that Dooyeweerd holds a particular view of the invisible church *(ecclesia invisibilis)* as the "supratemporal Body of Christ." My initial focus here is on the "institutional church"—the "temporal Church institution." Wider considerations follow from his view of the relation between the state and the "Body of Christ."

To ascertain the proper relation between the state and the institutional church, it is first necessary to understand the latter's structural principle. The church, he claims, is a pistically qualified and historically founded institutional community.[96] The historically formative power on which the church is founded is that of Christ as Word of God.[97] The church's leading function defines it as "an institutionally organized community of Christian believers in the administration of the Word and the sacraments."[98] Everything that the church does must be directed by its character as a community of faith.

The distinctive structural principle of the church is expressed in the character of its authority, which is the authority *of faith.* For this reason the church cannot model its authority structure on that of the state.[99] Dooyeweerd points out both that the officers of the church receive their authority only from Christ and that such authority is that of service to the Word, as distinct from the coercive authority of the state.[100] It is, however, a central implication of sphere sovereignty, as we saw, that *all* social structures receive their authority directly from God. It is also true that the church possesses penal (though not physically coercive) sanctions (e.g., excommunication), though these must be governed by the faith of the church, not by political principles.

The focus here is on the church's internal legal sphere. The notion that the church possesses a domain of law is not in conflict with the idea of a community based on faith, so long as the uniqueness of its existing law is borne in mind.[101] Just as with every kind of law, so also church law is characterized by a retributive harmonizing of interests. The fact that the church is a community of faith (and love) does not mean that norms of justice are inapplicable within it.[102]

Ecclesiastical law is an irreducible type. Since the material content of church law must reflect the distinctive faith qualification of the church, no church ought to submit its internal legal sphere to the public-legal authority of the state.[103] Included in the typical legal domain of the church are, for instance, its internal constitution, the competence of the various office holders, the content of the confession, its disciplinary procedures, and its diaconal duties.[104] So long as its functioning in these areas does not impinge upon either the public or civil law of the state it remains entirely within the domain of the church. Conflict between the legal spheres of church and state can only arise if one or the other attempts to overstep the boundaries of its competence. For example, a civil judge lacks the competence to decide whether an officer of the church is guilty of heresy, since it falls to the church alone to define what counts as *heresy*. He may only pronounce upon whether or not the officer had been fairly dismissed according to principles of civil law (such as "natural justice"). Civil law here "performs an enkaptic function" within the church's legal sphere.

The principle of legal sphere sovereignty clearly rules out the establishment of a particular church by the state, or the claiming of any public-legal authority by the church.[105] Since the church is a community of belief, that is, a *confessional* community, the idea of "a national church uniting the whole nation irrespective of fundamental differences of confession" is excluded.[106] The unity of the church cannot be based upon any external political criterion but only upon the internal criterion deriving from its qualifying function of faith.[107] It may indeed be the case that the spatial boundaries of local churches coincide with the politically determined boundaries of states or municipalities, but this is merely an example of an enkaptic interlacement and does not follow from the internal structural principle of the church. Such interlacements may in fact be positively harmful to the church. It is thus quite wrong for church boundaries to be *determined* (either by a church or by a political authority) according to political boundaries, for the latter kind are fixed according to public-legal criteria that are not definitive for the church and may hamper its work.[108]

The state must respect the juridical sphere sovereignty of the church. But this is compatible with the state's entering into various enkaptic interlacements with the church. Dooyeweerd discusses a case involving the question of a compulsory tax on all baptized members of the Dutch Reformed Church (Hervormde Kerk). He acknowledges that baptism "really establishes a juridical bond of an internal ecclesiastical nature." Yet because baptism takes place without a person's consent at infancy the church has no competence compulsorily to impose such a tax merely by virtue of baptism. Only the state has the power of compulsory taxation on account of its unique, coercive, public foundation. A person can leave the church but not the state. The Dutch Reformed Church, in this case, transgressed onto the state's legal sphere. An appeal to a civil court against the tax, lodged by a person baptized by the church but no longer wishing to remain a member, would thus be quite legitimate.[109] No violation of ecclesiastical sphere sovereignty would be involved if a civil judge ruled in favor of the appellant.

An example of an attempt on the part the church to move beyond its juridical sphere would be the traditional Roman Catholic conception that the legal regulation of all marriages belongs exclusively to the competence of the church. The church is indeed entirely within its rights in establishing its own regulations regarding marriages it performs. But these are necessarily restricted in application to members of that church, since the church lacks the public authority of the state. Apart from the fact that in the church's view marriage requires ecclesiastical sanction, marriage also fulfills nonecclesiastical public roles and is thus rightly enkaptically interlaced with the state's sphere of civil law.[110]

Another interesting question considered by Dooyeweerd in the context of his treatment of the church is whether Christian political parties are compatible with a proper recognition of the legal sphere sovereignty of both church and party.[111] He specifically rejects the idea of an "ecclesiastical party" in the sense of a political party that binds itself to a church confession, as the Dutch Catholic People's Party had done in its 1945 program. This involves an illegitimate subordination of the sphere sovereignty of the party to an outside body, and of the church's confession to a political party. By contrast, Dooyeweerd cited his own Antirevolutionary Party as rightly modeling the proper relationship between party and church. This had certainly bound itself to explicitly Christian political principles, on which the influence of a Calvinist confession was clearly evident, but it rejected any formal linkage with or subordination to any church.[112] A political party certainly functions in the faith aspect, but on this model it does so "not by means of a particular enkaptic binding of the party to a Church authority, but *according to its own inner nature*," namely, by defining for itself the content of its political faith.[113]

But does this imply, then, that the church should keep out of politics? In one specific sense it clearly does: the church, as a community qualified by its faith aspect, lacks competence to be able to "establish principles of a Christian policy or to bind its members to a particular Christian party." Dooyeweerd would thus cavil at the current tendency of church bodies to issue authoritative pastoral advice on concrete public policy questions. Yet in a deeper sense it does not. In a powerful sentence slipped into the above discussion but inviting clarification and amplification, he says: "True, the Church has the indispensable prophetic task to *oppose any manifestation of the spirit of apostasy in political life* and to remind the ... government that its authority derives from God and is subject to Him."[114]

This sentiment adds resonance to Dooyeweerd's keen inclination to underline the state's lack of competence with respect to church confessions. It is here that we encounter his distinctive, and somewhat problematic, conception of a "Christian State." A problem arises in his attempt to balance the insistence on the state's *confessional incompetence* with the necessary recognition that like all social structures the state also functions subjectively in the aspect of faith, on account of which it is impossible for it to maintain a stance of *religious neutrality*.[115] What does this subjective functioning of the state in the faith aspect imply? Many states may be led by false faiths, but it is possible for a state to be led by a genuinely Christian faith, yet without subscribing to any particular ecclesiastical confession. Rather a state functions Christianly in the aspect of faith by acknowledging divine revelation *within its internal political structure.* It is in a *political,* not an *ecclesiastical,* confession of faith that a state can function as a Christian State.[116] This political confession would involve, for example, recognizing God in the state's "public communal manifestations," such as parliamentary prayers, religious national anthems, perhaps even a reference to God in the constitution. In this way the state ought to perform a "Christian political integrating function" in the faith life of the nation, at least "so long as the public national opinion shows a Christian stamp."[117]

We may pose the question here whether Dooyeweerd has correctly—in terms of his own conceptions—identified the nature of the "political faith" that a state must inevitably express. How should a state "acknowledge divine revelation in its internal structure"? Is this not done adequately by committing itself to the divinely established political norm of *public justice* rather than by explicit invocation of Christian language in its official or ceremonial proceedings? If the state is incompetent to favor or disfavor ecclesiastical confessions, is it not also incompetent to favor or disfavor any explicitly confessional language at all? Of course it is possible that a state can, as a matter of fact, be a Christian State in the sense Dooyeweerd intends; and the Dutch state in the mid-twentieth century perhaps qualified as such. But, however inoffensive that might be to the general population, this seems inconsistent with his view of political and ecclesial sphere sovereignty.

My point is borne out by another important claim made by Dooyeweerd. As I noted, he clearly rules impermissible any granting of public-legal status to any institutional church. Indeed he also claims that one of the distinguishing features of a genuinely Christian state is precisely its *lack* of an ecclesiastical confession. A Christian state is one that also respects sphere sovereignty *in the realm of faith*.[118] But respecting sphere sovereignty in the realm of faith cannot only be taken to mean adopting an officially impartial stance toward different Christian denominational churches. It must also imply extending such official impartiality to all religious—indeed in principle all "worldviewish"—communities. Any official (dis)favoring of one worldview confession over another would seem to breach the recognition of pistical sphere sovereignty. And the question of whether public opinion "shows a Christian stamp" seems irrelevant here; these things should surely not be determined by public opinion—even Dooyeweerd's thick sense of public opinion—but by constitutional principle. I am suggesting, then, that the logic of Dooyeweerd's position should incline him to endorse a view of church-state relations closer to the American principle that the state should "pass no law respecting any establishment of religion" than to the "soft Establishment" model typical of many European states until the twentieth century (and remnants of which still survive in a few, for example, England).

This, however, does *not* imply that he should also endorse the currently prevailing liberal separationist interpretation of the relationship between church and state in American jurisprudence. Many observers have already argued, cogently in my view, that the central problem of this interpretation is its ideologically secularist conflation of the (legitimate and necessary) separation of the institutional competences of church and state with the (illegitimate) separation of religion and state.[119] I will not rehearse this specific debate here but simply locate a Dooyeweerdian approach as a particular version of the consociationalist model pursued to greater or lesser degrees in several European states, especially those influenced by Christian Democracy, during the course of the twentieth century.[120] I noted in chapter 2 that such a policy of equitable public pluralism had long been associated with Kuyperian neo-Calvinism and that it had significantly shaped Dutch public policy in a number of areas such as education, health, industrial relations, and broadcasting. Dooyeweerd's stance is an example of this consociational approach to public policy.[121]

The American liberal separationist stance is evidenced, for example, in the standard interpretation of the so-called Lemon test, which rules out any "excessive entanglements" between state and church.[122] This test has been used by courts to rule, for example, against the transfer to churches or faith-based organizations of public funds on the grounds that they have a "pervasively sectarian" rather than a public character. On the contrary, Dooyeweerd's model would regard as plainly discriminatory any inequitable treatment of churches or faith-based organizations in the disbursement of public funds for legitimate public activities such as running schools or welfare services.[123]

By contrast, the consociationalist view shared by Dooyeweerd is premised on the view that among the civil society institutions meriting various forms of protection and support from the state are not only churches but also many social institutions such as educational, welfare, charitable, workers', youth, broadcasting, and other organizations that choose to be governed by a specific religious ethos. Such protection and support ought, on this view, to be accorded to them on an equitable basis with their secular counterparts,[124] and each should also have equitable opportunities to shape the formation and administration of public policy.

The pertinent Dooyeweerdian insight here arises from the notion of sphere sovereignty. While it is common to treat the issue of religious or ideological pluralism separately from that of the pluralism of civil society institutions—the literatures have only recently started to meet—the notion of sphere sovereignty enables them to be treated in a conceptually unified way.[125] This is because one of the many competences arising from institutional sphere sovereignty is precisely the right to decide on the religious or ideological direction that will guide the institution. Put differently, civil society institutions possess the right to corporate religious liberty and its public expression. The onus must be on governments to make a compelling public interest case for confining the expression of that liberty rather than on the institutions themselves to beseech governments to cede it—as if it were in the gift of government in the first place. The liberal separationist view, operating from the unwarranted assumption that public governmental support for institutions like schools, hospitals, and social service agencies must be restricted to their supposed "secular purposes" is likely to lead to creeping, even systematic, infringements of the religious liberty of such institutions. In according rights to equitable public support and democratic participation to a wide range of religious or ideological standpoints, Dooyeweerd's theory is thus free of the kind of sectarian implications that can sometimes accompany religiously based theories. Indeed it lends support to the view that it is secular liberal separationism, with its compulsory exclusion of religious citizens and institutions from full participation in the public realm, that is the truly sectarian position.

The consociationalist model of equitable public pluralism might be thought to exclude in principle the idea of a Christian state. So let me explore whether any credibly legitimate sense of this term might be justified within Dooyeweerd's approach. As I noted, he holds that the presence of the Christian community in the world is not at all confined to the institutional church. The "Body of Christ" may be "supratemporal" in origin but is nevertheless present wherever the Christian faith exercises an influence, including within all and any social structures.[126] Now the state does not relate directly to the Body of Christ, since this is a spiritual community, but only to its particular expressions in (temporal) institutions, whether in, for example, schools or trade unions (or, indeed, in "the institutional church"). In each case the normal rules of engagement arising from sphere sovereignty apply. In a crucial sense, therefore, the normative legal relationship between state and church is no different from that between the state and any other institution: each should respect the other's sphere sovereignty (even when participating in an enkaptic interlacement). And the state respects the pistical sphere sovereignty—the convictional integrity—of institutions like schools, trade unions, political parties, and welfare agencies by recognizing their freedom to govern themselves according to their own directional convictions and not discriminating against them in any way when they do. Directly in the case of political organizations like parties or pressure groups and indirectly in the case of nonpolitical bodies like trade unions or churches, such bodies will quite legitimately enter democratic public debate and shape law and public policy. Insofar as they are Christian organizations, they will presumably seek to influence law and policy in accord with their Christian (political) convictions. In doing so they will, however, merely be exercising identical democratic rights to those of all other religious or worldview communities, whether Christian, humanist, Islamic, feminist, and so on. Where Christians are successful in exercising such democratic influence, there may be aspects of public policy, indeed of the constitutional structure itself, that seem "Christian"; and where "public national opinion shows a Christian stamp" (to use Dooyeweerd's phrase) these aspects may become quite prominent. So it appears that, as long as such influence does not rest upon or issue in any discriminatory policies toward other religious or worldview communities, there is indeed a legitimate, albeit limited, sense—the only one—in which Dooyeweerd could consistently and legitimately speak of a Christian state without compromising his endorsement of equitable public pluralism.

State and Economy

An especially illuminating example of the practical outworking of Dooyeweerd's conception of the role of the state with respect to other structures is found in his contribution to the debate over state regulation of industrial life in the Netherlands. It will be helpful to place this contribution in context by first sketching his broader conception of economic life.

In setting forth this conception Dooyeweerd finds the undifferentiated notion of "the economy" of limited use (on account of its potentially universalistic implications), instead organizing his analysis around the ideas of a distinct economic aspect of reality—of which the central norm is frugality[127]—and of economically qualified social structures and interlinkages. While all social structures (families, churches, states, etc.) and all interlinkages function economically, some are qualified by their economic aspect. The central example is the business enterprise, a voluntary community whose independent emergence is a salutary outcome of the breakdown of undifferentiated economic structures such as guilds and of the accompanying process of individualization—the emancipation of individuals from the confinements of these and other restrictive communal obligations. Out of this process emerges a realm of "free industrial life" in which individual economic initiative is allowed vastly expanded opportunities for expression but which also presents a new challenge of entrepreneurial risk.

Accordingly, Dooyeweerd defines the qualifying function of the differentiated modern business enterprise thus:

> The independent economic entrepreneurial function is inseparably bound to the principle of independent risk and mutual competition. The entrepreneurial profit is the remuneration, perfectly justified in and of itself, for the special economic services which the entrepreneurial system offers to society.[128]

Yet he immediately adds that profit seeking is not the essential purpose of a business. That purpose is the growth of the business in order to supply the needs of consumers, not only by providing for existing needs, but also by "intervening formatively in the human system of needs"—itself possible on account of differentiation and individualization—creating new products and services and so raising the overall level of economic welfare.[129]

This account should not be read as a naive empirical description of how modern business corporations actually operate but rather as a characterization of their normative vocation. Dooyeweerd is well aware of the profound deviations from this and other economic norms under modern liberal capitalism. His critique of classical liberal economic theory is trenchant. This theory, he argues, is a product of the individualism and scientism generated by the humanistic ground motive of nature and freedom.[130] It radically misconstrues not only the structural norms of economic life but also the very meaning of human freedom itself. As a result both of the triumph of economic liberalism in England and of the destruction of guilds and other intermediate structures in revolutionary France, a "thoroughly individualistic" conception of civil society took hold, mirrored in the actual development of capitalism. "Within a short time a new type of person appeared on the scene: the free entrepreneur who was no longer hampered in any of his undertakings. Economic life entered upon a period of immense expansion. But at the same time untold suffering awaited the working class."[131]

The rationalized and absolutized idea of free inter-individual relations dominated the entire industrial sector of Western society and gave it an extremely individualistic and merciless capitalistic form. . . . [U]nrestrained striving after separate interests gave rise to fierce antagonisms. . . . The process of unlimited one-sided technical rationalization in . . . industrial life sharpened the contrast between the interests of labor and capital to a real class struggle.[132]

The urban proletariat became "the victim of limitless exploitation"; labor was "debased . . . to a commodity."[133] "Family- and kinship-life of the laborers were denatured by the encroachment of impersonally rationalized industrial labor-relations."[134] Indeed Marx's analysis of capitalism appeared increasingly persuasive as "the civil-legal order with its basic principles of freedom and equality seemed to be but a legal cover for the deathly class struggle waged in 'society.'"[135]

The individualistic spirit driving these tendencies stands in "irreconcilable antithesis with the Christian idea of free inter-individual relations." Christianity must never seek to make peace with this "kingdom of darkness."[136] On the contrary, it must seek to stimulate and support the necessary countertendencies emerging in response to this individualistic spirit. These countertendencies are in fact but one manifestation—appearing in response to the excesses of nineteenth-century capitalism—of comprehensive, civilization-wide integrating tendencies occurring in modern society.[137] And while such tendencies are certainly required in modern society "for reasons of self-preservation,"[138] they are not in themselves simply corrective. Just as the processes of differentiation and individualization testify to the normative historical unfolding of created social potentials, so too the correlative processes of integration disclose new—and necessary—possibilities for human social interaction.

In the first place, the establishment of differentiated institutional communities—notably the state—and voluntary associations perform a vital integrating function.[139] The state, for example, integrates emancipated individuals into a new political community transcending religious, kinship, or ethnic ties, securing public-legal protection against a damaging economic individualism. And voluntary associations serve as the arena for endlessly varied modes of cooperation among free individuals pursuing numerous specific purposes.[140] Trade unions, in particular, serve to organize worker solidarity in order progressively to "elevate labor to an essential and equivalent partner in the process of production."[141]

The other major category of integrating tendencies is seen among the myriad forms of new interlinkage appearing in modern societies. Among the examples he considers (all too briefly) are the development of fashion, the expansion of science and technology, trade, and the growth of new forms of commercial contract law. Such "horizontal" integrating interlinkages not only come to be established within particular societies but also display an increasingly "expansive cosmopolitan" character.[142]

This "globalization" of integrating interlinkages is, in itself, a healthy development, he holds. Writing in the 1950s, Dooyeweerd did not, of course, use that term. Although he foresees the continual expansion of such tendencies and pays tribute to their likely salutary nature, like most other commentators at that time he could not anticipate the scale of economic injustices occasioned by distorted dimensions of late-twentieth-century economic globalization. But his trenchant critique of nineteenth-century economic liberalism lends itself quite readily to a contemporary critique of the drastic imbalance in the current expansion of the global economy: an enormous enlargement in the geographic scale of profit-driven economic exchanges proceeding apace without a corresponding expansion in the structures of social and political integration to protect vulnerable parties. The effect of this is a profound violation of what Dooyeweerd terms the principle of cultural economy, which, as noted, calls for a balanced historical disclosure of all the various social spheres and indicts any imperialistic expansion of one sector at the expense of others.[143] In later life Dooyeweerd himself recognized such dangers. In an informal interview held in 1974, he pointedly warned against the tendency toward the global concentration of economic power.

> The concentration-tendency has in our time acquired almost demonic traits. On this point history has confirmed Marx's "law of concentration." Here indeed a great danger threatens the identity of the nation *(volksbestaan)*. A Christian government has the undeniable task to intervene here, the moreso because this concentration is occurring in a way which is economically irresponsible. Here is a public interest and even a global interest, for the danger of power-concentrations is still greater because the economy is

increasingly becoming a global economy. This danger can only
be resisted through cooperation among governments in a supra-
national community.[144]

It was important to introduce Dooyeweerd's larger conceptions of
economic life before examining closely his specific analysis of the regulatory role of the state in industry, because the position he took on this
question in the 1950s was often perceived to reflect an anti-interventionist
bias in his thought. It was a subtle position revealing with special clarity
his understanding of the concrete policy implications of public justice.
The debate over the "public-legal organization of industry" (*publiekrechtelijke bedrijfsorganisatie*; henceforth PBO) preceded and followed the
passing of the 1950 Industrial Organization Act *(Wet op de bedrijfsorganisatie)*. Dooyeweerd's writings on this represent his most extensive recent
commentary on an issue of public policy.

The joint influence of nineteenth- and twentieth-century neo-
Calvinist and Catholic social thought created in the Netherlands a strong
current of opinion sympathetic to the pluralist principle of the independent self-government of societal structures, including industry.[145]
Whereas in nineteenth-century Britain matters such as the regulation of
competition, working conditions, and social insurance came to be seen
primarily as the responsibility of the state, in the Netherlands in the nineteenth and early twentieth century such matters were viewed as primarily
the responsibility of the private sphere of industry. The intention was
to avoid the excesses of an unregulated *laissez-faire* policy, not by direct
state regulation, but by stimulating the various participants in industrial
life to assume cooperative responsibility for their internal affairs. Initially
this led to the widespread development of nationwide collective bargaining agreements *(collectieve arbeidsovereenkomsten)* between national employers' and employees' organizations. In the 1920s the proposal that such
forms of industrial regulation should be supervised by the state began to
gain ground. In 1927 legislation was passed that was intended to supervise the development of these agreements.[146] However, several permanent
private organizations consisting of equal representation from employers'
and employees' organizations emerged, assuming direct responsibility
for regulating such agreements in entire sectors or "branches" of industry *(bedrijfstakken)*. Further many cartel agreements between employers

(ondernemersovereenkomsten), restricting competition, for example, also emerged, representing another expression of industrial self-government.

In the 1930s these private forms of industrial organization began to attract state ("public-legal") regulation. In 1935 the government acquired the power to make cartel agreements binding within an entire industrial sector, or to strike them down if these were against the public interest. And in 1937 this power was extended also to the provisions of collective bargaining agreements between employers and employees. This process culminated in the passing of the 1950 act, which instituted a new publicly recognized national body, the Social and Economic Council, consisting of equal representatives from employers and employees organizations, plus an equal proportion of independent experts appointed by the government. The council had two main functions: to formulate advice for the government regarding its socio-economic policies; and to supervise the institution of a complex structure of industrial boards with certain regulatory powers. These boards were of two kinds: some were horizontal, branchwide industrial boards *(bedrijfsschappen);* others were vertical, commodity-based boards *(produktschappen).* They were to be created where desired by the industrial organizations concerned, not imposed by the government. The regulatory powers of the horizontal boards covered technical areas such as product quality, social areas such as collective wage agreements, social insurance, training, and some limited economic areas such as conditions of sale. The vertical boards, however, would be granted regulatory competence also in the broad economic areas of production, marketing, and even price setting. The intention of such boards was to create a framework of public law within which such social and economic affairs could be regulated while respecting the principle of competition in industrial life. Although the boards were not directly supervised by the government, their regulations were subject to government approval and could be struck down if, for instance, they impeded fair competition. This provision was included to prevent the boards from becoming merely publicly sanctioned protective cartels.

The main ideological groups—Catholic, Calvinist, Liberal, and Socialist—took different positions on the PBO. The Catholics were generally in favor, regarding PBO as a healthy expression of the version of corporatism embodied in the encyclical *Quadragesimo Anno.* It honored the central principle of subsidiarity, leaving as much autonomy for lesser communities such as industry as possible while invoking the aid of the state in providing overall supervision according to the requirements of the common good. By contrast, many Protestants gave only qualified approval to PBO. Although generally not opposed to the principle of industrial organization behind it, they were concerned that it might undermine the independence of private industry. Least enthusiastic were the Liberals, who were concerned to protect the freedom of the individual enterprise from state interference. The Socialists, however, regarded PBO with favor, viewing it as a means whereby the state could more readily control industrial capitalism in the interests of labor while at the same time making possible a functional decentralization of public authority to lower organs of the state.

Against this background we can better appreciate Dooyeweerd's general conception of the relation between state and economy. What is now typically referred to as the field of political economy in fact embraces two distinct spheres of activity, namely, the internal and external economic functioning of the state. The former concerns the state's internal "housekeeping" *(staatshuishouding)* and includes activities such as raising revenue, procurement, or, exceptionally, operating an industry as a public utility.[147] The latter, the state's external or enkaptic functioning, concerns its civil- or public-legal regulation of *private* economic activity. This might include the civil law of contract, the declaration of collective bargaining agreements as binding, the establishment of a system of industrial arbitration, anticartel legislation, or social legislation, all of which are designed to ensure a just balancing of private economic interests.[148] It is a highly complex and increasingly extensive area of state activity since the state is bound to private economic activity "by a thousand ties."[149] The ambiguous term *volkshuishouding* (German: *volkswirtschaft*) must be interpreted in this specific sense rather than as the "totality of economic relationships" as in universalist conceptions.[150]

Dooyeweerd's main concern in the PBO debate was to safeguard the economically qualified sphere sovereignty of industry from the illicit encroachment of the state. He thought it essential to distinguish between the internal *economically qualified* juridical sphere of industry and the *public-legally qualified* sphere of the state. To explain this concern more fully we need to survey the main features of the PBO debate as he interpreted it. He distinguished two fundamental questions of principle in the debate.[151] The one most directly germane to this study can be summarized thus: was the public-legal authority of the proposed regulatory boards for the various branches of industry to be conceived of as an *extension* of the intrinsic authority of the already existing private industrial organizations, or as a *delegation* of the essentially public-legal authority of the state? In explaining why he held the latter view, we shall also encounter what to him was the second fundamental issue in the debate, namely, how was one to view the intrinsic nature of the private branch-wide industrial organizations from a normative structural viewpoint?

Regarding the first issue, Dooyeweerd's basic objection was to the corporatist implications of construing what were essentially nonpolitical societal relationships in private industrial life as foundations for the public authority of the state. He detected these corporatist overtones in both the socialist notion of functional decentralization and the Catholic whole-part conception of society. Moreover this whole-part conception also lay behind the views of the movement for Christian "solidarism," which attracted both Catholic and Protestant support. The essential problem in both socialist and Christian Solidarist conceptions was that the radical distinction between the distinctly public character of the state and the essentially private character of industrial life was being clouded.

Dooyeweerd ascribes an independent sphere of internal freedom and legal competence to the industrial enterprise. The structural principle of an industrial enterprise is that of an economically qualified, voluntary, organized community. Its internal juridical functioning ought always to remain subservient to its economic qualifying function, characterized by entrepreneurial risk and competition. Should the state attempt to encroach upon this internal, economically qualified juridical sphere, it would usurp the entrepreneurial function. Upholding the sphere sovereignty of industry does not consist merely in shoring up a position of independence for the *individual* enterprise.[152] Indeed Dooyeweerd seems more concerned with the sphere sovereignty of "industrial life" *(bedrijfsleven)* as a distinct realm of activity than that of the separate enterprises *(individuele ondernemingen)*. Dooyeweerd uses *bedrijf* to refer to a complex of enterprises.[153] Thus a *bedrijfstak* is a complex of enterprises within the same branch of industry, "an organization, qualified by the economic entrepreneurial function, of capital and labor in a complex of enterprises, which does not permit itself to be enclosed within the boundaries of the state."[154] An entire branch of industry has a distinctly qualified structure of its own and thus bears its own sphere sovereignty, which ought to be protected against state interference.

Rather curiously, Dooyeweerd suggests that the "center of gravity" (zwaartepunt) of industrial sphere sovereignty need not necessarily reside in the *individual* enterprise but may just as well be located in an entire branch of industry.[155] If, however, every social structure with its own structural principle possesses sphere sovereignty, then Dooyeweerd must, to be consistent, surely hold that each enterprise has a sphere sovereignty whose center of gravity lies within itself. It may enter into various relationships with an organized branch of industry, but it will not thereby lose any of its original sphere sovereignty, and nor will the sphere sovereignty of the latter necessarily take priority over that of the individual enterprise. He should therefore also hold that, just as the state must respect the sphere sovereignty of the organized branch of industry, so must this organized branch respect the sphere sovereignty of each individual enterprise making it up. Indeed the generalized concept of industrial sphere sovereignty sits uneasily with his theory of societal structures. He would not, for example, speak of "marital sphere sovereignty" as meaning anything other than the sphere sovereignty of individual marriage relationships. Nonetheless, a branch of industry can indeed be seen as having its own sphere sovereignty, and it is with this that we are mainly concerned.

Unlike an individual enterprise, a branch of industry is not a community but an *interlinkage*. It is a societal (maatschappelijk) network of intercommunal relationships between individual enterprises.[156] In Dooyeweerd's view, the conception prevailing in Christian Solidarist circles was that a branch of industry was a "natural community," and a relatively autonomous, organic part of the national whole organized in the state.[157] The Solidarists argued that a public-legal political status adhered to the permanent horizontal organizations within the branches of industry. In fact Dooyeweerd welcomed the emergence of these horizontal organizations, regarding their integrating function as indispensable as modern society became increasingly differentiated.[158] But their purpose should be to promote the particular interests of the branch of industry that they represented and to safeguard its sphere sovereignty. To regard them as bearers of public authority was to misunderstand their internal structure. And as networks of coordinated intercommunal relationships the organizations emerging from a particular branch of industry could only regulate their shared interests on the basis of *voluntary* agreement.[159]

We come now to Dooyeweerd's specific position on PBO. He was not, as is often supposed, opposed in principle to the introduction of some measure of public-legal industrial organization;[160] indeed he encouraged its extension.[161] However, he coupled this encouragement with the now-familiar warning that "by means of a public legal industrial organization, the State can only bind the industrial . . . relationships insofar as the latter are enkaptically interwoven with its own structure."[162] The Solidarists argued that the new organs emerging from particular branches of industry could exercise public legal authority in their own right. They represented natural communities that were parts of the state rather than independent individuality structures that could only be enkaptically bound by the state. The Solidarists and the Socialists held that public legal competence arose immediately from within industrial life itself. Dooyeweerd denies not only this but also the general assumption it betrayed, that the state may confer such competence upon intrinsically nonpolitical structures.[163] Because industry and agriculture are economically qualified productive sectors, their sphere sovereignty cannot include a public-legal competence. For "any public legal authority exercised by organs composed of representatives of organizations of employers and trade unions, is derived from the legislators." A public legal organization can only be legally qualified. The organs of such an organization only possess a "delegated autonomy," the limits of which are determined wholly by the requirements of the public interest. To confuse this autonomy with the economic sphere sovereignty of private industry and agriculture "must lead either to a deformation of public legal authority, or to an absorption of free industrial and agricultural life by the political sphere of the State."[164]

Here again we see his strong insistence on a sharp distinction between the "relative autonomy" of a part within a whole and the sphere sovereignty of a distinct individual whole. Autonomy is a property applicable only to the relationship of a part within a whole, such as a province or municipality within a state,[165] or a subsidiary of a larger corporation.[166] Such a part can never claim its own sphere sovereignty; the scope of its legitimate authority, moreover, is quite properly determined by the authoritative organs of the societal whole of which it is a part. Its competence is always derived, never original. Thus, for instance, no principled boundary can be set around municipal or provincial interests.[167] Equally, the degree of autonomy granted to an organ of PBO might eventually be whittled away as political circumstances required, just as was historically the case with Dutch municipal autonomy. It is the government's task to apportion such degrees of autonomy as is required by the public interest.[168] In the light of these considerations Dooyeweerd stresses that the government, in establishing the PBO, must take careful cognizance of the boundaries of industrial sphere sovereignty. For the autonomy of a PBO would itself give no adequate safeguard against violation of such sphere sovereignty.

One of Dooyeweerd's central objections to the PBO proposals arose because a PBO was envisaged as concerned with both social and economic affairs of industry. There is a general sense in which Dooyeweerd accepts this, namely, in the sense that all areas of societal life can in principle be enkaptically bound by the state in the public interest. Industrial life must be prepared to accept this also.[169] But while the state may enkaptically bind certain aspects of industrial life by means of PBO, it has no original competence to form the internal, economically qualified law of industry.[170] When the horizontal organization of a branch of industry is organized into a public-legal board it assumes the public-juridical qualification of the state. Thus a PBO can never be the bearer of *industrial* sphere sovereignty. The distinction between the sphere sovereignty of the organs of a branch of private industry and the relative autonomy of such organs once they have been organized under a PBO is crucial.

The next question is the extent to which public legal authority should be given to such private organs. Here a sharp distinction between *social* and *economic* affairs must be drawn.

> The former do indeed have an internal industrial legal aspect, but the emphasis undoubtedly falls on the acquisition of a social legal position for labor by which labor can no longer be treated as a commodity, as a mere object of exploitation. The regulation of labor conditions for an entire branch of industry (e.g. vocational training and retraining, pension settlements, measures against un-

employment initiated by industry, etc.) cannot be viewed as matters of internal industrial law. For *internal industrial law* as such is
always qualified by the *economic entrepreneurial vantage-point*. As
soon as the "social" concerns of industrial life are made subservient to the typical *economic destination* of industry, one would
eliminate whatever has been achieved since the end of the last century in the area of the social elevation of labor and regress to the
old liberal position.[171]

Social labor law must never be made dependent upon the results of the
individual enterprise, for this would be to place the hard-won "social
legal status" of the worker at risk.

The enterprise does not have a duty to grant workers a share in profits, since these depend on the results of economic competition. Nor does
it have a duty to allow workers to inspect company accounts.[172] Such decisions fall within the economically qualified function of the enterprise,
and beyond the area of social labor law. The PBO ought not, therefore,
to decide on such specifically economic matters. But whereas internal
industrial law, insofar as it concerns matters going beyond established
minimum wages and working conditions, should serve the entrepreneurial qualification of the enterprise, all social law should be guided by
the principle of "social justice" *(sociale gerechtigheid)*. This, Dooyeweerd
suggests, is a specific application of public justice within the field of
public administrative law. Included within the scope of administrative
law is "social law," regulating the administration of social security, safety,
collective bargaining agreements, and so on.[173]

It is on account of this "social-legal" qualification that Dooyeweerd
allows for *regulation of social labor law* by PBO. But he rejects the criticism that this implies an artificial, watertight separation between social
and economic industrial affairs.

Ever since the development of collective labor contracts, labor
law, as a special juridically qualified law with many bindings of
partly civil-legal, partly public-legal nature, could become established as its own legal sphere. While formed within industrial life
itself, it has nevertheless remained very closely intertwined with
internal industrial law, as is the case in reverse. Wages, working

conditions, etc., still remain in large measure connected with the prices of products, the volume of production, etc. in the branch of industry concerned, and also in the relation between branches of industry.[174]

Ultimately it is the necessity for social labor law to be universally applicable across an industry—if it is to be effective—that calls forth the inclusive public authority of the state. Only when the social legal position of the worker is not left dependent upon the economic performance of an individual enterprise is there any guarantee that public "social" justice will be rendered.[175] He states his central conclusion thus:

> All law that is typically qualified by the economic entrepreneurial function falls principally within this sphere of competence; all law, on the contrary, that is typically qualified by the public-legal principle of the public interest, falls within the original sphere of competence of the government, irrespective of whether this law was formed by the State legislature or rather by autonomous organs of a public-legal industrial organization.[176]

Sustaining a clear distinction between "social" and "economic" law within industry is crucial to Dooyeweerd's attempt to determine the boundaries of acceptable state intervention. Yet while this distinction does indeed seem plausible in principle it is not clear that he has applied it correctly throughout his account of industrial sphere sovereignty, and to conclude this section I briefly discuss why. Within the realm of the social legal sphere pertaining to workers, Dooyeweerd includes, as noted, such things as social security, safety regulations, and minimum wage levels but excludes, *inter alia,* the question of allocation of profits. In his view, therefore, while it may be quite feasible economically for a corporation to allocate a larger proportion of its profits to its workforce, the state is not competent to compel such an allocation of its economic surplus. However, he recognizes that the possibility of profit sharing and the level of minimum wages are in fact closely related to intrinsically economic factors.[177] In the case of the latter, it is clear that if an enterprise has a very low rate of productivity, then it simply may not be able to pay established minimum wages; indeed this is a common argument against legislating for it. State regulation of both these matters thus clearly restricts the range of possibilities open to an entrepreneur. Why does only one fall within the state's regulatory competence?

First, it is not obvious that one is necessarily an issue of public justice and thus within the state's field of competence while the other is not. In both cases workers could be held to have legitimate juridical claims. Nor is it obvious, second, that the question of the social legal status of workers could neatly be distinguished from that of the internal economic domain of the firm according to the distinction between public and private. For, given his use of the term *public,* it is not clear that profit sharing must necessarily remain a private economic affair. He argues that the possibility of profit sharing depends on the results of the individual enterprise, its rate of productivity, quantity of output, and so on. But then the ability of an enterprise to pay minimum wages is also dependent upon the results of this individual enterprise. What he is saying is that there should be a minimum level of wages that *ought not* to be left dependent upon such variable economic results. The level of minimum wages is an issue of justice that has a public dimension, since it concerns the social legal status of the worker. But if he is prepared to place this restriction on the range of entrepreneurial activity, why does he refrain from arguing that this range should be even further restricted by regulations governing the internal distribution of profits?

Here we must note the character of minimum wage legislation. Minimum wages constitute, in effect, a *fixed cost* of which all entrepreneurs must take account in their business activities. As long as an enterprise exists it can be required to pay minimum wages, just as it can be required to pay social insurance contributions, abide by (costly) pollution regulations, grant maternity leave, and so on. Such things all act as prior limits on economic activity, establishing a public framework of law within which such activity takes place. Such regulations enkaptically bind enterprises to various requirements of public justice. Although the level of minimum wages may vary according to occupation, age, or regional criteria, and thus not necessarily be equal for all within a state's territory, such criteria can be made universally applicable (e.g., by imposing a single universal level for all electricians). Thus minimum wage legislation can indeed be established by public law. I now argue that this is also true of profit sharing.

It is clear that a political authority cannot force an enterprise to make a profit. The level of profit depends upon the outcome of a multiplicity of economic decisions and other circumstances that the state cannot possibly orchestrate toward a specific outcome. Any regulation that presupposed the economic results of particular enterprises—for example, a general government regulation of product prices—would therefore be beyond the competence of the state. Similarly the state cannot regulate technical production methods except insofar as they have implications for worker safety, health, and so on. As noted, it is the irreducibly economic character of decisions like product price that leads Dooyeweerd to argue that they should be beyond the competence of any public body, whether central government or a decentralized organ such as PBO. To this extent at least his application of industrial sphere sovereignty seems justified.

But his argument against profit sharing is not conclusive. To require only *particular* enterprises or types of enterprises to share profits and thus to impose a public burden on some from which others were exempt would be discriminatory and would violate the principle of equitable treatment implicit in the notion of public justice. Similarly, offering subsidies to a particular concern but not to others could be objected to for the same reason (though it might exceptionally be justifiable in the public interest). Any profit sharing regulations imposed by the state would have to satisfy an appropriate criterion of universality. Such a criterion could be met by basing a profit sharing scheme on a proportionate standard. No scheme could in fact be based on an absolute quantitative standard. For to require all enterprises to distribute, say, $5,000 per year to each worker from corporate profits is simply to impose a fixed cost similar to minimum wages. Such a scheme would thus not be a *profit* sharing scheme at all. But a *proportionate* standard is conceivable. The state could for example require all corporations over a certain size to distribute, say, 15 percent of any annual profits among its employees. This would not represent a fixed cost but rather a compulsory, proportionate internal transfer payment. Such a regulation would not necessarily violate the internal economic freedom of the enterprise but would rather act as another prior limit within which economic activity would have to take place. There is no reason why a figure of 15 percent could not be applied universally. If so, then a proportionate profit sharing measure no more appears to violate industrial sphere sovereignty than does minimum wage legislation.[178]

Another of his applications of the concept of industrial sphere sovereignty also invites critical discussion, namely his view of industrial democracy. I began by noting that his definition of the leading function of an industrial enterprise is formulated exclusively from the perspective of the entrepreneur. Authority in an enterprise, he holds, while never unlimited, derives entirely from the provision of capital and the financial risk arising from this. Hence he opposes those forms of industrial democracy (strictly, codetermination, *medezeggenschap*) that confer a share of entrepreneurial authority—that is, authority to decide in economically qualified matters—upon representatives of employees.[179] He is supportive of consultative arrangements in which employees' representatives simply advise on economic matters and of employees sharing in decision making on social matters such as insurance. Nor does he rule out the possibility of such representatives having a measure of delegated managerial authority. As I noted earlier, he also regards the emergence of strong and independent trade unions as indispensable to the protection of workers' rights. But, in his view, granting a share in the exercise of the legal sphere sovereignty of an enterprise to those who have contributed no capital to it and who therefore bear no legally binding financial responsibility for its success is to misconceive the internal structure of the enterprise. For the state to compel this would be a "partial expropriation without compensation," a "theft by statute."[180]

In one of his earliest writings he remarks that the emergence of this form of capitalist economic organization at this historical juncture is not in itself wrong, and indeed he testifies to the realization of divinely given economic norms.[181] Arguably, this is a good example of what McIntire described as his uncritical acceptance of the normative character of modern Western social structures.[182] Yet already in 1926 he made clear that he was not opposed to codetermination for all time but only within the prevailing capitalist system. In a situation of *co-ownership*, codetermination would of course be appropriate. In such a case managerial authority would rightly be shared among all workers who held a stake in the enterprise. Indeed within the emerging cooperative movement, of which he speaks positively, codetermination is quite appropriate.[183] He does not object to the "experiments" in workers' cooperatives and the like already appearing but implies they are unlikely to succeed, since they work against the "logic of facts." Hence, although he concedes it is not possible to predict the course of future developments, he cautions against trying to "force" the historical pace.[184] Although confessing to be "very sympathetic" to co-ownership, he adds that "more than sympathy is necessary in order to lead historical development."[185]

Later in life his emphasis seems to have changed markedly. In another informal interview in 1974, he said:

> An enterprise is only good when it serves the interests of society. The limited company calls the enterprise into being. The workers are the natural partners of the capital owners. But workers are not members of the company as long as they have no shares. And that is why I propagate the idea of giving workers a sufficient share in the company so they can, as a group, have influence in the management of the company.[186]

While this is certainly a more enthusiastic endorsement of the idea of worker participation, it continues to make *membership* in the business community conditional on *ownership* of the capital. By contrast, Goudzwaard, who also favors the model of a producer cooperative, holds that workers are entitled to codetermination rights even in the absence of share ownership, simply by virtue of their own, indispensable contribution of labor.[187] Such a view arguably reflects a more compelling conception of business enterprises as genuine producer communities.

ELEVEN

CIVIL SOCIETY AND CHRISTIAN PLURALISM

MY AIM IN THIS CONCLUDING CHAPTER IS TO SUGGEST SOME
contributions that Dooyeweerd's version of normative institutional pluralism might make to contemporary civil society debates. The central
proposal is that his thought can point toward (if not yet fully deliver) a
richer and more coherent account than those currently on offer. My
analysis of his contributions is organized around the three core problems
in such debates identified in the first chapter: the definition and scope of
the concept of civil society, the relationship between civil society and the
state, and the utility of the concept of civil society for the project of social
critique. I proceed as follows. For the first problem I begin by identifying
and elaborating two central conceptual innovations in Dooyeweerd's social theory. I then review a range of recent definitions proposed in civil
society literature, locate Dooyeweerd's social theory in terms of the historical origins of civil society theorizing, and, finally, propose an alternative definition of civil society drawing on the two conceptual innovations
identified earlier. In the second section I prepare the ground for addressing the second and third problems by distinguishing between three
prevalent models of the purpose of civil society: the protective, the integrative, and the transformative. I then deploy my proposed Dooyeweerdian definition of civil society as an analytical tool to assess and develop
these models. My discussion of the integrative model occasions a commentary on Dooyeweerd's contribution to the second core problem, that

of the proper relationship between civil society and the state. The final core problem—the relation between civil society and social critique—is addressed as I assess the third, transformative model.

What Is Civil Society?

Among the many components of Dooyeweerd's complex social theory, two key conceptual innovations are especially illuminating for addressing the contested question of the definition and scope of the concept of civil society: the notion of irreducible institutional identity and the notion of the correlation between communities and interlinkages. I begin by elaborating the import of these two conceptual innovations, then critically review some recent attempts to delineate the concept of civil society, and finally propose an alternative definition appealing to a central, although undertheorized, Dooyeweerdian notion.

Irreducible Institutional Identity

A central conclusion of my discussion of Dooyeweerd's social ontology was that the claim that social structures possessed invariant structural principles is untenable. The implication that the specific normative structures of uniquely modern institutions such as business corporations or trade unions or territorial states were contained in principle in the *original* order of creation only waiting for historical disclosure cannot stand and obscures the sense in which social structures like these are variable, historical channels for the communal pursuit of specific, though universal, functional capacities rooted in (created) human nature.

But although the structural norms of particular types of community cannot be regarded as invariant in Dooyeweerd's sense, his account of the irreducible institutional identities (structural principles) of these types is nonetheless highly illuminating. This account turns essentially on the qualifying function (or structural purpose) of particular social structures—the specific human functional capacity to which the structure in question is designed to give organized communal expression.

Given the evident confusions that follow from the many attempts to deny the point, Dooyeweerd's argument that such capacities are themselves irreducible is at least a plausible working hypothesis: reasoning cannot be reduced to feeling; social interaction cannot be reduced to economic behavior; doing justice cannot be reduced to a mechanical balancing of interests; faith cannot be reduced to ethics. Accordingly, when humans organize institutional channels for the common exercise of such capacities, the institutions they establish possess a defining qualifying function that is irreducible to those of other types. The claim that "a state is not a family," for example, is not a mere figure of speech. States that function as families tend to succumb to damaging distortions like nationalism or nepotism, smothering or swindling their citizens.

It should be emphasized that "irreducibility" does not imply either "invariance" or "ubiquity." It is not meaningful to suggest that the structural norms for modern institutions like schools and businesses hold changelessly, as if they were valid even prior to the actual historical emergence of such institutions. Rather such norms come to exercise cultural holding power through a process of complex, often unruly, and vigorously contested historical development, and the normative validity they possess derives from their demonstrable necessity for a particular kind of (universal) human flourishing. This is to say that irreducible structural norms are discovered principally through long, careful, and critical reflection on historical experience.[1] Yet such normative validity is not finally grounded in the human subjective capacity to demonstrate such necessity or give concrete shape to such norms (i.e., to positivize them) but rather in the created imperatives of human nature itself.[2] Such experience seems to suggest that, for example, the structural purpose of a school, established to promote the formation of knowledge, character, and skill among children, is seriously twisted if it becomes a mere conduit for political propaganda or exclusively a preparation for employment. Or, a family existing to supply ethical nurture and security for its members will, experience suggests, become dysfunctional if its activities are entirely subordinated to the economic imperatives of a large corporation (or indeed of a family business). Equally, a state that is instituted to secure justice in the public realm of society will, history attests, instead promote injustice if it degenerates into a de facto arm of a governing party, a "military-industrial complex," powerful professional interests, or a kinship or ethnic group. Indeed where an institution's structural purpose has been fundamentally deformed we may conclude not merely that the institution in question is malfunctioning but that it has either dissolved or been transformed into a different type of institution entirely.

I have also argued that—with the exception of the family—Dooyeweerd's notion of the founding function of a social structure does not do the work he supposes it does. But his proposal that the definitive *qualifying function* or structural purpose of a social institution is what essentially defines its irreducible identity is, I suggest, his most original and illuminating pluralist contribution. The intent of his complex accounts of many particular structures is not merely classificatory. Rather identifying the distinctive structural purpose of an institution is essential both to discerning the requirements of its internal flourishing and to rendering it justice. Marriage partners or family members who understand their relationships to each other as just as another species of friendship will fail to fulfill the distinctive responsibilities and enjoy the distinctive benefits of marital or family life. Equally, unless we—and especially the state—know what a family is, we cannot adequately honor the rights, duties, and powers properly adhering to it; this kind of claim is at the heart of Dooyeweerd's complex theory of spheres of justice (legal sphere sovereignty). He acknowledges, of course, that his own accounts of the irreducible identities of structures are provisional and always open to debate (and I have proposed revisions to his accounts of both the state and the business corporation). But the valid implication of his approach is that such debates, whatever else they are about, will also need to be debates about such irreducible identities.

Dooyeweerd's insistence on the *equal normative status* of all social structures marks him out as an authentic inheritor of a salutary feature of the modern world with roots in Protestantism. The Reformation assertion of the spiritual equality of callings led to a radical questioning of the hierarchical social metaphysics underlying classical Thomism.[3] Reformation thinkers did not deny the necessity of obedience to divinely ordained social authorities like family, state, and church. Dooyeweerd also endorses the need for relations of authority and obedience in these three institutional communities (as well as in authoritative voluntary associations). Yet he holds that this is entirely compatible with the claim that social structures, while displaying diverse structures of authority, are, as he puts it, "axiologically equivalent." While the state, for example, exercises legal authority over social structures resident within its territory, this is a functionally limited authority and does not derive from any general metaphysical priority of supposedly "perfect" communities over "lesser" ones.

Finally, this pluralist claim is, above all, a claim regarding the *complementarity* of multiple types of social structure. It is not a claim about *mere* plurality, for a society populated merely by, say, numerous voluntary associations (as in Nozick's libertarian utopia), or one in which every structure is a dependent part of the political community (as in Plato's vision of the polis), would not remotely meet the communal aspirations and needs of a complex, multifaceted human nature. Nor is it a claim about mere diversity: not just *any* array of social structures will do; diversity in and of itself carries no particular normative weight. What matters is the *kind* of institutional diversity that a society displays, the specific forms of community or interlinkage to which it accords hospitality and support. Again, while Dooyeweerd's own accounts of the medley of humanly appropriate social structures are open to challenge, his claim that the multifunctional design of human nature calls for a plurality of differently qualified structures seems highly plausible.

The notion of the irreducible identity of institutions, centering on their unique structural purposes, is an innovative contribution to pluralist social theory.[4] It is important to repeat, however, that it does not imply that institutions pursue only *one* function. Dooyeweerd repeatedly insists that social structures, while qualified by one modal function, nevertheless function simultaneously in all modal aspects.[5] Every institution is multifunctional: the identity of a business may be defined by its economic function, but it also functions socially, juridically, ethically, and so on. Every level of functioning involves structural norms: a business exists in order to produce needed, tradable goods or services, but it is a multifaceted human community the members of which must be treated with respect (a social norm), paid fair wages (a juridical norm), and dealt with honorably (an ethical norm). The fact that the economic norm qualifies the business assuredly does not mean that considerations of profitability trump all others. Goudzwaard's claim that economic activity should be characterized by the "simultaneous realization" of multiple norms[6] is a helpful way to formulate what Dooyeweerd holds of all communities and interlinkages.

The Correlation of Communities and Interlinkages

A second important conceptual innovation is Dooyeweerd's analysis of the "indissoluble correlation" between (differentiated) communities and interlinkages. I just noted that the notion of irreducible institutional identity does not imply that social structures pursue only one function. Nor does it imply that social structures perform only *internal* functions. On the contrary, Dooyeweerd rightly insists that all social structures necessarily engage in numerous kinds of interlinkage with others (some of them enkaptic) and that these are indispensable to their flourishing; indeed many arise simply when a structure pursues its structural purpose. Parental discipline is essentially an internal function of the family. But children will not grow up as morally responsible persons if their families live in isolation from others or without extensive interactions with many other types of structure. The notion of irreducible identity does not imply self-sufficiency or self-enclosure; social structures are not fortresses pitted against invaders but institutionalized foci of functionally qualified responsibility. The concept of irreducibility here means that the multiple and necessary interactions among social structures should proceed in ways fitting to and respectful of the identities of each. This is the core of what Dooyeweerd means by insisting that such interactions should honor the sphere sovereignty of each structure.

As I showed in chapter 7, Dooyeweerd's assertion of the necessary correlation between and reciprocal presupposition of (differentiated) communities and interlinkages is the basis for his claim to have escaped the twin perils of individualism and universalism. Whereas each is guilty of absolutizing one or the other correlate, Dooyeweerd asserts the complete coherence of communal norms with the norm of individuality. Human beings need to belong to many complementary communities but also need a broad realm of legally protected personal freedom to engage in diverse pursuits, many of which will require establishing interlinkages with other individuals or other communities. The solidity and stability of communities—especially institutional communities—furnish the indispensable foundation for the cultivation of responsible personal freedom, while free and responsible persons bring inner resources of character, initiative, and talent to communities—both institutional communities and voluntary associations—without which such communities would either atrophy or become dysfunctional or oppressive.

An important theme in my expositions of Dooyeweerd has been the senses in which he, a penetrating critic of the humanistic foundation of modernity, can nevertheless enthusiastically celebrate some of its fundamental achievements. One of these senses is his identification of the modern processes of integration, individualization, and differentiation as examples of the normative historical disclosure of the cultural potentials of creation. It is, as I noted, a characteristic achievement of the modern world to have made possible an integration of formerly geographically isolated communities and a substantial extension of individualization for both persons and communities. Such individualization then effects the differentiation of communities, the clarification of their distinct structural purposes. These processes open up a vastly expanded realm of free interactions between individuals—who enjoy "civil-legal freedom and equality"—and between the communities and associations they freely form and sustain. He also observes that the existence of voluntary associations (themselves a species of community) presupposes the presence of free individuals capable of entering into novel forms of associative activity for specific purposes.

On the other hand, the freedom secured by individualization and differentiation is not absolute. Dooyeweerd's typical reference to freedom as "civil-legal" is intended to distinguish it from a modern*ist* presumption of unqualified moral autonomy; nor were the constraints on individual freedom prior to differentiation complete or necessarily oppressive. So to affirm modern individualization and differentiation is neither to accept all modern freedoms uncritically nor to deny that some premodern constraints (e.g., guild obligations) contributed, in their own context, to human flourishing. Nor, crucially, do individualization and differentiation undo the inherently and enduringly communal nature of differentiated social structures. Communal relationships, of many kinds, remain just as important in the modern as they were in the premodern world. Moreover—and this is a central claim of this chapter—free individuals and differentiated communities need to be interconnected in multiple ways: what Dooyeweerd calls "integrating tendencies" in the modern world are not neutral processes but, he proposes, necessary responses to the normative requirement for the creation of new kinds of cooperative interlinkages of many kinds among individuated individuals and communities.

It is true that in the modern world these are no longer inherited or ascribed but freely undertaken. All interlinkages are in principle, and should be in practice, voluntary partnerships among legally free and equal parties.[7] But neither interlinkages nor voluntary associations are to be conceived as purely instrumental to self-interested or self-posited individual ends. The possibility created by such freely initiated activities is new historical opportunities for cultural disclosure and social service, not openings for the expression of unconstrained and self-determining autonomy as implied in the humanistic personality-ideal. Individual economic enterprise, for example, carries with it from the very start the norms of the economic aspect and those of economic community correlated with it (noted above). The formation of workers' associations and, later, trade unions by emancipated guild members or peasants should not be construed merely as an act of self-defense but also as a historical vocation, pursuant to the social norm of solidarity. If these had not been established, formerly secure tradesmen or farm laborers would have been left wholly vulnerable to the unruly market forces of the early modern period (which, of course, is what many of them initially were).[8]

It is evident, then, that Dooyeweerd's understanding of voluntary associations—and indeed, by implication, of all interlinkages—reflects what, as noted earlier, Carney identifies as a distinctly Calvinian teleological view of the nature and purposes of human association. I described this view as "covenantal voluntarism," contrasting it with the "instrumental voluntarism" characteristic of much individualistic liberal thought. In this covenantal view, free and responsible persons voluntarily associate but pursuant to a particular human purpose or need arising from the normative design of human nature, not spun out of the arbitrary wills of the associates. Associational initiative is not an expression of radical moral autonomy but the fulfilling of a social vocation. Of course, those committed to modernist notions of moral autonomy might reply by saying that Dooyeweerd is celebrating the arrival of modern freedom only to hedge it around again with burdensome external constraints. The freedom to enter into voluntary relationships is, after all, an imposed obligation under another name. Dooyeweerd's response might then be to suggest that this disagreement reveals the conflict within social theory between two underlying religious ground motives and could only finally be addressed through dialogue at that deeper level. I return to this issue in the epilogue.

In the light of this interpretation of Dooyeweerd's conceptions of community, association, and interlinkage, we can now locate his social theory in relation to the emergence of modern theories of civil society. I have recorded Dooyeweerd's forceful repudiation of individualistic and economistic eighteenth-century conceptions of civil society. His objection is not to the distinction, presupposed in such theories, between state and society per se; indeed he regards this as a salutary outcome of the normative processes of societal differentiation and individualization.[9] His objection is rather to the flawed premises at the base of such theories, seriously skewing the early formulation of the distinction (and, indirectly, the early development of those processes). Such individualism generated an absolutization of interindividual relationships, an undermining of the normative reality of communal bonds, and a neglect of the indispensable norm of integration calling for individuated persons and communities to be brought into a variety of cooperative relationships.

Yet while Dooyeweerd rejects the individualistic and economistic presuppositions of the eighteenth-century originators of the modern concept of civil society, he powerfully affirms the progressive fruits of the processes of individualization and differentiation that preceded and made possible that modern concept. The process by which multiple functionally specific independent institutions emerged from the seventeenth to the nineteenth centuries was a salutary and irreversible civilizational watershed. It is clearly an essential presupposition of modern and contemporary notions of civil society, and Dooyeweerd affirms it.

A final point in assessing Dooyeweerd's understanding of civil society is his important recognition that the processes of individualization and differentiation both made possible and were facilitated by the emergence of the modern *state*. As Dooyeweerd repeatedly reminds us, the arrival of the state as a public institution—a *res publica*—required the dismantling of particularistic and overlapping feudal jurisdictions and the establishment of a single central political and military authority capable of establishing a uniform system of public and, crucially, *civil* law to which all citizens and institutions were equally subject and under which all had equal protection. In other words, the modern state actually made possible the arrival of civil society. The two were joined at birth and, as I shall point out below, they can no longer be separated. Dooyeweerd's analysis, then, suggests that the term *civil society* be reserved for societies that have undergone the progressive processes of differentiation and individualization.

If this analysis is broadly correct, it suggests that the term *civil* in the phrase "civil society" should be taken to refer to the dependence of the characteristically modern realm of free individual and communal activity on the cultural processes of individualization and differentiation, secured by the civil-legal equality guaranteed by the modern state. While it is important (as I noted in chapter 1) to identify the indispensable premodern conceptual foundations for the emergence of civil society, applying the term to premodern societies—as Ehrenberg does—anachronistically obscures this vital point. From a Dooyeweerdian perspective, then, the crucial transition is not the first appearance of a clear distinction between state and society, important though that was, but the establishment of the civil-legal freedom of persons and differentiated communities. This is not yet an adequate definition of *civil society*, only an identification of its essential historical conditions. I now want to show how these conditions point to a distinctive Dooyeweerdian definition of the concept.

An Alternative Definition

To bring out the significance of this definition I first need to explore further the contemporary examples of civil society discourse introduced in chapter 1. There I presented an outline sketch of some major currents of civil society discourse. Here I review some representative definitions of the concept found in that discourse.

All of them proceed from the common assumption that civil society is, as Dooyeweerd agrees, a product of modern freedom and differentiation. Beyond that, definitions vary considerably. Some seem to conceive civil society as virtually identical to an entire liberal democratic society. Pérez-Diaz, for example, defines it by "an institutional core consisting

of the following combination of political and socio-economic arrangements: a government which is limited and accountable and operates
under the rule of law; a market economy (implying a regime of private
property); an array of free, voluntary associations (political, economic,
social and cultural); and a sphere of public debate."[10] Most, however, isolate one or more dimensions of this description. Eberly emphasizes the
subpolitical location of civil society: it is "that sector of society in which
nonpolitical institutions operate—families, houses of worship, neighborhoods, civic groups, and just about every form of voluntary association
imaginable." Yet he recognizes that these institutions nevertheless serve
the wider purpose of compensating for or sustaining the economy and
the polity: they "mediate between the individual and the large megastructures of the market and the state, tempering the negative social tendencies associated with each; create important social capital; and impart
democratic values and habits."[11] Others lay emphasis instead on civil society as a potential source of political opposition. For Hall civil society is
"a particular form of society, appreciating social diversity and able to
limit the depredations of political power";[12] for Gellner it is "a cluster of
institutions and associations strong enough to prevent tyranny, but which
are, nevertheless, entered freely rather than imposed either by birth or by
awesome ritual."[13] Taylor also observes that the distinction between state
and civil society "has been central to the different forms of counter-
absolutist thinking" in the Western tradition.[14]

These and other definitions reveal considerable ambiguity in exactly
what types of institution or association properly fall within the concept.
Every definition includes voluntary associations and excludes the state,
but there is disagreement over whether the household and the market
should be included. For Eberly civil society embraces what Beem calls
the familiar American "triumvirate" of family, church, and neighborhood,[15] plus voluntary associations, but not the market. Many writers
exclude both household and market. Bryant is representative of many
writers in stipulating that civil society is composed of "the association
of citizens—social self-organization—between household and state and
aside from the market."[16] In the same vein, Ehrenberg defines it as "the
social relations and structures that lie between the state and the market."
Civil society "delineates a sphere that is formally distinct from the body

politic and state authority on one hand, and from the immediate pursuit of self-interest and the imperatives of the market on the other."[17]

A more precise and elaborate definition has been formulated by Cohen and Arato: civil society is "a sphere of social interaction between economy and state, composed above all of the intimate sphere (especially the family), the sphere of associations (especially voluntary associations), social movements, and forms of public communication." They go on to distinguish *civil, political,* and *economic* society. Modern civil society is "created through forms of self-constitution and self-mobilization" and is to be distinguished from "a political society of parties, political organizations, and political publics . . . and an economic society composed of organizations of production and distribution, usually firms, cooperatives, partnerships, and so on."[18] This is an illuminating definition. For example, distinguishing between a realm of self-constituted associations and political society helps guard against viewing bodies like voluntary welfare or educational associations or trade unions primarily in terms of their potential political role (whether supportive or oppositional), important though that may be. Likewise, distinguishing a realm of voluntary associative activity from a category of economic society oriented to production and distribution (presumably including market exchange) guards against the materialist assumption that the former are merely superstructural in relation to the latter.

Yet the description also generates several difficulties: on their definition, including the household is problematic, since families are not entirely self-constituted; embracing both families and social movements under the same general category of civil society risks conflating the distinctive social purpose and political import of each; restricting the designation of "self-constitution" to the institutions of civil society alone seems to exclude a priori that the institutions of both political and economic society may also admit of significant opportunities for meaningful participation and reform;[19] and excluding political parties, organizations, and publics from civil society undercuts much East European discourse that identified civil society with these very components.

While no definition can be expected to command universal assent, it will be instructive to observe—as I shall shortly—how those on offer reflect the influence of larger theoretical or ideological orientations. Eberly acknowledges that the skeptic, faced with so many contrasting definitions, will wonder whether the concept "merely serves as a useful rhetorical cover for essentially the same ideological debate that has been taking place for decades."[20] But he fails to follow through on this inadvertent but important insight. While it is not necessary to impute mere rhetorical intent to those employing the concept, it is enlightening to ask, as Beem puts it, what various theorists think civil society is *for.* I take up that evaluative task in the next section. But before I can do that I must first explain how Dooyeweerd's version of normative pluralism suggests a distinctive definition of the concept of civil society itself.

I propose to do so by using and developing Dooyeweerd's concept of interlinkages. Civil society, I suggest, can usefully be construed as *that realm of social interactions embracing the dense networks of interlinkages characteristic of a modern society.* As noted, the word *interlinkages* is a translation of the pregnant Dutch term *maatschapsverhoudingen,* which, in Dooyeweerd's usage, includes "interindividual" and "intercommunal" relationships. The force of this term lies in its contrast with the term *gemeenshapsverhoudingen,* which translates literally as "communal relationships" (but which I have normally rendered as "communities"). Communal relationships are relationships among members of a particular social structure, characterized by durability, internal unity, and authority. Interlinkages, by contrast, are essentially coordinate relationships, likely more transitory, among legally free and equal parties, whether persons or communities. While for Dooyeweerd communities of many kinds have always existed in human societies (whether differentiated or not), interlinkages are a distinctive product of modern societies, arising out of the processes of individualization and differentiation. Interlinkages are the characteristic form of societal interconnection in a differentiated culture.

On Dooyeweerd's account, the category of interlinkages already embraces a wide range of relationships: friendships, contracts, corporate agreements, associational confederations, political coalitions, strategic alliances, and so forth. I have already proposed supplementing this category with two additional types of relationships: first, relationships between individuals and communities ("individual-communal" interlinkages), which Dooyeweerd simply seemed to have overlooked; second, enkaptic interlacements between social structures (which, I suggested, are better viewed as a subclass of interlinkages characterized by relative permanence, intimacy, and proximity). Thus enriched, the term *inter-linkage* now embraces a vast and complex realm of interconnections between the discrete units of human society—persons and differently qualified communities—within a modern differentiated culture.

An analysis of communities is obviously a central dimension of any social theory. The particular strength of Dooyeweerd's analysis is its focus on their irreducible identities—especially the unique characteristics of their structural purposes—and the many dimensions of their internal functioning. As I will show, this focus can serve as an important reminder to civil society theorists to avoid conflating differently qualified communities or attributing to them structural purposes that do not belong to them, such as by looking to families to function primarily as "schools for civic virtue," or looking to trade unions or churches to function primarily as headquarters of political campaigns.

An analysis of interlinkages, I suggest, will constitute a second central dimension of social theory. Its focus will be on the myriad interactions among free persons and differentiated communities.[21] My proposal, then, is that the definitive focus of investigations of civil society is helpfully construed not as the investigation of the internal nature and functioning of communities but of the labyrinthine interconnectedness of communities and individuals—the sinews of a modern society rather than its muscles.

An important conclusion can now be ventured. As I showed, much contemporary discussion has taken the form of a quest to identify which *types* of community (household, voluntary, geographic, economic, cultural, political, religious, etc.) or which broad *sectors* of society (the market, public communications) ought to be embraced in the concept. The implication of my proposal is that this quest invites a different focus. What is of unique interest in the concept of *civil* society is not the types of community or societal sectors implied in it but the specific character of the *interactions*—interlinkages—among all of them. That specific character, I am suggesting, is shaped by the distinctively modern reality of individualization and differentiation. Interlinkages in a modern society hold between legally free and equal parties. The point of isolating and analyzing something called civil society is to understand the *normative requirements of modern interlinkages.*

An important terminological substitution will bring to the fore more fully the normative character of such interlinkages. I suggest that the limpid term *interlinkage* does not sufficiently convey the deeper normative intent of Dooyeweerd's analysis of how communities and persons relate to each other in a differentiated, free society. I noted that he conceives of the possibility of modern interlinkages, not as openings for the expression of unconstrained and self-determining individual autonomy or for the pursuit of essentially self-interested and self-posited goals, but rather as an unprecedented historical opportunity for the initiation of new forms of cultural disclosure and social service. Individualization and differentiation were spectacular cultural achievements, but they carried enormous risks of personal isolation, social fragmentation, and economic injustice in the absence of new cooperative ties.[22] As I have suggested, on a Dooyeweerdian reading the great achievement of modernity is not the liberation of autonomous, self-determining individuals from *any* necessary communal or moral bonds but the creation of the possibility of responsible, consensual expressions of interpersonal and intercommunal solidarity in a context of differentiation. Interlinkages can thus be construed as normative responses to the historical calling to establish new forms of integration, cooperation, and solidarity to replace the traditional social bonds typical of premodern societies.[23]

To capture this normative intent better, I propose to replace the term *interlinkages* with *interdependencies*. A relationship of interdependence is not a communal relationship uniting members in a durable social unity in which roles and responsibilities are given in the nature of the community itself, some of which (rightly) are assigned among unequal parties. It is rather a relationship of mutual service between free and responsible persons or communities. It is not a compulsory relationship but presupposes the equality of status and the possibility of mutual consent among the parties entering into it. As I noted, Dooyeweerd makes clear that an affirmation of interlinkages is not in any way based on the humanistic idea of the "self-sufficient, autarkical '*individuum*.'"[24] Thus entering into them is not a wholly unconstrained choice, since in so doing a person or community responds to a normative calling to engage in necessary cooperative service toward their personal or communal "neighbor." In this way persons and communities can exemplify the evocative Dutch term *dienstbaarheid* (serviceability), which I suggested in chapter 7 was a helpful way to denote the normative core of enkaptic interlacements. For Dooyeweerd the Christian idea of personal liberty upon which an affirmation of interlinkages is based is at bottom grounded in humankind's common subjection to "the central commandment of love."[25] The term *interdependencies* better captures this fundamental grounding.

Interdependencies can, of course, slide into unhealthy *dependencies,* which (outside of communities) are in principle illegitimate. This could occur, for example, when the unequal power or resources commanded by one or more interdependent parties are deployed by the stronger party at the expense of the legitimate interests of the weaker, overriding their formal legal equality of status. It is especially likely in the cases of what Dooyeweerd calls "unnatural" enkaptic interlacements. A prime example of this kind of distortion—which, as I noted, Dooyeweerd himself observed—was the unregulated labor market of the nineteenth century; the deregulated global financial markets today have dramatically exemplified it in our own. Indeed I specifically include market relationships in the category of interdependencies in order to insist that they too are subject to the controlling norm of equality of status among contracting parties. Workers obviously need businesses to supply jobs and consumers need businesses to supply products, but businesses are equally dependent on families, schools, health care institutions, and many other bodies to provide responsible and able-bodied workers. The notion of the "social embeddedness" of markets—of which I am here citing merely one instance—captures exactly my general claim about interdependencies.[26]

I want to emphasize that although interdependencies are not associations (which for Dooyeweerd belong to the category of communities) they are clearly a parallel instance of what I earlier called covenantal voluntarism and which I identified as a distinctive contribution of Calvinian social theory. In medieval Christian social thought, organic metaphors were invoked to characterize the normative social bonds necessary to keep the multiple parts of the social body functioning in harmony. But wedded as they are to unsupportable assumptions about natural hierarchy and subordination, such organic metaphors can no longer serve that purpose in a differentiated society characterized by civil-legal freedom and equality. The notion of covenantal voluntarism might be one of the motifs to which we need to appeal instead. It will not be enough to issue generalized appeals for the restoration of "community." This is partly because it is always essential to specify which kind of community is being invoked in any particular discussion, and the use of this hopelessly abstract term risks obscuring the very specific kinds of renewal or protection or correction needed for differently qualified kinds of community.[27] But appeals to "community" are also problematic because this is not the appropriate term to use to describe the numerous *interdependencies* required if contemporary societies are to recover and deepen a now widely fractured social cohesion and to attain a greater measure of public justice. Dooyeweerd's analysis suggests that the normative realization—simultaneously and equivalently—of multiple irreducible types of community and interdependency will be required to promote that end.

What Is Civil Society For? Three Models Assessed

I now want to suggest that it is possible to isolate three distinct (if partly overlapping) models of civil society marked by different answers to the question of the *purpose* of civil society: the *protective,* the *integrative,* and the *transformative.* My characterization and assessment of these models will facilitate an engagement with the second and third core problems in civil society debates identified above: the relationship between civil society and the state and the relationship between the concept of civil society and the project of social critique.

The protective model is best represented in the neo-Tocquevillian strand of discourse favored by American communitarians such as Eberly and social conservatives such as Berger and Neuhaus.[28] This model looks to the institutions of civil society as performing protective or remedial functions: the renewal of threatened social bonds, the generation of social capital, the nurturing of responsible citizens, and the promotion of civic harmony. This reflects a broader diagnosis that locates the principal source of social decay not in the polity or the economy but in culture, understood as the realm in which values and virtues are primarily reproduced.

Taylor and Beem represent a second strand, indebted in part to Hegel,[29] in which the focus is on the requirement to establish integrative connections between civil society institutions and the state. Civil society both serves the purpose of political integration and stands in need of the integrative role of the state. For Beem a theory of civil society cannot ignore "the necessity of politics." Taylor, noting the limits of the eighteenth-century idea of civil society as an extrapolitical realm of spontaneous order, suggests the need for a clearly political conception of civil society: a "separate" but not "self-sufficient" sphere, "incorporated into the higher unity of the state,"[30] in which independent economic and other associations are integrated more or less closely into the state. At the level of public policy, such integration involves a corporatist "interweaving of society and government to the point where the distinction no longer expresses an important difference in the basis of power or the dynamics of policymaking."[31] On this view, the primary purpose of civil society is the realization of a politically mediated social unity.

Cohen and Arato represent a third, transformative orientation. They conceive civil society "around a notion of self-limiting democratizing movements seeking to expand and protect spaces for both negative liberty and positive freedom and to recreate egalitarian forms of solidarity without impairing economic self-regulation."[32] On this view, while no wholesale systemwide transformation is envisaged, a chief purpose of civil society is to empower resistance to political and economic subordination and injustice and to facilitate the creation of a territory of democratic self-governance in which autonomy and equality can be recreated.[33]

I now want to illustrate how Dooyeweerd's comprehensive pluralistic account of multiple, irreducible types of community and the ramifying interdependencies in which each stand both enables an affirmation of valid insights in each of these three orientations and indicates how some of their respective limitations might be overcome.[34]

Civil Society as Protective

Consider first the *protective model* in which families, churches, neighborhoods, and voluntary associations are the focus of concern. In the first place, Dooyeweerd's accounts of the indispensable role of the institutional communities of marriage and family strongly endorse the call to safeguard the integrity of these "traditional" social institutions, which (when rightly ordered)[35] play a decisive role in the nurturing of mature and self-reliant persons capable of assuming many other social roles. Second, his account of voluntary associations affirms the arguments of those who call attention to their indispensability as arenas of social cooperation, schools of civic virtue, and bulwarks against governmental intrusion. Churches and many other religious communities can also advance these goals. Legally, and from the state's point of view, these possess the status of voluntary associations (except when "established"). Of course, they often regard themselves as institutional communities, and arguably they need to sustain this self-understanding if they are to advance those social goals (apart from their own internal reasons).

The notion of interdependencies I have proposed also points up the fact that it is never sufficient to view communities solely in terms of their internal communal activity. In the case of each of the communities highlighted in the protective model of civil society both their healthy internal life and their external benefits presuppose dense networks of interdependencies: between families and schools, families and religious associations, schools and voluntary associations, and so on. But such interdependencies will not subsist simply among these bodies themselves. Cooperative ties among numerous other types of community will also be essential: families and businesses, schools and businesses (local retailers), families and trade unions, governments and all of the above.

Obviously the full range and types of such interdependencies cannot remotely be cataloged here, as their range and diversity are so enormous. One illustration of their importance, however, is that other entity typically cited in the protective model, namely, the neighborhood. Dooyeweerd says little about this, but his analysis of the city suggests a fruitful way to understand its importance. In his view, as I noted, while the state is a community with a specific structural purpose, the city is not. I also showed how, by extension, the ramifying geographic phenomenon known as "society" is likewise not a community with a specific structural purpose. There is indeed such a thing as society, but it is not a community with a single, unifying normative end but rather an extremely complex network of enkaptic interlacements—or, as I now suggest, a complex network of interdependencies, some of which have an enkaptic character. Geographic neighborhoods such as villages or other localities with an acknowledged identity are microcosmic manifestations of society and can be similarly characterized.

Although Dooyeweerd does not say so in so many words, it follows from the thrust of his overall analysis that neighborhoods play a vital sustaining and integrating role in modern societies. Indeed beyond membership in communities like family and workplace, neighborhoods have often proved to be the most significant social nexus in many people's lives and the one whose loss is most felt if eroded. It is, therefore, necessary to identity them carefully and, especially, to avoid conflating them with local governments. As Dooyeweerd's analysis of the "metropolis" clearly shows, local governments are only one of the communities residing in the vicinity of a neighborhood. Reviving neighborhoods is a standard refrain of communitarians, but this is not identical to conferring more power on local governments. As a political community, local government is certainly responsible for promoting public justice within its locality, and this will indeed involve a task as potentially extensive (i.e., cross-sectoral) as that of a national state. For example, declining a planning application for a megastore whose arrival will likely decimate well-established and trusted local retailers, compel local residents to drive instead of walk, and, by emptying streets, undermine vital public space, would be a paradigmatic instance of enforcing neighborhood-level public justice.[36] On the other hand, local housing, community development, or job-creation programs controlled entirely from the town hall are likely to be paradigmatic cases of local statism. The distinction between enkaptic interlacements and part-whole relationships needs to be adhered to at the local level just as much as the national.

Dooyeweerd's categories, then, lead to an affirmation of the importance of protecting the many vulnerable social ecologies necessary for the sustenance of healthy families, religious communities, voluntary associations, and neighborhoods—the focus of the protective model. Now it can already be seen, however, that the protective model implies an integrative dimension, for example, especially insofar as local government performs the essential role of providing overall political coordination of neighborhoods, under the norm of public justice. Yet a major criticism of the protective model is that it takes insufficient account of the "necessity of politics." This neglect is evident in two representative formulations of the model.

David Green's neoconservative model, formulated in *Reinventing Civil Society: Welfare without Politics,* proposes to offload the great bulk of welfare provision currently delivered by government-controlled and publicly funded agencies like hospitals, to private voluntary associations.[37]Aspects of his critique of the bureaucratic, centralized welfare state would certainly converge with Dooyeweerd's attack on statism. But Green's account suffers from a reductive analysis of civil society in which exaggerated hopes are invested in one type of social structure, the voluntary association, buttressed by reinvigorated families. But these are only two of the many social structures that need to be revived if a problem like inadequate health care is to be addressed. And, crucially, since health care necessarily raises issues of *just distribution of resources,* public authorities will inevitably need to play an integrating role in guaranteeing, if not directly supplying, adequate provision. Green's retrieval of the model of the nineteenth-century British friendly society (a cooperative mutual aid association) is salutary, but his assumption that voluntarism plus families plus markets alone can solve the crisis of the welfare state—that one can have "welfare without politics"—is naive.[38]

Berger and Neuhaus's case for a much greater use of mediating structures in delivering desired public policy outcomes is not as influenced by the neoliberal economics shaping Green's, but it also insufficiently acknowledges the scale of the political intervention required if they are to fulfill that role. For example, the authors' salutary aim of reviving "people-sized" institutions rests on an assumption that bureaucratic and alienating "megastructures" like the state and large corporations cannot be significantly refashioned. But some versions of the continental European social market model suggest that corporations can indeed be constrained and guided toward more economically just outcomes, and without excessively enlarging the state. These limitations of the protective model will become clearer as we turn to the integrative model.

Civil Society as Integrative

Although the protective model already implies a limited recognition of the need for political integration, the integrative model has larger strategic horizons, concentrating primarily on the role of national governments in securing political unity among a diverse citizenry and its leading institutional sectors. Rather than expound this model at length, I want to try to show that Dooyeweerd's notion of public justice as the distinctive norm of the state helps frame a credible notion of political integration and cautions against some of the unwelcome corporatist tendencies of some versions of the integrative model. In elaborating this proposal I will also treat the second core problem identified above, the crucially important relationship between civil society and the state.

An important clarification is required at the outset. I have proposed a distinctive definition of civil society as the dense realm of interdependencies holding between the multiple communities and persons populating a differentiated society. I pointed out that, on my definition, the scope of civil society is not identified as a realm consisting of particular types of communities or sectors of society (familial, economic, social, cultural, political, etc.) but rather as a realm embracing interdependencies subsisting among all of them (and individual persons). Its focus is the normative requirements of interdependencies characteristic of a modern differentiated society. Now one of these communities in a differentiated society is, of course, the state itself. On its face, then, my definition seems to cut across the universal practice in civil society discourse of sustaining a sharp distinction between civil society and the state. Is this not too drastic a reconceptualization?

After all, there is a compelling reason why the distinction between state and civil society must be retained, and it arises, not surprisingly, from a unique property of the state. Note, first, that the *internal* relationships between the state and its members, and the state and its parts, would not count as interdependencies anyway; these are communal relationships, characterized by durability, internal unity, and authority. And they include all dimensions of the state-citizen relationship and the relationships between the state and its diverse organs, branches, and agencies. The state's activity within these relationships is its *internal* functioning, to be distinguished carefully from its *external* relationships both with nonpolitical communities and with persons in their nonpolitical capacities. Can these external (enkaptic) relationships be properly classified as "interdependencies"? On my definition it is evident that they cannot, for the simple reason that they are *compulsory*. Interdependencies hold between parties who stand to each other as legally free and equal parties, able to enter into voluntary partnerships, or not. But communities and persons do not stand to the state in this way. Uniquely among differentiated communities, the state is a compulsory community, not only in the sense that membership is compulsory for all residents in its territory, but also in the sense that conformity to its legal authority is simply mandatory. This unique property of the state, then, implies that not only are its internal communal relationships to its citizens (members) characterized by authority but so also are its external relations to its subjects. The state, then, cannot enter into what I have termed interdependencies.[39] My task now, then, is to examine the nature of the unique role played by the state in relation to the dense network of interdependencies I have defined as civil society and which in principle embraces all types of community and all sectors of society. There is an apparent oddity about this approach that must be noted straightaway. It seems to suggest that the state does not relate directly to individual communities or persons but only to the relationships (of interdependency) between them. Is the task of the state, then, to *relate to relationships?* On its face, this does seem implausible. However, when the essentially *adjudicative* nature of the state's role and the full extent of that role are further elaborated, it will be seen to be a coherent position.

Let me first indicate the sense in which I think Dooyeweerd's notion of public justice is conceptually innovative. On his account, the norm of public justice is not some subjective political maxim brought to the state from outside but arises from its very structural purpose. The state is defined as a public legal community, a community of public justice; this is its irreducible identity. The political community establishes an indispensable, substantial, yet specific and limited kind of relationship among its members. It does not embrace the entirety of their lives, even their social or public lives, for citizens are always more than their citizenship: human beings simultaneously occupy multiple individual and social roles, each of which serves to delimit the scope of the others. Nor do their responsibilities as citizens necessarily take precedence over the responsibilities arising from those other roles: the state is a *res publica,* but this does not imply a "republican" conception of citizenship, only that the state embraces the whole of the public as its members and exists to secure the public good. What membership in the state implies is entry into a community with a clearly circumscribed purpose: the creation and maintenance of a public order of just laws.

I explained in chapter 9 that Dooyeweerd describes the form of relationship established by the state among its citizens and subjects as "political integration." The kind of integration established by the state is a public-legal integration and not, for example, a religious, ethical, ethnocultural, or economic kind. It is worth briefly elaborating on each of these excluded alternatives. The state may not, first, impose, overtly or tacitly, a common religious (or secular) confession on its citizens, nor may it privilege one confession or church over others. Accordingly, as I noted, a consistent application of Dooyeweerd's position implies a rejection of the principle of religious establishment. Nor, second, may it legally impose purely ethical—as distinct from public-legal—obligations upon its citizens; it is beyond its power to mandate nonpolitical virtues among them. It may certainly require and stimulate adherence to the shared *political morality,* or civic virtue—respect for law, the capacity for political participation and critical deliberation, and so on—necessary for the sustenance and healthy functioning of the *political community* itself. Citizen virtues, then, have a specifically political referent. The virtues necessary for broader, nonpolitical ends such as social harmony (friendship), successful parenting, or industrious employment, for example, are not contained within or derived from the political virtues required for citizenship (they do not conflict with but support them), and so responsibility for their promotion falls chiefly to agents other than the state. Third, the state may not favor a particular ethnocultural group within its borders. I noted in chapter 10 that Dooyeweerd holds to a political conception of nationhood; nations are created in the process of state formation. Although he holds that the state ought to treat minority ethnic or cultural groups under the norm of public justice, this may not include according them special constitutional privileges, such as differential rights of citizenship.[40] Fourth and finally, the state may not seek to realize the kind of economic integrations among its citizens appropriate within a business corporation, as it would be doing when it attempted to treat them as its employees (or its customers). In pursuing any such objectives the state would be exceeding its legitimate competence and violating the sphere sovereignty of other structures, as well as the civil rights of individuals.

Public justice, then, is the definitive normative principle for all state activity, and it derives from the irreducible identity of the state as a public-legal community. Pursuing public justice requires the adjudication—the public-legal harmonization—of three things: the legitimate rights, duties, and powers of persons; the legitimate rights, duties, and powers of diverse social structures; and the distinct claims of the public interest. It also requires the creation of the necessary legal, administrative, or fiscal instruments pursuant to these three ends.

It is now necessary to specify this more closely in relation to the notion of interdependencies. Public justice, I propose, is the public-legal adjudication of those interdependencies that intersect with the public realm—of the realm of *public interdependencies.* Each of the three dimensions of public justice just listed can be characterized as a realm of interdependencies. This is easiest to see in the case of the public interest, which, as I have pointed out, is not an entity but essentially a realm of interactions. But it is also true of the first: the rights, duties, and powers of persons. Each of these three elements of the legal sphere of the person is inherently relational. Rights, for example, are not items of individual property but legal claims meaningful only within a political community that gives them positive form.[41] So when the state pursues its public justice task in relation to persons, it is in fact engaged in adjudicating their *relations* to other persons or communities. And the same applies to the rights, duties, and powers of social structures, on which I comment further below.

Not all interdependencies acquire a public dimension: the interdependency between a group of families and a local church congregation is not in itself public in character. But, in principle, any interdependency might enter the public realm and, where it generates an issue of justice, might stand in need of state action. The core task of the state, then, can be defined as the *adjudication of public interdependencies.* Two clarifications are in order. First, this proposal is not intended to extend the scope of the public justice role of the state beyond that already envisaged in earlier chapters. It is rather to *characterize* that role more precisely. Nor, second, is it to imply that the state's role touches interdependencies *as opposed* to communities. For while the state must respect the sphere sovereignty of communities, those communities are themselves implicated in numerous interdependencies, and when these acquire a public character political adjudication may be called for.[42]

The distinctive *pluralist* emphasis in this view of the role of the state is, of course, its impact upon diverse social structures. The state,

Dooyeweerd insists, lacks the authority to govern those responsibilities of social structures arising from their sphere sovereignty and is competent only to establish the *public-legal conditions* in which these can be fulfilled. These conditions, I am suggesting, are directed essentially to sustaining the public interdependencies subsisting among social structures. What might this involve?

In the first instance, it obviously requires the state *itself* to refrain from directly violating the sphere sovereignty of other social structures. It cannot responsibly adjudicate among persons and other social structures if *it* is treating them unjustly. Now simply abstaining from violations of sphere sovereignty would already imply a notable reorientation of the state's activities (in some states, a radical one). For example, structures like schools or hospitals, which often necessarily depend heavily upon public funding, have found themselves increasingly subjected to intrusive regulatory policies that seriously compromise their capacity for self-government and risk turning them into virtual organs of government. This, it is worth remarking, can follow from either neoliberal or liberal/social democratic policies. Neoliberal governments looking for substantial reductions in public expenditure in order to shrink bureaucracies and fund tax cuts have, ironically, found themselves imposing intrusive "audit cultures" on such structures, increasing rather than decreasing bureaucratic regulation. Liberal/social democratic governments have typically aimed rather at imposing equal provision and equal rights as a condition of public funding, necessitating extensive state regulation to ensure uniformity. But such institutions are not governmental in nature, and receipt of public funds does not make them so, or render them subservient to the purposes of government, however purportedly democratic. They certainly perform a public function: that is, they contribute vitally to purposes, such as public health or the generation of an educated citizenry, for which government is indeed finally responsible. But while government may legitimately lay down regulations designed to protect the public from harm or guarantee minimum acceptable professional standards, the mere performance of public functions by social institutions such as these does not entitle government to override the medical, educational, or other competences of such institutions.

Second, sustaining public interdependencies involves actively ensuring that social structures do not override and thereby possibly damage *each other's* legitimate sphere, that is, that the necessary public interdependencies among them do not degenerate into illicit dependencies. For example, tough regulatory action against illegitimate market domination by multinational drug companies or oligarchic energy suppliers would be entirely justified. It clearly falls within the public-legal role of the state to break up concentrations of societal power (or at least mitigate their public impact) where these substantially constrain the freedom of other institutions—in this case competitively disadvantaged medical or energy suppliers, and health care or energy purchasers—to pursue their own distinctive responsibilities and purposes.

So the defining purpose of the state—*its* sphere sovereignty—thus involves adjudicating the multiple claims arising from the public interdependencies of persons, social structures, and the public interest. Much more than a mere pragmatic "conciliation of interests" (as some political scientists have termed it) is implied here; rather a process of *normative political adjudication* among the numerous legitimate interests within the state's jurisdiction (and through the institutional channels of a representative, constitutional democracy).

We can now see how the apparent oddity of implying that the state relates not to particular persons and communities but to relationships falls away. I am considering the general integrating relationship between the state and civil society, and I have now defined *civil society* as a realm of relationships, of interdependencies. The public justice role of the state involves adjudicating among public interdependencies. To clarify this further, consider the following: the state is not normally expected to relate directly or in any privileged or exclusive way to *particular persons* or to *individual communities*. While, for example, it may institute a general policy of industrial support, including even tax advantages for general classes of industry or depressed regions, it is widely seen as bad practice—indeed discriminatory practice—to offer such benefits to favored individual companies or to industries within an electorally significant locality (such as a minister's electoral district).[43] Nor, moreover, is it the role of government to regulate or support the private aspects of *interdependencies,* such as, say, relations between an individual trade union and an individual company. Its core role is to regulate or support public interdependencies in general, to establish general public conditions necessary for persons and communities to sustain healthy interactions with each other, as determined by their unique identities, resources, and needs. The core of its adjudicative task involves justly interrelating the public interdependencies among all persons and communities within its territory.

An important implication emerging from the foregoing is that such a Dooyeweerdian model envisages a role for the state potentially as broad in *scope* as that assumed by many postwar social democratic states. Far from advocating merely a Christianized, group-sensitive version of the minimal state, Dooyeweerd holds that the state is in principle empowered to act within every sector of society, insofar as an issue of public justice has arisen. The qualification "public" is not intended to cordon off whole categories of social structures, such as business corporations or families or churches, or indeed individual pursuits, as if they were in principle immune from state action, but rather to identify a distinction between those aspects of the functioning of these bodies (or persons) that are essentially internal (or private)—that is, that inhere in their sphere sovereignty—and those aspects that are, or have become, public, in the sense that they impinge upon the legitimate rights of other structures, or upon those individual rights which essentially require public-legal protection, or upon the public interest.[44]

On Dooyeweerd's construal of the relationship between state and civil society, then, the decisive question is not first of all how *extensive* the scope of the state's role is—that is, the range of types of communities or societal sectors that may warrant the attention of the state—but rather how *intensive* state action is—that is, how scrupulously it respects the sphere sovereignty of the structures among which it has to adjudicate and the civil-legal freedom and equality of individual citizens. Such action must be so tailored as to respect and, where necessary, enhance the capacities and competences of other social structures, and of persons, to enjoy their own rights and exercise their own responsibilities and powers as far as is possible, balancing these in relation to the distinct claims of the public interest. As we saw, this was his intention in the postwar debate over state regulation of industry.

A Dooyeweerdian model would, then, certainly endorse the current aspiration to move beyond the outmoded default preferences for regulation by the state or by the market, as seen among, respectively, liberal/ social democratic and neoliberal/conservative thinkers. This obfuscating bipolarity is already under challenge where civil society institutions are proposed as a distinctive and relatively autonomous *third* sector alongside state and market.[45] Yet Dooyeweerd's model implies the need for a still more complex model in which the state is conceived as standing in a wide variety of adjudicative relationships to the many public interdependencies making up (what I have redefined as) the realm of civil society. In such a model, the qualitative differences between types of interdependency would be carefully attended to by policy makers, and both the content of policy and the appropriate policy instruments (permissive, proscriptive, regulatory, financial, etc., or some combination) and enforcement mechanisms would be chosen in a way appropriate to the special characteristics of the issue at stake.[46] If the state, however, driven by one leveling ideology or another, treats families like firms, universities like industrial training schools or research departments of business corporations, schools like party organs, charitable associations like businesses, religious communities like ethnic neighborhoods, public health systems like markets, and so on, then not only does it risk distorting the identity and skew the purposes of such bodies, but in all likelihood its own policies will simply fail. The notion of public justice suggests a model of "political integration" able both to avoid the complacency and naïveté of neoliberal and neoconservative approaches and to preempt the corporatist or statist tendencies of liberal/social democratic approaches.

Civil Society as Transformative

The final core question to be considered in this chapter is the extent to which a Dooyeweerdian notion of public justice has the potential to generate transformative possibilities that might extend beyond those envisaged under the integrative model. Earlier I cited Cohen and Arato as the chief representatives of the transformative model of civil society. In their conception, civil society is transformative in the sense that it functions as a site of democratic and egalitarian initiatives occurring relatively independently of the state and the economy, as well as in the sense that such initiatives might serve to "limit the depredations of political power" and perhaps bring about significant political change. In this discussion I have both these senses in mind but also a third, namely, the sense in which civil society itself—especially "bad civil society"—might be transformed by the state.

The foregoing discussions of the protective and integrative models of civil society make clear that Dooyeweerd's social theory has strong affinities with aspects of each. His theory generates a clear affirmation of the need to protect the sphere sovereignty of institutional communities and voluntary associations and the local social ecologies that sustain them. Equal emphasis is also laid on the need for the political integration of these and many other types of community and interdependency through the state's discharging of its responsibility for public justice at local and national levels. I already observed how the norm of public justice also serves as a corrective to the protective model. A narrow concentration on renewing traditional and local communities obscures the vulnerability of these and many other types of community to wider societal pressures (especially market forces), their need for direct or indirect public support (such as financial subsidy), and their involvement in larger networks of public interdependency that they themselves cannot sustain (such as transport systems) or regulate (such as the media). In each of these cases, public-legal action by the state alone will not be sufficient, but it will be indispensable. Another way to frame this correction of the protective model is to say that the state's integrating activity itself amounts to a protective function on behalf of the whole society.

I also observed how Dooyeweerd's insistence on the safeguarding of communal sphere sovereignty and personal freedom serves as a corrective to corporatist or other statist versions of political integration. While the role of the state can be *extensive*—potentially impinging upon every person, community, and interdependency—each of these needs to be protected against *intensive* projects of political integration.

It is evident already, then, that a Dooyeweerdian approach already contains a potentially significant transformative dimension. Many ingredients of a comprehensive critique of key deformations of modern society, and the role of the state in addressing them, have already been identified in this study. I have noted, for example, his profound repudiation of the humanistic philosophies of individualism and universalism and of Enlightenment doctrines of progress; his pointed critique of exploitative nineteenth-century industrial capitalism and its commodification of labor; his argument that classical liberal conceptions of the minimal state subverted the norm of public justice; his attacks on absolutist forms of political sovereignty and of totalitarian tendencies in the modern state not only under communism but also in the creeping statism of Western political systems; his assault on fascism as a reactionary and racist ideology.

Dooyeweerd's conception of the definitive role of the state as the promotion of public justice implies that potentially far-reaching structural reforms may be involved in the correction of substantial public injustices. Political integration may itself bring about significant transformation. Such reforms will not, however, necessarily line up with any one ideological tendency. As I just intimated, the critiques of absolutist and totalitarian tendencies are leveled at regimes of both right and left. Indeed the notion of public justice aims to resist capture by either tendency. For example, it equally insists on public-legal protection for traditional communities or business corporations as on public-legal regulation of markets in the interests of social justice.

Yet it must be acknowledged that overall, Dooyeweerd's social and political writings do not powerfully convey a transformative dynamic, whether initiated by the state or from within civil society itself. Four examples from earlier discussions bear this out. First, I noted that his view of authority relations in marriage reflected prevailing assumptions about natural male headship. In this he was, of course, no more culpable than most males of his generation, including—some would say especially—those of Calvinist persuasion. His writings were completed before feminist challenges made significant public impact, but there is little evidence of any critical curiosity on this question in his extensive—and otherwise illuminating—accounts of the nature of marriage.[47] Second, in considering his conception of nationhood and ethnicity, I drew attention to the absence of any systemic critique of the apartheid regime in South Africa of which he was well aware. Although he firmly repudiated racist ideology and did not offer succor to the regime, it is regrettable that he was unable to suggest philosophical resources to assist that much-needed Christian critique.[48] Third, I alluded to his insufficiently critical endorsement of the structure of the capitalist business enterprise as premised essentially on capital ownership, although I also noted his increasing sympathy for the model of the producer cooperative.

Each of these illustrates a point I briefly alluded to in chapter 7 in a critical discussion of the notion of the historical founding functions of social structures, their rootedness in various types of formative power. I suggested that a better focus of the study of such power than a quest for elusive founding functions would be a search for antinormative, distorted operations or distributions of formative power in various social contexts. Each of these is an example of Dooyeweerd's relative neglect of empirical distributions of power, a neglect perhaps stemming from his preoccupation with distributions of legal *authority*.

My fourth example is of the same kind. This is the absence of any serious reckoning with the vital role of oppositional political movements in his writings. I described earlier his appreciation of the role of the political party within a representative constitutional democracy. I also noted the deficiencies of his characterization of public opinion as overly oriented to elite classes. The problem with these otherwise illuminating accounts is that they are too static; they do not sufficiently convey the dynamic reality of citizens' democratic initiatives, the structural obstacles preventing them, or the institutional resistance they typically evoke. What is missing is the recognition of the assertion of the formative power of the citizenry as a necessary (though not definitive) dimension of politics; accordingly there is little attention to the vital importance of the distribution of political power within a political community, or of the role of oppositional movements in spurring major political reforms.[49] What we are offered resembles more an inventory of the many modal types of power rather than a characterization of the concrete operation of power; that is, a classification rather than a diagnosis. As a result we are left without clear guidance on the question of how politically to bring about the transformative redistributions of power (or authority or resources), which might be called for by the principle of public justice.

I suggest there may be five possible considerations that help explain the underdevelopment of the transformative potentials of Dooyeweerd's thought. The first is that he was writing in the context of a small, relatively prosperous and politically cohesive European state in the mid-twentieth century where large-scale structural transformations of the kind advocated by democratic socialism were less evidently necessary. In the postwar period especially, the tasks of reconstruction and the extension of the welfare state and industrial regulation certainly occasioned

vigorous debates—in which, as we have seen, he was also a participant—
but did not call for radical structural reforms. The second reason was
that he held the view that the biggest danger to the contemporary world
came from universalism rather than individualism; from the risks of absolutism and totalitarianism rather than from the dangers of unrestrained
libertarianism and capitalism. Given that he was writing in postwar Europe this is not hard to understand. But the consequence is that his critique of political domination is much more compelling and aggressive
than his critique of economic domination.

A third factor was his relative lack of expertise in the social sciences.
His mastery of contemporaneous European social philosophers was impressive, but he was unable to deploy very effectively the findings of empirical social science. This may explain why his detailed reflections on
the normative structures of particular types of community are not (as he
was well aware) adequately complemented by parallel analyses of what I
have called the normative requirements of modern interdependencies
(the special focus of macro-sociological studies). Further, although in his
early years he worked on economic matters as a civil servant, this was
only a brief spell, and he was never able to draw extensively on empirical
economic evidence. His economic thought is often searching but among
the least well developed areas of his social theory. While I have suggested
that his conception of the core structural purpose of the state is correct in
its essentials, I also concluded that his conception of the core structural
purpose of the business enterprise is too uncritical of classical liberal economic assumptions about ownership.

A fourth reason is that, for plausible historical reasons, he held to an
essentially reformist view of social change. He was a product of the Kuyperian "antirevolutionary" tradition, which, as I noted in chapter 2, was
established in opposition to the atheistic French revolutionary strategy of
comprehensive social reconstruction according to a rationally precon-
ceived plan. This was not a reactionary posture. Indeed Dooyeweerd specifically rejects any endorsement of reactionary tendencies in history and
aligns himself with those progressive ones that worked with the grain of
norms for historical development (integration, individualization, differentiation). Yet he held that normative progress had to reckon with the
stabilizing force of tradition, which resists drastic historical interruptions
and wholesale programs of social transformation, since these are likely to

precipitate as many new injustices as they resolve. While on this point I judge him to be essentially correct, his position leaves open the question of the appropriate pace of normative historical disclosure in particular historical contexts.

There is a fifth—arguably the deepest—explanation for why a transformational dynamic is somewhat muted in his social and political theory. This is his assumption regarding the historical effectivity of creational norms. While he holds that the consequences of the fall are radical and pervasive, his thought is nevertheless guided by the expectation that creational norms will "impinge upon" human behavior even in the face of humankind's overt spiritual rebellion. The point is not only that such norms are in principle *accessible* to human knowledge (itself a contested claim among theologians, of course), but that they are, over the long haul, *effective* regardless of what humans beings think they know. Persistent deviations from norms—the Bolshevik attempt to abolish the family, or unrestrained capitalist expansion, for example—will evoke countervailing forces in the direction of normativity: creation order will fight back. I will not offer here a general assessment of Dooyeweerd's expectation about creational effectivity, but I will suggest that such an expectation can lead to an underestimation of the concrete results of human fallenness in particular cases, and thus to an insufficiently critical posture toward the prevailing positive forms of particular communities and interdependencies.

Earlier I alluded to a lack of Augustinian bite in Dooyeweerd's critical social analysis. My suggestion is that all five factors discussed above may have played a role in explaining that deficiency, but perhaps especially the last. High expectations regarding what I called the historical effectivity of creation-based norms seem to have led him—in spite of his penetrating critique of the modern humanistic ground motive—to adopt a stance of presumptive affirmation toward existing social structures. Thinkers imbued with a more consistently Augustinian awareness of the pervasiveness and depth of human distortions of such norms—of what we might call the "effectivity of sin"—instead tend to adopt a stance of presumptive suspicion toward what fallen human creatures historically construct. Dooyeweerd strives to hold these two elements of the biblical ground motive in balance. Indeed he does not see them as standing in any essential tension. On the contrary, it is precisely an affirmation of the orderliness of creation that alone makes possible an accurate discernment of its distortedness. Yet a balance in a more Augustinian direction might have enabled him to countenance a more ambitious transformative social critique.[50]

The central conclusions of this chapter are as follows. First, the three most significant conceptual innovations in Dooyeweerd's Christian version of normative pluralism are the idea of irreducible institutional identity, the correlation between communities and interdependencies, and the principle of public justice as the core task of the state. I have explained the import of these innovations and suggested how they might assist contemporary theorizing on the concept of civil society. In particular, I showed how they suggest illuminating perspectives on three core problems surfacing in civil society discourse: the definition and scope of the concept of civil society, the relationship between civil society and the state, and the utility of the concept of civil society for the project of social critique. My account has sought to demonstrate that a Dooyeweerdian contribution includes both a novel understanding of the simultaneous pursuit of the norms of community and interdependency and a distinctive conception of the role of the state in relation to each.

Dooyeweerd was clearly aware that his own writings were no more than provisional explorations of the distinctive resources of a particular confessionally grounded philosophical movement that, at the end of his life, had only just begun to take shape as an established intellectual tradition. However, his very attempt to launch a project of Christian social and political theorizing intended to serve as a guide for political action inevitably raises for us again the question of the legitimacy and efficacy of employing religiously inspired discourse in a radically pluralistic and extensively secularized society. What prospects are there for a social theory and political orientation intentionally grounded in Christian faith to be taken seriously in such a context? With some brief Dooyeweerdian reflections on that question I close this study.

EPILOGUE

Religious Discourse in State and Civil Society

I NOTED IN CHAPTER 10 THAT ALTHOUGH DOOYEWEERD entertains a qualified notion of a Christian state, he nevertheless clearly rejects any discriminatory treatment of religion on the part of the state. It is one thing, however, to support a nonsectarian public policy toward religion but quite another to supply a genuinely *public* philosophy—one effectively addressed to a public audience and successfully illuminating the nature of the public good. Treating religiously or ideologically diverse communities equitably may indeed help preserve civic peace, but if those communities look to the state only for legal space to sustain their own self-referential tribal narratives, then the civic bonds holding the political community together will be tenuous. I noted that Dooyeweerd progressed from a view of his work as uniquely Calvinian to a broader ecumenical Christian aspiration. But what prospects are there that even a more ecumenical rendition of Christian pluralism might appeal beyond the community of those who accept Christian presuppositions? And how legitimate would it be even to try to launch such an appeal?

This question is taken up in Casanova's important analysis of the role of public religion in secularized modernity.[1] Casanova distills the principal valid insight in secularization theory. It is not, he shows, the now widely challenged claim that under conditions of secular modernity religion inevitably undergoes processes of both "decline" and "privatization." Recent evidence seems to demonstrate that neither are necessary outcomes of modernization. The valid insight in secularization theory is

rather that modernity is characterized by a process of institutional differentiation, which problematizes the authority and location of religion. A
secularized society is one in which religion and its institutional embodi-
ments no longer hold public sway over other sectors of society. But this
does not imply, he argues, that religion has accepted or must accept marginalization to the private sphere: religion in the modern world is undergoing "deprivatization" and can still legitimately play a public role. Utiliz-
ing Weberian and Habermasian categories, Casanova proposes that the
form of public influence appropriate to religion in the modern world is
the offering of "normative critique" of the "amoral" spheres of the economy and state, from a location in civil society. Not only are established
religions ultimately incompatible with the imperatives of modern differentiation, but former attempts by churches or religiously based political
movements to operate directly at the level of the "state" or at the level of
"political society" are incongruous with the reality of religious and cultural pluralism. The constraints of differentiation mean that effective
normative religious discourse is likely to issue from a base in civil society
alone.

The experience of Dooyeweerd's redoubtable forebear, Abraham
Kuyper, is highly pertinent to an assessment of Casanova's thesis. That
experience (summarized in chapter 2) offers powerful support for Casanova's rejection of the claims about religious decline or religious privatization. Yet it also suggests that Casanova's argument that the appropriate
location of modern public religion is in civil society *rather than* state or
political society need not follow. The neo-Calvinist movement under
Kuyper's leadership was a classic example of public religion under conditions of differentiation and religious pluralism. Yet it operated not only
from within civil society (churches, educational, labor, and other social
movements) but also at the level of *political society* as a Christian political
party (the ARP) and at the *state* level as a partner in successive coalition
governments. The Christian Democratic Party (CDA) into which the
ARP was incorporated in 1980 still exists and continues to enter government. Although the CDA continues to have its very legitimacy ques-
tioned by some of its secularist political opponents, its continuing presence generates no evidence of inherent incongruity with the imperatives
of a differentiated, religiously pluralist society. Indeed one of the distinctive policy emphases of the CDA remains precisely its defense of the legal

protection of religious pluralism in the face of policies advocated by secularist parties that would have the effect of undermining such pluralism.

It is true that Kuyper was certainly regarded as a divisive figure by his political and ecclesial foes, but, arguably, he was no more guilty of that charge than many of the prominent humanist liberals and socialists of his time. Indeed it could be suggested that he was *less* divisive in view of the fact that he openly recognized religious and ideological difference and sought to accommodate it explicitly in law and public policy rather than suppress it in the interests of a spurious national unity.[2] His ambition was not simply the protection of his own confessional community but *the renewal of the whole nation, in the light of a distinctive vision of the public good*. And his views, although deeply objectionable to many, were perfectly intelligible; he seemed no less successful than his ideological rivals in projecting a public philosophy in the sense defined above. For him the political meaning of confessional pluralism meant the creation of space in which rival public philosophies could respectfully contend in the public square.

Dooyeweerd's philosophical work was inspired by the same spirit and guided by the same strategy. I ventured earlier that the salience of many of his conclusions regarding the rights and responsibilities of social institutions and the state could be and indeed have been recognized by those who cannot accept his underlying ontological framework or the religious convictions that shaped that framework. I want now briefly to explain how, even within his own terms, such recognition is possible.

In chapter 3 I introduced Dooyeweerd's transcendental critique of theory, which concludes that theorizing in every scholarly discipline is profoundly shaped by deep, often hidden presuppositions of an essentially religious nature. But this claim about the foundational role played by religion is not intended to apply merely to the activity of theorizing but is advanced as an assertion about the fundamental nature of the human condition. In politics, as in every other sphere of life, participants are substantially, if unwittingly, influenced by powerful underlying religious convictions, whether theistic or secularist. This has been interpreted by some of Dooyeweerd's critics as implying a fideistic incommensurability across perspectival divides, on account of which contending perspectival communities are, after all, engaged finally in self-referential narrative confession rather than in genuine intercommunal communication—in mere expression rather than dialogue. But this is far from Dooyeweerd's intention. His *theoretical* ambition is to create conditions conducive to the honest recognition of religious difference, not in order to bring intellectual exchange to a halt in a fruitless tribal standoff, but rather precisely to facilitate better dialogue across deep perspectival divides. When applied to *politics* this requires, again, not a denial or suppression of perspectival differences but an open dialogue about their origins and implications. The goal is the promotion of a more constructive form of political communication premised on mutual respect between adherents of rival positions, in order to allow a *more just conciliation* among advocates of contending policy stances.

The clearest statement of this Kuyperian strategy came in his contribution to the debate over the spiritual dimensions of postwar reconstruction in the Netherlands, to which I alluded in chapter 10. To the consternation of many, he argued against exploiting the historical interruption of the war as an opportunity to leave behind the vexing confessional divides of the prewar era and in favor of upholding those very differences but in the context of a truly *public* debate about national reconstruction. Such public debate was possible because every human being not only holds to particular religious convictions but also inhabits the *same created order* and so shares in common human experiences arising from that order, in spite of even radical religious differences in interpreting such experiences. By employing what, without too much distortion, may be termed a Protestant version of natural law, he holds that communication across deep presuppositional divides is eminently possible and desirable. At the level of theory, this enables him to account for the fact that social and political theories rooted in presuppositions wholly incompatible with his own can nevertheless produce a whole range of valid insights, of which, as I noted, he makes frequent use. At the level of politics, it serves as the deeper basis of his expectation that political consensus on issues of law and policy is in principle attainable and worth striving for. When citizens act politically, they do so—wittingly or not—in response to the same underlying imperatives rooted in the created foundation of social order. However deep their perspectival differences, they can therefore *potentially* recognize each other as engaged in a common struggle for (what Dooyeweerd calls) public justice. The impinging reality of the need for political community will, he wagers, make itself felt through common strivings for justice (however differently defined) and shared institutional constraints (however variously encountered) discernible in principle by all.

The current resurgence of political religion worldwide—in important respects a source of hope and renewal, in others a cause of profound disquiet—suggests that Dooyeweerd's account of political consensus, formulated in his time and with his own national context in view, may be worth revisiting in our time, when safeguarding the destinies of both our national and global contexts seem to demand a depth of reflection that our political culture has, for too long, imagined it could do without:

> If the postwar "dialogue" is to contribute to the spiritual renewal of our nation, it must penetrate to that depth dimension of human life where one can no longer escape oneself. . . . Only when men have nothing to hide from themselves and from their counterparts in the discussion will the way be opened for a dialogue that seeks to convince rather than repel.[3]

APPENDIX 1

Dooyeweerd's Conception of the Task of Social Philosophy

IN CHAPTER 3 I INTRODUCED DOOYEWEED'S "THEORY OF theory"—his hugely ambitious "transcendental critique of theoretical thought." I noted that this critical project was launched not for its own sake or to do down rivals but to clear the way for the development of constructive philosophical work in many fields. This book outlines the substantive content of that work in social and political philosophy. Here I outline the basic methodology it implies for the field of social philosophy.

For Dooyeweerd the task of social philosophy is the critical, systematic elucidation of the invariant normative structural principles undergirding the actually existing institutions populating modern society. We saw in chapter 3 that the burden of the transcendental critique is to demonstrate, through an analysis of the structure of theoretical thought, the inescapable determination of such thought by pretheoretical commitments of a religious character (ground motives). This determination takes place, Dooyeweerd asserts, through the medium of a transcendental ground-Idea, a theoretical Idea (or complex of Ideas) that is immediately generated by a religious ground motive, and which frames the fundamental concepts of philosophy. Philosophy is a distinctive branch of theoretical thought in that it examines not any single part of reality but its total structure.[1] The foundational philosophical concepts of which such a total account is composed in turn determine the basic concepts of each of the special disciplines, or, as Dooyeweerd calls them, "sciences."[2]

Dooyeweerd holds that philosophy comprises five mutually presup-posing fundamental areas of investigation: the transcendental critique, the theory of modal aspects, the theory of structures of individuality, epistemology, and philosophical anthropology.[3] The methodological problem now under discussion arises in the field of epistemology, which investigates the structures of the various forms of human knowledge, in-cluding theoretical knowledge.[4] It is one of the central tasks of episte-mology to reflect on the methodologies appropriate for each different science. This involves, among other things, indicating the role played by philosophy in such methodologies. An epistemology will point to the indispensable role of the philosophical subdisciplines, the *special philosophies*—the philosophies of history, economics, law, language, bi-ology, and so on—in each of the special sciences. These special philoso-phies will thus presuppose a conception of the appropriate methodology for their field, supplied by epistemology. Special philosophies analyze the fundamental ontic structures of their own area of reality, while general philosophy analyzes the structures of the totality of reality (time, mo-dality, individuality, etc.). The central preoccupation of the special phi-losophies is with the modal and typical structures specifically related to their field. Thus, for example, economic philosophy will be focused on the structure of the economic aspect and the design of economically quali-fied structures of individuality, whereas general philosophy will concern itself with the coherence between the economic aspect and all the other aspects and between economically qualified structures and other kinds of individuality structures. The special philosophies therefore cannot be reliably pursued apart from such a general philosophy, nor can a general philosophy avoid having implications for each of these particular areas.[5] Philosophical reflection is a seamless robe, whether or not a philosopher is aware of it.

These special philosophies must be distinguished from the *special sciences,* economics, biology, law, physics, and so on, each of which fo-cuses on a particular modal aspect.[6] Dooyeweerd's claim is that the latter are all conceptually founded in a special philosophy.[7] In view of the fact that philosophical concepts are themselves conditioned by religious ground motives, this is therefore also a claim that the special sciences are (indirectly) religiously determined. Religion conditions science but through the intermediary of a philosophical framework. In contrast to the positivist conception of scientific objectivity, widely influential when he wrote, Dooyeweerd holds that no science can be, or ought to strive to be, religiously neutral, since it is precisely religious commitment that makes the scientific enterprise possible at all. Far better to acknowledge its influence openly than to succumb to it unwittingly, and so uncritically.[8]

A special *science* could only be autonomous with respect to philosophy if a specific aspect of *reality* could be investigated without considering its coherence with other aspects. But since all the aspects of reality are mutually cohering, scientific analysis of each of them must take account of their coherence with all the others.[9] We can see, therefore, how Dooyeweerd's integral ontology of cosmic time necessarily implies an interdisciplinary methodology of scientific research in which philosophy plays the conceptually determinative role: consequently, "an interpenetration of philosophy and special science is inescapable."[10]

What, then, is the relation between the philosophical concepts underpinning all special sciences and the empirical investigations carried out by those sciences? Dooyeweerd rejects any version of what he terms "speculative metaphysics," by which he means any attempt to impose philosophical constructions in a priori fashion on empirical reality. This he regards as completely incompatible with his own "integral empirical method."[11] Rejecting the charge that the philosophical concepts he employs are a priori constructions, he insists that he acquired them by means of critical philosophical analysis of empirical reality itself. Philosophy is not to be classed as a purely "theoretical" discipline in distinction from the "empirical" disciplines. It is neither simply deductive nor inductive, though it may involve both these logical tools. All systematic analytical investigation is both theoretical in character and empirical in object.[12]

One of the most fundamental philosophical issues on which special scientists will necessarily have to adopt a position is the delimitation of the field of investigation appropriate to their enterprise. Empirical phenomena obviously do not present themselves neatly parcelled up into such fields complete with labels attached. Since every phenomenon displays every modal aspect, the practitioner of these sciences will have to make a choice about which of these to abstract for purposes of scientific research. Biologists will need a criterion of "the biotic," economists a criterion of "the economic," and so on. These criteria cannot be arrived at apart from a view of the relation of one field to all the others, and this can only be supplied by an overarching philosophical view aspiring to take in the whole of reality.

Such scientists will also need to be able to distinguish between various *typical* structures that function in, say, the biotic or economic aspects. The specific structure and laws of a modal aspect can only be analyzed by examining concrete existents, each of which has a typical structure. To analyze the juridical aspect, for example, a legal theorist must be able to distinguish between the different types of law found within a variety of societal structures (e.g., constitutional law in the state, ecclesiastical law in the church, industrial law in the corporation or between corporations, international law among states). The general modal concept of law cannot in itself supply these distinctions. What is necessary is a grasp of the typical structures within which law functions. For example, the general concept of law in itself tells us nothing about the specific content of state law. For this we need to grasp the structure of the state itself.[13] It thus appears that every special science will be indebted to philosophy for both modal and typical concepts, which it inevitably, if unwittingly, must assume.[14]

The main feature of the general relation between philosophy and the special sciences applies also to that between social philosophy and empirical sociology.[15] Actually, Dooyeweerd prefers the term *positive sociology* (not to be confused with positiv*ist* sociology) to empirical sociology since, as we noted, he holds that philosophy too is an empirical discipline.[16] The science of empirical sociology depends upon basic concepts given by social philosophy. Dooyeweerd's "integral empirical method" implies a continuous mutual interaction between the two fields, with positive sociology supplying the data upon which social philosophy reflects, in order, in turn, to generate the concepts that positive sociology must use. Throughout this interactive process social philosophy itself depends upon broader concepts given by a general philosophical framework, which concepts are in turn forged out of reflection on empirical reality.

We can now state what this implies for the field of investigation of positive sociology. Dooyeweerd distinguishes in *NC* between two different areas of sociological investigation.[17] First, there is the *special science* of sociology that investigates the structure of the *social aspect*. This is on par with other "modal" sciences like physics, chemistry, psychology, economics, law, theology, and so on. The scope of the modal science of sociology is indicated by the nuclear moment of the social aspect, namely, "intercourse," and its task is to examine the various modal norms of social intercourse, such as politeness, respect, and so on.[18] Some modal sciences are natural sciences; some (e.g., economics, law, or ethics) have as their object particular aspects of human societal life. The latter are "special social sciences."[19] Sociology understood as the science of the social aspect is thus one of the special social sciences, since it investigates merely one modal aspect of (a multimodal) human society. Dooyeweerd's distinction between the "social" as a modal aspect and the "societal" as a realm of institutions must continually be kept in mind.[20]

Second, there is the *totality science* of sociology that takes into its purview the entire range of typical *societal structures*.[21] Its object of research is defined not with reference to a specific modal aspect but rather with reference to the comprehensive or "total" structure of human society, which displays all aspects.[22] To grasp this total structure requires a standpoint that can be provided only by social philosophy.[23] Social philosophy investigates the invariant ontic order of social structures, their structural principles, while the totality science of positive sociology investigates the variable concrete forms of these structures in the light of a philosophical view of their ontic order.[24] The social philosophy that Dooyeweerd elaborates, in over five hundred pages of the third volume of the *NC* and in many other writings, is intended to serve as the foundation both for this totality science and for the various special social sciences (including the modal science of the social aspect).[25]

The basic challenge of the totality science of positive sociology is to attain "a theoretical total view of human society."[26] Such a view cannot be acquired merely by synthesizing the results of the special social sciences.[27] Attempts to acquire a "total view" apart from an integrative social philosophy will inevitably lead to the conscious or unconscious singling out of one particular modal aspect and attempts to explain the whole of society in terms of that aspect alone. This is a standing temptation, one easily succumbed to on account of the phenomenon of the "sphere universality," or "ubiquity," of every modal aspect. Precisely because every social structure functions in, for example, the economic aspect, it appears prima facie plausible to seek explanatory accounts of their concrete functioning in terms of economic causality alone. Such theories are indeed reckoning with what Dooyeweerd calls "indubitable states of affairs," but they are doing so at the cost of inflating the explanatory power of the economic aspect out of all proportion. They are guilty of a gross form of exaggeration, an "absolutization" of the economic aspect. And, as we have seen, aspectual absolutization leads necessarily to reductionism. Indeed the presence in Dooyeweerd's time of many competing schools within sociology—mechanism, biologism, psychologism, evolutionism, economism, and so on—was for him testimony to such absolutization.[28]

We are now in a position to see how the role that Dooyeweerd attributes to social philosophy can be more precisely specified as the provision of answers to the three "transcendental" questions facing all comprehensive philosophical frameworks.[29] These questions correspond to the three "transcendental basic problems of theoretical thought" lying at the base of all philosophies. The *first question* can be put thus: is there some fundamental ontological structure underlying all the diverse social structures that are distinguished for theoretical purposes? In theorizing about society, each structure needs to be abstracted from the others in order to grasp its typical character. Yet the object of a social philosophy is to construct a total view of society. To do this the different structures need subsequently to be compared with one another. What makes such comparison possible is that all of them are ontically grounded in the universal order of cosmic *time;* that is, they all function in all the "temporal" modal aspects. This is the "basic denominator" by which they can be compared.[30] The *second question* asks, what is the relationship between these diverse typical structures? All typical structures are rooted in the same ontic order, but this very order confers on each type an irreducible distinctiveness. The answer is that they relate to each other in terms of *sphere sovereignty,* "an inner sovereignty of each structure within its own orbit," balanced, however, by the enkaptic interlacement of each with others.[31] The *third question* asks, what is the *"radical unity"* of all social structures? This is only to be found "in the central religious community of mankind."[32] It is this answer that leads to a repudiation of all "universalistic" conceptions of social structures that attribute their unity to their status as parts of a single, all-embracing community such as nation or state. Dooyeweerd's denial that any *temporal* community can embrace all others in this way is a crucial component of his social pluralism (though in chapter 6 I expressed a doubt about the importance of that claim). These, then, are the three fundamental questions facing the totality science of sociology whose solution is the task of a social philosophy.[33]

APPENDIX 2

Dooyeweerd on Natural Law and Legal Positivism

DOOYEWEERD CLAIMS THAT HIS THEORY OF THE NATURE of law is an alternative to both legal positivism and natural law theory. The position he took in the 1920s and 1930s in this long-standing debate is distinctive (although the terms of the debate have, of course, changed significantly since then). Legal positivism, he holds, denies the inherently normative character of law and reduces it to its observable manifestations in particular legal systems, while the natural law theory needlessly posits a transcendent sphere of binding valid law in addition to positive law. Indeed he insists that there is only one kind of valid law—positive law—but that this ought to conform to normative legal principles inherent in the juridical aspect.[1] Legal principles and positive law are not two independent legal systems but are inseparably connected and mutually presupposing.[2] On the one hand, positive law without legal principles is a contradiction in terms, but on the other, the validity of legal rules depends on legal principles actually being positivized.[3]

The difference between his position and legal positivism is quite evident, but his critique of natural law theory, especially that of Thomas Aquinas, invites further comment.[4] It is important to bear in mind that what Thomists term "natural law" embraces an entire metaphysic and is thus to be compared not simply with his analysis of the legal or juridical aspect but also with his whole ontology. Here, however, we are concerned with the specifically jurisprudential implications of natural law theory.

Dooyeweerd's view of natural law is of special interest since in his early writings he was ready to describe the Calvinist legal theory he sought as a natural law theory.[5] By the time of *WdW* he had virtually abandoned the term, employing it only in a restricted and specialized natural scientific sense.[6] Even in his early writings, however, he distinguishes a Calvinist view of natural law sharply from a Thomistic one. The Thomistic idea of natural law as the participation of human reason in eternal law issuing from the divine mind is ruled out by his Calvinist "law-idea" *(wetsidee)*, which conceives law as an expression of divine will, an absolute boundary between God and creature.[7] Later, he refines and supplements this critique with his new concepts of modal aspect and individuality structure.[8] The former enables him more clearly to distinguish the juridical and ethical or moral spheres[9] and to argue that irreducible divine norms apply in each. The latter he presents as an alternative to the metaphysical concept of substance, which underpins the teleological idea operative within Thomistic natural law theory.

Finally, he gradually develops the notion that normative legal principles are "dynamic," in contrast to the "abstract," "static" principles of "scholastic" natural law.[10] They are "dynamic" because the juridical aspect, like all aspects, participates in the cultural "opening process." This implies two things. First, the requirement of positivization of legal principles is a necessary moment within the juridical aspect itself. It points to its historical analogy; indeed all positivization is, as noted in chapter 5, rooted in the historical aspect. New historical circumstances require new positivizations; for instance, the ban on interest in canon law was lifted when economic conditions changed.[11] Second, new legal principles emerge, appearing when the normative anticipatory moments in the juridical aspect are disclosed.[12]

The idea that positivization is inherent in the very nature of law is central to his critique of Thomism as a "dualistic" theory (a critique that he acknowledges is indebted to Kelsen).[13] The fundamental issue centers on the concept of validity. Thomistic natural law principles are different from what he terms "normative legal principles" in that they are regarded as "valid" irrespective of whether they have been established in positive law. This implies that there are actually *two* genuinely valid systems of law. Indeed, as Rommen, a defender of natural law, points out, it is precisely because natural law principles are independently valid that they are seen by defenders of the Thomistic theory as capable of functioning as a normative criterion by which a positive law can be critically evaluated and, if in contravention of natural law, declared null and void; here natural law "breaks" positive law.[14] The judicial nullification of many Nazi laws by German courts in the aftermath of World War II is often cited here as a classic example in support of natural law theory.

Dooyeweerd's objection (at least as faithfully represented by his successor Hommes) would be that the idea of natural law possessing real validity implies that, insofar as natural law and positive law share the same content, there would exist two valid laws with the same area of validity: natural law would thus render positive law otiose. Or, if natural law were allowed to "break" positive law, a significant element of uncertainty would be introduced into the legal system.[15] In Hommes's view, what was occurring in the German example was not that judges were "breaking" positive law with natural law but rather that they were appealing to widely acknowledged normative legal principles, such as "natural justice."[16]

This is not the place for a detailed discussion of whether Dooyeweerd has accurately represented Thomistic natural law theory or whether his critique is persuasive.[17] His attack on legal positivism is certainly more damning than that on Thomistic natural law theory. Indeed he pays tribute to the latter's "imperishable" contribution to legal theory in having demonstrated its need for recognition of material principles of law standing above the arbitrary will of legislators.[18] When viewed against the background of the variety of historical schools of legal philosophy, there is no doubt that the affinities between his theory of law and natural law theory are far more significant than the differences between them.

NOTES

Unless otherwise indicated, translations from Dutch sources are my own.

INTRODUCTION

1. Several publications proceeded from conferences held on the centenary of Kuyper's Stone Lectures at Princeton Seminary, delivered in 1898. See, e.g., Luis E. Lugo, ed., *Religion and Pluralism in Public Life: Abraham Kuyper's Legacy for the Twenty-first Century* (Grand Rapids: Eerdmans, 2000); *Markets and Morality*, vol. 5, no. 1 (2002); Cornelius Van der Kooi and Jan de Bruijn, eds., *Kuyper Reconsidered: Aspects of His Life and Work* (Amsterdam: VU Uitgeverij, 1999). Two other significant works appeared in the same year: Peter Heslam, *Creating a Christian Worldview: Abraham Kuyper's Lectures on Calvinism* (Grand Rapids: Eerdmans; Carlisle: Paternoster, 1998); James Bratt, ed., *Abraham Kuyper: A Centennial Reader* (Grand Rapids: Eerdmans, 1998). Kuyper's 1898 lectures were published as *Lectures on Calvinism* (Grand Rapids: Eerdmans, 1931). The Abraham Kuyper Center for Public Theology was established at Princeton Seminary in 2002 under the leadership of Max Stackhouse.

2. Calvinism is cited as a fruitful source of pluralist thinking by William Galston in *The Practice of Liberal Pluralism* (New York: Cambridge University Press, 2005), 23.

3. Many of Dooyeweerd's works have been translated (or republished when already translated) as *The Collected Works of Herman Dooyeweerd*, for many years a project of the Dooyeweerd Centre for Christian Philosophy based at Redeemer University College in Ontario (www2.redeemer.ca/dooyeweerd) and published by the Edwin Mellen Press.

4. See, e.g., C. T. McIntire, "Herman Dooyewerd in North America," in *Reformed Theology in America*, ed. David F. Wells (Grand Rapids: Eerdmans, 1985), 172–185.

5. By this I mean an affirmation of a plurality of original sources of law among many social institutions, not the system whereby various religious communities in a multireligious state have jurisdiction over certain spheres of personal law.

One.   Christianity, Civil Society, and Pluralism

1. It may be doubted whether what "recurred" here was the same question. Many argue that the concept of civil society is essentially modern and that applying it to premodern societies is anachronistic. I address this question in chapters 5 and 11. This chapler adapts material from Jonathan Chaplin, "Civil Society and the State: A Neo-Calvinist Perspective," in *Christianity and Civil Society: Catholic and Neo-Calvinist Perspectives*, ed. Jeanne Heffernan Schindler (Lanham, MD: Lexington Books, 2008), 67–96.

2. Oliver O'Donovan, *The Desire of the Nations: Rediscovering the Roots of Political Theology* (Cambridge: Cambridge University Press, 1996), 193.

3. See John Witte, Jr., *The Reformation of Rights: Law, Religion and Human Rights in Early Modern Calvinism* (Cambridge: Cambridge University Press, 2007).

4. Brian Tierney, *Religion, Law and the Growth of Constitutional Thought, 1150–1650* (Cambridge: Cambridge University Press, 1982).

5. Kuyper offered an enthusiastic (indeed hagiographical) statement of exactly this line of thought in both his first Stone Lecture (chapter 1 of *Lectures on Calvinism* [Grand Rapids: Eerdmans, 1931]) and his 1874 speech, "Calvinism: Source and Stronghold of our Constitutional Liberties," in *Abraham Kuyper: A Centennial Reader*, ed. James Bratt (Grand Rapids: Eerdmans, 1998), 279–322. For a more reliable analysis of the sources, see Witte, *The Reformation of Rights*.

6. See R. H. Tawney, *Religion and the Rise of Capitalism* (Harmondsworth: Penguin, 1926).

7. Subsections in this introduction allude to P. B. Evans et al., *Bringing the State Back In* (Cambridge: Cambridge University Press, 1985).

8. Don E. Eberly, ed., *The Essential Civil Society Reader: Classic Essays in the American Civil Society Debate* (Lanham, MD: Rowman and Littlefield, 2000). Contributors include Robert Nisbet, Alan Wolfe, Robert Bellah, Gertrude Himmelfarb, Jean Bethke Elshtain, Amitai Etzioni, Peter Berger, Richard Neuhaus, James Q. Wilson, Francis Fukuyama, Michael Sandel, Mary Ann Glendon, and William Galston. Robert K. Fullwinder, ed., *Civil Society, Democracy, and Civic Renewal* (Lanham, MD: Rowman and Littlefield, 1999), is another representative work in this genre. See also Christopher Wolfe, ed., *The*

Family, Civil Society, and the State (Lanham, MD: Rowman and Littlefield, 1998).

9. See Jean L. Cohen and Andrew Arato, *Civil Society and Political Theory* (Cambridge, MA: MIT Press, 1992), the first part of which contains a comprehensive survey of European and Latin American developments up to the early 1990s; John Keane, ed., *Civil Society and the State: New European Perspectives* (London: Verso, 1988). For other European-oriented assessments, see John A. Hall, ed., *Civil Society: Theory, History, Comparison* (Cambridge: Polity, 1995); Charles Taylor, "Invoking Civil Society," in *Philosophical Arguments* (Cambridge, MA: Harvard University Press, 1995), 204–224; Víctor Pérez-Díaz, ed., *Markets and Civil Society: The European Experience in Comparative Perspective,* European Civil Society (New York: Berghahn Books, 2009).

10. E.g., Paul Hirst, *Associative Democracy: New Forms of Economic and Social Governance* (Amherst: University of Massachusetts Press, 1994); and *From Statism to Pluralism: Democracy, Civil Society and Global Politics* (London: UCL Press, 1991). See also Mark E. Warren, *Democracy and Association* (Princeton: Princeton University Press, 2001).

11. Iris Marion Young, *Justice and the Politics of Difference* (Princeton: Princeton University Press, 1990); Chantal Mouffe, *The Democratic Paradox* (New York: Verso, 2000).

12. E.g., John Keane, *Global Civil Society* (Cambridge: Cambridge University Press, 2003); Mary Kaldor, *Global Civil Society: An Answer to War* (Cambridge: Polity, 2003).

13. Peter L. Berger and Richard John Neuhaus, *To Empower People: From State to Civil Society,* 20th Anniversary Edition, ed. Michael Novak (Washington, DC: AEI, 1996). The classic 1977 essay on mediating structures, which this 1996 volume celebrates, is not an especially "neoconservative" document. Neuhaus was content to be known as a social conservative, but Berger is less easy to categorize. Their respective reflections on the essay in this 20th anniversary volume reveal diverse political leanings. For a clearer neoconservative statement, see Michael Novak, *Is There a Third Way?* (London: IEA Health and Welfare Unit, 1998).

14. Amitai Etzioni, ed., *New Communitarian Thinking: Persons, Virtues, Institutions, and Communities* (Charlottesville: University of Virginia Press, 1995), esp. Etzioni's contribution, "Old Chestnuts and New Spurs, " 24 ff.; Amitai Etzioni, ed., *The Essential Communitarian Reader* (Lanham, MD: Rowman and Littlefield, 1998); Henry Tam, *Communitarianism: An Agenda for Politics and Citizenship* (London: Macmillan, 1998). Etzioni has written a searching critique of neoliberal economics, *The Moral Dimension: Toward a New Economics* (New York: Free Press, 1988).

15. John Ehrenberg, in *Civil Society: The Critical History of an Idea* (New York: New York University Press, 1999), chapter 7, also suggests that East European civil society theorists chose this term over *democracy* because of the systematic distortion of that term by the "people's democracies."

16. Christopher Beem, *The Necessity of Politics: Reclaiming American Public Life* (Chicago: University of Chicago Press, 1999).

17. See also Govert Buijs et al., eds., *Civil Society. Tussen oud en nieuw* (Amsterdam: Aksant, 2009).

18. Ehrenberg, *Civil Society: The Critical History of an Idea,* chapters 4–6.

19. He notes too that Ferguson, while observing the emergence of such a sphere, also launched a moral protest against its damaging social effects.

20. "Medieval political thought gave rise to an involved corporate theory of intermediate bodies but located them all within the oneness of God. The continuing drive to think in terms of the most comprehensive levels of association made it impossible to develop a theory of civil society that could stand independent of theology. The Greeks had tried to organize everything around the polis; medieval writers centered their thinking around God's organization of the cosmos" (Ehrenberg, *Civil Society: The Critical History of an Idea,* 41). But this fails to notice that substantial degrees of institutional autonomy—more significant than the "considerable local activity" that Ehrenberg himself observes—were seen as entirely compatible with God's cosmic sovereignty.

21. Ehrenberg, *Civil Society: The Critical History of an Idea,* 42; he notes that Aquinas was a partial exception to this (46–48).

22. Taylor, "Invoking Civil Society," 209.

23. Ibid., 211.

24. Michael Banner, "Christianity and Civil Society," in *Alternative Conceptions of Civil Society,* ed. Simone Chambers and Will Kymlicka (Princeton: Princeton University Press, 2002), 113–130. Both affirmations are underplayed by Ehrenberg. The first (solidarity) is developed by Buijs into a comprehensive geneaology of civil society in which "agape" is central rather than (as in my treatment and most others') social pluralism. For Buijs the drive toward civil society was not first the plurality of institutions but rather the emergence of associations of indiscriminate social care. Govert Buijs, "Agape and the Origins of Civil Society," in *Philosophy Put to Work: Contemporary Issues in Art, Society, Politics, Science and Religion,* ed. H. G. Geertsema et al., Amsterdam Christian Studies (Amsterdam: VU University Amsterdam, 2008), 18–50.

25. Chambers and Kymlicka, eds., *Alternative Conceptions of Civil Society;* Nancy L. Rosenblum and Robert C. Post, eds., *Civil Society and Government* (Princeton: Princeton University Press, 2002). Both appear in the Ethikon Series in Comparative Ethics.

26. In Rosenblum and Post, eds., *Civil Society and Government*, 223–254.

27. Writing in the early 1990s, David Hanley, in *Christian Democracy in Europe: A Comparative Perspective* (New York: Pinter, 1994), 2, suggests that the explanation for the general scholarly neglect of Christian Democracy is that "governing parties have become boring for political scientists." We wait to see whether their less predictable recent fortunes in Europe will revive scholarly interest. In addition to Hanley, see Stathis N. Kalyvas, *The Rise of Christian Democracy in Europe* (Ithaca: Cornell University Press, 1996); Emiel Lamberts, ed., *Christian Democracy in the European Union, 1945–1995* (Leuven: Leuven University Press, 1997); Thomas Kselman and Joseph A. Buttigieg, eds., *European Christian Democracy: Historical Legacies and Comparative Perspectives* (Notre Dame: University of Notre Dame Press, 2003).

28. Among the minority of those who are familiar with this tradition, several regard it with suspicion: religiously inclined American neoconservatives tend to view it as naively statist, while Christian socialists and liberationists dismiss it as irredeemably deferential to (American) liberal capitalism. Evidence supporting both of these judgments is not difficult to garner from the governing records of Christian Democratic parties in Europe and Latin America.

29. Academic indifference, however, has also reflected the fact that Christian democratic parties have frequently been interpreted as merely a sanctimonious rendition of moderate conservatism, social liberalism, social democracy, or simply catchall centrism, meriting no sustained separate attention. Kees van Kersbergen, *Social Capitalism: A Study of Christian Democracy and the Welfare State* (New York: Routledge, 1995) challenges this conventional interpretation, identifying a distinctive Christian democratic conception of the welfare state, "social capitalism," which cannot be satisfactorily accommodated under any of these categories, and the distinctiveness of which lies partly in its efforts to implement the principle of subsidiarity in the organization of public welfare provision.

30. The principal contributors to Christian democratic thought came from the leadership of the nineteenth- and twentieth-century movements of social and political Catholicism and from groups of Catholic intellectuals steeped in Thomist social philosophy, both of which have shaped and in turn been shaped by the official social doctrine emanating from the Vatican. Among their leading intellectual representatives are the French neo-Thomist philosopher Jacques Maritain, the French personalist Emmanuel Mounier, the German solidarists Heinrich Pesch and Oswald Von-Nell Breuning, and Johannes Messner and Heinrich Rommen.

31. Jacques Maritain, *Man and the State* (Chicago: University of Chicago Press, 1951), 23.

32. Jacques Maritain, *Integral Humanism: Temporal and Spiritual Problems of a New Christendom,* trans. Joseph W. Evans (Notre Dame: University of Notre Dame Press, 1973), 163–164. In the first major analysis of Christian Democracy in English, Michael Fogarty characterized the original vision of the Christian democratic movement as pluralistic in both a "horizontal" and a "vertical" sense: in its affirmation of the vital role of multiple, qualitatively distinctive communities and associations, independent of the state; and in its support for consociationalist responses to ideological pluralism (*Christian Democracy in Western Europe, 1820–1953* [Notre Dame: University of Notre Dame Press, 1957], 41–100). I refer to the consociationalist theme later.

33. Pius XI, *Quadragesimo Anno* (1931), reprinted in *Two Basic Social Encyclicals* (Washington, DC: Catholic University Press, 1943), paragraphs 78–79 (henceforth cited as *QA*). For discussions of subsidiarity, see Kenneth L. Grasso, "Beyond Liberalism: Human Dignity, the Free Society and the Second Vatican Council," in *Catholicism, Liberalism, and Communitarianism,* ed. Kenneth L. Grasso et al. (Lanham, MD: Rowman and Littlefield, 1995), 29–58; Christopher Wolfe, "Subsidiarity: The 'Other' Ground of Limited Government," in Grasso et al., eds., *Catholicism, Liberalism, and Communitarianism,* 81–96; Jonathan Chaplin, "Subsidiarity and Sphere Sovereignty: Catholic and Reformed Conceptions of the Role of the State," in *Things Old and New: Catholic Social Teaching Revisited,* ed. Frank P. McHugh and Samuel M. Natale (Lanham, MD: University Press of America, 1993), 175–202.

34. Max Stackhouse, "Christianity, Civil Society and the State: A Protestant Response," in Rosenblum and Post, eds., *Civil Society and Government,* 254–264. There are other representatives of this Protestant view (e.g., Emil Brunner, John Luther Adams), but I believe Kuyper's formulation is the most original and substantial.

35. Ibid., 256. For an application of his view to debates on globalization, see Max Stackhouse, "General Introduction," in *God and Globalization,* vol. 1, *Religion and the Powers of the Common Life,* ed. Max Stackhouse with Peter J. Paris (Princeton: Trinity Press International, 2000), 1–52; and Max Stackhouse, *God and Globalization,* vol. 4, *Globalization and Grace* (New York: Continuum, 2007).

36. Such convergence, in the writings of Dooyeweerd and Catholic philosopher Yves Simon, is explored in David T. Koyzis, "Towards a Christian-Democratic Pluralism: A Comparative Study of Neothomist and Neocalvinist Political Theories" (Ph.D. dissertation, University of Notre Dame, 1986).

37. Stackhouse, "Christianity, Civil Society and the State," 257.

38. For surveys of various strands of normative pluralism, see Robert Nisbet, *The Social Philosophers* (St. Albans, Herts.: Paladin, 1976), chapter 6; An-

thony Black, *Guilds and Civil Society in European Political Thought from the Twelfth Century to the Present* (London: Methuen, 1984); David Nicholls, *The Pluralist State,* 2nd ed. (New York: St. Martins, 1994); Paul Hirst, ed., *The Pluralist Theory of the State* (New York: Routledge, 1989); Stanislaw Ehrlich, *Pluralism: On and Off Course* (Oxford: Pergamon, 1982).

39. On Gierke, see Jonathan Chaplin, "Toward a Social Pluralist Theory of Institutional Rights," *Ave Maria Law Review* 3 (2005): 147–170.

40. See Ralph Bowen, *German Theories of the Corporative State* (New York: Whittlesey House, 1947); Matthew Elbow, *French Corporative Theory, 1789–1948: A Chapter in the History of Ideas* (New York: Columbia University Press, 1953).

41. G. W. F. Hegel, *Philosophy of Right,* trans. T. M. Knox (Oxford: Oxford University Press, 1967), 250–256; George Heiman, "The Sources and Significance of Hegel's Corporate Doctrine," in *Hegel's Political Philosophy,* ed. Z. A. Pelczinski (Cambridge: Cambridge University Press, 1971), 111–135. Hegel, of course, is notoriously difficult to classify. He might be located on the more statist wing of organicist pluralism. Notwithstanding his animus toward romanticism, his theory of corporations and indeed the wider theories of "mediation" and "civil" society within which they are framed share the reintegrative aims of the organicists. What sets him apart from them and the romanticism many of them had imbibed is his speculative rationalism. Beem ventures, unpersuasively, that a major strand of contemporary American civil society theorizing displays Hegelian influences; Beem, *The Necessity of Politics,* chapter 7.

42. Some might counter that such theories are not *characteristically* pluralist since their pluralism is a relatively minor theme in an overall perspective dominated by, for instance, concepts of human rights, distributive justice, or the divine origin of political authority; and it is certainly the case that the pluralist note is struck more loudly in some Catholic and Calvinist thinkers than others. Yet there is, I think, a sufficiently extensive body of explicitly pluralist reflection within these two Christian traditions to count as a school in its own right. I should add, too, that much other modern Christian social and political thought does not count as pluralist in my sense, even though few Christian writers (at least in the West) seem to reject it outright.

43. Not all strands would equally endorse, or even share, all such concerns. Contemporary radical democratic pluralists, especially, might cavil at being characterized in these ways. Perhaps they amount to a sixth postmodern version of normative pluralism.

44. Hirst, *Associative Democracy,* 20–22.

45. "Anti-statist" should not be read as "anti-state." Some classic pluralists, such as anarchist socialists, are anti-state; but most pluralists, and almost all civil society theorists, both modern and contemporary, are not.

46. I explicate these two centrally important categories further in chapter 2.

47. Dooyeweerd did not use the term *pluralism* to describe his own social and political thought, though he does at times apply the term appreciatively to others. The reason for this was a desire to distinguish himself from contemporaneous "political pluralists" such as Harold Laski or G. D. H. Cole in England or Leon Duguit in France, whose ideas were current when he was writing but whom he regarded as having lapsed into syndicalist tendencies that undermined the concept of the state as a public institution. See Herman Dooyeweerd, *De crisis der humanistische staatsleer in het licht eener calvinistische kosmologie en kennistheorie* (Amsterdam: Ten Have, 1931), 121, 125; and "Het vraagstuk van het organisch kiesrecht in een nieuwe stadium," in *Almanak van het Studentencorps aan de Vrije Universiteit* (Amsterdam, 1935), 105–121. For an analysis of Laski from a Dooyeweerdian perspective, see Bernard Zylstra, *From Pluralism to Collectivism: The Development of Harold Laski's Political Thought* (Assen: Van Gorcum, 1968). Not surprisingly, Dooyeweerd also did not refer to himself as a theorist of civil society, though he does comment on others' use of the term. See Herman Dooyeweerd, *A New Critique of Theoretical Thought*, 4 vols., trans. D. H. Freeman and W. S. Young (Lewiston, NY: Edwin Mellen Press, 1997), 3:587 ff. Henceforth cited in the text and notes as *NC*. (*NC* was originally published by Presbyterian and Reformed Publishing Co., 1953–58.)

Two.   Dooyeweerd in Context

1. See J. van der Kroef, "Abraham Kuyper and the Rise of Neo-Calvinism in the Netherlands," *Church History* 17 (1948): 316–344; Dirk Jellema, "Kuyper's Attack on Liberalism," *Review of Politics* 19 (1957): 472–485; G. J. Westra, "Confessional Political Parties in the Netherlands, 1813–1946" (Ph.D. dissertation, University of Michigan, 1972); C. den Hollander, *Christian Political Options* (The Hague: AR-Partijstichting, 1979); H. E. S. Woldring and D. Th. Kuiper, *Reformatische maatschappijkritiek. Onwikkelingen op het gebied van sociale filosofie en sociologie in de kring van het Nederlandse protestantisme van de 19e eeuw tot heden* (Kampen: J. H. Kok, 1980), 19–66; James W. Skillen and Stanley W. Carlson-Thies, "Religion and Political Development in Nineteenth-Century Holland," *Publius: The Journal of Federalism* 12 (Summer 1982): 43–64; Michael Wintle, *Pillars of Piety: Religion in the Netherlands in the Nineteenth Century, 1813–1901* (Hull: Hull University Press, 1987); Luis E. Lugo, ed., *Religion, Pluralism and Public Life: Abraham Kuyper's Legacy for the Twenty-first Century* (Grand Rapids: Eerdmans, 2000), pt. 1; Cornelis van der Kooi and Jan

de Bruijn, eds., *Kuyper Reconsidered: Aspects of His Life and Work* (Amsterdam: VU Uitgeverij, 1999).

2. Abraham Kuyper, *Lectures on Calvinism* (Grand Rapids: Eerdmans, 1961). See also H. R. Van Til, *The Calvinistic Concept of Culture* (Philadelphia: Presbyterian and Reformed Publishing Co., 1959); and S. U. Zuidema, "Common Grace and Christian Action in Abraham Kuyper," in *Communication and Confrontation: A Philosophical Appraisal and Critique of Modern Society and Contemporary Thought,* trans. Harry Van Dyke (Toronto: Wedge, 1972), 52–105.

3. I pass by the question of whether this was an accurate construal of the then-dominant "scholastic" conception of nature and grace. It obviously applies much less to post–Vatican II conceptions. Nor does it apply without substantial qualification to pre-Conciliar conceptions of thinkers such as Jacques Maritain, whose 1936 *Integral Humanism* represents an important "integralist" statement of this relationship.

4. W. F. De Gaay Fortman et al., eds., *Philosophy and Christianity. Philosophical Essays Dedicated to Professor Dr. Herman Dooyeweerd* (Amsterdam: North Holland, 1965), 18.

5. James W. Skillen, "From Covenant of Grace to Equitable Public Pluralism: The Dutch Calvinist Contribution," *Calvin Theological Journal* 31 (1996): 67–96.

6. See Skillen and Carlson-Thies, "Religion and Political Development in Nineteenth-Century Holland," 43–64; Kenneth Gladdish, *Governing from the Centre: Politics and Policy-Making in the Netherlands* (London: Hurst and Co.; The Hague: SDU, 1991), chapter 2.

7. Hans Daalder summarizes the breadth of his reforming achievements thus: "Within a score of years he organized (or helped to organize) a militant daily newspaper (1872), an Anti-School Law League (1872) consciously modeled on the British Anti-Corn Law League, a massive petition movement against a new Liberal School Bill (1878) which obtained over 300,000 signatures at a time when the electorate was only a little over a third of this figure, a political party, the Anti-Revolutionary Party (1879), which proclaimed resistance against the world of 1789 and pioneered modern mass-party organization techniques in the Netherlands, an independent Calvinist University (1880) which provided the movement with its future intelligentsia; and finally a separate church organization" ("The Netherlands: Opposition in a Segmented Society," in *Political Oppositions in Western Democracies,* ed. Robert A. Dahl [New Haven: Yale University Press, 1966], 200–201).

8. Harry Van Dyke, "How Kuyper Became a Christian Democrat," *Calvin Theological Journal* 33 (1998): 420–443; H. E. S. Woldring, "Kuyper's Formal and

Comprehensive Conceptions of Democracy," in Van der Kooi and De Bruijn, eds., *Kuyper Reconsidered*, 206–227.

9. Skillen and Carlson-Thies, "Religion and Political Development in Nineteenth-Century Holland," 43. Confirmation of this critique of the association of modernization with declining attachment to religion is found in José Casanova, *Public Religions in the Modern World* (Chicago: University of Chicago Press, 1994).

10. Skillen and Carlson-Thies, "Religion and Political Development in Nineteenth-Century Holland," 55.

11. Marcel E. Verburg, *Herman Dooyeweerd. Leven en werk van een Nederlands christen-wijsgeer* (Baan: Ten Have, 1989); George Puchinger, "Prof. Dr. Herman Dooyeweerd (1894–1977)," in H. G. Geertsema et al., eds., *Herman Dooyeweerd 1894–1977. Breedte en actualiteit van zijn filosofie* (Kampen: Kok, 1994), 11–27.

12. This was published as *De ministerraad in het Nederlandsche staatsrecht* (The Cabinet in Dutch Constitutional Law) (Amsterdam: Vrije Universiteit, 1917).

13. This influence continued after his death, within the Christian Democratic Appeal (CDA) formed in 1980 out of a merger of the Catholic People's Party, the ARP, and the CHU. Dooyeweerd's ideas are visible in a 1990 report produced by the CDA's research institute, the title of which, *Public Justice*, is a central motif in his theory of the state. See Wetenschappelijk Instituut voor het CDA, *Publieke gerechtigheid. Een christen-democratische visie op de rol van de overheid in de samenleving* (Houten: Bohn Stafleu Van Loghum, 1990). This report sets out, partly for reasons of party unity, to synthesize familiar Catholic themes—social justice, solidarity, subsidiarity—with distinctive ideas from neo-Calvinism. It still functions as a point of reference for the policy thinking of the research institute but less evidently so for the policies of CDA in parliament or government. The newer Christen Unie (CU) party is reviving interest in Dooyeweerd's thought.

14. *De beteekenis der wetsidee voor rechtswetenschap en rechtsphilosophie* (Kampen: J. H. Kok, 1926).

15. This was the Gereformeerde Kerk, founded by Kuyper in 1892, as an alternative to the established Hervormde Kerk.

16. Its first chair was D. H. Th. Vollenhoven, Dooyeweerd's brother-in-law and lifetime intellectual collaborator. Vollenhoven published several major works of Christian philosophy and exercised an influence within Calvinist philosophical circles second only to Dooyeweerd. The Association for Calvinist Philosophy, which attracted hundreds of members in short order, published three academic journals, of which the most significant was the scholarly journal *Philosophia Reformata*, which continues today.

17. Puchinger, "Prof. Dr. Herman Dooyeweerd," 25.

18. See Herman Dooyeweerd, *Encyclopedie der rechtswetenschap*, vols. 1–4 (Amsterdam: Studentenraad van de Vrije Universiteit, 1966). Henceforth cited as *EN*. Volume 1 has been translated as *Encyclopedia of the Science of Law*, ed. Alan Cameron and trans. Robert K. Knudsen (Lewiston, NY: Edwin Mellen Press, 2002).

19. In addition to his professional academic roles, Dooyeweerd served as chair of the Protestant Christian Reclasseringsvereniging from 1938 to 1953 and of the Juliana Hospital of Amsterdam from 1938 to 1954. He also gave numerous public speeches to a range of academic, social, and political organizations, many of which are published. He was also an accomplished pianist.

20. John Kraay, "Successive Conceptions in the Development of the Christian Philosophy of Herman Dooyeweerd," *Philosophia Reformata* 44 (1979): 137–149; 45 (1980): 1–40.

21. See Albert Wolters, "The Intellectual Milieu of Herman Dooyeweerd," in *The Legacy of Herman Dooyeweerd*, ed. C. T. McIntire (Lanham, MD: University Press of America, 1985), 1–19; and F. L. R. Sassen, "Dutch Philosophy," *Encyclopedia of Philosophy* 5 (1967): 441–442.

22. J. Glenn Friesen has recently argued that the mystical philosophy of Franz Von Baader (1765–1841) was a major influence on Dooyeweerd's thought. See J. Glenn Friesen, "The Mystical Dooyeweerd: The Relation of His Thought to Franz Von Baader," *Ars Disputandi* 3 (2003), www.arsdisputandi.org/publish/articles/000088/index.html/; and "Dooyeweerd, Spann and the Philosophy of Totality," *Philosophia Reformata* 70 (2005): 2–22. D. F. M. Strauss contests this in "Intellectual Influences upon the Reformational Philosophy of Dooyeweerd," *Philosophia Reformata* 69 (2004): 151–181.

23. See Thomas E. Willey, *Back to Kant: The Revival of Kantianism in German Social and Historical Thought* (Detroit: Wayne State University Press, 1978).

24. Wolters, "The Intellectual Milieu of Herman Dooyeweerd," 10.

25. Dooyeweerd, *NC*.

26. Wolters, "The Intellectual Milieu of Herman Dooyeweerd," 15.

27. Ibid., 14.

28. Dooyeweerd, *NC*, 1:v.

29. See Wolters, "The Intellectual Milieu of Herman Dooyeweerd," 10–17; Calvin G. Seerveld, "Dooyeweerd's Legacy for Aesthetics: Modal Law Theory," in C. T. McIntire, ed., *The Legacy of Herman Dooyeweerd*, 41–79: 55–64, 74 n. 48; Dirk Jellema, "The Philosophy of Vollenhoven and Dooyeweerd": pt. 2, "Dooyeweerd and Hartmann," *Calvin Forum* (May 1954): 192–194; pt. 3, "A New Synthesis-Philosophy," *Calvin Forum* (October 1954): 31–33.

30. See Heiman, "The Sources and Significance of Hegel's Corporate Doctrine," in *Hegel's Political Philosophy*, ed. Z. A. Pelczynski (Cambridge: Cambridge University Press, 1971), 111–135, esp. 113.

31. Wolters, "The Intellectual Milieu of Herman Dooyeweerd," 16.

32. See A. L. Conradie, *The Neo-Calvinistic Concept of Philosophy: A Study in the Problem of Philosophic Communication* (Natal: Natal University Press, 1960); Vincent Brümmer, *Transcendental Criticism and Christian Philosophy: A Presentation and Evaluation of Herman Dooyeweerd's "Philosophy of the Cosmonomic Idea"* (Franeker: T. Wever, 1961); K. Kuypers, "Herdenking van Herman Dooyeweerd," *Jaarboek van de Koninklijke Nedelandse Akademie van Wetenschappen* 3 (1977), 1–8; Marcel E. Verburgh, *Herman Dooyeweerd. Leven en werk van een Nederlands christen-wijsgeer* (Baarn: Ten Have, 1989).

33. Kuyper, *Lectures on Calvinism*, 133. Elsewhere, and not always consistently, Kuyper emphasized the common ground shared by thinkers having different religious presuppositions. See Zuidema, "Common Grace and Christian Action in Abraham Kuyper."

34. See Herman Dooyeweerd, "Het Calvinistische beginsel der souvereiniteit in eigen kring als staatkundig beginsel," *Nederland en Oranje* 4 (1923): 98–99, 185–189; 5 (1924): 8–15, 27–31, 71–76; *Calvinisme en natuurrecht* (Amersfoort: Wijngen, 1925); and *De beteekenis der wetsidee voor rechtswetenschap en rechtsphilosophie* (Kampen: J. H. Kok, 1926).

35. See Herman Dooyeweerd, *In the Twilight of Western Thought: Studies in the Pretended Autonomy of Theoretical Thought* (Philadelphia: Presbyterian and Reformed Publishing Co., 1960), 113–156.

36. Dooyeweerd, *NC*, 2:176.

37. Dooyeweerd, *De crisis*, 185.

38. Dooyeweerd, *Calvinisme en natuurrecht*, 2–3.

39. Henceforth cited in the text as *WdW.*

40. Dooyeweerd, *NC*, 1:524. His exaugural address delivered at the Free University in 1965 proposed that his philosophy was really founded on a "reformed-ecumenical ground motive." See his "Het oecumenisch-reformatisch grondmotief van de wijsbegeerte der wetsidee en de grondslag van de Vrije Universiteit," *Philosophia Reformata* 31 (1966): 3–15.

41. For partly contrasting readings, see Lambert Zuidervaart, "Good Cities or Cities of the Good? Radical Augustinianism, Societal Structures, and Normative Critique," in *Radical Orthodoxy and the Reformed Tradition: Creation, Covenant and Participation*, ed. James K. A. Smith and James H. Olthuis (Grand Rapids: Baker Academic, 2005), 135–150; and Jonathan Chaplin, "Suspended Communities or Covenanted Communities?: Reformed Reflections on the Social Thought of Radical Orthodoxy," in Smith and Olthuis, eds., *Radical Orthodoxy and the Reformed Tradition*, 151–182.

Three.   Religion and Philosophy

1. Dooyeweerd was well versed in the history of that debate. A substantial early series of articles treated it in depth: "In den strijd om een christelijke staatkunde. Proeve van een fundering der Calvinistische levens- en wereldbeschouwing in hare wetsidee," *Antirevolutionaire Staatkunde* 1 (1924–1925): 7–25, 62–79, 104–118, 161–173, 189–200, 228–244, 309–324, 433–460, 489–504, 528–542, 581–598, 617–634; 2 (1926): 244–265, 425–445; (quarterly) 1 (1927): 142–195.

2. In the twentieth century some of the most serious thinking on the relation of Christianity and philosophy has come from the neo-Thomist and neo-Calvinist traditions. On the relation between reason and faith in the tradition of John Calvin in particular, see Hendrik Hart et al., eds., *Rationality in the Calvinian Tradition* (Lanham, MD: University Press of America, 1983); and Alvin Plantinga and Nicholas Wolterstorff, eds., *Faith and Rationality* (Notre Dame: University of Notre Dame Press, 1983). For a classic introduction to a neo-Thomist understanding of Christian philosophy, see Étienne Gilson, *Christian Philosophy: An Introduction,* trans. Armond Maurer (Toronto: Pontifical Institute for Mediaeval Studies, 1993). For an official restatement, see John Paul II, *Fides et Ratio* (Chicago: Pauline Books and Media, 1998). For works that address the history of Christianity's relation to philosophy, see Colin Brown, *Christianity and Western Thought: A History of Philosophers, Ideas and Movements* (Downers Grove, IL: InterVarsity Press, 1990); and Jacob Klapwijk et al., eds., *Bringing into Captivity Every Thought: Capita Selecta in the History of Christian Evaluations of Non-Christian Philosophy* (Lanham, MD: University Press of America, 1991); Robert Sweetman, ed., *In the Phrygian Mode: Neo-Calvinism, Antiquity and the Lamentations of Reformed Philosophy* (Lanham, MD: University Press of America, 2007).

3. René van Woudenberg, *Gelovend denken. Inleiding tot een christelijke filosofie* (Amsterdam: Buijten and Schipperheijn; Kampen: Kok, 1992), 1–2. The Dutch title, *Gelovend denken,* translates as "believing thinking." Dooyeweerd's approach anticipates "postfoundational" approaches such as Michael Polanyi, *Personal Knowledge: Towards a Post-Critical Philosophy* (London: Routledge, 1962), esp. chapter 10 ("Commitment"); and Charles Taylor's notion of "background frameworks" shaping moral discourse in *Sources of the Self: The Making of Modern Identity* (Cambridge, MA: Harvard University Press, 1989); see also Taylor's *A Secular Age* (Cambridge, MA: Harvard University Press, 2007). For a postmodern statement, see William Connolly, *Why I Am Not a Secularist* (Minneapolis: University of Minnesota Press, 1999).

4. See Vincent Brümmer, *Transcendental Criticism and Christian Philosophy: A Presentation and Evaluation of Herman Dooyeweerd's "Philosophy of the Cosmonomic Idea"* (Franeker: T. Wever, 1961). For works on epistemology or on broader issues of the relation between faith and reason, drawing in varying degrees on or critically responding to Dooyeweerd, see Roy Clouser, *The Myth of Religious Neutrality: An Essay on the Hidden Role of Religious Belief in Theory*, rev. ed. (Notre Dame: University of Notre Dame Press, 2005); Ronald A. Kuipers, *Critical Faith: Toward a Renewed Understanding of Religious Life and Its Public Accountability* (Amsterdam: Rodopi, 2002); Hendrik Hart and Kai Nielsen, *Search for Community within a Withering Tradition: Conversations between a Marxian Atheist and a Calvinian Christian* (Lanham, MD: University Press of America, 1990). On Dooyeweerd's transcendental method and his transcendental critique in particular, see Robert D. Knudsen, "The Religious Foundation of Dooyeweerd's Transcendental Method," in *Contemporary Reflections on the Philosophy of Herman Dooyeweerd*, ed. D. F. M. Strauss and Michelle Botting (Lewiston, NY: Edwin Mellen Press, 2000), 272–285; Jan Hoogland, "De uitdrukkingskracht van de transcendentale denkkritiek," *Philosophia Reformata* 59 (1994): 114–136; Lambert Zuidervaart, "The Great Turning Point: Religion and Rationality in Dooyeweerd's Transcendental Critique," *Faith and Philosophy* 21 (2004): 65–89; H. G. Geertsema, "The Inner Reformation of Philosophy and Science and the Dialogue of Christian Faith with a Secular Culture: A Critical Assessment of Dooyeweerd's Transcendental Critique of Theoretical Thought," in *Christian Philosophy at the Close of the Twentieth Century: Assessment and Perspective*, ed. Sander Griffioen and Bert M. Balk (Kampen: J. H. Kok, 1995), 11–28; Roy Clouser, "The Transcendental Critique Revisited and Revised," *Philosophia Reformata* 24 (2009): 21–47.

5. Clouser, *The Myth of Religious Neutrality*.

6. If Dooyeweerd can be said to have developed a Christian "apologetics" this is its aspiration rather than to attempt any kind of rational "proof" of faith, an enterprise he rejected in principle. See Jonathan Chaplin, "Herman Dooyeweerd," in *New Dictionary of Christian Apologetics*, ed. Campbell Campbell-Jack and Gavin McGrath (Downers Grove, IL: InterVarsity Press, 2006), 224–226.

7. Dooyeweerd, *NC*, 1:3–34.

8. Ibid., 1:34.

9. Ibid., 1:34–35.

10. Ibid., 1:37.

11. Ibid., 1:37–38.

12. Ibid., 1:38. This does not imply a rejection of "dogma" per se. It has its rightful place in the confessions of the church. It does not have a place in philo-

sophical discourse, however. Dooyeweerd would thus have difficulty with a particular aspect of the Thomistic view, advanced for example in John Paul II's *Fides et Ratio,* that faith convictions (such as the authoritative teachings of the church) may place *external* boundaries around what (theoretical) reason may conclude. Dooyeweerd would say that such convictions should mold the *foundations and internal process* of reasoning itself, in a way I shortly explain. There are many other aspects of this document, however, with which he would be in broad agreement. For two responses to the encyclical from the school known as Reformed Epistemology (not to be confused with Dooyeweerd's approach), see Nicholas Wolterstorff's and Alvin Plantinga's contributions to "Faith and Reason: Philosophers Respond to Pope John Paul II's Encyclical Letter *Fides et Ratio,*" *Books and Culture* 5, no. 4 (1999): 29, 32. See also Wolterstorff's earlier formulation of his position in Nicholas Wolterstorff, *Reason within the Bounds of Religion* (Grand Rapids: Eerdmans, 1976). For additional debates on the issue, see Eduardo J. Echeverria, *"Fides et Ratio:* The Catholic and the Calvinist: Prospects for Rapprochement," *Philosophia Reformata* 65 (2000): 72–104. Echeverria writes as a Catholic philosopher trained in Dooyeweerd's philosophy. Roy Clouser responds in "Reason and Belief in God," *Philosophia Reformata* 68 (2003): 36–68.

13. In fact such an Idea really consists of three related Ideas comprising answers to the three "transcendental basic problems" confronting all philosophical frameworks. These questions concern, respectively, the *coherence,* the *totality,* and the *Origin* of all reality. Dooyeweerd, *NC,* 1:41 ff.

14. It may nevertheless be the *case* that theory rests on such assumptions, as several of the authors cited in note 4 above argue at length.

15. Dooyeweerd, *NC,* 1:59.

16. Herman Dooyeweerd, *Grenzen van het theoretisch denken,* ed. Marcel E. Verburg (Baarn: Ambo, 1986) (Geschiedenis van Wijsbegeerte in Nederland, vol. 20), 131.

17. Dooyeweerd, *NC,* 1:59–61. A "motive" is not merely an intellectual "motif." See Ralph Vunderink, "Ground Motifs—A Modest Revision," in Strauss and Botting, eds., *Contemporary Reflections on the Philosophy of Herman Dooyeweerd,* 157–177. For an evocative discussion of Dooyeweerd's way of reading the history of philosophy, see William V. Rowe, "Vollenhoven's and Dooyeweerd's Appropriation of Ancient Greek Philosophy," in Sweetman, ed., *In the Phrygian Mode,* 213–229.

18. Dooyeweerd also claims that at the most fundamental level there are only *two* communal spirits at work in the human race: the power of the Spirit of God, which acts redemptively in human beings to restore the fallen creation, and the "spirit of apostasy," or rebellion against the Creator, leading to

the idolatrous worship of various dimensions of creaturely reality, as revealed in theoretical "absolutizations." By "apostasy" Dooyeweerd does not mean the repudiation of the Christian (or any other) confession but rather humankind's repudiation of its Creator in the fall. Between these two is a radical, unbridgeable "antithesis" (a notion I explain further below).

19. Herman Dooyeweerd, *Roots of Western Culture*, ed. Mark Vander Vennen and Bernard Zylstra, trans. J. Kraay (Toronto: Wedge, 1979), 20. Henceforth cited as *Roots*. "The old conflict continued to characterize this religious ground motive: the principle of blind fate governing the eternal flux of all individual forms in the cyclical stream stood over against the principle of the supernatural, rational, and immortal form, itself not ruled by the stream of becoming." For a critique of this account of Greek thought and culture, indicating its dependence on certain now-dated sources (in particular, Nietzsche's *The Birth of Tragedy*), see A. P. Bos, "Het grondmotief van de Griekse cultuur en het titanische zin-perspectief," *Philosophia Reformata* 51 (1986): 117–137.

20. Dooyeweerd suggests that this ground motive "introduces an internal split into the creation motive by distinguishing the natural and the supranatural and by restricting the scope of fall and redemption to the supranatural" and thereby "robs the scriptural ground motive of its integral and radical character" (*Roots*, 116–117)—a more polemical statement of what he articulates more guardedly elsewhere. It is obviously a contestable judgment. He even asserts, extraordinarily, that the scholastic ground motive conflicts with the biblical ground motive "at every point." For a critique of Dooyeweerd's account of the scholastic ground motive, especially with regard to the thought of Thomas Aquinas, see J. A. Aertsen, "'Uit God zijn Alle Dingen'. Enkele overwegingen bij de 700ste sterfdag van Thomas van Aquino," *Philosophia Reformata* 39 (1974): 102–155.

21. Dooyeweerd, *Roots*, 151.

22. Ibid., 148–185, and *NC* 1:169–495; see Johan van der Hoeven, "Dooyeweerd en de geschiedenis van de moderne wijsbegeerte," in *Herman Dooyeweerd 1894–1977. Breedte en actualiteit van zijn filosofie*, ed. H. G. Geertsema et al. (Kampen: J. H. Kok, 1994), 255–274.

23. Dooyeweerd, *NC*, 1: 69.

24. Ibid., 1:70; 93–94. See note 13 above. This is Dooyeweerd's translation of the Dutch term *wetsidee* (lit., "law-idea").

25. Ibid., 1:88.

26. See, e.g., Dale K. Van Kley, "Dooyeweerd as Historian," in *A Christian View of History*, ed. George Marsden and Frank Roberts (Grand Rapids: Eerdmans, 1984), 139–179; William Young, "Herman Dooyeweerd," in *Creative*

Minds in Contemporary Theology, ed. Phillip Hughes (Grand Rapids: Eerdmans, 1966), 270–306; and Vunderink, "Ground Motives," 162–177.

27. Bob Goudzwaard, *Capitalism and Progress: A Diagnosis of Western Society,* trans. Josina Van Nuis Zylstra (Grand Rapids: Eerdmans, 1979); and Egbert Schuurman, "The Technological Culture between the Times," in Griffioen and Balk, eds., *Christian Philosophy at the Close of the Twentieth Century,* 185–200, suggest how this relationship might be characterized.

28. Dooyeweerd, *NC,* 1:114. An "apostate" ground motive generates an internal "dialectic" (or necessary contradiction) because its exaggeration ("absolutization") of some dimensions of reality evokes a corrective response from other dimensions. The correction is a result of the operation of the power of the created order itself.

29. Dooyeweerd, *NC,* 1:511–515.

30. Ibid., 1:522.

31. Ibid., 1:116.

32. Ibid., 2:60.

33. Ibid., 1:117, 119, 2: 73; cf. 1:527.

34. Ibid., 1:118.

35. Ibid., 1:523.

36. Ibid., 1:118.

37. Ibid., 1:119.

38. Dooyeweerd, *Roots,* 28. See also *NC,* 1:507. For a popular statement, see Albert M. Wolters, *Creation Regained: Biblical Basics for a Reformational Worldview* (Grand Rapids: Eerdmans, 1985).

39. Dooyeweerd, *Roots,* 28–29.

40. The closest parallel to this term in Thomism is not what Thomas calls "divine law," which is law revealed in Scripture and tradition, but "eternal law," the law by which God sustains the whole universe. Dooyeweerd does not endorse this (originally Augustinian) notion without qualification.

41. Dooyeweerd, *Roots,* 30.

42. Ibid., 33. Elsewhere, these "rays" are characterized more technically as human capacities or "functions" corresponding to the fifteen "modal aspects" of reality, introduced in the next chapter.

43. Dooyeweerd, *NC,* 2:248, 246.

44. Dooyeweerd, *Roots,* 30–31. Original emphasis.

45. Ibid., 30.

46. Ibid., 33.

47. Ibid., 36.

48. Ibid., 37; original emphasis. Cf. *NC,* 2:33, 335.

49. Dooyeweerd, *Roots*, 59; cf. 60.

50. Dooyeweerd, *NC*, 2:257, 262.

51. Dooyeweerd, *Roots*, 37.

52. Dooyeweerd, *NC*, 3:507.

53. Ibid., 2:33.

54. Ibid., 2:262.

55. Ibid., 2:35.

56. Ibid., 2:33–34.

57. Dooyeweerd, *Roots*, 37.

58. Dooyeweerd, *NC*, 2:262.

59. Dooyeweerd, *Roots*, 37.

60. Ibid., 38.

61. They seem akin to what MacIntyre calls first principles, which function not only as the objects but also as the starting points of philosophical discussion. See Alasdair MacIntyre, *First Principles, Final Ends, and Contemporary Philosophical Issues* (Milwaukee: Marquette University Press, 1990). This work is also reprinted in Kelvin Knight, ed., *The MacIntyre Reader* (Notre Dame: University of Notre Dame Press, 1989), 170–201. MacIntyre regards such principles as having attained clarity in a process of long-standing philosophical contestation. Dooyeweerd does not tell us how his Ideas appear, only that they arise "immediately" from religious ground motives. While MacIntyre might be pressed to disclose how religious convictions shape first principles (a matter on which he seems strangely reticent), Dooyeweerd's account suffers from a vagueness that MacIntyre's account partly dispels.

62. Dooyeweerd, *NC*, 1:506.

63. On these, see Johan van der Hoeven, "In Memory of Herman Dooyeweerd: Meaning, Time and Law," *Philosophia Reformata* 43 (1978): 130–144, on which this section draws.

64. Dooyeweerd, *NC*, 1:101.

65. Ibid., 1:4. "Meaning-as-being" can perhaps be read as a modern rendition of the Augustinian and Bonaventurian notion of creature-as-sign. I am grateful to Michael De Moor for pointing out this parallel.

66. Van der Hoeven, "In Memory of Herman Dooyeweerd," 137.

67. Dooyeweerd, *NC*, 2:31; cf. 1:9–10, 97; 2:33–35.

68. Ibid., 1:97. A further distinction is introduced at this point. The radical dependency of the cosmos, its "meaning character," is apparent in the fact that the entire cosmos both "expresses" and "refers to" a transcendent origin (God) (*NC*, 1:4). Expression and reference denote the two fundamental dimensions of the religious relation between reality and its Origin; or better, the two *movements* within what is an essentially dynamic relationship, termed by Geertsema

the "concentric" and the "transcendental" movements, respectively (H. G. Geertsema, "Transcendentale openheid. Over het zinkarakter van de werkelijkheid in de wijsbegeerte van H. Dooyeweerd," *Philosophia Reformata* 35 [1970]: 25–56, 132–155). Humans occupy a central place in both dimensions of this relationship. *Concentrically,* created reality can be seen as the expression of a central religious unity. The complexity and diversity of the cosmos expresses the coherence of the cosmos; the cosmos as such is an expression of the human heart or "selfhood" in which it is religiously concentrated; and the human selfhood is an expression of the image of God (Dooyeweerd, *NC,* 1:3–4; cf. 2:307). *Transcendentally,* created reality can be seen as pointing toward an Origin that transcends it. The cosmos "refers" beyond itself to an Origin (God), the ultimate source of its existence and structure (*NC,* 1:3–4). The idea of an Origin is not, Dooyeweerd acknowledges, the special property of Christian or even theistic philosophical frameworks; all philosophies presuppose an idea of Origin, whether they are aware of it or not. Only Christian philosophies, however— those governed by the biblical ground motive—are able to acknowledge the *absolute transcendence* of the origin with respect to the cosmos. Non-Christian philosophers, of whatever stripe, have inevitably sought an Origin *within* the cosmos itself, within the realm of meaning, an ultimately untenable standpoint (*NC,* 1:9).

69. Dooyeweerd, *NC,* 1:28. Wolters, however, notes that in conceiving of time as a "general ontological principle of continuity," Dooyeweerd may have been influenced by Heidegger's *Being and Time,* a work with which he was familiar. See Wolters, "The Intellectual Milieu of Herman Dooyeweerd," 15.

70. Van der Hoeven, "In Memory of Herman Dooyeweerd," 139.

71. Dooyeweerd, *NC,* 1:28. Or, a "cosmonomic" side and a "factual" side.

72. Ibid., 1:29.

73. Ibid., 1:24, 28.

74. Ibid., 1:29.

75. Dooyeweerd further distinguishes between the *coherence* of the cosmos and its *unity* (or "radical unity"). As noted, the concentration point of creation is located in the heart or religious center of humanity—originally unfallen humanity, but since the fall Jesus Christ as the "new religious root of creation." It is here that the "religious root unity" of creation is found (*NC,* 2:32). The unity of the cosmos is the point at which its religious meaning is concentrated. The concepts of meaning, time, and unity are inseparable: "In time, meaning is broken into an incalculable diversity, which can come to a radical unity only in the religious center of human existence." He then adds: "For this is the only sphere of our consciousness in which we can transcend time" (1:31). The religious root unity of the cosmos turns out to lie beyond time. Dooyeweerd thus

draws a fundamental distinction *within* the created cosmos between the temporal and the supratemporal spheres, assigning diversity (and coherence) to the former and unity to the latter. The human heart, his religious center, also lies beyond time; the heart is "supratemporal." Human beings are only able to experience the religious unity expressed in the diversity of their functions by concentrating on their Origin. This concentration of temporal diversity must rise above such diversity and thus, Dooyeweerd concludes, transcend time: "How could man direct himself toward eternal things, if eternity were not 'set in his heart'?" (1:31 n.1). Critics have pointed to the "unreformed" Platonic residue in this notion of supratemporality. See, e.g., James H. Olthuis, "Dooyeweerd on Religion and Faith," in *The Legacy of Herman Dooyeweerd: Reflections on Critical Philosophy in the Christian Tradition*, ed. C. T. McIntire (Lanham, MD: University Press of America, 1985), 21–40; and A. Brüggemaan-Kruijff, "Tijd als omsluiting, tijd als ontsluiting," *Philosophia Reformata* 46 (1981): 119–163; 47 (1982): 41–68.

76. Van der Hoeven, "In Memory of Herman Dooyeweerd," 142.

77. This is the title of the first Dutch edition of *NC*.

78. Dooyeweerd, *NC*, 1:93–94.

79. Ibid., 1:99.

80. "As sovereign Origin, God is not subjected to the law. On the contrary this subjectedness is the very characteristic of all that which has been created, the existence of which is limited and determined by the law" (ibid., 1:99 n.1).

81. Ibid., 1:518.

82. Ibid., 1:508.

83. Ibid., 1:96.

84. Ibid., 1:105, 2:8.

85. Ibid., 1:105. "Potentiality itself resides in the factual subject-side; its principle, on the contrary, is the cosmonomic-side of time. The factual subject-side is always connected with individuality (actual as well as potential), which can never be reduced to a general rule. But it remains bound to its structural laws, which determine its margin or latitude of possibilities" (ibid.).

Four.   Plurality, Identity, Interrelationship

1. The suggestion that "events" or "acts" are best so described seems implausible, though I shall not explore the question here. A South African philosopher with an affinity for Dooyeweerd's approach, H. G. Stoker, proposed a different account of the "cosmic dimension" of events, which, he argued, is not adequately accounted for in terms of the categories of individuality and mo-

dality. H. G. Stoker, "Die kosmiese dimensie van gebeurtenisse," *Philosophia Reformata* 29 (1964).

2. For a sympathetic reading (and comparison with the thought of Mekkes), see J. D. Dengerink, "In het krachtveld van het scheppingswoord. Over de modaliteiten: haar fundamentele verscheidenheid, samenhang en eenheid," *Philosophia Reformata* 59 (1994), 137–157. For a critique, see René van Woudenberg, "'Aspects' and 'Functions' of Individual Things," *Philosophia Reformata* 68 (2003), 1–13. For a reply, see H. G. Geertsema, "Analytical and Reformational Philosophy: Critical Reflections Regarding R. van Woudenberg's Meditation on 'Aspects' and 'Functions,'" *Philosophia Reformata* 69 (2004): 53–76.

3. See Michael Oakeshott, *Experience and Its Modes* (Cambridge: Cambridge University Press, 1933). John Finnis, *Natural Law and Natural Rights* (Oxford: Clarendon Press, 1980), 85 ff. Finnis's basic forms of the good are life, knowledge, play, aesthetic experience, sociability, practical reasonableness, and religion.

4. Jacob Klapwijk, *Purpose in the Living World: Creation and Emergent Evolution,* trans. and ed. Harry Cook (Cambridge: Cambridge University Press, 2008), chapter 7.

5. Or "modal spheres," or "modalities of meaning"; the terms are synonymous.

6. Dooyeweerd, *NC*, 1:3, 24. The modal aspects are "modalities of cosmic meaning" (1:24), differentiations or "refractions" of the "fullness of meaning."

7. Ibid., 2:7. See chapter 3 n. 77.

8. Ibid., 2:101–102; cf. 1:16, 31; 2:25.

9. Ibid., 2:8; cf. 2:3–4.

10. Ibid., 1:3.

11. Ibid., 2:84. Similarly, biotic life is a distinct modality not a concrete phenomenon (2:108, 110). Nor, further, is it a metaphysical substance. Dooyeweerd wrote an extensive critique of the Thomistic concept of substance, the burden of which was to argue that it was incompatible with his notion of meaning, since the latter implies the radical dependence of all existence upon the Origin, while the concept of substance entails a "religious depreciation of the individual." See "De idee der individualiteits-structuur en het Thomistisch substantiebegrip. Een critisch onderzoek naar de grondslagen der Thomistische zijnsleer," *Philosophia Reformata* 8 (1943): 65–99; 9 (1944): 1–41.

12. Dooyeweerd, *NC*, 1:102.

13. Ibid., 1:102.

14. Ibid., 2:49 ff., 107 ff.

15. E.g., Erwin Laszlo, *Introduction to Systems Philosophy: Toward a New Paradigm for Contemporary Thought* (New York: Harper and Row, 1972).

Dooyeweerd does not discuss such theories, but he would likely hold that they rightly acknowledge what he terms modal "sphere universality" (explained below) but at the cost of compromising modal "sphere sovereignty."

16. Dooyeweerd, *NC*, 2:49–50.

17. The earlier aspects are the "substratum" of the later aspects, the later are the "superstratum" of the earlier (ibid., 2:51–52). Yet Dooyeweerd never speaks of "lower" and "higher" aspects; as Van der Hoeven notes, the modal order is an order of succession, not of subordination (Johan van der Hoeven, "In Memory of Herman Dooyeweerd: Meaning, Time and Law," *Philosophia Reformata* 43 [1978]: 140). This repudiation of a hierarchical ordering among irreducible levels of being is one significant philosophical difference between Dooyeweerd and Thomism.

18. Dooyeweerd, *NC*, 2:51. See also Lambert Zuidervaart, "The Great Turning Point: Religion and Rationality in Dooyeweerd's Transcendental Critique," *Faith and Philosophy* 21 (2004): 65–89.

19. The numerical aspect has a special place since it lacks any substratum spheres; no spheres precede it. Similarly the pistical aspect is unique since it has no superstratum; no spheres follow it. These are "terminal spheres" (Dooyeweerd, *NC*, 2:52).

20. Ibid., 2:53–54, 186–188.

21. Ibid., 2:75.

22. Ibid., 2:79.

23. Ibid., 2:86.

24. Ibid., 2:97.

25. Ibid., 2:99.

26. Ibid., 2:107.

27. Ibid., 2:110–111.

28. Ibid., 2:80.

29. Ibid., 2:195. I explain this in some detail in chapter 5.

30. Ibid., 2:126. I examine the implications of this for economics in chapter 11.

31. Ibid., 2:140–141. I allude to this aspect in chapter 6.

32. Ibid., 2:66.

33. Ibid., 2:128.

34. Ibid., 2:129. This aspect is considered at length in chapter 9.

35. Ibid., 2:158. I compare this aspect with the juridical aspect in chapter 9.

36. Ibid., 2:304.

37. Ibid., 1:3.

38. Ibid., 2:331.

39. Ibid., 2:57. The nuclear moments cannot be identified apart from the analogies clustered around them and from which they are inseparable. Indeed

it is precisely by identifying the analogies as analogies that the task of identifying modal kernels proceeds.

40. Ibid., 2:66.

41. Ibid., 2:194–232.

42. So it is perfectly valid to assert, for example, as one medieval historian does, that "the middle ages were born out of a death," that is, the death of the Roman Empire. J. B. Morrall, *Political Thought in Medieval Times* (London: Hutchinson University Library, 1958), 1.

43. The term *scientific reductionism* typically means reductionism in the natural sciences. An example would be the development of "theories of everything," that is, theories seeking to explain the totality of reality in terms of merely physical or even mathematical interactions.

44. See Appendix 1 for a survey of Dooyeweerd's general account of social scientific disciplines.

45. Or sometimes "natural laws." Here "law" is the translation of the Dutch term *wet* (and "natural laws" of *natuurwetten*). This language parallels the distinctly modern natural scientific sense of "natural law" rather than the classical sense of "that which is in accord with right reason," which embraces what Dooyeweerd calls "norms."

46. Dooyeweerd, *NC*, 2:189 n.1.

47. Ibid., 1:237.

48. Ibid., 2:238. Dooyeweerd holds that such agency is nevertheless rationally founded (2:156, 237–238). That is, "postlogical" normative agency is "founded in" the human capacity for logical analysis, the ability to make distinctions; the logical aspect is foundational with respect to all those following it in the modal order of succession. This aspectual (or "functional") sense of logical is, however, a more restricted notion of "rationality" than that operative in Thomistic natural law theory. Dooyeweerd argues that the Thomist sense is too wedded to the "pagan" Greek notion of logos. For a critique of Dooyeweerd's interpretation, see J. A. Aertsen, "'Uit God zijn Alle Dingen'. Enkele overwegingen bij de 700ste sterfdag van Thomas van Aquino," *Philosophia Reformata* 39 (1974): 102–155.

49. For a critique of the idea that there is a distinct "ethical aspect" and an argument that "ethics" addresses issues of right conduct across every normative aspect, see M. D. Stafleu, "Philosophical Ethics and the So-Called Ethical Aspect," *Philosophia Reformata* 72 (2008): 151–164.

50. His use of the specifically legal term *positivization* here is potentially misleading, since it makes responsible human action sound too much like the process of legislating. It needs to be kept in mind, therefore, that positivization is involved in every kind of human functioning, including things as diverse as

speaking grammatically, parenting sensitively, running a business efficiently, or campaigning against poverty.

51. It is, therefore, surprising that his critical assessments of seriously deformed aspects of modern Western culture often seem to lack Augustinian bite. I return to this point in chapter 11.

52. Dooyeweerd, *NC*, 3:54–56.

53. Dooyeweerd also refers to them as "total structures" or "totalities," by which he means integrated, internally unified structured wholes.

54. Dooyeweerd, *NC*, 2:556.

55. Ibid., 2:558.

56. Ibid., 1:29.

57. Ibid., 2:557.

58. The difference between a "thing" and a "social relationship" is explored in the next chapter.

59. Klapwijk states the difference between "modal laws" and "type laws" thus: "Modal laws . . . are laws that are level-bound, determinative of the functions and characteristics of entities on any organizational level of reality. Type laws, in Dooyeweerd's view, are not level-bound. They are laws that are typical for entities as a whole. He calls them typical because they put their stamp to a collection of entities, thus typifying the group. In short, type laws are laws that determine the specific identity of a class of entities" (*Purpose in the Living World*, 247–248).

60. Dooyeweerd, *NC*, 3:97.

61. I discuss Dooyeweerd's view of the nation and the family in chapter 10.

62. Dooyeweerd, *NC*, 3:53 ff., 90 ff.

63. Ibid., 3:56.

64. Ibid., 3:55–56.

65. Ibid., 3:266 ff.

66. In chapter 9 I explain how for Dooyeweerd the term *legal* immediately implies that of *justice*.

67. Some of these relationships, it turns out, are also themselves individuality structures, but I will not comment on those here.

68. Dooyeweerd, *NC*, 3:637.

69. The coherence of the *modal* diversity of the cosmos is guaranteed by the sphere universality of each modal aspect. And because all individuality structures function in all these aspects, sphere universality is already one way in which they cohere. This modal coherence, however, cannot account for the ways in which individuality structures relate to one another *as structural wholes*.

70. Dooyeweerd, *NC*, 3:627.

71. We can see here how such transference could either enhance or confine the effectiveness of the business (and the family)—a minor but instructive illustration of a point to be discussed shortly, namely, how an interlacement could be "unnatural."

72. Dooyeweerd, *NC*, 3:634.

73. There are in fact two kinds of part-whole relations, "the internal homogeneity of the parts in a homogenous aggregate" (such as the relation between a class and its identical members) and "the internal heterogeneity of the parts in a non-homogenous total structure." Dooyeweerd, *NC*, 3:638; emphasis omitted. The significant contrast is between an enkaptic relation and the latter kind of part-whole relation.

74. Dooyeweerd, *NC*, 3:637–638.

75. Ibid., 3:638–639.

76. Ibid., 3:639.

77. Ibid.

78. It "exceeds the boundaries of its internal structural principle in this enkaptic function within another thing." Ibid.

79. Enkaptic interlacements give rise to what Dooyeweerd terms "phenotypical variations" or "variability types" among structures (a notion I define in the next chapter). They are the "nodal points" of such variations. These variations arise not from the internal structure of a thing but from its external relation to its environment; and they are multiple and complex. Where an individuality structure relates enkaptically to another, we encounter phenotypical variations (*NC*, 3:633). A marriage regulated under civil law is such a phenotype. The civil regulation is not part of its enduring structure—it is absent in earlier societies, and might disappear from existing Western societies—but is only a feature of marriages within modern states having systems of civil law.

Five.   A Philosophy of Cultural Development

1. Further critical revisions will also be proposed as I take up his theory of the structural principle of the state in chapters 8 through 11.

2. Dooyeweerd also refers to this as the "retrocipatory" direction of time.

3. Thus the transcendental direction is also called the "anticipatory" direction of time.

4. H. G. Geertsema, "Transcendentale openheid. Over het zinkarakter van de werkelijkheid in de wijsbegeerte van H. Dooyeweerd," *Philosophia Reformata* 35 (1970): 132.

5. If they did they would be "anticipations." Dooyeweerd, *NC*, 2:181.

6. Ibid., 2:182.

7. Ibid., 2:182–183.

8. Ibid., 2:182. Since the process takes place over time, examples will thus be found where, at particular historical periods, the anticipatory analogies of a particular modal aspect have not yet been opened up. In such cases the structure of this modal aspect remains "closed," appearing only in a "rigid, restrictive function." When, however, the anticipations are disclosed "the modal meaning is deepened and expresses itself in an expansive or deepened function (2:184). The opening up of the "anticipatory structure" of a modal aspect (i.e., the opening up of its "anticipatory spheres") takes place under the guidance of the later aspect that is anticipated. In the case of personal accountability in law the ethical aspect guides or opens up the juridical aspect. We can thus speak of "guiding" or "directing" functions and "guided or directed" functions.

9. Ibid., 2:181 n.1. The Dutch term *ontsluitingsproces* can also be rendered as "unfolding process" or "opening process."

10. On this, see M. D. Stafleu's helpful corrective to Dooyeweerd's account: "Time and History in the Philosophy of the Cosmonomic Idea," *Philosophia Reformata* 73 (2008): 154–169.

11. Ibid. 2:184–185.

12. A. Brüggemann-Kruijff, "Tijd als omsluiting, tijd als ontsluiting," *Philosophia Reformata* 47 (1982): 44.

13. In the case of the disclosure of a prenormative (e.g., physical) aspect by another prenormative aspect (e.g., biotic) humans play no role. But the opening up of the *normative anticipations* in an aspect, whether this aspect is prenormative or normative, necessarily presupposes human intervention. Humans are thus responsible for the opening up both of anticipations in the normative aspects to later normative aspects and of anticipations in the prenormative aspects to the normative aspects. Dooyeweerd, *NC*, 2:336; see also Geertsema, "Transcendentale openheid," 134.

14. Put more technically, the distinction between the ontic and the historical does not coincide with that between the law-side and the subject-side of cosmic time.

15. Dooyeweerd, *NC*, 2:188–190.

16. Ibid., 2:193.

17. Ibid., 1:68–69; 2:195, 200.

18. Ibid., 2:69.

19. Ibid., 2:197–198.

20. Ibid., 2:198, 230. As noted in the previous chapter rationality ("reflection") plays a crucial and foundational role in historical action.

21. Ibid., 2:69, 229–230.

22. Ibid., 2:198, 231. For broader reflection on culture informed by Dooye-weerd, see Sander Griffioen, *Moed voor cultuur. Een actuele filosofie* (Amsterdam: Buijten and Schipperheijn, 2003).

23. Calvin G. Seerveld, "Dooyeweerd's Legacy for Aesthetics: Modal Law Theory," in *The Legacy of Herman Dooyeweerd: Reflections on Critical Philosophy in the Christian Tradition*, ed. C. T. McIntire (Lanham, MD: University Press of America, 1985), 76 n.60.

24. In Thomism humankind's religious vocation, while also encompassing (indeed "perfecting") everything pertaining to the "natural end" of humanity, is seen as culminating in the attainment of the supernatural "beatific vision," whereas for Dooyeweerd—who rejects the nature/supernature distinction—it culminates in participation in the eschatological renewal and reaffirmation of the created (natural) order.

25. Dooyeweerd, *NC*, 2:264; cf. 285–288.

26. C. T. McIntire, "Dooyeweerd's Philosophy of History," in McIntire, ed., *The Legacy of Herman Dooyeweerd*, 97. Specifically, as we have seen, it appeals both to his conception of history as a modal aspect and to his wider theory of the normative dimension of the process of disclosure. The Idea of cultural development points us to the opening of the *anticipatory moments of the historical aspect,* that is, to ways in which this aspect anticipates later ones.

27. Dooyeweerd, *Roots,* 67.

28. Dooyeweerd, *NC,* 2:247–248.

29. Ibid., 2:196.

30. As noted, the term *disclosure* points to the intimate relationship between the cultural vocation of man and the modal opening process. Contra McIntire ("Dooyeweerd's Philosophy of History," 93, 97–98), the two are not the same since the opening process takes place in part without human cultural action (Geertsema, "Transcendentale openheid," 135–137). The cultural vocation of man involves the "normative opening process" (or "disclosure of normative meaning"). This means the opening up both of the normative analogies ("normative anticipatory moments") within prenormative aspects and of the anticipatory moments within the normative aspects (Dooyeweerd, *NC,* 2:336). Strictly, this normative opening process is still not yet *identical* to cultural development. The process takes place *as* humans fulfill their cultural vocation. In culturally forming the natural and human environments humans are engaged in opening up the normative anticipatory moments of all the modal aspects. Thus the cultural or historical aspect is "the *nodal point* of the entire process of disclosure in the normative anticipatory spheres of the other aspects" (2:191).

31. This point is implicitly made in Bob Goudzwaard, *Capitalism and Progress: A Diagnosis of Western Society,* ed. and trans. Josina Van Nuis Zylstra

(Toronto: Wedge; Grand Rapids: Eerdmans, 1979), a particularly creative application of Dooyeweerd's idea of cultural disclosure.

32. Dooyeweerd, *NC*, 2:292.

33. Ibid. 2:297.

34. See Dooyeweerd, *NC*, 3:320; and Geertsema, "Transcendentale openheid," 139.

35. Geerstema, "Transcendentale openheid," 144–146.

36. Ibid., 146; See also J. D. Dengerink, *De zin van de werkelijkheid. Een wijsgerige benadering* (Amsterdam: Vrije Universiteit Uitgeverij, 1986), 214.

37. Dooyeweerdian philosophers of technology have attempted to remedy this gap. See, e.g., Hendrik van Riessen, *The Society of the Future* (Philadelphia: Presbyterian and Reformed Publishing Co., 1952); Egbert Schuurman, *Technology and the Future* (Toronto: Wedge, 1980); Ad Vlot, "Cultuur- en techniekfilosofie," in *Kennis en werkelijkheid. Tweede inleiding tot een christelijke filosofie*, ed. René van Woudenberg (Amsterdam: Buijten and Schipperheijn, 1996), 203–235; Kees Boersma et al., eds., *Aan Babels stromen. Een bevrijdend perspectief op ethiek en techniek* (Amsterdam: Buijten and Schipperheijn, 2002).

38. Dooyeweerd, *NC*, 2:259 ff.

39. Ibid., 2:259.

40. That is, if they are to experience "any normative dynamics, any deepening of the meaning of a primitive culture" (ibid., 2:260).

41. Ibid. Later we shall see that Dooyeweerd also speaks of "integrating tendencies" in a modern, differentiated society.

42. Ibid., 2:275.

43. Ibid., 2:261.

44. Ibid.

45. Ibid., 2:274–275. See Calvin G. Seerveld, "Dooyeweerd's Idea of Historical Development: Christian Respect for Cultural Diversity," *Westminster Theological Journal* 58 (1996): 41–61.

46. Dooyeweerd, *De crisis*, 65.

47. Dooyeweerd, *NC*, 2:269; see also Herman Dooyeweerd, "The Criteria of Progressive and Reactionary Tendencies in History," in *Verslag van de plechtige viering van het honderdvijftig-jarig bestaan der Koninklijke Nederlandse Akademie van Wetenschappen* (Amsterdam: North Holland, 1958), English text, 213–228; French text, 139–154; Dutch text, 61–77.

48. Dooyeweerd, *Roots*, 78; see also McIntire, "Dooyeweerd's Philosophy of History," 102.

49. He would no doubt regard Islamic attempts to introduce Sharia law into states where civil liberties and religious toleration currently prevail as a "reactionary" abandonment of the differentiation of church and state. For a

consideration of how in liberal democracies private tribunals engaging in Alternative Dispute Resolution might yet legitimately appeal to aspects of Sharia law, see Jonathan Chaplin, "Legal Monism and Religious Pluralism: Rowan Williams on Religion, Loyalty and Law," *International Journal of Public Theology* 2 (2008): 418–442.

50. Dooyeweerd, *Roots,* 81.

51. Ibid., 80–81. The inevitable result is a countercultural reaction in which suppressed spheres "protest" against their subordination to the dominant sphere, a process that also testifies to divine judgment in history (84–86).

52. Max Weber, "Religious Rejections of the World and Their Directions," in *From Max Weber: Essays in Sociology,* ed. H. H. Gerth and C. Wright Mills (New York: Oxford University Press, 1946), 323–359, esp. 328, 334, 339. See José Casanova, *Public Religions in the Modern World* (Chicago: University of Chicago Press, 1994), 20–21, for a brief account of Weber on differentiation. Dooyeweerd is critical of Weber's sociological positivism (as manifested, for example, in his theory of the state) but does not interact directly with his writings on differentiation. It remains unclear whether he developed his own theory in conscious contrast to Weber's.

53. McIntire, "Dooyeweerd's Philosophy of History," 101–104.

54. Dooyeweerd, *Roots,* 79.

55. Sander Griffioen, "De betekenis van Dooyeweerds ontwikkelingsidee," *Philosophia Reformata* 51 (1986): 83–109; 105.

56. Dooyeweerd, *Roots,* 79.

57. McIntire, "Dooyeweerd's Philosophy of History," 104.

58. As Dengerink has also observed; see J. D. Dengerink, *Critisch-historisch onderzoek naar de sociologische ontwikkeling van het beginsel der "souvereiniteit in eigen kring" in de 19e en 20e eeuw* (Kampen: J. H. Kok, 1948), 195–200.

59. Griffioen, "De betekenis van Dooyeweerds ontwikkelingsidee," 90–91.

60. McIntire, "Dooyeweerd's Philosophy of History," 104.

61. For a thoughtful treatment of the question drawing on but moving beyond Dooyeweerd, see Jacob Klapwijk, "Pluralism of Norms and Values: On the Claim and the Reception of the Universal." *Philosophia Reformata* 59 (1994): 158–192.

62. The interpretation of this order is also supported on occasion by scriptural references, though by the time of *NC* he was much less inclined to do this.

63. McIntyre, "Dooyeweerd's Philosophy of History," 104.

64. Dooyeweerd, *NC,* 2:281.

65. Ibid., 2:356–362.

66. Dooyeweerd, *In the Twilight of Western Thought*, 112; see also Griffioen, "De betekenis van Dooyeweerds ontwikkelingsidee," 105–106.

67. One might triangulate him in relation to, say, Alasdair MacIntyre and Charles Taylor. Less of a cultural pessimist than the former, his critique of the sources of the modern self is more trenchant than the latter. His overall assessment of modernity is also more religiously attuned than that of either, bearing comparison with that of Jacques Maritain, for instance, *Integral Humanism: Temporal and Spiritual Problems of a New Christendom*, trans. Joseph W. Evans (Notre Dame: University of Notre Dame Press, 1973). Comparison can also be made with the work of Eric Voegelin; in this regard, see Bernard Zylstra, "Voegelin on Unbelief and Revolution," in *Een staatsman ter navolging*, ed. W. F. De Gaay Fortman et al. (The Hague: Antirevolutionary Party, 1976), 155–165.

68. Zuidervaart notes that Dooyeweerd was intentionally modern in another sense, namely, in his post-Kantian conception of philosophy as "critical." See Lambert Zuidervaart, "The Great Turning Point: Religion and Rationality in Dooyeweerd's Transcendental Critique," *Faith and Philosophy* 21 (2004): 65–89. We might further say that since this critical stance was also directed toward modern foundationalist epistemologies he can also be said to have anticipated postmodern concerns in this specific sense.

Six. A Philosophy of Social Pluralism

1. Dooyeweerd, *NC*, 3:263. See Appendix 1 for a fuller account of his view of social philosophy. This chapter draws on material in Jonathan Chaplin, "Dooyeweerd's Notion of Societal Structural Principles," *Philosophia Reformata* 60 (1995): 16–36.

2. Ibid., 1:538; see also 3:263–264.

3. Ibid., 3:171.

4. Ibid., 2:557.

5. Ibid., 3:56: The qualifying function is "the ultimate point of reference for the internal structural coherence of . . . .[an existent]," grouping its various aspects in a "typical" way.

6. Ibid., 3:59. Put technically, it guides or opens up the earlier functions (the "anticipatory spheres") of the structure.

7. Ibid., 3:56, 59–60.

8. Ibid., 3:60.

9. Roy Clouser, *The Myth of Religious Neutrality: An Essay on the Hidden Role of Religious Belief in Theories*, rev. ed. (Notre Dame: University of Notre Dame Press, 2005), 279. We may also ask whether the notion of internal desti-

nation is as different from the Aristotelian idea of internal teleology as Dooyeweerd holds. His claim that there is a genuine distinction here is central to his
critique of Thomistic social thought. If the difference is not, after all, fundamental, then an important element in this critique is vitiated.

10. A type "has the character of a law" (Dooyeweerd, *NC*, 3:97).

11. Ibid., 3:80, 94. This attempt to classify human constructions such as
social structures under what appear to be biological categories will strike many
as surprising and unpromising. That is, the use of the language of "radical
types," "genotypes," and "phenotypes" may seem to fit when distinguishing between genus, species, and subspecies in the plant and animal kingdoms but
straightforwardly reductionist when applied to social realities. Dooyeweerd's
plausible argument that social relationships are not qualified by biological laws
but operate under normative laws does not entirely dispel this worry.

12. Ibid., 3:83: "This criterion delimits the ultimate *genera* of the structures of individuality. . . . [T]hey circumscribe invariable structural orbits of
individuality whose further typical articulation is dependent on them."

13. Ibid., 3:53 ff., 83, 88–90 ff.

14. In ordinary human ("naive") experience we encounter three radical
types of a non-normative qualification, each circumscribing a kingdom: first,
the kingdom of physically qualified kinds of matter, things, and events; second, the biotically qualified kingdom of plants and their "bio-milieu"; third,
the psychically qualified kingdom of animals, their symbiotic relationships,
form products, and milieu (ibid. 3:83). Importantly, Dooyeweerd denies that
human beings constitute a distinct radical type. Humans function in all aspects
but do not have a qualifying function.

15. More technically, in social structures (not necessarily in things) the
qualifying function reveals a "retrocipatory type of individuality," as distinct
from an "original" or an "anticipatory" type (Dooyeweerd, *NC*, 3:90–92).

16. Dooyeweerd expresses this point technically by saying that the "genotypical character of the qualifying function" of a social structure is determined
by its founding function.

17. Kent Zigterman, in "Dooyeweerd's Theory of Individuality Structures
as an Alternative to a Substance Position, Especially That of Aristotle" (M.Phil.
thesis, Institute for Christian Studies, 1977), 86–90. As types they also have the
character of a law. Yet they are not part of the internal structural principle, and
the fact that, as noted, they can be "unnatural" (Dooyeweerd, *NC*, 3:93) means
they cannot *themselves* be laws. Zigterman's suggestion that variability types
can be compared to positive law is supported by an examination of what Dooyeweerd terms "societal forms," to which I return later. I suggest that variability
types are most consistently viewed as variations on the subject-side of reality.

18. Interlacements are not an optional extra but are "a necessary requirement for the realization of the inner nature of a thing."

19. Dooyeweerd, *NC*, 1:538; see also 3:263–264.

20. Ibid., 3:97. Drawing on Zigterman, "Dooyeweerd's Theory of Individuality Structures," 76–82, C. Ouwendorp, in "Het probleem van het universele en individuele," *Philosophia Reformata* 59 (1994): 29–57, has noted the ambiguity in Dooyeweerd's language at this point. He seems in this quotation to identify the subject-side of reality with atypical subjectivity, or unique individuality. Yet normally he speaks of the subject-side precisely as that which is subject to (typical) law. This appears to suggest the identification of the law-subject distinction with the universal-individual distinction, which conflicts with his view that individual things are never wholly unique but always exist in the framework of universal law (52).

21. The subject-object relation should not be confused with the "law-subject relation." The latter points to the fact that all existents are subject to the law of creation. The former is a special kind of relation *between* existents. It is a relation between law-governed subjects; and the relation itself is governed by law. There is a (creational) law that orders subjects (= creatures) to be related to each other as subjects (= active agents) and objects (= passive recipients).

22. Dooyeweerd, *NC*, 3:104; 3:56–58.

23. Ibid., 3:107.

24. Ibid., 3:109 ff.

25. Ibid., 3:138.

26. See also Dooyeweerd, *De crisis*, 111 ff.

27. Dooyeweerd, *NC*, 3:89.

28. Ibid., 3:207.

29. Ibid., 3:122–123; see also Dooyeweerd, *De crisis*, 122.

30. Dooyeweerd, *NC*, 3:198.

31. Sander Griffioen, "De betekenis van Dooyeweerds ontwikkelingsidee," *Philosophia Reformata* 51 (1986): 104.

32. Ibid., 105.

33. We might further suggest that the state's structural principle will in time require that such a bureaucracy be established. This could serve as an example of the internal opening process within a social structure, its historical growth toward maturity.

34. Griffioen, "De betekenis van Dooyeweerds ontwikkelingsidee," 106.

35. This third sense of cultural diversity is, I think, embraced in what Griffioen and Mouw term "contextual plurality" and which they distinguish from both "associational" and "directional" plurality. See Richard Mouw and Sander Griffioen, *Pluralisms and Horizons: An Essay in Christian Public Philosophy* (Grand Rapids: Eerdmans, 1993), 16–18, 130–157.

36. Dooyeweerd, *NC*, 2:274–275; 3:580–583, 587–589.

37. Imagine, for instance, a prosperous urban Western Christian trying to reach consensus on the obligations of children to parents with a Christian resident of a poor traditional African village. I am not suggesting this is impossible, only very difficult.

38. Dooyeweerd, *NC*, 3:174. I noted Dooyeweerd's suggestion that enkaptic interlacements between differently qualified structures give rise to phenotypical variations. It seems obvious that he is referring here to a very similar phenomenon, although the linkage between these two terms is undeveloped. Presumably if the two are not identical societal forms are simply a special case of phenotypical variation.

39. Ibid., 3:173–174.

40. The same difficulty is apparent as Dooyeweerd is expounding the general nature of positivization, where he writes: "In the historical and post-historical aspects the laws acquire a concrete sense through human positivizing of divine normative principles. The human formative will is then to be conceived of as a subjective moment on the law-side of these spheres themselves" (*NC*, 2:239). This elliptical formulation seems to imply that humans participate in making—as distinct from positivizing or concretizing—the law to which they are subject. Now it is certainly consistent to hold that the requirement laid upon humans to engage in positivizing is itself on the law-side, specifically, as Dooyeweerd puts it, on the law-side of the historical aspect. As Johan van der Hoeven expresses it in "Wetten en feiten. De 'Wijsbegeerte der Wetsidee' temidden van hedendaagse bezinning op dit thema," in *Wetenschap, wijsheid, filosoferen*, ed. P. Blokhuis et al. (Assen: Van Gorcum, 1981), 119: "the response-character of the subject-side is an outworking of the law-side itself." But this need not, and on my reading should not, be taken to imply that Dooyeweerd intends to claim that humans are the authoritative source of the normative laws to which they are subject. This is exactly the assertion driving the humanistic freedom-nature motive, which he specifically repudiates.

41. Charles Taylor, *Hegel* (Cambridge: Cambridge University Press, 1975), 570–571.

42. Dooyeweerd, *NC*, 2:557.

43. Ibid., 1:105; see 1:187; 2:238, 551.

44. He specifically distinguishes his own position from that of Maurice Hauriou, whose notion of the "institutional ideas" of a community confuses "internal structural principles" with "speculative neo-Platonic Ideas"; *NC*, 3:578.

45. See Zigterman, "Dooyeweerd's Theory of Individuality Structures," 98.

46. This is true even if it is held that "law" lies within the realm of created order and not above it, as Dooyeweerd does. He would endorse Aristotle's

rejection of Plato's notion of ideal forms existing independently of any of their concrete instantiations, and his own position is evidently closer to Aristotle's idea of a telos *internal* to an existent.

47. Dooyeweerd, *NC*, 3:170.

48. Rooted as they are in the divine order of cosmic time, constant structures of individuality "cannot be subject to genesis and evolution, [but] it is only their *realization* in changeable individuals which permits a genetic investigation according to specific scientific viewpoints. Ideovariations (mutations) which occur within the vegetable or animal kingdoms cannot give rise to new *structural principles*, but only to *individuals* which exhibit a specific geno-type not realized before" (Dooyeweerd, *NC* 3:94; original emphasis). Modal and typical laws are principles of possibility, transcendental conditions for the factual existence of things. Individual existents make their actual appearance at particular moments in time. When they appear they realize or actualize only what the enduring order of creation makes possible. The typical structural principles rooted in that order are the ontic framework within which genetic processes occur. Jacob Klapwijk summarizes Dooyeweerd's general position precisely: "That the temporal disclosure of events in the world could be accompanied by idionomic novelty, with new law structures becoming functional, seems unfitting to Dooyeweerd. . . . [W]hat time has disclosed must have been enclosed in time from its very beginning. All structures that time has brought to expression—the biological species included—must have been, in one way or another, enclosed in the cosmic time order. The cosmic time order brings to expression the a priori and universal validity of all those structures that are grounded in the creation order" (*Purpose in the Living World: Creation and Emergent Evolution*, trans. and ed. Harry Cook [Cambridge: Cambridge University Press, 2008], 236). Chapter 12 of *Purpose in the Living World* is a critique of Dooyewerd's biological essentialism (238). "Type laws" (what Dooyeweerd calls typical structural principles) are real and identifiable, says Klapwijk, but "they are not to be identified with irreducible essences that originated from an original creating Word" (253). Klapwijk alludes to the position of Vollenhoven, Dooyeweerd's closest philosophical colleague, who rejected the idea of invariant type laws rooted in an original creation order (254–258).

49. Nicholas Wolterstorff, *Until Justice and Peace Embrace* (Grand Rapids: Eerdmans, 1983), 62–63. Wolterstorff's critique interacts principally with Dooyeweerd's shorter and less technical work, *Roots of Western Culture*, and does not engage with his extensive account of structural principles in *NC*. Nonetheless, it serves to voice a widely held view, both within and beyond the Christian community.

50. Wolterstorff, *Until Justice and Peace Embrace*, 63.

51. Ibid., 63n.

52. My response to Wolterstorff draws on Paul Marshall's review of *Until Justice and Peace Embrace* in *Philosophia Reformata* 50 (1985): 89–93; see esp. 92.

53. An argument along such lines is found in James W. Skillen, "Politics in One World," *Philosophia Reformata* 66 (2001): 117–131.

54. The question then arises whether the function of public justice is administered *at all* in such societies. Dooyeweerd's reply to that question is touched on in the next chapter.

55. Of course, what may be arguable in respect of the state might not be arguable with respect to other kinds of social structures. A wide-ranging series of research programs, focusing on the numerous kinds of structures present in a variety of cultures, would lie ahead if the general argument were to be fully sustained. The bulk of Dooyeweerd's own empirical research was in the field of law, so it is not surprising that it is in this field that the most extensive developments of his work have taken place.

56. J. D. Dengerink formulates the issue with a distinct accent in *De zin van de werkelijkheid. Een wijsgerige benadering* (Amsterdam: Vrije Universiteit Uitgeverij, 1986), 179; see also his "Structuur en persoon," *Philosophia Reformata* 51 (1986): 38, 43. He suggests that "new structural laws" do indeed emerge in history, but these are to be seen neither as "supplements" to an already given reality nor as filling in a kind of structural "vacuum" in reality. Rather, they represent the "disclosure of possibilities which are, by virtue of the creation-word, really given in reality" (Dengerink, *De zin van der werkelijkheid,* 179). The opening process and the differentiation process "are not limited to the factual side of reality, but apply also to the law side. . . . [A]s a consequence of human activities, we can speak of a progressive disclosure of the law side of reality. There are all kinds of structural laws that only come into force in an articulated way in the course of the history of creation" (182). So far this is broadly consonant with Dooyeweerd's own accounts. Both view humans as the agents of the disclosure of these new structural laws, though not the source of the possibility of such disclosure. And both hold that disclosure of "new" structural laws is indeed itself a creational norm to which human beings must respond. For both, disclosure involves more than a continual sustaining of an originally complete order but also the unfolding of new possibilities enclosed within that original order (121, 131). (See also Hendrik Hart, *Understanding Our World: An Integral Ontology* [Lanham, MD: University Press of America, 1984], 105–107.) However, Dengerink employs the term *new* in a way not found explicitly in Dooyeweerd. For Dengerink, "new" indicates "only now in force" (though not ontically unprecedented). The subtle difference here is between a view in which

all societal structural principles are *already given* in the original order of creation, waiting to be positivized at the appropriate historical period (Dooyeweerd) and one in which (at least some of) these structural principles are *given only when disclosed* (Dengerink). But for Dengerink too only God is the "giver." "New" structural principles, he suggests, are already enclosed in the creation-Word, but this is now conceived as embracing past, present, and future. On its face this seems a plausible way to circumvent the problem of structural invariance, since it avoids implying the existence of "laws without subjects." Genuinely new structural principles can arise in history. But it invites the separate theological criticism that divine providence is now being absorbed into divine creation. Not every providential action of God in history is an act of creation.

57. For example, Hendrik Hart, "Creation Order in Our Philosophical Tradition: Critique and Refinement," in *An Ethos of Compassion and the Integrity of Creation,* ed. Brian J. Walsh et al. (Lanham, MD: University Press of America, 1995), 67–96. In a response to Hart Johan van der Hoeven claims (rightly in my view) that Hart has misread Dooyeweerd's notions of order and law ("Portrayal of Reformational Philosophy Seems Unfair," in Walsh et al., eds., *An Ethos of Compassion,* 109–114). Hart develops his view further in "Notes on Dooyeweerd, Reason, and Order," in *Contemporary Reflections on the Philosophy of Herman Dooyeweerd,* ed. D. F. M. Strauss and Michelle Botting (Lewiston, NY: Edwin Mellen Press, 2000), 125–146. Students of Hart (especially Kuipers, Dudiak, and Ansell) defend and explore Hart's view of creation order in Ronald A. Kuipers and Janet Catherina Wesselius, eds., *Philosophy as Responsibility: A Celebration of Hendrik Hart's Contribution to the Discipline* (Lanham, MD: University Press of America, 2002).

58. A summary of his anthropology is given in Herman Dooyeweerd, "De leer van de mens in der Wijsbegeerte der Wetsidee," *Correspondentiebladen* 7 (1942): 133–144, a work that appears in English as "The Theory of Man: Thirty-two Propositions on Anthropology" (Institute for Christian Studies, Toronto, n.d.). The first volume of his *Reformatie en scholastiek in de wijsbegeerte,* elaborating his philosophical anthropology, was published in 1949 (Franeker: Wever). For discussions of his anthropology, see Gerrit Glas, "Ego, Self and the Body: An Assessment of Dooyeweerd's Philosophical Anthropology," in *Christian Philosophy at the Close of the Twentieth Century: Assessment and Perspective,* ed. Sander Griffioen and Bert M. Balk (Kampen: J. H. Kok, 1995), 67–78; Gerrit Glas, "Filosofische antropologie," in *Kennis en werkelijkheid. Tweede inleiding tot een christelijke filosofie,* ed. René van Woudenberg (Amsterdam: Buijten and Schipperheijn, 1996), 86–142; Gerrit Glas, "Persons and Their Lives: Reformational Philosophy on Man, Ethics and Beyond," *Philosophia Reformata* 71 (2006): 31–52; M. D. Stafleu, "Being Human in the Cosmos," *Philosophia Refor-*

mata 56 (1991): 101–131; P. Blosser, "Reconnoitering Dooyeweerd's Theory of Man," *Philosophia Reformata* 58 (1993): 192–209; Willem J. Ouweneel, "Supra-temporality in the Transcendental Anthropology of Herman Dooyeweerd," *Philosophia Reformata* 58 (1993): 210–220; Govert Buijs et al., eds., *Home respondens. Verkenningen rond het mens-zijn* (Amsterdam: Buijten and Schipperhijn, 2005). James H. Olthuis proposes a postmodern rendering of a Dooyeweerdian anthropology in "Be(com)ing: Humankind as Gift and Call," *Philosophia Reformata* 56 (1993): 153–172; and "Of Webs and Whirlwinds: Me, Myself and I," in Strauss and Botting, eds., *Contemporary Reflections*, 31–48.

59. Wolterstorff, *Until Peace and Justice Embrace*, 59. Original emphasis.

60. Jacques Maritain, *Man and the State* (Chicago: University of Chicago Press, 1951), 13.

61. Here I utilize suggestions in Hart, *Understanding Our World*, 275–292; and Dengerink, *De zin van de werkelijkheid*, 179–183, 329–331, 338–354.

62. Later I argue that natural human communities also need such formation. Both types are equally established by human positivizing activity.

63. This term refers to what Dooyeweerd describes as "inter-individual and inter-communal relationships," treated further in subsequent chapters.

64. See Dooyeweerd, *NC*, 3:192–193.

65. Ibid., 3:197–198.

66. M. D. Stafleu defends the idea of "subjective pre-logical functioning" in "associations" (what Dooyeweerd terms "communities") in "On the Character of Social Communities, the State and the Public Domain," *Philosophia Reformata* 69 (2004): 126.

67. Dooyeweerd, *NC*, 3:492–500; see also J. Zwart, "De staatsleer van Herman Dooyeweerd," *Philosophia Reformata* 45 (1980): 137; Dengerink, *De zin van de werkelijkheid*, 254, 349–350.

68. Dooyeweerd, *NC*, 3:499–500.

69. On the other hand, the fact that communities lack prelogical subjective functioning need not warrant the conclusion, advanced by Hart on grounds I find unpersuasive, that they lack *any* subjective functioning. See *Understanding Our World*, 284–285, where Hart claims that societal structures are normatively structured, enkaptic *relationships between persons* (enkaptic structural wholes); a school, for example, "is an organization, that is, an organized, inter-actional, interrelation of persons in a specific environment, such that the interaction has organizational centricity." They are not, however, "functors" (Hart's term for "individuality structures"), because they do not function subjectively in the first four functional levels (modal aspects) (284–285). "No existing functor can be devoid of dimensions of physicality. For in that case we would have a functor incapable of acting effectually" (109; cf. 220). But to restrict "effectual

action" to entities having a physical foundation seems reductive. Behind Hart's position is the view that each functor in a higher realm must incorporate the capacity for subjective physical functioning into its own subjective functioning (101). I do not see the force of the "must" here. Hart rightly wishes to avoid a "substantialization of . . . social totalities as though they were themselves persons who can be treated as such." He adds: "But persons cannot hide behind institutions" (285). But affirming the subjective (normative) functioning of communities does not imply any such substantialization, or that persons can escape their communal responsibilities. I agree with Hart that persons should not be viewed as "parts" of societal wholes and that the "members" of a societal whole are, strictly speaking, not persons as such but rather persons functioning in specific roles (mother, citizen, etc): "as mothers and citizens, people are, in these functions, integrated into wholes such as families and states" (220). This is a helpful formulation, but it does not exclude that the wholes into which functioning persons are thereby integrated are capable of "effectual action," thus qualifying as functors.

70. Dooyeweerd, *NC*, 3:198.

71. Ibid., 3:296–297.

72. Ibid.

73. "Human acts, with their threefold intentional direction (viz. the knowing, the volitional and the imaginative directions), may assume the most different structures of individuality. The act of praying is typically qualified as an act of faith[;] . . . the act of aesthetical imagination is typically qualified in the aesthetical aspect of experience, etc." (Dooyeweerd, *NC*, 3:88).

74. Ibid., 3:296.

75. Maurice Mandelbaum, "Societal Facts," in *Modes of Individualism and Collectivism*, ed. J. O'Neill (London: Heineman, 1973), 227, makes a similar point. In a debate on "methodological individualism," he notes that "sociological concepts cannot be translated into psychological concepts without remainder." See also Steven Lukes, *Individualism* (Oxford: Blackwell, 1973), chapter 17. For a view parallel to Dooyeweerd's, see Alan Carter, "On Individualism, Collectivism and Interrelationism," *Heythrop Journal* 31 (1990): 23–38.

76. Dooyeweerd, *NC*, 3:299. Original emphasis.

77. Ibid., 3:88.

78. Dooyeweerd sees each of these human acts as a distinct individuality structure, functioning simultaneously in all aspects.

79. Dooyeweerd, *NC*, 3:88–89.

80. Dengerink, *De zin van de werkelijkheid*, 340–342.

81. I leave open here (for lack of competence as much as space) the question whether or not my decision to retain the Dooyeweerdian notion of universal human functional capacities is compatible with an evolutionary conception of human nature (theistic or otherwise) according to which entirely unprecedented *functional capacities* arise in history—as, for example, in notions of "emergence" found in versions of systems theory. This seems to be (or be compatible with) the position of Klapwijk, who says of the process of "hominization": "The neo-cortex, already enlarged in *Homo erectus,* appears to have grown out into a receiver dish tuned in to the signals from the Eternal. In the depths of his consciousness the earth creature hears a voice, a voice calling him to respond and to take responsibility: 'Adam, where are you?'" (*Purpose in the Living World,* 166). This seems to allude to the temporal emergence of the irreducibly human function of faith. Whether or not this idea is philosophically or theologically plausible (it could not be resolved by science), I would certainly reject modernist variants of emergence according to which certain functions become *redundant* at certain historical junctures—namely, according to secularization theory, the function of faith.

82. Dengerink, *De zin van de werkelijkheid,* 181, 348–349.

83. See note 48 above for Klapwijk's description of Dooyeweerd's "type essentialism."

84. The notion of universal human capabilities developed by Amartya Sen and applied constructively by Martha Nussbaum has some parallels with my proposal here and carries with it potentially quite radical political implications.

85. For a restatement of the classical Christian position, see Christopher C. Roberts, *Creation and Covenant: The Significance of Sexual Difference in the Moral Theology of Marriage* (London: T. & T. Clark, 2007).

86. I am not suggesting that philosophy is the only or the primary source of information relevant to such debates (or that public debates take the form of philosophical discourse). For many adherents to religious traditions the authority of a text or an institution would be more important, and likely decisive.

Seven.   A Medley of Social Structures

1. This type seems to include structures of a quite disparate nature. It is not clear that a category including families, trade unions, political parties, and schools will be greatly useful. In fact it is the detailed account of the structural principle of each of these genotypes that does the clarifying work.

2. Dooyeweerd, *NC*, 3:176–191.

3. Ibid., 3:176.

4. While his later attempt at such an explanation does elaborate the content of the distinct notions of transcendental societal category and typical structural principle, the precise sense in which they are related remains obscure; see *NC*, 3:565–569.

5. The term *interlinkages* is proposed in L. Kalsbeek, *Contours of a Christian Philosophy: An Introduction to Herman Dooyeweerd's Thought,* ed. Bernard Zylstra and Josina Zylstra (Toronto: Wedge, 1975), 260, and was coined by Bernard Zylstra. It is an attempt to capture the meaning of the Dutch term *maatschapsverhoudingen* (used in *WdW*), for which no exact English equivalent exists. In chapter 11 I propose an alternative term. *Communities* is a translation of *gemeenschapsverhoudingen,* more literally rendered as "communal relationships." The Dutch terms *gemeenschap* and *maatschap* parallel the German terms made famous in Ferdinand Tönnies's book *Gemeinschaft und Gesellschaft* (1887), first translated into English by Charles P. Loomis as *Fundamental Concepts of Sociology (Gemeinschaft und Gesellschaft)* (New York: American Book Company, 1940) and reprinted as *Community and Society* (East Lansing: Michigan State University Press, 1957). But Dooyeweerd specifically rejects Tönnies's "antithetic" distinction between community as organically unified whole and society as fictional and arbitrary association (*NC*, 3:184–186).

6. Dooyeweerd, *NC*, 3:177–178.

7. Ibid., 3:181. This is not of course offered as anything like a complete analysis of the problem of social equality. For a clarification of his idea of equality, see Bernard Zylstra, *From Pluralism to Collectivism: The Development of Harold Laski's Political Thought* (Assen: Van Gorcum, 1968), chapter 6.

8. Ibid., 3:178.

9. I noted earlier that this reading of undifferentiated communities has been challenged.

10. Ibid., 3:580–581.

11. Ibid., 3:581–582.

12. Ibid., 3:582–583.

13. Ibid., 3:583.

14. Ibid., 3:587. What Dooyeweerd terms the "norm of integration" (described in chapter 5) is, initially, the vocation for formerly geographically separated groups to interact with each other to widen their cultural horizons, to "integrate." This is distinct from the "integrating tendencies" he is now discussing, and which are the necessary complement to individualization and differentiation. Yet the latter can in effect be seen as a later expression of a norm of integration more broadly conceived.

15. Ibid., 3:588.

16. Ibid., 3:588–589. Presumably, the subcategory of relationships between individuals and communities should also be included here; call them "individual-communal" relationships.

17. Ibid., 3:590.

18. Ibid.

19. Ibid., 3:592–593. For critical accounts of contemporary globalization partly informed by Dooyeweerd's thought, see Bob Goudzwaard, *Globalization and the Kingdom of God* (Grand Rapids: Baker, 2001); Jonathan Chaplin, "God, Globalization and Grace: An Exercise in Public Theology," in *The Gospel and Globalization: Exploring the Religious Roots of a Globalized World,* ed. Michael W. Goheen and Erin G. Glanville (Vancouver: Regent College Publishing/ Geneva Society, 2009), 49–68, and other chapters in that book.

20. Dooyeweerd, *NC,* 3:179.

21. Dutch *verbanden* (German *Verbande*). Thus only those communities *(gemeenschappen)* that are "organized" are styled *verbanden.* This point is obscured in Sander Griffioen and René van Woudenberg, "Theorie van sociale gemeenschappen," in *Kennis en werkelijkheid. Tweede inleiding tot een christelijke filosofie,* ed. René van Woudenberg (Amsterdam: Buijten and Schipperheijn, 1996), 248 ff.

22. Dooyeweerd, *NC,* 3:405.

23. This is another term alluding to the "nuclear moment" of the historical aspect.

24. Dooyeweerd followed the conventions of his time in also holding that in marriage authority resides in the husband.

25. Dooyeweerd, *NC,* 3:179–180.

26. At least it is one involving responsible human decision. Which is not to say that it is a wholly autonomous act. In Catholic moral theology, for example, procreation is a primary purpose of marriage, so that partners are not morally "free" to decide not to try to have children. I suspect Dooyeweerd would endorse this position, though perhaps not the distinct view proscribing contraception.

27. This is not true of marriage, which certainly occasions a physical, sexual connection between partners and opens up the possibility of biological reproduction but seems not to be founded either in that connection or in those possibilities.

28. It would thus be erroneous to suggest that all social structures share the same founding function, as distinct from being founded in the same modal aspect. This is technically formulated in terms of the notion of modal types of individuality, introduced in chapter 8.

29. Dooyeweerd, *NC*, 2:261.

30. Ibid., 2:275.

31. Ibid., 3:346–347.

32. Ibid., 3:347.

33. Ibid., 3:348–349, 357 n. 3. The exception is that the functions of the natural communities are not taken over. Such communities are only artificially "intersected" by the undifferentiated unit (3:347).

34. Ibid., 3:348–349.

35. Ibid., 3:350–357, 367.

36. Ibid., 3:362.

37. Ibid., 3:364.

38. Ibid., 3:358.

39. This is not the only objection that can be leveled against Dooyeweerd's account. See, e.g., Calvin G. Seerveld, "Dooyeweerd's Idea of Historical Development: Christian Respect for Cultural Diversity," *Westminster Theological Journal* 58 (1996), 41–61.

40. Naturally such a conclusion is elicited from a chain of reasoning assuming Dooyeweerd's acceptance of the biblical ground motive. However, if what he terms "states of affairs" really do impress themselves upon people irrespective of their ground motives he would have reason to expect at least some people of different religions or worldviews to be able to recognize those possibilities as genuinely emancipatory.

41. Undifferentiated primitive communities also have an institutional character. See Dooyeweerd, *NC*, 3:187–188.

42. Regarding the church, Dooyeweerd notes that many children are baptized into a church and remain members at least until old enough to choose to leave. Dooyeweerd suggests that churches rejecting infant baptism do not qualify as institutions. But this overlooks the fact that intensive membership is indeed often expected of all adult church members, irrespective of when they were baptized. Joining the church is surely supposed to be a lifelong commitment, even though the commitment may wane or even disappear. (Dooyeweerd's view certainly rules out any voluntaristic understanding of the church, which, as many sociologists have pointed out, seems to characterize the practice of many American Protestants if not necessarily the official stance of their church authorities.)

43. See note 5 above.

44. The Dutch term *autoritaire* (which appears in *WdW*; see also Dooyeweerd, *Verkenningen in de wijsbegeerte, de sociologie and de rechtsgeschiedenis*, 2nd ed., ed. J. Stellingwerff [Amsterdam: Buijten and Schipperheijn, 1967; first

edition published 1962], 132), of which "authoritarian" is a literal translation, should not be read here as carrying the negative connotation of this English word. A better rendition would be "authoritative" (which also contrasts more naturally with "associative" rather than "associatory"). On this, see M. D. Stafleu, "On the Character of Social Communities, the State and the Public Domain," *Philosophia Reformata* 69 (2004): 125–139.

45. Dooyeweerd, *NC,* 3:191. Of course it is easy to think of examples of each of these types that are "authoritarian" in the bad sense. But Dooyeweerd would hold that these are examples of the abuse of the legitimate function of authority in each case. His intriguing views on workers' cooperatives are noted in chapter 10.

46. Ibid., 3:189–190.

47. Ibid., 3:581.

48. Ibid., 594–595. Dooyeweerd may have taken the word *rationalizing* from Weber but here gives it a rather different meaning, i.e., something like "organization informed by scientific thought," which, within appropriate bounds, is "destined to disclose and to realize the potentialities and dispositions inherent in social relations according to the divine world-order."

49. Ibid., 3:571. Dooyeweerd further characterizes the relation between the purpose and structure of voluntary associations in terms of the category "societal form," which embraces both "genetic" and "existential" forms (3:570–573). The genetic form of a voluntary association is the contract. Associations are originated by means of a voluntary contractual agreement between independent parties. Purpose plays a "constitutive" role in this contractual genetic form of voluntary associations in that the particular purpose for which they were created will normally be specified in the articles of association (3:572). But this purpose never coalesces with the structural principle of a voluntary association, which cannot be reduced to its genetic form.

50. Ibid., 3:574–575.

51. Ibid., 3:578–579.

52. Ibid., 3:574.

53. Ibid., 3:288. Such an emphasis echoes the insistence in official Catholic social teaching on the centrality of the family to society.

54. Ibid., 3:661.

55. Ibid., 3:93.

56. Ibid., 3:174.

57. Ibid., 3:174–176.

58. The family business is a phenotype of the genotype business corporation, which falls within the radical type of economically qualified voluntary associations.

59. Dooyeweerd, *A Christian Theory of Social Institutions*, 66. I have corrected the translation here, substituting "lifesphere" (= *levenssfeer*) for "structural characteristics." The next sentence in the translation is therefore also misleading. It reads: "These types of structural characteristics, however, are not of a subjective character." It should read: "The structural types themselves, however, are not of a subjective character." The point is that an antinormative interlacement can damage the subject-side of a concrete social structure but cannot tamper with the typical structural principle itself, since this is on the law-side. Indeed only with reference to the structural principle can such damage be actually identified as antinormative.

60. Dooyeweerd, *NC*, 3:93.

61. Or should determine it: a military government would be an example of a part (the army) controlling the whole (the state).

62. I also identified a third kind, "individual-communal relationships."

63. One of Dooyeweerd's concerns in making this distinction is to insist on the difference between enkaptic and whole-part relationships. The latter, he suggests, exist between structures having the same typical structural principle. But after all this seems to misstate his intention. A whole-part relationship is not properly characterized as one existing between two entities having the same typical structure but rather as one existing within one and the same concrete ("factually existing") structure.

64. The other two are symbiotic enkapsis, especially evident in biological organisms, such as in parasitic relationships between animals and plants and occurring between two structures either of different radical type or of different genotypes within the same radical type; and subject-object enkapsis, manifested between animals or vegetables and their "objective formations," such as a snail's shell, or between humans and the product of their labor (*NC*, 3:648–650).

65. Dooyeweerd, *NC*, 3:640–641. Among cultural artifacts, for instance, a sculpture is irreversibly founded in, say, the marble from which it is made, but the marble is not founded in the sculpture. In this type of enkapsis one structure opens up various functions of another. Such examples of enkaptic relationships generally occur between structures of different radical or genotype.

66. Ibid., 3:648. In the natural world this is a case of a relation of reciprocal dependence between an individuality structure and an environment, such as that between a biological organism and its environment. This relation is not one of irreversible foundational enkapsis, because the environment also needs the organism. Its biotic or psychic object functions are dependent on the subjective functioning of the organism.

67. This is exclusively found in the state, which I examine in chapter 10.

68. Johan van der Vyver suggests that (what I am calling) functional subservience is a feature only of one type of enkaptic interlacement, namely, "unifying enkapsis." See his "The Jurisprudential Legacy of Abraham Kuyper and Leo XIII," *Markets and Morality* 5, no. 1 (2002): 218. This term is indeed used by Dooyeweerd at one point (Dooyeweerd, *A Christian Theory of Social Institutions,* 67; the term translates *"unierende"* in *Verkenningen in de wijsbegeerte, de sociologie, and de rechtsgeschiedenis,* 104). However, Dooyeweerd does not define unifying enkapsis there specifically as functional subservience, nor does he contrast it with other types in such terms. Moreover, as far as I am aware, the category "unifying enkapsis" does not appear anywhere else in Dooyeweerd's writings, is not clearly defined, and is not integrated with his much more extensive account in the third volume of *NC.* (*Verkenningen in de wijsbegeerte,* composed of lectures presented to a student audience, was first published in 1947. It was reprinted in 1962, after the appearance of *NC,* but with only minor revisions. Dooyeweerd seems not to have taken the opportunity to clear up the categorial ambiguity.) In my view it is clear from that longer account that he regards functional subservience as definitive of all enkaptic interlacements.

69. Dooyeweerd, *NC,* 3:306–307, 322–324. Presumably Dooyeweerd would include common law marriage here. And there is no reason to believe that he would not recognize single-parent families, existing due to death or divorce, as genuine families. Whether he would regard children born from casual or forced sexual encounters as members of a family is not clear. If so, then "marriage" would not be necessary for there to be a "family."

70. Dooyeweerd suggests further that marriage and family are not only interlaced with each other but also each interlaced with other structures. For example, the family may be enkaptically interlaced with social classes or religious and political communities, causing the family's internal sphere of communal thought (its logical function) to reveal certain prejudices derived from these affiliations (3:289); its attitudes will reveal it as a "typical working class" or "solidly conservative" family. The family here performs an enkaptic function in the sense that it lends the support of its family solidarity to the larger group concerned. Similarly, the family's emotional life will be conditioned by the same sort of affiliations (3:295). But first Dooyeweerd does not tell us whether this is an example of foundational or correlative enkapsis, and it is difficult to see how it could be either; neither irreversibility nor any mutual presupposition is involved here; and second, social classes do not, for Dooyeweerd, have structural principles, whereas in an enkaptic interlacement both parties must have. If by religious and political communities Dooyeweerd means churches and

political parties, then we may be able to speak of a genuine enkaptic interlacement here. But even if this is the case there is, third, the problem of identifying which structure is functionally subservient. Again, functional subservience does not seem a particularly enlightening concept. The same conclusion emerges from his examples of correlative enkaptic relationship between family or marriage and interlinkages (3:655–657) and of irreversible foundational relationship between the family and church and state (3:658–659).

71. Dooyeweerd, *NC*, 3:658. This type of enkaptic relationship is thus termed genetic foundational enkapsis.

72. Dooyeweerd also mentions the foundational and correlative enkaptic interlacements between differentiated interlinkages. International trade, for example, is irreversibly founded in transport, while the free market and economic competition are enkaptically related in a correlative sense (*NC*, 3:661). But the same question applies here too.

73. The same applies to voluntary associations, which are in turn "irreversibly founded" in differentiated interindividual relationships.

74. Dooyeweerd, *NC*, 3:659–660.

75. Compare Dooyeweerd's treatment of the enkaptic interlacement between natural communities and undifferentiated primitive communities. Although the primitive community substantially conditions the natural communities within it, these natural communities never actually become its parts but at most "perform an enkaptic function" within it. This, he suggests, is a case of an irreversible foundational enkaptic relationship: primitive communities cannot exist without natural communities, but the reverse does not apply (*NC*, 3:653). The organized primitive community avails itself of the functions of the natural community in its internal operations. The natural community supplies a biotically founded bonding, which the organized community exploits in order to sustain its own unity and power (see 3:339 ff., 535 ff.). It seems we finally do have an example of a relation of unilateral functional subservience, a genuinely enkaptic interlacement according to Dooyeweerd's definition. Disappointingly, it occurs in the least plausible of all his accounts of particular social structures.

76. At one point Dooyeweerd seems inadvertently to acknowledge this. He suggests that the fact that one structure is enkaptically founded in another does not after all mean that enkaptic binding is only one-way. This point is connected to the transcendental correlativity of communities and interlinkages. The case under discussion happens to be the foundational enkaptic relationship between a community (the state) and interlinkages. The transcendental correlativity between these two categories means that although the enkaptic relationship is an irreversible foundational one, nevertheless there is a mutual enkaptic binding present (*NC*, 3:660). The same also applies in the case of the

irreversible foundational enkaptic relationship between voluntary associations and interindividual relationships (3:658). But conceding this point seems completely to undermine his general conception of an enkaptic interlacement as *unilateral* functional subservience.

77. Pius XI, *QA*, paragraph 80.

78. See Jonathan Chaplin, "Subsidiarity and Sphere Sovereignty: Catholic and Reformed Conceptions of the Role of the State," in *Things Old and New: Catholic Social Teaching Revisited,* ed. Frank P. McHugh and Samuel M. Natale (Lanham, MD: University Press of America, 1993), 180.

79. J.-Y. Calvez and J. Perrin, *The Church and Social Justice,* trans. J. R. Kirwan (Chicago: Henry Regnery, 1961), 332.

80. Dooyeweerd, *Roots,* 121–133.

81. See my "Toward an Ecumenical Social Theory: Revisiting Herman Dooyeweerd's Critique of Thomism," in *That the World May Believe: Essays on Mission and Unity in Honour of George Vandervelde,* ed. Michael Goheen and Margaret O'Gara (Lanham, MD: University Press of America, 2006), 215–238.

82. In fact the hierarchical social metaphysics underlying the classical formulation of subsidiarity has in any case receded into the background of Catholic social teaching since Vatican II. The "personalist" cast of the social encyclicals of John Paul II has even further relativized this hierarchical social theory (even while John Paul II seemed to reaffirm a hierarchical ecclesiology).

83. This is what Mary Ann Glendon refers to, in a discussion of the family, as "connectedness." See her "The Missing Dimension of Sociality," chapter 5 of *Rights Talk: The Impoverishment of Political Discourse* (New York: Free Press, 1991).

84. J. D. Dengerink, *De zin van de werkelijkheid. Een wijsgerige benadering* (Amsterdam: Vrije Universiteit Uitgeverij, 1986), 227. Dooyeweerd himself also uses this term on occasion.

85. See Hendrik Hart, *Understanding Our World: An Integral Ontology* (Lanham, MD: University Press of America, 1984), 218–221, for an alternative formulation of this point.

86. This section draws particularly on chapter 3 of J. D. Dengerink, *Critisch-historische onderzoek naar de sociologische ontwikkeling van het beginsel der "souvereiniteit in eigen kring" in de 19e en 20e eeuw* (Kampen: J. H. Kok, 1948).

87. The accounts in James W. Skillen, "The Development of Calvinistic Political Theory in the Netherlands, with Special Reference to the Thought of Herman Dooyeweerd" (Ph.D. dissertation, Duke University, 1974); and Gordon J. Spykman, "Sphere-Sovereignty in Calvin and the Calvinist Tradition," in *Exploring the Heritage of John Calvin,* ed. D. E. Holwerda (Grand Rapids: Baker,

1976), 163–208, underplay the significance of this organicism; Dengerink, in *Critisch-historish onderzoek*, is more reliable here but unpersuasively attributes the influence of organicism to Kuyper's "nature-supernature" dualism.

88. Abraham Kuyper, *Lectures on Calvinism* (Grand Rapids: Eerdmans, 1961), 53.

89. Dengerink, *Critisch-historish onderzoek*, 111.

90. Abraham Kuyper, *The Problem of Poverty*, ed. James W. Skillen (Grand Rapids: Baker, 1991), 69. This volume is a translation of Kuyper's 1891 address titled *Het sociale vraagstuk en de christelijk religie* (Amsterdam: J. A. Wormser).

91. Frederick S. Carney, "Associational Thought in Early Calvinism," in *Voluntary Associations*, ed. D. R. Robertson (Richmond: John Knox, 1966), 39–53. It is instructive to note that while Dooyeweerd appreciatively identifies Althusius as the first Calvinist to have formulated the principle of sphere sovereignty (*NC*, 3:663) Kuyper pointedly distances himself from Althusius and instead cites "Languet" as the more reliable early representative of authentically Calvinist political thought. See Abraham Kuyper, *Antirevolutionaire staatkunde*, 2 vols. (Kampen: J. H. Kok, 1916), 1:652–654. "Languet" was probably Mornay; see Quentin Skinner, *The Foundations of Modern Political Thought*, 2 vols. (Cambridge: Cambridge University Press, 1978), 2:305 n. 3. Kuyper here cites Gierke as responsible for creating the unfortunate impression of Althusius as the principal representative of an essentially unified movement of early Calvinist political thought. It is likely that Kuyper was misled by Gierke's interpretation of Althusius as a secularizing thinker. (See Otto von Gierke, *The Development of Political Theory*, trans. Bernard Freyd [London: George Allen and Unwin, 1939]; a translation of *Johannes Althusius und die Entwicklung der Naturrechtlichen Staatstheorien*, 4th ed. [Breslau, 1929].) Thus Kuyper traces the lineage of his own thought to other, supposedly more orthodox Calvinist writers of the period. Carney's suggestion that a distinctive Calvinist associationalist theory emerged from a group of writers at this time, of whom Althusius was simply the "culminating theorist," does allow the possibility that Kuyper might have derived pluralist inspiration from sources other than Althusius. For a more reliable reading of Althusius, see James W. Skillen, "The Political Theory of Johannes Althusius," *Philosophia Reformata* 39 (1974): 171–190. The most comprehensive recent study of Althusius is Thomas O. Huegelin, *Early Modern Concepts for a Late Modern World: Althusius on Community and Federalism* (Waterloo, ON: Wilfred Laurier University Press, 1999). See also John Witte, Jr., *The Reformation of Rights: Law, Religion and Human Rights in Early Modern Calvinism* (Cambridge: Cambridge University Press, 2007), chapter 3.

92. Carney, "Associational Thought in Early Calvinism," 43, 46.

93. Ibid., 49–50.

94. Note that for these early Calvinists not only are the church and the political association constituted and limited by covenant, but all human associations are covenantal in nature: all are theaters of human response to the call of God to service and to justice. The same theme recurs in the Puritan writers. As Gardner notes, "for the Puritans all forms of community are fundamentally covenantal" (except the family, he adds). See E. Clinton Gardner, *Justice and Christian Ethics* (Cambridge: Cambridge University Press, 1995), 105.

95. Carney, "Associational Thought in Early Calvinism," 52.

96. Commenting on Puritanism, Graham Maddox puts it this way: "The covenant is not merely a voluntary congress of autonomous individual persons, but is grounded upon supra-personal authority." See his *Religion and the Rise of Democracy* (London: Routledge, 1996), 153.

97. Kuyper, *The Problem of Poverty*, 259.

98. Kuyper did not consistently hold this position.

99. Here Kuyper is continuing a line of thought found in his Dutch Calvinist predecessor Groen van Prinsterer, who in turn derived it in part from the Lutheran J. F. Stahl, an adherent of the Historical school of law. See Dengerink, *Critisch-historisch onderzoek,* chapters 1–2; and A. J. Van Dyke, *Groen van Prinsterer's Lectures on Unbelief and Revolution* (Toronto: Wedge, 1989). Kuyper's conception of the state also reflects this organicist influence, but I will not explore it here. (See Peter Heslam, *Creating a Christian Worldview: Abraham Kuyper's Lectures on Calvinism* (Grand Rapids: Eerdmans; Carlisle: Paternoster, 1998), chapter 6; Dengerink, *Critisch-historisch onderzoek,* 118–121; Skillen, *The Development,* 225–273). Dooyeweerd rejects the organicist traces in Kuyper's view of the nation and develops a different position, noted in chapter 10.

100. In "Het Calvinistische beginsel der souvereiniteit in eigen kring als staatkundig beginsel," Dooyeweerd honors Kuyper's contribution but also suggests some (not all) of its shortcomings.

101. Dooyeweerd, *NC,* 3:171.

102. Ibid., 3:285.

103. Herman Dooyeweerd, *De strijd om het souvereiniteitsbegrip in de moderne rechts- en staatsleer* (Amsterdam: H. J. Paris, 1950), 52.

104. Dooyeweerd, *Roots,* 48.

105. Dooyeweerd, *NC,* 3:535; emphasis added.

106. Ibid.

107. In what seems like an important concession to the "scholastic" view, however, Dooyeweerd does suggest that this equivalence is compatible with the idea that some structures are more "important" or "fundamental" than others.

As we have seen, institutional communities—state, church, and family—are more important than, for example, voluntary associations. Indeed the church, after all, has a "completely exceptional position" as an institution of regenerating grace. He asserts that the "light of eternity will always glow in the sanctuary of this particular Christian community" (*NC*, 3:535–536).

108. Dooyeweerd, *NC*, 3:694 ff.

109. Ibid., 3:699–780. Although this notion is not fully developed in *NC* it is seen not as an afterthought but as "the indispensable keystone" of the entire theory of enkapsis. This is because it is under this category that Dooyeweerd includes the human body itself. The notion is foundational to his philosophical anthropology. Other cases of enkaptic wholes exist in the three primary kingdoms (physical, vegetable, animal) and in the products of animal formation (3:697–698).

110. Ibid., 3:696.

111. Ibid., 3:697.

112. This suggests the possibility of a critique of the oppressive nature of a totalitarian society in terms of radically distorted interlacements, or intercommunal interlinkages generally. Later I note how a parallel critique of a society excessively dominated by market interlinkages might also be developed.

113. Dooyeweerd, *NC*, 3:582.

114. Dooyeweerd, *A Christian Theory of Social Institutions*, 84–85.

115. Alternatively we might say that his view suggests the possible development of a distinctive "enkaptic" variant of the system concept.

116. For Dooyeweerd's accounts of the different senses of the terms *individualism* and *universalism*, see *NC*, 3:167–168; and Herman Dooyeweerd, "De wijsgerige achtergrond van de moderne democratische reactie tegen het individualisme," *Mededeelingen* 4 (1939): 7–10. Gierke employs the same contrast; it seems possible that Dooyeweerd adapted it from him. See John D. Lewis's abridged translation of Otto von Gierke, "The Basic Concepts of State-Law and the Most Recent State-Law Theories," in J. D. Lewis, *The Genossenschaft-Theory of Otto von Gierke: A Study in Political Thought*, University of Wisconsin Studies in the Social Sciences and History 25 (Madison: University of Wisconsin, 1932), 179; cf. 166–168.

117. Dooyeweerd, *NC*, 3:183.

118. Both individualism and universalism have appeared in thinkers directed by each of the three nonbiblical ground motives. It would be wrong to suppose, for instance, that the pagan ground motive alone generates universalistic social theories while modern humanism produces exclusively individualistic ones.

119. *Dooyeweerd, NC*, 3:183.

120. Ibid., 3:182.

121. Ibid., 3:183.

122. Ibid., 3:193.

123. Ibid., 3:194.

124. Herman Dooyeweerd, *Verkenningen in de wijsbegeerte, de sociologie en de rechtsgeschiedenis*, 211.

125. Dooyeweerd, "De wijsgerig achtergrond van de moderne democratische reactie tegen het individualisme," 10.

126. Dooyeweerd, *NC*, 3:280; see also Dooyeweerd, *EN*, 2:137–139, 185–189.

127. Dooyeweerd, *NC*, 3:168.

128. Ibid., 3:595–596.

129. Ibid., 3:196.

130. Dooyeweerd, *A Christian Theory of Social Institutions*, 68.

131. Dooyeweerd, *NC*, 3:163, 167.

132. Ibid., 3:194–195.

133. Ibid., 3:195.

134. Herman Dooyeweerd, "De overspanning van het begrip 'natuurlijke gemeenschap' en het sociologisch universalisme," *Almanak van het Studentencorps aan de Vrije Universiteit* (1951): 216–229.

135. Dooyeweerd, *NC*, 3:195. The point is famously argued by Reinhold Niebuhr in *Moral Man and Immoral Society* (New York: Charles Scribner's Sons, 1960).

136. Dooyeweerd, *NC*, 3:167.

137. Ibid., 3:783–784.

138. Ibid., 3:169.

139. Ibid., 3:196.

140. For a defense of Dooyeweerd's position, see D. F. M. Strauss, "The Central Religious Community of Mankind in the Philosophy of the Cosmonomic Idea," *Philosophia Reformata* 37 (1972): 58–67.

141. Dooyeweerd, *NC*, 3:195.

Eight.   The Identity of the State

1. The theorists whose writings Dooyeweerd cites to illustrate this judgment are principally German, French, and Dutch social, political, and legal theorists writing in the nineteenth century and the first four decades of the twentieth century. See Kenneth Dyson, *The State Tradition in Western Europe: A Study of an Idea and an Institution* (Oxford: Martin Robertson, 1980), 81–185, for the climate in which some of these thinkers were writing.

2. Dooyeweerd, *De crisis.*

3. Jacques Maritain, *Integral Humanism: Temporal and Spiritual Problems of a New Christendom,* trans. Joseph W. Evans (Notre Dame: University of Notre Dame Press, 1973). For an even closer parallel, see John H. Hallowell, *The Decline of Liberalism as an Ideology: With Particular Reference to German Politico-Legal Thought* (London: Kegan Paul, Trench, and Trubner, 1946). Later, modernity critics such as Leo Strauss, Eric Voegelin, George Grant, and Alasdair MacIntyre were to present comparable analyses of the demise of modern political philosophy.

4. Dooyeweerd, *NC,* 3:381.

5. Ibid., 3:380.

6. Ibid., 3:381–382.

7. Ibid., 3:380–381.

8. Quoted in Dooyeweerd, *NC,* 3:382.

9. Ibid., 3:161, 169. For a postwar analysis of sociological schools that in some ways resembles Dooyeweerd's, see Don Martindale, *The Nature and Types of Sociological Theory* (Boston: Houghton Mifflin, 1960).

10. Dooyeweerd, *De crisis,* 6–8, 10–11, 30.

11. Dooyeweerd, *NC,* 3:161.

12. Ibid., 3:158.

13. Ibid., 3:176.

14. Dooyeweerd, *Roots,* 207; Eric Voegelin, *The New Science of Politics* (Chicago: University of Chicago Press, 1952), offers a parallel critique.

15. Dooyeweerd, *Roots,* 61.

16. Ibid., 65. The historicist attitude toward the state was clearly articulated by Herman Heller, who explicitly denied the possibility of discovering a transhistorical structure of the state. Heller's fear was of taking "the momentary state" to be the absolute standard for all states. In his view political categories are inevitably historically changeable, even when those categories are definitions of the functions and structure of the state. A political structure valid for one historical society will be impossible to apply in another (Dooyeweerd, *NC,* 3:390). There is an affinity between Heller's view and that of Wolterstorff, discussed in chapter 6.

17. Ibid., 3:157.

18. Ibid., 3:158, 171.

19. See James H. Olthuis, *Facts, Values and Ethics,* 2nd ed. (Assen: Van Gorcum, 1968), for a development of Dooyeweerd's view of the fact-value relationship.

20. Dooyeweerd, *NC,* 3:175. Dooyeweerd's point, of course, is that these companies were not genuine states. He misses an opportunity to record that

this is a case of an "unnatural" enkaptic interlacement, which produces in-justice.

21. H. G. Geertsema, "Which Causality? Whose Explanation?" *Philosophia Reformata* 62 (2002): 173–185.

22. Dooyeweerd, *NC*, 3:159–160.

23. See Herman Dooyeweerd, "De sociologishe verhouding tussen recht en economie in het probleem van het zgn: 'economische recht,'" in *Opstellen op het gebied van recht, staat en maatschappij aangeboden aan Prof. Dr. A. Anema en Prof. Dr. P. A. Diepenhorst bij hun afscheid van de Vrije Universiteit door oud-leerlingen* (Amsterdam: Bakker, 1949): 221–265; 256–257.

24. Dooyeweerd, *NC*, 3:453.

25. Dooyeweerd, *Roots*, 198.

26. Ibid.

27. See Leo Strauss, "What is Political Philosophy?" in *What Is Political Philosophy? and Other Studies* (Westport, CT: Greenwood Press, 1973), 9–55.

28. Dooyeweerd, *Roots*, 207–208. For a more technical critique drawing on Dooyeweerd, see Paul Marshall, "Mathematics and Politics," *Philosophia Reformata* 45 (1979): 113–136. Similar concerns are expressed in M. Sartori, "Concept Misinformation in Comparative Politics," *American Political Science Review* 64 (1970): 1033–1053.

29. Dooyeweerd, *NC*, 3:175–176.

30. Ibid., 3:386–387. In the same vein Ludwig Waldecker denied any qualitative difference between the state and businesses or municipalities; Harold Laski regarded the state as comparable to a miners' federation; Hans Kelsen viewed it merely as a "logical system of legal norms" (ibid.).

31. Ibid., 3:384.

32. Ibid., 3:401.

33. The relationship between political science and political philosophy (or theory) parallels that between the "totality science" of "positive sociology" and "social philosophy" (outlined in Appendix 1). The parallel is not complete because political science studies only one specific societal individuality-structure, the state, whereas positive sociology studies the totality of such structures. Political science is not a modal science; there is no "political aspect." The state is qualified by its juridical or legal aspect, and this makes for a very close relationship between the modal science of law (and legal philosophy) and political science. But political science cannot be reduced to a mere branch of legal science because the state is a structure of individuality that functions in all the modal aspects. Dooyeweerd's account of the state does have a decidedly legal orientation, but this can be explained as a consequence of his professional specialization rather than as a necessary feature of his general theory. For a proposal to

distinguish the legal aspect from a putative "political aspect," see M. D. Stafleu, "On the Character of Social Communities, the State and the Public Domain," *Philosophia Reformata* 69 (2004): 125–139.

34. Skillen has outlined some implications of Dooyeweerd's political theory for the contemporary discipline of political science as a whole. The fact that the state functions in all modal aspects is one possible basis for understanding at least some of the diversity of the discipline. See James W. Skillen, "Towards a Comprehensive Science of Politics," *Philosophia Reformata* 53 (1988): 33–58. An abridged version of Skillen's essay is reprinted in Jonathan P. Chaplin and Paul Marshall, eds., *Political Theory and Christian Vision: Essays in Memory of Bernard Zylstra* (Lanham, MD: University Press of America, 1994), 57–80. The notion of the modal aspects of the state provides a theoretical basis for an "encyclopaedia of political science" by which the proliferating subdisciplines in contemporary political science can be placed in a coherent framework. We can identify the various subdisciplines within political science—political geography, biopolitics, political culture, political discourse, political sociology, political economy, political ideology, and so on—as investigations into the modal functions of the state. Conceived thus these increasingly fragmented subdisciplines could be enabled to move toward a recognized division of labor and equipped with the capacity to communicate with each other by employing a coherent set of categories.

35. Dooyeweerd, *NC*, 3:467–508; see also Dooyeweerd, *De crisis*, 142–147.

36. Dooyeweerd, *NC*, 3:499.

37. Ibid., 3:500. These are two examples of prenormative functions, but they should not be conceived naturalistically, as if the state were subject, for example, to physical or climatological causation; see Dooyeweerd, *De crisis*, 143–144.

38. Dooyeweerd, *NC*, 3:485.

39. Ibid., 3:486.

40. Ibid., 3:479–480.

41. J. Zwart, "De staatsleer van Herman Dooyeweerd," *Philosophia Reformata* 45 (1980): 109–139; 137.

42. Dooyeweerd, *NC*, 3:397.

43. Ibid., 3:397–398.

44. See A. P. D'Entrèves, *The Notion of the State: An Introduction to Political Theory* (Oxford: Clarendon, 1967), for a parallel argument that the state cannot be based purely on force or power.

45. Dooyeweerd, *NC*, 3:381.

46. Ibid., 3:398.

47. Ibid., 3:411; cf. Dooyeweerd, *De crisis,* 80–81.

48. Griffioen questions my interpretation in Sander Griffioen, "Dooye-weerds programma voor de sociale wetenschap," in *Herman Dooyeweerd 1894–1977. Breedte en actualiteit van zijn filosofie,* ed. H. G. Geertsema et al. (Kampen: J. H. Kok, 1994), 146, 163.

49. Sheldon Wolin, *Politics and Vision* (Boston: Little, Brown, 1960), 3.

50. In his usage "organization" seems virtually synonymous with "forma-tion." But there are surely more ways to form something than to organize it.

51. Dooyeweerd, *NC,* 2:275.

52. Ibid., 3:423.

53. "The word 'organization' must derive all its structural meaning from the individuality structure of an organized community" (Dooyeweerd, *NC,* 3:410).

54. Ibid., 3:411.

55. Ibid., 3:413.

56. Ibid., 3:414. Apparently *two* forms of power seem to be involved here: "organization," which is historical, and "the sword," which is physical. I clarify this point presently.

57. H. H. Gerth and C. Wright Mills, eds. and trans., *From Max Weber: Es-says in Sociology* (New York: Oxford University Press, 1946), 78.

58. Ibid., 77.

59. The particular structure of government is, he holds, not determined by the structural principle but is only one factual implementation of it, a point to which I return later; see Dooyeweerd, *NC,* 3:412.

60. Quentin Skinner, *The Foundations of Modern Political Thought,* 2 vols. (Cambridge: Cambridge University Press, 1978), 2:351–353.

61. Herman Dooyeweerd, *De strijd om het souvereiniteitsbegrip in de mo-derne rechts- en staatsleer* (Amsterdam: H. J. Paris, 1950), 6.

62. Dooyeweerd, *NC,* 3:412.

63. Ibid., 2:252.

64. By contrast, neither the medieval feudal kingdoms nor the ancient Asiatic empires nor the Merovingian Empire can be described as states. The latter, for example, was no more than a *"res regia."* "The historicistic view, which levels out these radical differences and speaks of gentilitial, tribal and feudal 'states,' may not be called 'empirical' since it ignores undeniable empirical states of affairs" (Dooyeweerd, *NC,* 3:412).

65. Partial confirmation is found in Gerhard Ritter, "The Origins of the Modern State," in *The Development of the Modern State,* ed. Heinz Lubasz (New York: Macmillan, 1964), 13–25; Martin van Creveld, *The Rise and Decline of the*

State (Cambridge: Cambridge University Press, 1999), chapter 2. Like Weber, however, both accentuate the quest for a monopoly of *power* on the part of emerging early modern states. Dooyeweerd's analysis is closer to that of D'Entrèves, who by contrast emphasizes the emergence of the state as a unified system of *law;* see D'Entrèves, *The Notion of the State,* chapter 5.

66. Herman Dooyeweerd, *Publiek- en privaatrecht* (Amsterdam: Uitgave Studentenraad, Vrije Universiteit, 1963), 49.

67. Here again we see an example of a fundamentally negative judgment on undifferentiated communities, confirming my view that it is inconsistent of Dooyeweerd also to hold that it was somehow normative for societies to pass through such a stage. On the other hand, this negative verdict on the extent to which these undifferentiated communities were able to promote "public justice" may well need revising. As on several occasions his systematic point is clear and plausible, but his historical analyses are found wanting.

68. This point, incidentally, still stands if we redescribe the historical aspect as the "formative" or "techno-formative."

69. Herman Dooyeweerd, *A Christian Theory of Social Institutions,* ed. John Witte, Jr. and trans. Magnus Verbrugge (La Jolla, CA: Herman Dooyeweerd Foundation, 1986), 90.

70. Dooyeweerd, *NC,* 3:416.

71. Ibid., 3:416–417.

72. Ibid., 3:417.

73. Ibid., 3:536–539.

74. Ibid., 3:538.

75. Ibid., 3:609–610.

76. Ibid., 3:544 ff.

77. Ibid., 3:435.

78. Ibid., 3:436.

79. Ibid., 2:70–271.

80. Ibid., 3:414.

81. James W. Skillen, "The Development of Calvinistic Political Theory in the Netherlands, with Special Reference to the Thought of Herman Dooyeweerd" (Ph.D. dissertation, Duke University, 1974), 405.

82. Dooyeweerd, *NC,* 3:420.

83. Ibid., 3:421.

84. Dooyeweerd, *Roots,* 88.

85. Ibid., 89.

86. Dooyeweerd, *NC,* 3:419.

87. Ibid., 3:422.

88. Yet this subservience of political power to law does not make power into anything other than power. A function does not compromise its irreducible character when it "anticipates" or is "opened up" by another

89. Dooyeweerd, *NC,* 3:434. The allusion is to Augustine's well-known phrase from Book IV, chapter 4, of *City of God,* ed. David Knowles (Markham, ON: Penguin, 1972), 139, hardly a complete statement of Augustine's view of the state.

90. Romans 13:1–5; 1 Peter 2:13; Revelation 13:10; see Dooyeweerd, *NC,* 3:423.

91. Dooyeweerd, *NC,* 3:506.

92. Ibid., 3:423–424.

93. Herman Dooyeweerd, "Arbeidsrecht, intern bedrijfsrecht en de juridische grenzen der souvereiniteit in eigen kring," *Antirevolutionaire Staatkunde* 24 (1954): 177–191; 185.

94. Dooyeweerd, *Roots,* 59–60; and "Arbeidsrecht, intern bedrifsrecht," 184.

95. Thus it turns out that although humans cannot introduce "new" structural principles in history new ones can be introduced by divine providence.

96. Indeed one might surmise that if God himself had the right to threaten death to Adam and Eve on pain of disobedience, he could surely build such a right into the original structural principle of the state.

97. This, it will be observed, brings me very close to a Thomist, rather than an Augustinian, account of the "natural" origin of the state.

98. Van Creveld identifies some early historical variations in *The Rise and the Decline of the State,* chapter 1. Note that in my formulation I implicitly accept that the state will "necessarily" emerge. This indicates my acceptance of Dooyeweerd's claim that the state is indeed an institutional community rather than a mere voluntary association.

99. This was also the proposal of Dooyeweerd's colleague K. J. Popma. However, in *Venster op de wereld* (Kampen: J. H. Kok, 1968), 132–136, Popma makes the further claim that as a post-fall necessity coercion is "alien" to the nature of the state. In contrast, I would say that in a post-fall situation coercion is a normative necessity for the state to realize its creational purpose.

100. Dooyeweerd, *NC,* 3:600–601.

101. Ibid.

102. See Jacques Maritain, *Man and the State,* trans. Doris C. Anson (Chicago: University of Chicago Press, 1951), 188 ff. Dooyeweerd does not explore this possibility, though others influenced by him have. See, e.g., James W.

Skillen, *With or Against the World? America's Role among the Nations* (Lanham, MD: Rowman and Littlefield, 2005); Justin Cooper, "David Mitrany's Functionalist World Order," in Chaplin and Marshall, eds., *Political Theory and Christian Vision*, 121–141; Justin Cooper, "The State, Transnational Relations, and Justice: A Critical Assessment of Competing Paradigms of World Order," in *Sovereignty at the Crossroads*, ed. Luis Lugo (Lanham, MD: Rowman and Littlefield, 1996), 3–27; Bob Goudzwaard, *Globalization and the Kingdom of God* (Grand Rapids: Baker, 2001). It is interesting to note Kuyper's speculative view that in an unfallen creation, while "mechanical" states would not be needed, something resembling a world political authority would have emerged "naturally" on the basis of patriarchal structures (Abraham Kuyper, *Lectures on Calvinism* [Grand Rapids: Eerdmans, 1961], chapter 3; see Skillen, "The Development of Calvinistic Political Theory," 240–247).

103. Events since the early 1990s seem to confirm the urgent need for an international political authority both with binding public-legal competence (UN Security Council resolutions are already supposed to be legally binding on member-states) and sufficient coercive power to enforce them (UN authorization of military intervention in Iraq in 1990 and in Haiti suggests that this may be slowly evolving). Even the NATO authorization of intervention in Kosovo seemed consistent with this internationalizing trend. But the unauthorized U.S.-led invasion of Iraq in 2003 represented a setback in this development.

104. Emil Brunner, *Justice and the Social Order*, trans. M. Hottinger (London: Lutterworth, 1945), 188.

105. This criticism has been suggested by A. M. Donner, in "Bijdrage tot de discussie over de staatstaak," in *Rechtsgeleerde opstellen door zijn leeringen aangeboden aan Prof. Dr. H. Dooyeweerd t.g.v. zijn 25-jarig hoogleraarschap* (Kampen, J. H. Kok, 1951), 180, with respect to Dooyeweerd's account of the state's leading function, but this is to hit the wrong target; the point seems better directed against his account of its founding function.

106. Thus in Dooyeweerd's technical terminology its leading function displays an "original" and not a "retrocipatory" type of individuality.

Nine.   The Just State

1. Dooyeweerd, *NC*, 3:435.

2. See above chapter 2 n. 18 for the full citation. See also Alan Cameron's valuable "Editor's Introduction" to the English translation.

3. This forms the basis for a history of legal thought by his successor at the Free University of Amsterdam. See H. J. van Eikema Hommes, *Major Trends*

in the History of Legal Philosophy, trans. P. Brouwer and J. Kraay (Amsterdam: North Holland, 1979). For commentary on Dooyeweerd's use of legal history, see S. Faber, "Dooyeweerd en de rechtsgeschiedenis," in *Herman Dooyeweerd 1894–1977. Breedte en actualiteit van zijn filosofie,* ed. H. G. Geertsema et al. (Kampen: J.H. Kok, 1994), 77–87.

4. See, e.g., Herman Dooyeweerd, "Calvinism and Natural Law," in Herman Dooyeweerd, *Essays in Legal, Social and Political Philosophy,* ed. Alan Cameron and trans. Albert Wolters (Lewiston, NY: Edwin Mellen Press, 1997): 3–38; "De universaliteit der rechtsgedachte en de idee van den kultuurstaat," *Almanak van het Studentencorps aan de Vrije Universiteit* (1928): 103–121; "De structuur der rechtsbeginselen en de methode der rechtswetenschap in het licht der wetsidee," in *Wetenschappelijke bijdragen, aangeboden door hoogleeraren der Vrije Universiteit ter gelegenheid van haar 50-jarig bestaan 20 October, 1930* (Amsterdam: De Standaard, 1930), 223–266; "De bronnen van het stellig recht in het licht der wetsidee: een bijdrage tot opklaring van het probleem inzake de verhouding van rechtsbeginsel en positief recht," *Antirevolutionaire Staatkunde* 4 (1930): 1–59, 224–263, 325–362; 8 (1934): 57–94; "De theorie van de bronnen van het stellig recht in het licht der wetsidee," *Handelingen van de Vereeniging voor Wijsbegeerte des Rechts* 19 (1932) 1:1–28; 2:1–10, 24–31; *Recht en historie* (Assen: Hummelen, 1938); *Publiek- en privaatrecht* (Amsterdam: Uitgave Studentenraad, Vrije Universiteit, 1963).

5. Two useful overviews and contextualizations are J. Zwaart, "Rechts- en staatsfilosofie," in *Kennis en werkelijkheid. Tweede inleiding tot een christelijke filosofi,* ed. René van Woudenberg (Amsterdam: Buijten and Schipperheijn, 1996), 293–309; and A. Soeterman, "Dooyeweerd als rechtsfilosoof," in Geertsema et al., eds., *Herman Dooyeweerd,* 28–49.

6. These fundamental concepts are either "elementary" or "complex," a distinction Dooyeweerd adopts from Stammler (Dooyeweerd, *EN,* 3:10). The elementary concepts refer to the analogical (retrocipatory and anticipatory) moments of the juridical aspect. The retrocipatory moments yield concepts that refer to elements necessarily present in every existing legal system (3:11–93). They include, for example, the concepts of area of validity (spatial analogy), legal causality (physical), legal will (psychic), legal power (historical), legal intercourse (social), and legal interest (economic). The anticipatory moments, by contrast, appear only in legal systems that have undergone a process of cultural disclosure, in which the meaning of the juridical aspect is "deepened" by the opening up of its ethical and faith anticipations. In such systems the additional concepts of good faith, equity (ethical), and guilt (faith), for example, come to be recognized in practical jurisprudence. This process of disclosure occurs only in the transition from primitive legal orders to differentiated

orders. They testify to the dynamic nature of the juridical aspect. The modern concept of legal guilt, for instance, is a normative advance on primitive notions of illegality. In primitive legal orders the individual is seen as a dependent part of the community, whereas under modern civil law—emerging coterminously with societal differentiation—the individual is liberated from such communities and held personally responsible for his actions (Dooyeweerd, *Recht en historie*, 50–51). The anticipatory moments are thus not transhistorical, abstract rational ideas applicable within every positive legal order (Dooyeweerd, *EN*, 3:51). Dooyeweerd adds that the concepts they generate are embraced within the theoretical Idea of law, but this notion seems to play no significant role in those aspects of his legal theory pertaining to his political theory. In addition to "elementary" concepts of law, there is also a series of "complex" concepts, which are "categorial relations" uniting all the elementary concepts (*EN*, 3:98 ff.). The principal examples are the relations of legal norm to legal fact, legal subject to legal object, and subjective right, which receive extensive treatment. The major systematic works of Hommes, Dooyeweerd's successor at the Free University, follow his thought very closely. See H. J. van Eikema Hommes, *De elementaire grondbegrippen der rechtswetenschap* (Deventer: Kluwer, 1971); and *De samengestelde grondbegrippen der rechtswetenschap* (Zwolle: Tjeenk Willink, 1976). See also J. D. Dengerink, "Enkele beschouwingen over het proces van het rechtsvorming," *Rechtsgeleerd Magazijn Themis* 5 (1959): 429–460.

7. One of the most significant turns out to be "legal power," or "competence." It attracts an extensive discussion in the *Encyclopaedia* (in a section developing an extensive earlier study from 1930–1934). Its focus, the problem of the sources of positive law, is identified by Dooyeweerd as the central problem in legal theory, and I treat it further shortly.

8. Positivization, it will be recalled, occurs in every normative aspect, not just the juridical.

9. Dooyeweerd, *EN*, 3:111–114.

10. Dooyeweerd, *NC*, 2:151 ff. For a critique of Dooyeweerd's idea that there is a moral "aspect," see M. D. Stafleu, "Philosophical Ethics and the So-Called 'Ethical Aspect,'" *Philosophia Reformata* 72 (2008): 151–164.

11. Dooyeweerd, *NC*, 2:140–163.

12. Dooyeweerd, *EN*, 3:128; see also O. J. L. Albers, *Het natuurrecht volgens de Wijsbegeerte der Wetsidee. Een kritische beschouwing* (Nijmegen: Janssen, 1955), 13–16.

13. Dooyeweerd, *NC*, 2:130.

14. Ibid., 2:134.

15. Ibid., 2:131.

16. Ibid., 2:132; see also Dooyeweerd, *EN*, 3:4.

17. Dooyeweerd, *NC,* 2:129.

18. Ibid., 2:134.

19. Dooyeweerd, *EN,* 3:28.

20. Ibid.

21. Dooyeweerd, *NC,* 2:135.

22. Ibid., 2:128.

23. Ibid., 2:66, 128.

24. Dooyeweerd, *EN,* 3:27.

25. Dooyeweerd, *NC,* 2:135.

26. Ibid. 2:131.

27. Dooyeweerd, *De crisis,* 188.

28. Calvin G. Seerveld, "Modal Aesthetics: Preliminary Questions with an Opening Hypothesis," in *Hearing and Doing: Philosophical Essays Dedicated to H. Evan Runner,* ed. J. Kraay and A. Tol (Toronto: Wedge, 1979), 290.

29. Dooyeweerd, *NC,* 2:135.

30. Ibid., 2:135–136.

31. Dooyeweerd, however, is critical of the way Aristotle related them to society; see Dooyeweerd, *NC,* 3:212–214; 2:135; *Publiek- en privaatrecht,* 52.

32. Dooyeweerd, *NC,* 2:212.

33. Ibid., 3:445.

34. Herman Dooyeweerd, "Die Philosophie der Gesetzidee und ihre Bedeutung für die Rechts- und Sozialphilosophie," *Archiv für Rechts- und Sozialphilosophie* 53 (1967): 1–30, 465–513; 474.

35. Dooyeweerd, *NC,* 2:130.

36. Ibid., 3:129; my emphasis.

37. J. D. Dengerink makes a similar move in *De zin van de werkelijkeid. Een wijsgerige benadering* (Amsterdam: Vrije Universiteit Uitgeverij, 1986), 227–230.

38. Paul Tillich, *Love, Power, and Justice: Ontological Analyses and Ethical Applications* (New York: Oxford University Press, 1954), 63–64. This passage was brought to my attention by Bernard Zylstra.

39. Dooyeweerd, *NC,* 3:283; see also *De Crisis,* 148 ff.

40. Herman Dooyeweerd, "Sociology of Law and Its Philosophical Foundations," in *Truth and Reality: Philosophical Perspectives on Reality Dedicated to Professor H. G. Stoker,* ed. H. J. J. Bingle et al. (Braamfontein: De Jong's Bookshop, 1971), 60–61.

41. Ibid., 3.

42. A. M. Honóre's notion of the justice of special relations approximates Dooyeweerd's idea of juridical sphere sovereignty. Honóre notes the existence of particular claims, which members of a family have upon each other on

382   Notes to Pages 195–196

account of the "special relations" obtaining between them. It would be unfair, for instance, for a father to disinherit his child even if the child was not in need, because this would violate their special relation. This example of justice cannot be embraced in the wider general concept of social justice because it "upholds not the claims of man as man but only of man standing in a special relation to some particular fellow-man." A. M. Honóre, "Social Justice," in *Essays in Legal Philosophy*, ed. R. S. Summers (Oxford: Blackwell, 1970), 61–94.

43. For Dooyeweerd's discussion of the narrower concept of legal personality, see also *EN*, 3:111–113, 155–165.

44. Dooyeweerd, *NC*, 3:282. In Dooyeweerd's more technical terms, legal competence is the "legal power of an organ to give form to the supra-arbitrary legal principles in juridical declarations of will," that is, the power to positivize legal principles; see also Dooyeweerd, *EN*, 3:21.

45. Dooyeweerd, "Sociology of Law and Its Philosophical Foundations," 67.

46. Dooyeweerd, *EN*, 3:102 ff. For analyses of Dooyeweerd's theory of rights, see Paul Marshall, "Dooyeweerd's Empirical Theory of Rights," in *The Legacy of Herman Dooyeweerd: Reflections on Critical Philosophy in the Christian Tradition*, ed. C. T. McIntire (Lanham, MD: University Press of America, 1985), 119–142; John Witte, Jr., "The Development of Dooyeweerd's Concept of Rights," in *Political Theory and Christian Vision: Essays in Memory of Bernard Zylstra*, ed. Jonathan P. Chaplin and Paul Marshall (Lanham, MD: University Press of America, 1994), 27–55. For elaborations and applications of the theory, see the following by Paul Marshall: *Human Rights Theories in Christian Perspective* (Toronto: Institute for Christian Studies, 1983); "Justice and Rights: Ideology and Human Rights Theories," in *Norm and Context in the Social Sciences*, ed. Sander Griffioen and Jan Verhoogt (Lanham, MD: University Press of America, 1990), 129–158; "Universal Human Rights and the Role of the State," in *Sovereignty at the Crossroads*, ed. Luis E. Logo (Lanham, MD: Rowman and Littlefield, 1966), 153–175. See also the Catholic response to Marshall in the latter volume by Joseph Boyle.

47. Dooyeweerd, *EN*, 3:106.

48. Dooyeweerd, *NC*, 3:283. Dooyeweerd accounts for this ontologically in terms of the fundamental coherence between the modal and typical structures of cosmic time. A neglect of the typical structures of individual entities amounts to a violation of the specific character of the modal aspects as well. It is not possible to respond adequately to the modal norms rooted in the juridical aspect while ignoring the individualized norms for the plurality of typical ways in which the juridical aspect expresses itself in various societal structures.

49. Ibid., 3:664–693.

50. Dooyeweerd, "De bronnen van het stellig recht in het licht der wetsidee"; see also the third and fourth volumes of *EN*.

51. Dooyeweerd, *NC*, 1:553.

52. Ibid., 3:668.

53. See Dooyeweerd, *EN*, 5:62 ff.

54. Dooyeweerd, *NC*, 3:665.

55. Ibid., 667–668.

56. Ibid., 3:669.

57. Ibid.

58. Ibid., 3:670.

59. See note 71 below.

60. Michael Walzer, *Spheres of Justice* (New York: Basic Books, 1984), 19.

61. Ibid., 127.

62. Ibid., 119.

63. See above, chapter 5.

64. Walzer, *Spheres of Justice*, 319.

65. Ibid., 9, 318–319.

66. Ibid., 28.

67. Ibid., 31, 39, 61–62, 281–282.

68. Dooyeweerd, *NC*, 3:435.

69. Ibid., 3:536.

70. Ibid., 3:435. See also Herman Dooyeweerd, "The Christian Idea of the State," in Herman Dooyeweerd, *Essays in Legal, Social, and Political Philosophy* (Lewiston, NY: Edwin Mellen Press, 1997), 149–150. (English translation first published by Craig Press, Nutley, NJ, 1975.)

71. This position seems to exclude what has sometimes been termed "legal pluralism," which, as noted in chapter 2, refers to a devolution of public-legal authority within selected areas (notably family law) to relatively autonomous courts governing diverse religious or ethnic communities, as applies in India, for example. I think Dooyeweerd would have principled objections to such a system, although he would be aware of the need for sensitivity in changing a culturally and historically rooted system like this. "Legal pluralism" in this sense is not an instance of "legal sphere sovereignty," since the latter protects the legal autonomy of distinct institutions (including churches, mosques, etc.) but not that of wider communities defined religiously or ethnically. See Jonathan P. Chaplin, "Legal Monism and Religious Pluralism: Rowan Williams on Religion, Loyalty and Law," *International Journal of Public Theology* 2 (2008): 418–442.

72. This concept seems to have been suggested to him by his critical study of Smend's theory of integration; see Dooyeweerd, *De crisis,* 64 ff.

73. Dooyeweerd, *NC,* 3:437.

74. Ibid.; emphasis added.

75. Ibid.

76. My use of the term *subject* is in keeping with Dooyeweerd's usage of the term. When drawing attention to people's political and civil rights and duties he uses the term *citizen (burger).*

77. Or "nation"; the terms are used synonymously. I explore his view of "people" and "nation" further in chapter 10.

78. Dooyeweerd, *NC,* 3:438.

79. Ibid., 3:436.

80. Ibid.

81. Ibid., 3:438; emphasis added.

82. Dooyeweerd, *Publiek- en privaatrecht,* 50.

83. Ibid., 50.

84. James W. Skillen, "The Development of Calvinistic Political Theory in the Netherlands, with Special Reference to the Thought of Herman Dooye-weerd" (Ph.D. dissertation, Duke University, 1974), 422.

85. Dooyeweerd, *EN,* 5:54.

86. Dooyeweerd, *Publiek- en privaatrecht,* 51; *Verkenningen in de wijsbe-geerte, de sociologie en de rechtsgeschiedenis,* 2nd ed., ed. J. Stellingwerff (Amsterdam: Buijten and Schipperheijn, 1967), 160 ff.; see Otto von Gierke, *Community in Historical Perspective,* ed. Anthony Black and trans. Mary Fischer (Cambridge: Cambridge University Press, 1990), 11.

87. Dooyeweerd, *Roots,* 186.

88. Ibid., 52.

89. Ibid., 54.

90. Herman Dooyeweerd, "De Sociologische verhouding tussen recht en economie in het probleem van het zgn. 'economisch recht,'" in *Opstellen op het gebied van recht, staat en maatschappij aangeboden aan Prof. Dr. A. Anema en Prof. Dr. P. A. Diepenhorst bij hun afscheid van de Vrije Universiteit door oud-leerlingen* (Amsterdam: Bakker, 1949), 236–237.

91. It is worth adding here that, analagously, *jus specificum,* which is private communal law, finds its transcendental correlate in that "specific" law created by interlinkages but falls outside the scope of civil law, such as a private agreement between two persons to engage in a joint task. These are not usually considered examples of "law" at all, but, as we have seen, Dooyeweerd holds that all social relationships, even those as seemingly ephemeral as such private agreements, have their own juridical dimension.

92. Dooyeweerd's concern about ethnically or religiously based "legal pluralism" would be the risk of subverting these foundational legal principles.

93. Dooyeweerd, *NC*, 3:451.

94. Dooyeweerd, *EN*, 5:55. Dooyeweerd cites an example of an appeal lodged against expulsion from a particular association before a Dutch civil court (Dooyeweerd, *NC*, 3:684–685). The claimant, while chairing a public meeting, had permitted an insulting expression to be used against the members of an association and subsequently was expelled on the grounds of one of the society's articles of association prohibiting members from endangering its reputation. The association tried to defend its exclusive competence in the matter of the expulsion and argued that the civil judge lacked competence in the case. However, since the claimant did not request reinstatement of membership but only damages on grounds of alleged unlawfulness of the expulsion, the judge decided to hear the case. He concluded that the expression concerned had indeed endangered the society's reputation on account of its insulting character and so rejected the claim for damages. The basis of the judge's decision in this case was not the formal ground of conformity to internal articles of association but the *material* civil legal ground of the actual insulting character of the expression. The judge held that the latter fell within the court's civil legal competence since the members of the association had the ordinary civil right not to be insulted. This right was not dependent on their membership in the association but rather on their status as independent legal subjects. Consequently the decision of the judge was not made on the basis of the association's typical internal communal law. If it had been, the judge would have acted *ultra vires*. Had the judge come to the material conclusion that in fact the expression was not insulting, he could still only have ruled in the plaintiff's favor on the basis of the criterion of unfair dismissal, which as a material criterion of civil law falls within the judge's sphere of competence.

95. *NC*, 3:441.

96. Herman Dooyeweerd, *De strijd om het souvereiniteitsbegrip in de moderne rechts- en staatsleer* (Amsterdam: H. J. Paris, 1950), 7.

97. Ibid., 5.

98. Dooyeweerd, "De bronnen van het stellig recht in het licht der wetsidee," 28.

99. Dooyeweerd, *De strijd*, 50.

100. Dooyeweerd, *NC*, 3:394 n. 3.

101. Dooyeweerd, *Roots*, 132.

102. Dooyeweerd, *NC*, 3:442.

103. H. J. van Eikema Hommes, "The Material Idea of the Law-State," *Philosophia Reformata* 43 (1978): 49–60; and David S. Caudill, "The Rechtsstaat:

Magic Wall or Material Necessity?" *Houston Journal of International Law* 4 (1982): 169–188.

104. Dooyeweerd, *Publiek- en privaatrecht*, 55.

105. Ibid.

106. Dooyeweerd, *De strijd*, 50; emphasis added.

107. Ibid., 52.

108. Dooyeweerd, *EN*, 3:115–117.

109. Dooyeweerd, *De crisis*, 180, 195.

110. Dooyeweerd, *NC*, 3:439; and *Publiek- en privaatrecht*, 50.

111. Dooyeweerd, *De crisis*, 153–154.

112. Dooyeweerd, *NC*, 3:477.

113. Ibid., 3:477.

114. Ibid., 3:477, 598–589.

115. Ibid., 155–160.

116. Dooyeweerd, *De crisis*, 152–153. Dooyeweerd would probably venture that since the principle of making governments accountable to popularly elected representative bodies is now firmly established in modern constitutions it would be "reactionary" to seek to restore some form of monarchical or aristocratic government. Robert Kraynak alludes to this possibility in *Christian Faith and Modern Democracy* (Notre Dame: University of Notre Dame Press, 2001).

117. Dooyeweerd, *NC*, 3:605–624.

118. Dooyeweerd rejects the implication, however, that a pluralism of party viewpoints in any way implies "relativism" as regards political truth (*NC*, 3:607–609).

119. Dooyeweerd, *NC*, 3:609. Thus what unifies a party is not a church confession but shared "political" conviction. Dooyeweerd defended the possibility—and in certain circumstances, the necessity—of Christian political parties (3:620–624) and was a lifelong member of one, but he denied that parties should be defined as essentially religious organizations or parts of or subject to a church. Strictly, parties are qualified by their moral aspect—"the moral bond of political conviction"—not by their faith aspect, though their political principles might quite legitimately be grounded in a statement of religious faith (3:613–615). I return to this point when discussing the relation between church and state in chapter 10.

120. Ibid., 3:611–613, 618.

121. Ibid., 3:616–617.

122. Ibid., 3:623.

123. This is the primary manifestation of the "logical function of the state" (*NC*, 3:489–492).

124. Dooyeweerd, *NC*, 3:492.

125. Dooyeweerd, *NC*, 3:491.

126. Dooyeweerd elsewhere mentions, in passing, the influential role of pressure groups like the nineteenth-century English Anti-Corn Law League. But this hardly qualifies as a "popular" movement.

127. In *Man and the State* (Chicago: University of Chicago Press, 1951), 139–146, Jacques Maritain styles these "prophetic shock minorities" and notes their importance in a political community.

128. Dooyeweerd, *Publiek- en privaatrecht,* 55.

129. See Dooyeweerd, *Publiek- en privaatrecht,* 152; and *De strijd,* 58.

130. By contrast, the Thomists Maritain and Simon held just such a view. See, e.g., Jacques Maritain, *Christianity and Democracy,* trans. Doris C. Anson (New York: Charles Scribner's Sons: 1944); Yves Simon, *Philosophy of Democratic Government* (Chicago: University of Chicago Press, 1951).

131. A. K. Koekkoek, *Bijdrage tot een christen-democratische staatsleer* (Deventer: Kluwer, 1982), 22–24, 28.

132. Dooyeweerd himself argues that absolutism was influenced by streams of thought within the humanistic ground motive; see "The Contest over the Concept of Sovereignty," in Dooyeweerd, *Essays in Legal, Social and Political Philosophy,* 101–120.

133. See Herman Dooyeweerd, "De wijsgerige achtergrond van de moderne democratische reactie tegen het individualisme," *Mededeelingen van de Vereeniging voor Calvinistische Wijsbegeerte* 4 (1939): 10.

Ten.   An Active, Limited State

1. This chapter draws on material in Jonathan Chaplin, "'Public Justice' as a Critical Political Norm," *Philosophia Reformata* 72 (2007): 130–150.

2. Dooyeweerd, *NC*, 3:467–508.

3. Ibid., 3:483.

4. Ibid., 3:481.

5. Ibid., 3:205. I will not assess the accuracy of Dooyeweerd's reading of Aristotle on the point.

6. Ibid., 3:452.

7. Ibid., 3:416.

8. Ibid., 3:661–662. This is an additional feature of enkaptic relationships between state and other structures, which may be either of the "correlative" type (Dooyeweerd gives no example of this) or the "irreversible foundational" type (as in the case of differentiated interindividual relationships and voluntary associations).

9. Ibid., 3:662.

10. Ibid., 3:445–446.

11. Dooyeweerd, *WdW*, 3:401, 395.

12. James W. Skillen, "The Development of Calvinistic Political Theory in the Netherlands, with Special Reference to the Thought of Herman Dooyeweerd" (Ph.D. dissertation, Duke University, 1974), 422.

13. J. D. Dengerink, *De zin van de werkelijkheid. Een wijsgerige benadering* (Amsterdam: Vrije Universiteit Uitgeverij, 1986), 350, 361 n.140.

14. Another way to put this is to say that public justice implies an *equitable* treatment of juridical interests. It rules out, however, any leveling or equalizing of such interests, since these differ according to the specific character of the interest-possessing sphere, and, as we have noted, their relative value at any one time will depend on prevailing circumstances. We have already noted that equality is an indispensable concept in the field of civil law and that Dooyeweerd is reluctant to extend its political application any further. Regrettably, his critique of the concept of political equality implied here is undeveloped. An initial attempt to develop it is found in Bernard Zylstra, *From Pluralism to Collectivism: The Development of Harold Laski's Political Thought* (Assen: Van Gorcum, 1968), 191–201. For comparable critiques, see Julius Stone, "Justice not Equality," in *Justice,* ed. Eugene Kamenka and Alice Ehr-Soon Tay (London: Edward Arnold, 1979), 97–115; John Charvet, "The Principle of Equality as a Substantive Principle of Society," *Political Studies* 17 (1969): 1–13.

15. This is an example of the state's recognition of the legal interests of a social institution. Examples of such recognition of the rights of *persons* would be protecting women or children against exploitation in the labor market, or reversing racially discriminatory practices in employment or housing.

16. In his Dutch writings he also employs, interchangeably, the terms *algemeen belang* (general interest) and *algemeen welzijn* (general welfare or common good).

17. Dooyeweerd, *NC,* 3:443; emphasis added. This charge is supported by Gerhard Niemeyer, whose examples are rather more convincing than Dooyeweerd's; see his "Public Interest and Private Utility," in *The Public Interest,* ed. C. J. Friedrich (New York: Atherton, 1966), 1–13.

18. Dooyeweerd, *NC,* 3:444.

19. Ibid., 3:438.

20. Ibid., 3:442; see also Herman Dooyeweerd, *Publiek- en privaatrecht* (Amsterdam: Uitgave Studentenraad, Vrije Universiteit, 1963), 48.

21. Dooyeweerd, *NC,* 3:445.

22. Herman Dooyeweerd, "Omvang en aard van de staatstaak," *Mededeelingen van de Vereeniging voor Calvinistische Wijsbegeerte* (September 1953): 4–6.

23. Dooyeweerd, *NC*, 3:444–445.

24. Herman Dooyeweerd, "De sociologische verhouding tussen recht en economie in het probleem van het zgn. 'economisch recht,'" in *Opstellen op het gebied van recht, staat en maatschappij aangeboden aan Prof. Dr. A. Anema en Prof. Dr. P. A. Diepenhorst bij hun afscheid van de Vrije Universiteit door oud-leerlingen Amsterdam* (Amsterdam: Bakker, 1949), 238.

25. Dooyeweerd, *NC*, 3:446; emphasis added.

26. Dooyeweerd, *EN*, 3:68–71.

27. Dooyeweerd, *Publiek- en privaatrecht*, 46.

28. He might also argue that such a process of maximization would not necessarily guarantee that the distribution of interest satisfactions would be a just one, since, as a familiar argument against utilitarianism claims, increasing the total sum of private interests is compatible with distributing benefits inequitably.

29. See Brian Barry, "The Use and Abuse of 'The Public Interest,'" in Friedrich, ed., *The Public Interest*, 195.

30. On this, see M. D. Stafleu's helpful remarks on the "public intersubjective network of social intercourse" making up the public realm, in "On the Character of Social Communities, the State and the Public Domain," *Philosophia Reformata* 69 (2004): 136–137.

31. And it is, I suggest, at least partly convergent with what Thomist political thought refers to as the "common good." There isn't space for a full comparison of these two terms. The two are not identical in meaning or scope, and the "common good" is often read as embracing state acitivities, which, for Dooyeweerd, clearly go beyond its proper competence.

32. Herman Dooyeweerd, "Het typisch stuctuurprincipe van de staat en de leer der staatsdoeleinden," *Weekblad voor Privaatrecht, Notarisambt en Registratie* 92, no. 4701 (December 1961): 507–515.

33. Dooyeweerd, *NC*, 3:444.

34. See Dooyeweerd, *Publiek- en privaatrecht*, 45.

35. Dooyeweerd, *NC*, 3:445–446. The problem of the internal functions/external relations distinction arises again in this passage. Dooyeweerd suggests that the task of the state cannot be externally delimited because it "functions in all aspects of . . . reality." But this cannot be the reason why the task of the state cannot be delimited externally. The real reason is that the state relates to *other social structures* with leading functions in various modal aspects (e.g., economically qualified enterprises, ethically qualified families). The reason why the state plays a role in education is not because the state *itself* functions in the logical aspect. Its own internal logical functioning is displayed in, for example,

"public opinion," or rational policy making, or in its "political communication," not in its educational policy.

36. Ibid., 3:425–433; cf. Dooyeweerd, "Het typisch structuurprincipe"; and "Omvang en aard der staatstaak."

37. Dooyeweerd, *NC*, 3:426–427.

38. Ibid., 3:60; original emphasis.

39. Ibid., 3:425.

40. Ibid., 3:433; original emphasis.

41. Herman Dooyeweerd, "Een Rooms-Katholiek visie op de Protestants-Christelijke denkbeelden inzake bedrijfsorganisatie en de recente discussie over de grenzen der overheidstaak," *Antirevolutionaire Staatkunde* 22 (1952): 65–79, 97–122. See also "Omvang en aard van de staatstaak." Dooyeweerd first introduced the typical/atypical distinction in an article in 1952 and then again in 1953 in a lecture responding to critics, one of whom held that his view of the state's task was too narrowly juridical. See A. M. Donner, "Bijdrage tot de discussie over de staatstaak," in *Rechtsgeleerde opstellen door zijn leerlingen aangeboden aan Prof. Dr. H. Dooyeweerd t.g.v. zijn 25-jarig hoogleraarschap* (Kampen: J. H. Kok, 1951), 181–182, on this point. The distinction failed to find its way into the third volume of *NC*.

42. Dooyeweerd, "Een Rooms-Katholiek visie," 73; original emphasis.

43. See Dooyeweerd, "Omvang en aard van de staatstaak," 6.

44. Dooyeweerd, "Een Rooms-Katholiek visie," 73.

45. A. C. De Ruiter, *De grenzen van de overheidstaak in de Antirevolutionaire staatsleer* (Kampen: J. H. Kok, 1961), 117.

46. E.g., Dooyeweerd, *NC*, 3:445–446.

47. The same problem has been recognized by H. J. Strauss, whose proposed alternative is rather to conceive of these ("atypical") activities as justified by the state's responsibility for promoting the "emancipation of cultural interests" *(beskawingsbelange)*; call this "cultural emancipation." The state has a duty positively to promote the cultural advancement of its people, by enhancing their ability to "positivize cultural norms," i.e., to assume increasing responsibilities in the various cultural sectors such as education, industry, the arts, or politics. Cultural emancipation must not conflict with public justice or sphere sovereignty but cannot be reduced to them (H. J. Strauss, "Nie-staatlike owerheidstaak in beskawingsamenhang," *Philosophia Reformata* 30 [1965]: 198–204). At times Dooyeweerd seems to come close to this position. The state's task, he suggests, includes measures to "support, renew and stimulate" non-state communities such as families, industries, and so on, "insofar as they are necessary to the health of the nation" *(volkskracht)* (Dooyeweerd, *De crisis*, 182). A similar

suggestion has been made by Woldring, who conceives of the state's sphere sovereignty as embracing this wider task: "The idea of 'sphere sovereignty' . . . does not in the first place concern the *boundaries* of the task of government, but the government's *calling* according to the structural principle of the state. Precisely in recognizing the structural identity of societal relationships, the state is called to do everything to foster the possibilities for disclosure which are possessed by the participants of these structures" (H. E. S. Woldring, "Venster op de samenleving," in *Het leven beschouwd. Facetten van het werk van Prof. Dr. K. J. Popma,* ed. Paul Koning [Kampen: J. H. Kok, 1974], 220–248; 245). Woldring is here taking the further step of regarding the state's duty to *recognize* the sphere sovereignty of other structures as implying a duty to *maximize* the possibilities of their being able to exercise such sphere sovereignty. This invites a question: must the state do "everything" possible to this end? Is not this a recipe for precisely the kind of overweening, collectivist state that Dooyeweerd's theory is designed to curtail? (The same question may be posed against an influential official Catholic definition of "the common good," issued at Vatican II, as embracing "the sum of those conditions of the social life whereby men, families, and associations more adequately and readily may attain their own perfection" [*Gaudium et spes,* paragraph 74]). Dooyeweerd's view suggests a more modest definition of the task of the state. Strauss's idea of cultural emancipation seems closer to Dooyewerd's intentions at this point because it retains a clear distinction between performing this task and honoring sphere sovereignty, with the latter functioning as a brake on the former. Strauss's principle is as follows: cultural emancipation, within the constraints of societal sphere sovereignty. Woldring, however, derives the wider emancipatory task from political sphere sovereignty itself, which suggests that sphere sovereignty cannot function as an independent restraint on state action. His principle is, cultural emancipation, as an outworking of sphere sovereignty. Strauss's proposal is only one way of conceptualizing those aspects of the task of the state that appear not to fall within the scope of juridical integration of the private legal interests of persons and structures. The suggestion proposed by another of his critics, Donner, is that the task of the state should be defined as the establishment of "public order" (see Donner, "Bijdrage tot de discussie over de staatstaak," 183–184). Dooyeweerd would regard this is an unacceptably vague notion. "Public interest" is clearly preferable to "public order" because, as intimated earlier, although its implications for public policy cannot be defined in the abstract, it does have substantive content. It includes a definite area of social life within its scope— the "public realm"—and clearly excludes others—those evidently falling within the internal spheres of particular communities, for example.

48. Dooyeweerd, *Roots*, 82; original emphasis.

49. For a definition of the nation indebted to Dooyeweerd, see David T. Koyzis, *Political Visions and Illusions: A Survey and Christian Critique of Contemporary Ideologies* (Downers Grove, IL: InterVarsity Press, 2003), chapter 4.

50. Dooyeweerd, *Roots*, 82; original emphasis.

51. It is worth observing that, while Dooyeweerd expresses a desire to preserve the "scriptural-Calvinistic formation" of the Dutch nation, he offers generous tribute to the role of Dutch humanism in the formation of the national character, writing, for example, that "from a purely historical point of view [humanism] has done more for the recognition of public freedom for religious convictions than did seventeenth-century Calvinism" (*Roots*, 83).

52. Dooyeweerd, *NC*, 3:472. See my defense, in chapter 5, of the idea that social structures "function subjectively," i.e., as agents.

53. Ibid., 3:436.

54. Ibid., 3:470. He enters this important qualification: "It may be that the latter has not yet attained to the position of an independent state, or that it has lost this position. Every national community has the potency to become a real state. This explains why, at least in a democratic constitution, the so-called *'pouvoir constituant,'* i.e., the original political competence, can only belong to the nation." He quickly adds that this is not an endorsement of the doctrine of "popular sovereignty," which was "nothing but a speculative ideology lacking any contact with political reality" (3:470–471).

55. Ibid., 3:470. This view of the nation places him much closer to the "modernist" school of theories of nationalism, according to which nations are the products of the state-building enterprise of modernity, than to the "primordialist" school, which holds instead that the distinguishing features of a national culture—e.g., language—sometimes antedate the birth of, or even the aspiration toward, a state. It also clearly distances him from the "integralist" (or organicist) notion of national self-determination.

56. Ibid., 3:470.

57. Ibid., 3:469, 470.

58. Ibid., 3:468. Organicist theories seize upon the fact that the state does indeed function in the biotic aspect: it is a "political form of life," a "vital community" (3:494–495). In my view, however, this is not "original" but "retrocipatory" functioning. This is because, as I argued in chapter 6, it is not "subjective" functioning.

59. Ibid., 3:470. Dooyeweerd also adds that an undifferentiated "primitive folk community" cannot be considered a real "nation" (3:468).

60. Ibid., 3:469.

61. Ibid., 3:469.

62. Ibid., 3:467.

63. Ibid., 3:469–470.

64. Ibid., 3:470.

65. Ibid., 3:471.

66. Ibid., 3:488.

67. Ibid., 3:493.

68. Ibid., 3:494. Rather artificially, and controversially, Dooyeweerd further suggests that such feeling will also produce a sense of "national military power" (3:493–494). He balances that, however, with the statement that a "demonic joy in 'the strong state' with its powerful army is entirely in conflict with a Christian love of country" (3:471)—one of many statements evoked by the experience of Nazism.

69. Ibid., 3:471.

70. Dooyeweerd, "De overspanning van het begrip 'natuurlijke gemeenschap' en het sociologisch universalisme," 227–228.

71. Dooyeweerd's position is comparable to that of Jacques Maritain in *Man and the State,* trans. Doris C. Anson (Chicago: University of Chicago Press, 1951), 4–9. Maritain recognizes the existence of pre-political national communities, calling them "ethico-social" communities rooted in birth and lineage, and accords them somewhat greater intrinsic value than does Dooyeweerd. But he also proposes that, once a political society (state) is established, it then tends to create a new, inclusive national community, which transcends, and may perhaps incorporate, preexisting national communities. It is in this sense that "the Nation does not become a State. The State causes the Nation to be" (8).

72. For an approach to multiculturalism informed by public justice, see Jonathan Chaplin, "Beyond Multiculturalism—But to Where? Public Justice and Cultural Diversity," *Philosophia Reformata* 73 (2008): 190–209; and Hans-Martien Ten Napel, "The Concept of a Multicultural Democracy: A Preliminary Christian-Philosophical Appraisal," *Philosophia Reformata* 71 (2006): 145–153.

73. Dooyeweerd, *NC,* 3:488. The term *peace* here probably suggests the idea of harmonization.

74. Ibid., 3:488–489.

75. Ibid., 3:472. This observation occasions a point of wider significance for Dooyeweerd's social theory. The normative duties laid upon us on account of our many institutional affiliations can never *ultimately* be in conflict, even though their conflicting demands may occasion considerable personal pain:

"There can be no question of a real *collisio officiorum* in the normative relations of love. Such a conflict is precluded by the cosmic principle of sphere sovereignty" (3:473). This point would be more plausible if Dooyeweerd had clearly distinguished between contrasts arising from the diverse imperatives arising from *creational normativity* and the real conflicts generated by *antinormative* (fallen) human behavior. Of course, both are intermingled in any concrete situation of moral choice.

76. Ibid., 3:497.

77. Ibid., 3:495.

78. Ibid., 3:497.

79. Ibid., 3:496.

80. "It is undeniable that up till now the cultural and political abilities of the negro have proved to be relatively small in comparison with those of the white and yellow races, though there are remarkable individual exceptions, and though we must not forget that hereditary dispositions are flexible and capable of disclosure by a good education" (*NC*, 3:497). The sources he cites here were already dated when *NC* appeared, for instance, Sorokin, *Contemporary Sociological Theories* (1938), 223 ff.; and R. B. Dixon, *The Racial History of Man* (1923), 518.

81. Dooyeweerd, *NC*, 3:497. This passage could have been written no later than 1958, when the third volume appeared. Yet the odious and oppressive character of the regime was already abundantly clear by then, and even some Calvinist leaders in South Africa who had supported the regime (notably Beyers Naudé) were only shortly after that to embark upon their painful rupture with the regime and the Dutch Reformed Church, which supplied its theological legitimation. What is more, this passage was *added* to *NC* (the English translation) and was not present in the Dutch version (*WdW*) published in 1935.

82. Dooyeweerd, *NC*, 3:265; cf. 3:344.

83. Ibid., 3:269–271.

84. Ibid., 3:292 n. 1.

85. Ibid., 3:292.

86. Ibid., 3:300.

87. Ibid., 3:275–304.

88. Ibid., 3:286–288.

89. Ibid., 3:276.

90. Dooyeweerd, "Arbeidsrecht, intern bedrijfsrecht," 182.

91. Dooyeweerd, *NC*, 3:276, 281.

92. Dooyeweerd, *De crisis*, 182.

93. Dooyeweerd, *NC*, 3:281.
94. Dooyeweerd, "Arbeidsrecht, intern bedrijfsrecht," 186–187.
95. Dooyeweerd, *NC*, 3:281.
96. Ibid., 3:536.
97. Ibid., 3:537–539.
98. Ibid., 3:539.
99. Ibid., 3:545.
100. Ibid., 3:543–544.
101. Ibid., 3:554, 557.
102. Ibid., 3:556.
103. Ibid., 3:544–545.
104. Dooyeweerd, *EN*, 3:51.
105. Dooyeweerd, *De crisis*, 176.
106. Dooyeweerd, *NC*, 3:540.
107. Ibid., 3:541–542.
108. Ibid., 3:559–561.
109. Ibid., 3:689–691. His judgment here is clearly determined by his Protestant view of baptism. In the sacramentalist view, the question of "consent" would be seen as irrelevant to this case.
110. Ibid., 3:555.
111. Ibid., 3:620–624.
112. In the same way, the party sought a situation in which the state itself was to be "bound to divine ordinances [not] through the judgment of any Church but *in the conscience* both of the government and the subject" (Dooyeweerd, *NC*, 3:622; emphasis added). It is worth noting that although in its early years it had in fact benefited from tacit or explicit endorsement from *Gereformeerde* ministers, officially it rejected the idea that churches were entitled to offer such endorsement.
113. Ibid., 3: 622; original emphasis. As noted, Dooyeweerd denies that a party is *qualified* by its faith aspect—it is rather qualified by its moral aspect—but this is compatible with asserting that it also *functions in* the faith aspect (indeed it necessarily does so even if it makes no explicit statement of political faith).
114. Dooyeweerd, *NC*, 3:620–621; original emphasis. The example of the Barmen Declaration made by the German Confessing Church under the Nazi regime might well have been in his mind.
115. Ibid., 3:503.
116. Ibid., 3:503–504.
117. Ibid., 3:505.

118. Ibid., 3:505.

119. The literature on this issue is extensive. Titles influenced more or less by a neo-Calvinist approach include John Witte, Jr., *Religion and the American Constitutional Experiment: Essential Rights and Liberties* (Boulder, CO: Westview Press, 2000); Wolterstorff's contribution to Robert Audi and Nicholas Wolterstorff, *Religion in the Public Square* (Lanham, MD: Rowman and Littlefield, 1997); Stephen V. Monsma and J. Christopher Soper, eds., *Equal Treatment of Religion in a Pluralistic Society* (Grand Rapids: Eerdmans, 1998); James W. Skillen, *Recharging the American Experiment: Principled Pluralism for Genuine Civic Community* (Grand Rapids: Baker, 1994).

120. The more or less consociationalist Dutch and German models are compared with three Anglo-Saxon alternatives in Stephen V. Monsma and J. Christopher Soper, *The Challenge of Pluralism: Church and State in Five Democracies* (Lanham, MD: Rowman and Littlefield, 1997).

121. For an American account of such an approach, see Charles L. Glenn, *The Ambiguous Embrace: Government and Faith-Based Schools and Social Agencies* (Princeton: Princeton University Press, 2000).

122. *Lemon v Kurzman*, 403 U.S. 607 (1971).

123. Thus his position undoubtedly supports the so-called Charitable Choice provisions of the American 1996 Welfare Reform Act, which aim to remove just such discriminatory practices.

124. Some proponents of the consociationalist view argue that *all* social institutions (e.g., even supposedly "neutral" public schools or media outlets) are guided by some kind of implicit religious ethos or ideological tendency. I will not explore that large claim here, but to the extent that it can be made good, the argument for equitable public treatment is rendered that much stronger.

125. A good example of this integrated approach is Skillen, *Recharging the American Experiment,* which draws on a Dooyeweerdian model. He refers to the former as "confessional pluralism" and the latter as "structural pluralism" and shows how the former is a vitally important outworking of the latter. Another work influenced by a neo-Calvinist approach is Mouw and Griffioen, *Pluralisms and Horizons: An Essay in Christian Public Philosophy.*

126. Dooyeweerd, *NC,* 3:534–536.

127. "The sparing or frugal mode of administering scarce goods, implying an alternative choice of their destination with regard to the satisfaction of human needs," and proscribing "an excessive or wasteful satisfaction of a particular need at the expense of other more urgent needs" (*NC,* 2:66, 128). Arguably, the inclusion of the notion of scarcity in this definition concedes too much to modern neo-classical economics. This is why Goudzwaard, an influential

economist working in the neo-Calvinist tradition, defines the core of economic functioning instead as "stewardship" or "fruitfulness" (Bob Goodzwaard, *Capitalism and Progress: A Diagnosis of Western Society,* ed. and trans. Josina Van Nuis Zylstra [Toronto: Wedge; Grand Rapids: Eerdmans, 1979], 212).

128. Dooyeweerd, *Vernieuwing en bezinning,* 201–202. An alternative to this definition has been suggested by Goudzwaard, who defines an enterprise essentially as a "work community," of which the preferred legal structure is a "producer cooperative" (*Capitalism and Progress,* 216–219). Now Dooyeweerd also holds that the enterprise is a "community," and, as I note shortly, draws implications from this that move in the direction advocated by Goudzwaard.

129. Dooyeweerd, *Vernieuwing en bezinning,* 201 ff. Writing in the late 1940s, Dooyeweerd is quite aware of the danger of excessive profits in a free market, as a result of cartels, for example. He seems less aware of the danger of consumerism, however, suggesting that, in a free market system, "the consumer remains fully and personally responsible for the choice of the manner in which he will satisfy his needs. Industrial freedom is inseparably related to spiritual freedom and human responsibility."

130. Dooyeweerd, *NC,* 3:595–596.

131. Dooyeweerd, *Roots,* 196.

132. Dooyeweerd, *NC,* 3:595–596.

133. Dooyeweerd, *Roots,* 197.

134. Dooyeweerd, *NC,* 3:596.

135. Ibid., 3:19; see also 3:458. Dooyeweerd adds: "[Marx's] analysis is still extremely important" (196). He also makes clear that he does not accept that the class concept—with its implication of necessary social conflict—can be an adequate basis for a sociological analysis of society. Classes are real—they are the product of complex economic interlinkages—but the concept cannot be used as the basis for a comprehensive causal explanation of structures of society. See Dooyeweerd, *Roots,* 199–206.

136. Dooyeweerd, *NC,* 3:596.

137. Ibid., 3:588–603. See chapter 7 n. 14 above.

138. Dooyeweerd, *NC,* 3:596.

139. Ibid., 3:588.

140. Ibid., 3:571.

141. Ibid., 3:576, 597.

142. Ibid., 3:592–593, 590

143. For arguments along these lines drawing on some of Dooyeweerd's insights, see Bob Goudzwaard, *Globalization and the Kingdom of God* (Grand Rapids: Baker, 2001); Jonathan Chaplin, "God, Globalization and Grace: An Exercise in Public Theology," in *The Gospel and Globalization: Exploring the*

Religious Roots of a Globalized World, ed. Michael W. Goheen and Erin G. Glanville (Vancouver: Regent College Publishing/Geneva Society, 2009), 49–68.

144. "De actualiteit van de schepping. Gesprek met Prof. Dr. H. Dooyeweerd" (interview held on 9 May 1974), Stichting "Internationaal Christelijk Studiecentrum" (mimeograph), 6.

145. See G. J. Balkenstein, "The Netherlands Industrial Organization Act 1950," *University of Pennsylvania Law Review* 106 (1958): 499–524; B. M. Telderstichting, *De publiekrechtelijke bedrijfsorganisatie in Nederland* (The Hague: Martinus Nijhoff, 1958); J. P. Windmuller, *Labor Relations in the Netherlands* (Ithaca: Cornell University Press, 1969).

146. Here, it might be noted, was an instance of what Dooyeweerd observed to be a general phenomenon of the state necessarily taking an increasingly active civil-legal role in the process of "horizontal integration" of societal relationships; see Dooyeweerd, *De crisis,* 163–165.

147. Dooyeweerd, *De crisis,* 177 n. 1.

148. See Herman Dooyeweerd, "Inzage in de bedrijfsboekhouding door de arbeidersvertegenwoordigers in de particuliere onderneming," *Antirevolutionaire Staatkunde* 1 (1924–1925): 291–306; 298, 305–306.

149. Dooyeweerd, *De crisis,* 178–179.

150. Dooyeweerd, "De sociologische verhouding tussen recht en economie in het probleem van het zgn. 'economisch recht,'" 248.

151. Dooyeweerd, "Een Rooms-Katholiek visie," 99; and Herman Dooyeweerd, *Vernieuwing en bezinning om het reformatische grondmotief,* ed. J. A. Oosterhoff (Zutphen: J. B. van der Brink, 1959), 205–206.

152. See Dooyeweerd, *De crisis,* 152.

153. Herman Dooyeweerd, "Enkele opmerkingen inzake de 'Richtlijnen' betreffende een toekomstige bedrijfsorganisatie" (Mimeograph, 1944), 4.

154. Dooyeweerd, *Vernieuwing en bezinning,* 201.

155. Dooyeweerd, "Arbeidsrecht, intern bedrijfsrecht," 185.

156. Dooyeweerd, *Vernieuwing en bezinning,* 207.

157. Dooyeweerd, *NC,* 3:597.

158. Ibid., 3:596.

159. Dooyeweerd, *Vernieuwing en bezinning,* 207.

160. Dooyeweerd, "Arbeidsrecht, intern bedrijfsrecht," 189.

161. Dooyeweerd, *NC,* 3:599.

162. Ibid.

163. Dooyeweerd, "Arbeidsrecht, intern bedrijfsrecht," 189; *Vernieuwing en bezinning,* 203, 205; *NC,* 3:598.

164. Dooyeweerd, *NC,* 3:598–599.

165. Dooyeweerd, *Vernieuwing en bezinning,* 201.

166. Ibid., 206.

167. Dooyeweerd, "Enkele opmerkingen inzake de 'Richtlijnen' betreffende een toekomstige bedrijfsorganisatie," 2.

168. Dooyeweerd, *Vernieuwing en bezinning,* 205; "Een Rooms-Katholiek visie," 106.

169. Dooyeweerd, *Vernieuwing en bezinning,* 204.

170. Dooyeweerd, "Arbeidsrecht, intern bedrijfsrecht," 180–181; see also Herman Dooyeweerd, "De sociologische verhouding tussen recht en economie in het probleem van het zgn. 'economisch recht,'" 247.

171. Dooyeweerd, *Vernieuwing en bezinning,* 212–213; original emphasis.

172. Dooyeweerd, "Inzage in de bedrijfsboekhouding door de arbeidersvertegenwoordigers in de particuliere onderneming."

173. Dooyeweerd, *Publiek- en privaatrecht,* 57–58. It is not entirely clear why a new term *(social)* is necessary to demarcate this field of public law.

174. Dooyeweerd, "Een Rooms-Katholiek visie," 107.

175. Dooyeweerd, *Vernieuwing en bezinning,* 213.

176. Dooyeweerd, "Een Rooms-Katholiek visie," 117.

177. Dooyeweerd, "Inzage in de bedrijfsboekhouding door de arbeidersvertegenwoordigers in de particuliere onderneming," 296–297.

178. It should be emphasized, however, that this proves not that the distinction between social and economic law is invalid, but only that Dooyeweerd seems in this case to have drawn the boundary incorrectly.

179. See Herman Dooyeweerd, "De band met de beginsel. Inzake het vraagstuk der medezeggenschap," *Nederland en Oranje* 7 (1926): 2–18, 33–40; Herman Dooyeweerd, "Tweeërlei kritiek. Om de principiele zijde van het vraagstuk der medezeggenschap," *Antirevolutionaire Staatkunde* 2 (1926): 1–21; Dooyeweerd, *De crisis,* 177–178; and Herman Dooyeweerd, "Het Amsterdamsche Rapport inzake de medezeggenschap van het personeel in de gemeentebedrijven en -diensten," *Antirevolutionaire Staatkunde* 8 (1932): 71–86, 121–132, 152–168.

180. Dooyeweerd, "De band met de beginsel," 15–16.

181. Dooyeweerd, "Inzage in de bedrijfsboekhouding door de arbeidersvertegenwoordigers in de particuliere onderneming," 294–295; see also "De band met de beginsel," 14–15.

182. See C. T. McIntire, "Dooyeweerd's Philosophy of History," in *The Legacy of Herman Dooyeweerd: Reflections on Critical Philosophy in the Christian Tradition,* edited by C. T. McIntire (Lanham, MD: University Press of America, 1985), 104.

183. Dooyeweerd, "De band met de beginsel," 35–36.

184. Dooyeweerd, "Tweeërlei kritiek," 5–8.

185. Dooyeweerd, "Het Amsterdamsche Rapport inzake de medezeggen-schap van het personeel in de gemeentebedrijven en diensten," 168 n.3. Dooye-weerd's qualified stance contrasts with that of another influential pluralist, Otto von Gierke, who was an enthusiastic advocate of producer cooperatives and other related forms of economic "fellowship." See Gierke, *Community in Historical Perspective,* ed. Anthony Black and trans. Mary Fischer (Cambridge: Cambridge University Press, 1990), esp. 221 ff.

186. Excerpt from Magnus Verbrugge's 1974 interview with Dooyeweerd published in *Public Justice Report* 26, no. 3 (2003), Center for Public Justice, Annapolis, MD, 9. Dooyeweerd's proposal for worker share ownership was op-posed by the Dutch Christian trade union movement because it would, they supposed, risk creating a materialistic attitude among workers and expose them to too great a financial risk.

187. *Capitalism and Progress,* 216–217. See also the work of another Dooye-weerdian economist, Alan Storkey, *A Christian Social Perspective* (Leicester: Inter-Varsity Press, 1979), 334–364. Both Goudzwaard and Storkey cite appre-ciatively the work of George Goyder, especially *The Responsible Company* (Ox-ford: Blackwell, 1961) and *The Just Enterprise* (London: André Deutsch, 1987). I have concentrated on the question of whether codetermination is compatible with the internal structure of the enterprise rather than on whether the *state* has the legal competence to impose it. Dooyeweerd denies the latter, while Goyder affirms it. But it seems possible that a case in support of such legislation could be developed along the same lines as that proposed above in support of profit-sharing legislation. See also M. J. Verkeerk and A. Zijlstra, "Philosophical Analysis of Industrial Organizations," *Philosophia Reformata* 68 (2003): 101–122, which applies the notion of enkaptic interlacements to business enterprises.

Eleven.   Civil Society and Christian Pluralism

1. As I noted earlier, from certain perspectives, including religious ones, "experience" is seen as requiring confirmation, interpretation, or correc-tion by a canonical text or a religious authority, or both. In the Christian tra-dition this is typically the case with what Dooyeweerd calls the institutional communities—state, church, marriage, and family. For him experience is not interpreted via a supposed neutral reason but in the light of one or other reli-gious ground motive. I return to this point in the epilogue.

2. This, it will be evident, is a formulation that Thomists might well be able to endorse as a possible definition of natural law—except that they would

want to insert the term *rational* in it.

3. Classical Thomism always asserted the ultimate spiritual equality of *persons* made in the divine image but construed this as compatible with inherited or assigned social rankings mirroring the hierarchy of being. I have noted that contemporary Catholic social thought no longer prioritizes this construal. It is, for instance, absent from the following representative statement by Pope John Paul II: "the social nature of man is not completely fulfilled in the State, but is realized in various intermediary groups, beginning with the family and including economic, social, political and cultural groups which stem from human nature itself and have their own autonomy, always with a view to the common good" (*Centesimus Annus,* paragraph 13). My own reading of Dooyeweerd converges closely with this statement.

4. I develop this point in Jonathan Chaplin, "The Concept of 'Civil Society' and Christian Social Pluralism," in *The Kuyper Center Review,* vol 1.: *Politics, Religion, and Sphere Sovereignty,* ed. Gordon Graham (Grand Rapids: Eerdmans, 2010), 14–33.

5. Nor does the notion imply that social structures engage in only one kind of concrete activity. Dooyeweerd's distinction between structure and purpose enables him to distinguish those activities that are inherent to an institution's identity (e.g., the state passing a law) from those that are contingent and transient (e.g., the state building a dike). Note also that both are examples of the state's multifunctionality.

6. Bob Goudzwaard, *Capitalism and Progress: A Diagnosis of Western Society,* ed. and trans. Josina Van Nuis Zylstra (Toronto: Wedge; Grand Rapids: Eerdmans, 1979), 65, 205 ff. The phrase was originally formulated by T. P. Van der Kooy, as Goudzwaard acknowledges.

7. This is not at all to say that all such interlinkages are of a legal kind. International fashion, Internet discussion groups, and missionary activity, for example, are not.

8. See Dooyeweerd, *Roots,* 196–197.

9. Albeit one subsequently distorted by reductionist nineteenth-century positivist and Marxist sociological theory. See Dooyeweerd, *Roots,* 192 ff.

10. Víctor Pérez-Díaz, "The Possibility of Civil Society: Traditions, Character and Challenges," in *Civil Society: Theory, History, Comparison,* ed. John A. Hall (Cambridge: Polity, 1995), 81.

11. Don E. Eberly, ed., *The Essential Civil Society Reader: Classic Essays in the American Civil Society Debate* (Lanham, MD: Rowman and Littlefield, 2000), 7. This is close to Peter L. Berger and Richard John Neuhaus's definition in *To Empower People: The Role of Mediating Structures in Public Policy* (Wash-

ington, DC: American Enterprise Institute, 1977).

12. John A. Hall, "In Search of Civil Society," in *Civil Society: Theory, History, Comparison* (Cambridge: Polity, 1995), 25.

13. Ernest Gellner, "The Importance of Being Modular," in Hall, ed., *Civil Society*, 42.

14. Charles Taylor, "Invoking Civil Society," in *Philosophical Arguments* (Cambridge, MA: Harvard University Press, 1995), 223.

15. Christopher Beem, *The Necessity of Politics: Reclaiming American Public Life* (Chicago: University of Chicago Press, 1999), 18.

16. Christopher G. A. Bryant, "Civic Nation, Civil Society, Civil Religion," in Hall, ed., *Civil Society*, 148.

17. John Ehrenberg, *Civil Society: The Critical History of an Idea* (New York: New York University Press, 1999), 235.

18. Jean L. Cohen and Andrew Arato, *Civil Society and Political Theory* (Cambridge, MA: MIT Press, 1992), ix.

19. Like many writers with roots in the European left, they attribute the capacity for "self-constitution" only to the institutions of civil society because they view states and markets as rigid bureaucratic structures essentially resistant to substantial refashioning. Ironically, conservatives Berger and Neuhaus share this pessimism about bureaucratic "megastructures" like states and corporations. See Berger and Neuhaus, *To Empower People*.

20. Eberly, *The Essential Civil Society Reader*, 6.

21. For Dooyeweerd these two kinds of analysis are distinct but finally inseparable since an analysis of particular communities is incomplete until their interrelations with others is examined. There are, of course, other central dimensions of the enterprise of social theory, e.g., the analysis of social change; or of the processes by which social structures are constructed and reproduced by social agents—what Dooyeweerd calls positivization of norms (and which has certain parallels with what Anthony Giddens calls "structuration" in *Central Problems in Social Theory* [London: Macmillan, 1979], chapter 2).

22. And, as Dooyeweerd compellingly argues, the celebration of unconstrained autonomy in individualistic social theories provided fatal legitimation for such risks. Whether or not individualization and differentiation were originally able to yield wholesome cultural fruit depended in large part on the vigor and extent of the interrelationships that free and responsible persons and communities—including, of course, the state—were capable of establishing. The modern record is, at best, profoundly ambiguous, and the parallel dilemma facing contemporary late-modern societies undergoing rampant individualization and lopsided globalization is no less acute

23. This, it may be noted, is an important Tocquevillian theme: voluntary

associations in an egalitarian society serve as replacements for the "secondary powers" that supplied status and protection in the ancien régime. Dooyeweerd's concerns, however, range wider than Tocqueville's.

24. See discussion in chapter 6 above.

25. Ibid.

26. See David S. Woods, "Reconceptualizing Economics: The Contributions of Karl Polanyi," in *Political Theory and Christian Vision: Essays in Memory of Bernard Zylstra,* ed. Jonathan P. Chaplin and Paul Marshall (Lanham, MD: University Press of America, 1994), 247–266. It might be countered here that to describe an arena dominated by competition, such as a market, as a realm of cooperative *inter*dependencies is implausible. It is certainly counterintuitive, but this, perhaps, is only testimony to the continuing hegemonic power of individualistic economic thought. For alternative models of economics, see Goudzwaard, *Capitalism and Progress;* Amitai Etzioni, *The Moral Dimension: Toward a New Economics* (New York: Free Press, 1990); Herman E. Daly and John B. Cobb, *For the Common Good* (Boston: Beacon Press, 1994).

27. For a pointed critique of such generalized invocations of "community," see Raymond Plant, *Politics, Theology and History* (Cambridge: Cambridge University Press, 2001), chapter 10.

28. See above, chapter 1.

29. Taylor, "Invoking Civil Society"; and Beem, *The Necessity of Politics.*

30. Taylor, "Invoking Civil Society," 222.

31. Ibid., 206.

32. Cohen and Arato, *Civil Society and Political Theory,* 17–18.

33. Interestingly, it is precisely because Ehrenberg does envisage such a systemwide socialist transformation, led by the state, that he relativizes the transformative potentials of civil society; Ehrenberg, *Civil Society,* esp. chapter 9. While Cohen and Arato represent the Habermasian left, Ehrenberg remains within the Marxist tradition.

34. I stress that my aim here is illustrative and is not at all a comprehensive reckoning with civil society theorizing.

35. This is not to suggest that traditional forms of the family are necessarily "rightly ordered." Here I do not address the question of what precise positive forms of family or other traditional communities are most conducive to personal and communal well-being.

36. See Jonathan Chaplin, "Street-Level Justice: Governing Metropolitan Public Space," *Comment* 16 December 2005, www.cardus.ca/comment/article/301/.

37. London: IEA Health and Welfare Unit, 1993.

38. Ironically, it was British governments substantially influenced by such

neoconservative aspirations—Mrs. Thatcher's and its successors—that from 1979 to 1997 presided over the most extensive centralization of British public services for a generation. Thatcher's ambition to increase the efficient use of public expenditure and so make possible substantial tax cuts led, unintentionally but inexorably, to the imposition of an intrusive "audit culture" on successive areas of public policy, including notably education and health. For a penetrating critique of the impact of Thatcherism on this point, see Simon Jenkins, *Accountable to None: The Tory Nationalization of Britain* (Harmondsworth: Penguin, 1995). Jenkins was initially a devotee of Thatcher.

39. Thus enkaptic interlacements involving the state cannot be interdependencies as these presuppose equal legal status. So it is now necessary to modify my earlier redefinition (in chapter 6) of enkaptic interlacements as a *sub*category of intercommunal interlinkages. It now appears that they constitute an *overlapping* category. That is, while many enkaptic interlacements are indeed interdependencies, those involving the state cannot be because they are regulated by a compulsory authority and not entered into between legally equal parties. (Dooyeweerd observes that there is yet another, separate class of relationships in which the state is involved that falls *outside* its sphere of compulsory legal authority, namely, those in which the state acts on a par with any other citizen, for instance, as a purchaser in economic markets. See *NC*, 3:481–482.)

40. I suggest, however, that a regime of differential rights, possibly including self-government, may indeed be justifiable when a vulnerable minority group experiencing historically rooted injustice (such as aboriginal communities in Canada) faces the threat of assimilation or continuing marginalization. This is not the only argument for granting aboriginal sovereignty. Another is that in Canada such sovereignty was originally possessed by Canadian First Nations and then illegally suppressed by the Canadian government and must now be restored. See Hans-Martien Ten Napel, "The Concept of a Multicultural Democracy: A Preliminary Christian-Philosophical Appraisal," *Philosophia Reformata* 71 (2006): 145–153; Jonathan Chaplin, "Beyond Multiculturalism—But to Where? Public Justice and Cultural Diversity," *Philosophia Reformata* 73 (2008): 190–209.

41. See Paul Marshall, *Human Rights Theories in Christian Perspective* (Toronto: Institute for Christian Studies, 1983). Examples of the obligation of the state to give public-legal protection to individual rights would include the definition and defense of civil rights (such as freedom of speech and association), social rights (such as entitlements to income support), and arguably also cultural rights (such as language rights). Elsewhere Marshall also argues that the category of (legal) *human* rights should be reserved only for the first of

these; see his "Universal Human Rights and Role of the State," in *Sovereignty at the Crossroads,* ed. Luis E. Lugo (Lanham, MD: Rowman and Littlefield, 1996), 153–175. It can also be noted that, in principle, a variety of types of law could be used to defend individual rights: constitutional, administrative, civil, common, or statute; or, indeed, a variety of policy instruments. Dooyeweerd's model does not prescribe entrenching particular rights in a constitutional bill of rights, nor does it exclude it, although it would be unfavorable to ceding wide latitude on substantive matters to judicial discretion.

42. Dooyeweerd would hasten to add that what I have called interdependencies themselves possess sphere sovereignty on account of their possession of distinct internal structural principles. As I suggested earlier, however, this is to multiply the number of distinct normative principles populating the social world beyond what is necessary (thus evoking the application of Occam's razor). As I have insisted, interdependencies do indeed have a normative character, but the content of that normativity is sufficiently determined by the structural principles of the various parties to an interdependency.

43. Nationalizing an entire industry—say, a natural monopoly—is not a case of such individual treatment, whereas full or partial public ownership of selected individual companies is. For a Dooyeweerdian critique of industrial corporatism, see Sander Griffioen, *Facing the New Corporatism* (Toronto: Christian Labour Association of Canada, 1980).

44. Yet Dooyeweerd's caution that the term *public interest* can easily be abused to justify intrusive interventions in personal freedom or communal sphere sovereignty needs to be heeded. Appeals to the public interest should therefore be disciplined by such considerations. I noted that Dooyeweerd's account of the relationship between the public interest and sphere sovereignty lacks precision but interpreted him to intend that the public realm does indeed have its own interest, which must be balanced *alongside* the interests of persons and communities. So sphere sovereignty and personal freedom do not represent sectors of immunity from public-legal attention. Rather political adjudication involves a just and prudential balancing among these three distinct sources of legitimate public claims.

45. In Dutch Christian democratic thought since the 1980s the state is distinguished both from the market and from what is termed the societal *middenveld,* the realm of nonprofit mediating structures that ought not to be incorporated into regulatory regimes or subjected to efficiency audits only appropriate for the competitive business sector. Communitarians such as Etzioni, for example, also propose a threefold distinction between regulation by state, market, and community, though this begs the question of whether or not the market sector contains bodies that we might call "communities" (businesses and trades

unions, on Dooyeweerd's construal at least), and why the state is not one. For an analysis of the relationship between these three sectors, see Alan Wolfe, *Whose Keeper?: Social Science and Moral Obligation* (Berkeley: University of California Press, 1989).

46. This, of course, is what often happens already; among other things, Dooyeweerd's model suggests an account of why.

47. Dooyeweerd, *NC*, 3:266–342.

48. While it is inappropriate to criticize a philosopher for not also being a political activist, a more critical questioning stance might have led Dooyeweerd to seek evidence from activists like Naudé who knew firsthand what "separate development" meant for the black peoples Dooyeweerd described as "primitive." Dooyeweerd's own "integral-empirical method" in social theory, requiring "continuous confrontation" with empirical states of affairs, surely involves a rigorous search for that kind of evidence, especially from the experience of those actually undergoing oppression.

49. In an interview held in 1974, however, he does acknowledge the possible need for civil disobedience where states violate their calling.

50. I am not, however, suggesting that Augustine himself held a "transformative" stance. On the contrary, he denied the possibility of upward moral progress in a fallen world. See Oliver O'Donovan's illuminating discussion in "Augustine's *City of God* XIX and Western Political Thought," *Dionysius* 11 (1987): 89–110. I am saying, however, that, *in the hands of a robust Calvinist like Dooyeweerd* driven by a strongly affirming stance toward the created order, a sharper Augustinian bite might have generated a more consistently critical social analysis. Henk Geertsema has suggested to me that a significant factor explaining this limitation is that Dooyeweerd accounts for human *evil* primarily in terms of "absolutization." That is, he conceives of evil as the absolutization of particular aspects in creation, resulting from our (idolatrous) exaggeration of their relative significance. Behind this lies his tendency to analyze the structure of reality in terms of the categories of *unity* and *diversity*. Absolutization, then, amounts to a distortion of creational unity by attributing undue significance to one of its diverse parts. The limitations of such a confining conceptual framework for interpreting the complexity and mystery of human evil are clear.

Epilogue

1. José Casanova, *Public Religion in the Modern World* (Chicago: University of Chicago Press, 1994), chapters 2 and 8. See also David Herbert, *Religion*

and Civil Society: Rethinking Public Religion in the Contemporary World (London: Ashgate, 2003); and Sander Griffioen, "Secularisme en secularisatie," *Philosophia Reformata* 73 (2008): 71–84.

2. See James W. Skillen and Stanley W. Carlson-Thies, "Religion and Political Development in Nineteenth-Century Holland," *Publius: The Journal of Federalism* 12 (Summer 1982): 43–64; John L. Hiemstra, *Worldviews on the Air: the Struggle to Create a Pluralistic Broadcasting System in the Netherlands* (Lanham, MD: University Press of America, 1997).

3. Dooyeweerd, *Roots*, 6. See also Jonathan Chaplin, *Talking God: The Legitimacy of Religious Public Reasoning* (London: Theos, 2009).

Appendix 1   Dooyeweerd's Conception of the Task of Social Philosophy

1. Dooyeweerd, *NC*, 1:542.

2. The term *sciences* is equivalent to the Dutch term *wetenschappen* and the German term *wissenschaften*. In Dooyeweerd's usage, it includes the natural, the social, and the human sciences. For him too the latter would embrace literature, linguistics, even theology.

3. Dooyeweerd, *NC*, 1:541–542.

4. He held a very different view of the scope of epistemology to that prevailing in current analytic philosophy. For treatments of or informed by his epistemology, see Hendrik Hart, "Dooyeweerd's Gegenstand Theory of Theory," in *The Legacy of Herman Dooyeweerd: Reflections on Critical Philosophy in the Christian Tradition*, ed. C. T. McIntire (Lanham, MD: University Press of America, 1985), 143–166; H. G. Geertsema, *Het menselijk karakter van ons kennen* (Amsterdam: Buijten and Schipperheijn, 1992); René van Woudenberg, "Theorie van het kennen," in *Kennis en werkelijkheid. Tweede inleiding tot een christelijke filosofie* (Amsterdam: Buijten and Schipperheijn, 1996), 21–85; and the references in notes 2 and 12 in chapter 3 above.

5. Dooyeweerd, *NC*, 1:544–545.

6. Herman Dooyeweerd, *A Christian Theory of Social Institutions*, ed. John Witte, Jr. and trans. Magnus Verbrugge (La Jolla, CA: Herman Dooyeweerd Foundation, 1986), 33.

7. See *NC*, 1:545–566, where Dooyeweerd states that the sciences ought, however, to strive to be free from social or cultural influences, which conflict with the character of science itself.

8. Dooyeweerd, *A Christian Theory of Social Institutions*, 46. I remark

later in this Appendix on the sense in which Dooyeweerd's social philosophy might be framed as "critical" in the different sense that its research programs should be oriented to the critical exposure of social injustice or oppression (as in "critical theory"). Regrettably, this is a possibility on which Dooyeweerd says next to nothing, in spite of the fact that his own social philosophy was profoundly informed by the experience of Kuyperian emancipation movements, as well as by his own early wrestling with the impact of religion on law and public policy. Frustration with this lacuna is expressed in Lourens M. du Plessis, "Function and Role of the State," in *The Challenge of Marxist and Neo-Marxist Ideologies for Christian Scholarship*, ed. John C. Vander Stelt (Sioux Center, IA: Dordt College Press, 1982), 149–186. For a corrective move, see Brad Breems, "The Service of Sociology: A Lighter Cloak or a Sturdier Iron Cage?" in *Marginal Resistance: Essays Dedicated to John C. Vander Stelt*, ed. John Kok (Sioux Center, IA: Dordt College Press, 2001), 253–272. Nicholas Wolterstorff discusses Dooyeweerd's position in chapter 8, "Theory and Praxis," of *Until Justice and Peace Embrace* (Grand Rapids: Eerdmans, 1981). A notable example of what a critical social theory drawing on Dooyeweerdian insights might look like is Bob Goudzwaard, *Capitalism and Progress: A Diagnosis of Western Society*, ed. and trans. Josina Van Nuis Zylstra (Toronto: Wedge; Grand Rapids: Eerdmans, 1979).

    9. Dooyeweerd, *NC*, 1:548.

    10. Ibid., 1:565.

    11. Ibid., 1:548.

    12. Ibid., 1:565; see 1:250–251, 557.

    13. Ibid., 1:553.

    14. Dooyeweerd does not assume, of course, that every special science, still less every special scientist, will actually or consciously possess a *coherent* view of these underlying concepts. Indeed a substantial part of his critical engagements with other social theorists is to bring to the surface profound *incoherencies*, especially "antinomies," at that underlying philosophical level. This conception of interdisciplinarity is not intended as a description of what social theorists actually do but as a regulative ideal for the successful pursuit of theoretical work.

    15. See Dooyeweerd, *NC*, 3:157–163, 168–176, 262–265.

    16. Ibid., 3:263–264.

    17. Ibid., 3:157.

    18. Disappointingly, Dooyeweerd says very little about this modal science. Elaine Botha proposes "care" or "concern" as the modal kernel of the social aspect. See Elaine Botha, *Sosio-kulturele metavrae: 'n ensiklopedies-wysgerige ondersoek na enkele grondbegrippe in die cologie en ander sosio-kulturele*

wetenskappe (Amsterdam: Buijten and Schipperheijn, 1971), 126. See M. D. Stafleu, "Philosophical Ethics and the So-Called Ethical Aspect," *Philosophia Reformata* 72 (2008): 151–164, for a parallel proposal. See R. Kuiper, "Human Identity and Reformational Social Philosophy," *Philosophia Reformata* 96 (2004): 14–37, for an elaboration of the relationship between social philosophy and philosophical anthropology. Kuipers argues that Dooyeweerd's account of the social aspect neglects the "primary social norms" of "individuation" and "socialization."

19. Dooyeweerd, *NC*, 3:162–163.

20. All the more because he himself all too frequently uses the term *social* when he clearly means "societal" (e.g., Dooyeweerd, *NC*, 3:174).

21. Dooyeweerd, *NC*, 3:264.

22. A clearer, if less elegant, designation of this totality science might have been "societology."

23. Or, perhaps, "societal philosophy."

24. Dooyeweerd, *A Christian Theory of Social Institutions*, 59.

25. Dooyeweerd, *NC*, 3:157.

26. Ibid., 3:158, 163.

27. Ibid., 3:158.

28. Dooyeweerd, *A Christian Theory of Social Institutions*, 35–36. Thomist philosophers have developed parallel critiques of these various expressions of sociological reductionism; see, e.g., Johannes Messner, *Social Ethics: Natural Law in the Western World* (St. Louis: B. Herder, 1965), 5–12.

29. Dooyeweerd, *NC*, 3:168–169, 263.

30. Ibid., 3:169.

31. Ibid., 1:170. In fact both of these properties are determined by the order of cosmic time.

32. Ibid., 3:168–170.

33. For an assessment of Dooyeweerd's conception of social science, see Sander Griffioen, "Dooyeweerds programma voor de sociale wetenschappen," in *Herman Dooyeweerd 1894–1977. Breedte en actualiteit van zijn filosofie*, ed. H. G. Gertseema et al. (Kampen: J. H. Kok, 1994), 143–171. Varying critical elaborations or applications of a Dooyeweerdian methodology in social science and social philosophy are found in D. F. M. Strauss, "Philosophy and Sociology," *Philosophia Reformata* 44 (1979): 150–182; James W. Skillen, "Herman Dooyeweerd's Contribution to the Philosophy of the Social Sciences," *Journal of the American Scientific Affiliation* 31 (1979): 20–24; Richard A. Russell, "Philosophy and Sociology," in *A Reader in Sociology: Christian Perspectives*, ed. C. P. De Santo et al. (Scottsdale: Herald Press, 1980); Paul Marshall and Robert Vander Vennen, eds., *Social Science in Christian Perspective* (Lanham, MD: University

Press of America, 1988); Paul Marshall et al., eds., *Stained Glass: Worldviews and Social Science* (Lanham, MD: University Press of America, 1989); Sander Griffioen and Jan Verhoogt, eds., *Norm and Context in the Social Sciences* (Lanham, MD: University Press of America, 1990); Govert Buijs, ed., *Als de olifanten vechten* (Amsterdam: Buijten and Schipperheijn, 2001); Bruce Wearne, "Deism and the Absence of Christian Sociology," *Philosophia Reformata* 68 (2003): 14–35.

Appendix 2   Dooyeweerd on Natural Law and Legal Positivism

1. Herman Dooyeweerd, "De bronnen van het stellig recht in het licht der wetsidee. Een bijdrage tot opklaring van het probleem inzake de verhouding van rechtsbeginsel en positief recht," *Antirevolutionaire Staatkunde* 4 (1930): 19; see also H. J. van Eikema Hommes, "The Function of Law and the Role of Legal Principles," *Philosophia Reformata* 39 (1974): 77–81; P. B. Cliteur, "Rechtsbeginselen. Tussen natuurrecht en rechtspositivisme," *Philosophia Reformata* 49 (1984): 57–70; and A. Soeterman, "Dooyeweerd als rechtsfilosoof," in *Herman Dooyeweerd 1894–1977. Breedte en actualiteit van zijn filosofie*, ed. H. G. Geertsema et al. (Kampen: J. H. Kok, 1994), 28–49, which places Dooyeweerd's position in the context of earlier and contemporary debates in legal philosophy and argues that the two poles of naturalism and legal positivism between which Dooyeweerd sought to position himself have now been largely transcended.

2. Dooyeweerd, *EN,* 4:225.

3. Ibid., 3:22, 25.

4. See, e.g., H. A. Rommen, *The Natural Law: A Study in Legal and Social History and Philosophy,* rev. ed., trans. T. R. Hanley (St. Louis: B. Herder, 1947); and A. P. D'Entrèves, *The Notion of the State: An Introduction to Political Theory* (Oxford: Clarendon, 1967), for accounts of natural law theory.

5. See Herman Dooyeweerd, "Het Calvinistische beginsel der souvereiniteit in eigen kring als staatkundig beginsel," *Nederland en Oranje* 4 (1923): 98–99, 185–189; 5 (1924): 8–15, 27–31, 71–76; *Calvinisme en natuurrecht* (Amersfoort: Wijngen, 1925); and *De betekenis der wetsidee voor rechtswetenschap en rechtsphilosophie* (Kampen: J. H. Kok, 1926).

6. See O. J. L. Albers, *Het natuurrecht volgens der Wijsbegeerte der Wetsidee. Een kritische beschouwing* (Nijmegen: Janssen, 1955).

7. Ibid., 9–11.

8. Ibid., 39, 96–109.

9. See Alan Cameron, "Dooyeweerd on Law and Morality—A Test Case,"

Victoria University of Wellington Law Review 28 (1998): 263–281.

10. Ibid., 44–45, 52–53, 115–117.

11. Dooyeweerd, *EN,* 4:21–22.

12. Ibid., 3:22. Dooyeweerd in fact suggests that the lifting of the ban on interest also represents the appearance of a new legal principle. However, this seems not to be an example of the new disclosure of an anticipatory moment but only of a positivization of an existing principle in new conditions.

13. Ibid., 1:94–96; 2:128–129, 255–256.

14. Rommen, *The Natural Law,* 261–262.

15. See Hommes, "The Function of Law and the Role of Legal Principles," 79–80; and *Major Trends in the History of Legal Philosophy,* 57–59.

16. Hommes, "The Function of Law and the Role of Legal Principles," 80.

17. He appears, for example, to have exaggerated its static, unhistorical and rationalistic aspects; for more reliable accounts, see A. P. D'Entrèves, *Natural Law: An Historical Survey* (New York: Harper and Row, 1951), 43–44; Rommen, *The Natural Law,* 52–54, 216 ff.; and John Finnis, *Natural Law and Natural Rights* (Oxford: Clarendon, 1980), 22–49, 281–290.

18. Dooyeweerd, "De bronnen van het stellig recht in het licht der wetsidee," 30.

BIBLIOGRAPHY

Works by Herman Dooyeweerd

"Het Calvinistische beginsel der souvereiniteit in eigen kring als staatkundig beginsel." *Nederland en Oranje* 4 (1923): 98–99, 185–189; 5 (1924): 8–15, 27–31, 71–76.

"Inzage in de bedrijfsboekhouding door de arbeidersvertegenwoordigers in de particuliere onderneming." *Antirevolutionaire Staatkunde* 1 (1924–1925): 291–306.

"In den strijd om een christelijke staatkunde. Proeve van een fundering der calvinistische levens- en wereldbeschouwing in hare wetsidee." *Antirevolutionaire Staatkunde* 1 (1924–1925): 7–25, 62–79, 104–118, 161–173, 189–200, 228–244, 309–324, 433–460, 489–504, 528–542, 581–598, 617–634; 2 (1926): 244–265, 425–445; (quarterly) 1 (1927): 142–195.

Calvinisme en natuurrecht. Amersfoort: Wijngen, 1925.

"De band met de beginsel. Inzake het vraagstuk der medezeggenschap." *Nederland en Oranje* 7 (1926): 2–18, 33–40.

"Het oude probleem der christelijke staatkunde." *Antirevolutionaire Staatkunde* 2 (1926): 63–84.

"Tweeërlei kritiek. Om de principieele zijde van het vraagstuk der medezeggenschap." *Antirevolutionaire Staatkunde* 2 (1926): 1–21.

De betekenis der wetsidee voor rechtswetenschap en rechtsphilosophie. Kampen: J. H. Kok, 1926. [Inaugural address.]

"De oorsprong van de anti-these tusschen Christelijke en Humanistische wetsidee en hare beteekenis voor de staatkunde." *Antirevolutionaire Staatkunde* (quarterly) 1 (1927): 73–107.

"De universaliteit der rechtsgedachte en de idee van den kultuurstaat." *Almanak van het Studentencorps aan de Vrije Universiteit* (1928): 103–121.

"De strijd om de grondslagen ven het volkenrecht." *De Volkenbond* 4 (1929): 316–320.

"De structuur der rechtsbeginselen en de methode der rechtswetenschap in het licht der wetsidee." In *Wetenschappelijke bijdragen, aangeboden door hoogleeraren der Vrije Universiteit ter gelegenheid van haar 50-jarig bestaan 20 October, 1930*, 223–266. Amsterdam: De Standaard, 1930.

"De bronnen van het stellig recht in het licht der wetsidee. Een bijdrage tot opklaring van het probleem inzake de verhouding van rechtsbeginsel en positief recht." *Antirevolutionaire Staatkunde* 4 (1930) (quarterly): 1–59, 224–263, 325–362; 8 (1934): 57–94.

De crisis der humanistische staatsleer in het licht eener calvinistische kosmologie en kennistheorie. Amsterdam: Ten Have, 1931.

"Het Amsterdamsche rapport inzake de medezeggenschap van het personeel in de gemeentebedrijven en -diensten." *Antirevolutionaire Staatkunde* 8 (1932): 71–86, 121–132, 152–168.

"De theorie van de bronnen van het stellig recht in het licht der wetsidee." *Handelingen van de Vereeniging voor Wijsbegeerte des Rechts* 19 (1932) 1:1–28; 2:1–10, 24–31.

"Het vraagstuk van het organisch kiesrecht in een nieuw stadium." *Almanak van het Studentencorps aan de Vrije Universiteit* (Amsterdam, 1935): 105–121.

De Wijsbegeerte der Wetsidee. 3 vols. Amsterdam: H. J. Paris, 1935–1936.

"De wijsgeerige grondslagen van het fascisme." *Handelingen van de Vereeniging voor Wijsbegeerte des Rechts* 24 (1937) 2:58–65.

Recht en historie. Assen: Hummelen, 1938.

"De wijsgerige grondslag der democratie." *Handelingen voor de Vereeniging voor Wijsbegeerte des Recht* 25 (1938) 2:33–42, 59–61.

"De wijsgerige achtergrond van de moderne democratische reactie tegen het individualisme." *Mededeelingen van de Vereeniging voor Calvinistische Wijsbegeerte* 4 (1939): 7–10.

"De 'Théorie de l'institution' en de staatsleer van Maurice Hauriou." *Antirevolutionaire Staatkunde* 14 (1940): 301–347; 15 (1941): 42–70.

"De leer van de mens in der Wijsbegeerte der Wetsidee," *Correspondentiebladen* 7 (1942): 133–144. [Published in English as "The Theory of Man: Thirty-two Propositions on Anthropology" (Institute for Christian Studies,Toronto, n.d.)].

"De idee der individualiteits-structuur en het Thomistisch substantiebegrip. Een critisch onderzoek naar de grondslagen der Thomistische zijnsleer." *Philosophia Reformata* 8 (1943): 65–99; 9 (1944): 1–41.

"Enkele opmerkingen inzake de 'Richtlijnen' betreffende een toekomstige bedrijfsorganisatie." Mimeograph. 1944.

"De verhouding van individu en gemeenschap rechtswijsgeerig bezien." *Algemeen Nederlands Tijdschrift voor Wijsbegeerte en Psychologie* 39 (1946): 5–12.

"Een nieuw geschrift over Hauriou's leer der 'Institution.'" *Bestuurswetenschappen* 2 (1948): 1–15.

Transcendental Problems of Philosophic Thought: An Inquiry into the Transcendental Conditions of Philosophy. Grand Rapids: Eerdmans, 1948.

"Het historisch element in Groen's staatsleer." In *Groen's "Ongeloof en Revolutie,"* edited by L. C. Suttorp et al., 89–98. Wageningen: Zomer en Keuning, 1949.

"De sociologische verhouding tussen recht en economie in het probleem van het zgn. 'economisch recht.'" In *Opstellen op het gebied van recht, staat en maatschappij aangeboden aan Prof. Dr. A. Anema en Prof. Dr. P. A. Diepenhorst bij hun afscheid van de Vrije Universiteit door oud-leerlingen,* 221–265. Amsterdam: Bakker, 1949.

"De vooronderstellingen van ons denken over recht en samenleving in de crisis van het moderne historisme." *Rechtsgeleerd Magazijn Themis* (1949): 193–248.

De strijd om het souvereiniteitsbegrip in de moderne rechts- en staatsleer. Amsterdam: H. J. Paris, 1950. [English version in *Free University Quarterly* 1 (1951): 85–106.]

"De overspanning van het begrip 'natuurlijke gemeenschap' en het sociologisch universalisme." *Almanak van het Studentencorps aan de Vrije Universiteit* (1951): 216–229.

"Een Rooms-Katholieke visie op de Protestants-Christelijke denkbeelden inzake bedrijfsorganisatie en de recente discussie over de grenzen der overheidstaak." *Antirevolutionaire Staatkunde* 22 (1952): 65–79, 97–122.

"Omvang en aard van de staatstaak." *Mededeelingen van de Vereeniging voor Calvinistische Wijsbegeerte* (September 1953): 4–6.

A New Critique of Theoretical Thought. 4 vols. Translated by D. H. Freeman and W. S. Young. Amsterdam: H. J. Paris; Philadelphia: Presbyterian and Reformed Publishing Co., 1953–1958. [Revised and enlarged translation of *De Wijsbegeerte der Wetsidee.*]

"Arbeidsrecht, intern bedrijfsrecht en de juridische grenzen der souvereiniteit in eigen kring." *Antirevolutionaire Staatkunde* 24 (1954): 177–191.

"Een nieuwe Rooms-Katholieke visie op de staat en het recht." *Antirevolutionaire Staatkunde* 25 (1955): 289–303.

"The Criteria of Progressive and Reactionary Tendencies in History." In *Verslag van de plechtige viering van het honderdvijftig-jarig bestaan der Koninklijke Nederlandse Akademie van Wetenschappen.* Amsterdam: North Holland, 1958. [English text: 213–228; French text: 139–154; Dutch text: 61–77.]

Vernieuwing en bezinning. Om het reformatorisch grondmotief. Edited by J. A. Oosterhoff. Zutphen: J. B. van der Brink, 1959. [Edited collection of articles first appearing in the weekly *Nieuw Nederland,* 1944–1948.]

In the Twilight of Western Thought: Studies in the Pretended Autonomy of Philosophical Thought. Philadelphia: Presbyterian and Reformed Publishing Co., 1960.

Review of B. de Goede, "De staatsvrije sfeer." *Rechtsgeleerd Magazijn Themis* 80 (1961): 177–182.

"Het typisch structuurprincipe van de staat en de leer der staatsdoeleinden." *Weekblad voor Privaatrecht, Notarisambt en Registratie* 92, no. 4701 (December 1961): 507–515.

Publiek- en privaatrecht. Amsterdam: Uitgave Studentenraad, Vrije Universiteit, 1963. Collegediktaat.

Encyclopaedie der rechtswetenschap. Vols. 1–4. Amsterdam: Studentenraad van de Vrije Universiteit, 1966.

"Het oecumenisch-reformatisch grondmotief van de Wijsbegeerte der Wetsidee en de grondslag van de Vrije Universiteit." *Philosophia Reformata* 31 (1966): 3–15.

"Die Philosophie der Gesetzidee und ihre Bedeutung für die Rechts- und Sozialphilosophie." *Archiv für Rechts- en Sozialphilosophie* 53 (1967): 1–30, 465–513.

Verkenningen in de wijsbegeerte, de sociologie en de rechtsgeschiedenis. 2nd ed. Edited by J. Stellingwerff. Amsterdam: Buijten and Schipperheijn, 1967. [First edition published 1962.]

"Na vijfendertig jaren." *Philosophia Reformata* 36 (1971): 1–12.

"Sociology of Law and Its Philosophical Foundations." In *Truth and Reality: Philosophical Perspectives on Reality Dedicated to Professor H. G. Stoker,* edited by H. J. J. Bingle et al., 55–73. Braamfontein: De Jong's Bookshop, 1971. [First published 1964.]

"Introduction by the Editor-in-Chief, Prof. Herman Dooyeweerd." In *The Idea of a Christian Philosophy: Essays in Honour of D. H. Th. Vollenhoven. Philosophia Reformata* 38 (1973): 5–16; and Toronto: Wedge, 1973: 5–16.

"De actualiteit van de schepping. Gesprek met Prof. Dr. H. Dooyeweerd." Edited by Sander Griffioen. Unpublished interview, 9 May 1974. Distributed by Stichting Internationaal Christelijk Studiecentrum, Utrecht.

The Christian Idea of the State. Translated by J. Kraay. Nutley, NJ: Craig Press, 1975. [First published 1936 in Dutch.]

Interview in J. M. van Dunne et al., *Acht civilisten in burger,* 35–67. Zwolle: W. E. J. Tjeenk Willink, 1977.

Roots of Western Culture: Pagan, Secular and Christian Options. Edited by
M. Vander Vennen and B. Zylstra. Translated by J. Kraay. Toronto: Wedge,
1979. [Translation of chapters 1–3 of *Vernieuwing en Bezinning*, 1959.]
Herman Dooyeweerd. Grenzen van het theoretisch denken. Edited by M. E. Ver-
burg. Geschiedenis van Wijsbegeerte in Nederland 20. Baarn: Ambo, 1986.
A Christian Theory of Social Institutions. Edited by J. Witte, Jr. Translated by
M. Verbrugge. La Jolla, CA: Herman Dooyeweerd Foundation, 1986.
[Translation of "Grondproblemen der wijsgerige sociologie," in *Verkennin-
gen in de wijsbegeerte, de sociologie en de rechtsgeschiedenis,* 69–146. First
published 1947.]
The Collected Works of Herman Dooyeweerd. General editor D. F. M. Strauss.
Lewiston, NY: Edwin Mellen Press, 1996–. www2.redeemer.ca/dooyeweerd.
Christian Philosophy and the Meaning of History. Edited by D. F. M. Strauss.
[*The Collected Works of Herman Dooyeweerd,* Ser. B, vol. 1.] Lewiston, NY:
Edwin Mellen Press, 1996.
"Calvinism and Natural Law." In Herman Dooyeweerd, *Essays in Legal, Social,
and Political Philosophy,* edited by Alan Cameron and translated by Albert
Wolters. Lewiston, NY: Edwin Mellen Press, 1997, 3–38.
Essays in Legal, Social, and Political Philosophy. Edited by Alan Cameron. Trans-
lated by Albert Wolters. [*The Collected Works of Herman Dooyeweerd,*
Ser. B, vol. 2.] Lewiston, NY: Edwin Mellen Press, 1997.
Political Philosophy. Edited by D. F. M. Strauss. [*The Collected Works of Herman
Dooyeweerd,* Ser. D, vol. 1.] Lewiston, NY: Edwin Mellen Press, 2004.
Reformation and Scholasticism in Philosophy. Vol 1., *The Greek Prelude.* Edited
by Robert K. Knudsen, D. F. M. Strauss, and Albert M. Wolters. Translated
by Ray Togtmann. [*The Collected Works of Herman Dooyeweerd,* Ser. A,
vol. 5.] Lewiston, NY: Edwin Mellen Press, 2004.

OTHER WORKS

Aertsen, J. A. "'Uit God zijn Alle Dingen'. Enkele overwegingen bij de 700ste
sterfdag van Thomas van Aquino." *Philosophia Reformata* 39 (1974):
102–155.
Albers, O. J. L. *Het natuurrecht volgens de Wisjsbegeerte der Wetsidee. Een kritische beschouwing.* Nijmegen: Janssen, 1955.
Althusius, Johannes. *The Politics of Johannes Althusius.* Translated and abridged
by Frederick S. Carney. Boston: Beacon Press, 1964.
Aquinas, Thomas. *Selected Political Writings.* Edited by A. P. D'Entrèves and
translated by J. G. Dawson. Oxford: Blackwell, 1959.

Archibald, Katherine. "The Concept of Social Hierarchy in the Writings of St. Thomas Aquinas." *Historian* 12 (1949–1950): 28–54.

Aris, Reinhold. *A History of Political Thought in Germany from 1789 to 1819.* London: Frank Cass, 1965.

Aristotle. *The Politics.* Translated by Ernest Barker. Oxford: Oxford University Press, 1958.

Audi, Robert, and Nicholas Wolterstorff, eds. *Religion in the Public Square.* Lanham, MD: Rowman and Littlefield, 1997.

Balkenstein, G. J. "The Netherlands Industrial Organization Act 1950." *University of Pennsylvania Law Review* 106 (1958): 499–524.

Banner, Michael. "Christianity and Civil Society." In *Alternative Conceptions of Civil Society,* edited by Simone Chambers and Will Kymlicka, 113–130. Princeton: Princeton University Press, 2002.

Barker, Ernest. "Introduction." In Otto von Gierke, *Natural Law and the Theory of Society.* Translated by Ernest Barker, ix–xci. Cambridge: Cambridge University Press, 1934.

Barnard, F. M. *Herder's Social and Political Thought: From Enlightenment to Nationalism.* Oxford: Clarendon, 1965.

Barnard, F. M., and R. A. Vernon. "Socialist Pluralism and Pluralist Socialism." *Political Studies* 25 (1977): 474–490.

Barry, Brian. "The Use and Abuse of 'The Public Interest.'" In *The Public Interest,* edited by C. J. Friedrich, 191–204. New York: Atherton, 1966.

Basden, Andrew. "Brief Comments on Stafleu's Proposal for a New Political Aspect." *Philosophia Reformata* 70 (2005): 70–75.

Beem, Christopher. *The Necessity of Politics: Reclaiming American Public Life.* Chicago: University of Chicago Press, 1999.

Berger, Peter L., and Richard John Neuhaus. *To Empower People: The Role of Mediating Structures in Public Policy.* Washington, DC: American Enterprise Institute, 1977.

———. *To Empower People: From State to Civil Society.* 20th Anniversary Edition. Edited by Michael Novak. Washington, DC: AEI, 1996.

Black, Anthony. *Guilds and Civil Society in European Political Thought from the Twelfth Century to the Present.* London: Methuen, 1984.

———. *State, Community and Human Desire: A Group-Centred Account of Political Values.* Hemel Hempstead: Harvester/Wheatsheaf, 1988.

———. "Editor's Introduction." In Otto von Gierke, *Community in Historical Perspective,* edited by Anthony Black, xiv–xxx. Cambridge: Cambridge University Press, 1990.

Blosser, Philip. "Reconnoitering Dooyeweerd's Theory of Man." *Philosophia Reformata* 58 (1993): 192–209.

Boersma, Kees, et al., eds. *Aan Babels stromen. Een bevrijdend perspectief op ethiek en techniek.* Amsterdam: Buijten and Schipperheijn, 2002.

Bos, A. P. "Het grondmotief van de Griekse cultuur en het titanische zinperspectief." *Philosophia Reformata* 51 (1986): 117–137.

Botha, Elaine. *Sosio-kulturele metavrae: 'n ensiklopedies-wysgerige ondersoek na enkele grondbegrippe in die colologie en ander socio-kulturele wetenskappe.* Amsterdam: Buijten and Schipperheijn, 1971.

Bowen, Ralph. *German Theories of the Corporative State.* New York: Whittlesey House, 1947.

Bratt, James, ed. *Abraham Kuyper: A Centennial Reader.* Grand Rapids: Eerdmans, 1998.

Breems, Brad. "The Service of Sociology: A Lighter Cloak or a Sturdier Iron Cage?" In *Marginal Resistance: Essays Dedicated to John C. Vander Stelt,* edited by John Kok, 253–272. Sioux Center, IA: Dordt College Press, 2001.

Breitling, Rupert. "The Concept of Pluralism." In *Three Faces of Pluralism,* edited by Stanislaw Ehrlich and Graham Wootton, 1–19. Farnborough: Gower, 1980.

Briefs, Goetz A. "The Economic Philosophy of Romanticism." *Journal of the History of Ideas* 2 (1941): 297–300.

Brown, Colin. *Christianity and Western Thought: A History of Philosophers, Ideas, and Movements.* Downers Grove, IL: InterVarsity Press, 1990.

Brüggemann-Kruijff, A. "Tijd als omsluiting, tijd als ontsluiting." *Philosophia Reformata* 46 (1981):119–163; 47 (1982): 41–68.

Brümmer, Vincent. *Transcendental Criticism and Christian Philosophy: A Presentation and Evaluation of Herman Dooyeweerd's "Philosophy of the Cosmonomic Idea."* Franeker: T. Wever, 1961.

Brunner, Emil. *Justice and the Social Order.* Translated by M. Hottinger. London: Lutterworth, 1945.

Bryant, Christopher G. A. "Civic Nation, Civil Society, Civil Religion." In *Civil Society: Theory, History, Comparison,* edited by John A. Hall, 136–157. Cambridge: Polity Press, 1995.

Buijs, Govert. "Agape and the Origins of Civil Society." In *Philosophy Put to Work: Contemporary Issues in Art, Society, Politics, Science and Religion,* edited by H. G. Geertsema et al., 18–50. Amsterdam Christian Studies. Amsterdam: VU University Amsterdam, 2008.

———, ed. *Als de olifanten vechten.* Amsterdam: Buijten and Schipperheijn, 2001.

Buijs, Govert, et al., eds. *Home respondens. Verkenningen rond het mens-zijn.* Amsterdam: Buijten and Schipperheijn, 2005.

Buijs, Govert, et al., eds. *Civil Society. Tussen oud en nieuw.* Amsterdam: Aksant, 2009.

Calvez, Jean-Yves, and Jacques Perrin. *The Church and Social Justice.* Translated by J. R. Kirwan. Chicago: Henry Regnery, 1961.

Cameron, Alan. "Dooyeweerd on Law and Morality—A Test Case." *Victoria University of Wellington Law Review* 28 (1998): 263–281.

Camp, Robert L. *The Papal Ideology of Social Reform: A Study in Historical Development, 1878–1967.* Leyden: E. J. Brill, 1969.

Carney, Frederick S. "Associational Thought in Early Calvinism." In *Voluntary Associations,* edited by D. B. Robertson, 39–53. Richmond: John Knox, 1966.

Carter, Alan. "On Individualism, Collectivism and Interrelationism." *Heythrop Journal* 31 (1990): 23–38.

Casanova, José. *Public Religions in the Modern World.* Chicago: University of Chicago Press, 1994.

Caudill, David S. "The Rechtsstaat: Magic Wall or Material Necessity?" *Houston Journal of International Law* 4 (1982): 169–188.

Cawson, Alan. *Corporatism and Political Theory.* Oxford: Blackwell, 1986.

Chambers, Simone, and Will Kymlicka, eds. *Alternative Conceptions of Civil Society.* Princeton: Princeton University Press, 2002.

Chaplin, Jonathan. "How Much Cultural and Religious Pluralism Can Liberalism Tolerate?" In *Liberalism, Multiculturalism and Toleration,* edited by J. Houghton, 32–49. London: Macmillan, 1993.

———. "Subsidiarity and Sphere Sovereignty: Catholic and Reformed Conceptions of the Role of the State." In *Things Old and New: Catholic Social Teaching Revisited,* edited by Frank P. McHugh and Samuel M. Natale, 175–202. Lanham, MD: University Press of America, 1993.

———. "Suspended Communities or Covenanted Communities?: Reformed Reflections on the Social Thought of Radical Orthodoxy." In *Radical Orthodoxy and the Reformed Tradition: Creation, Covenant and Participation,* edited by James K. A. Smith and James H. Olthuis, 151–182. Grand Rapids: Baker Academic, 2005.

———. "Toward a Social Pluralist Theory of Institutional Rights." *Ave Maria Law Review* 3 (2005): 147–170.

———. "Toward an Ecumenical Social Theory: Revisiting Herman Dooyeweerd's Critique of Thomism." In *That the World May Believe: Essays on Mission and Unity in Honour of George Vandervelde,* edited by Michael Goheen and Margaret O'Gara, 215–238. Lanham, MD: University Press of America, 2006.

———. "Herman Dooyeweerd." In *New Dictionary of Christian Apologetics*, edited by Campbell Campbell-Jack and Gavin McGrath, 224–226. Downers Grove, IL: InterVarsity Press, 2007.

———. "'Public Justice' as a Critical Political Norm." *Philosophia Reformata* 72 (2007): 130–150.

———. "Beyond Multiculturalism—But to Where? Public Justice and Cultural Diversity." *Philosophia Reformata* 73 (2008): 190–209.

———. "Civil Society and the State: A Neo-Calvinist Perspective." In *Christianity and Civil Society: Catholic and Neo-Calvinist Perspectives*, edited by Jeanne Heffernan Schindler, 67–96. Lanham, MD: Lexington Books, 2008.

———. "Legal Monism and Religious Pluralism: Rowam Williams on Religion, Loyalty and Law." *International Journal of Public Theology* 2 (2008): 418–442.

———. "God, Globalization and Grace: An Exercise in Public Theology." In *The Gospel and Globalization: Exploring the Religious Roots of a Globalized World*, edited by Michael W. Goheen and Erin G. Glanville, 49–68. Vancouver: Regent College Publishing/Geneva Society, 2009.

———. *Talking God: The Legitimacy of Religious Public Reasoning*. London: Theos, 2009.

———. "The Concept of 'Civil Society' and Christian Social Pluralism." In *The Kuyper Center Review*, vol. 1: *Politics, Religion, and Sphere Sovereignty*, edited by Gordon Graham, 14–33. Grand Rapids: Eerdmans, 2010.

Chaplin, Jonathan P., and Paul Marshall, eds. *Political Theory and Christian Vision: Essays in Memory of Bernard Zylstra*. Lanham, MD: University Press of America, 1994.

Chapman, John W. "Voluntary Associations and the Political Theory of Pluralism." In *Voluntary Associations*, edited by J. R. Pennock and J. W. Chapman, 87–118. New York: Atherton, 1969.

Charles, Rodger, and Duncan Maclaren. *The Social Teaching of Vatican II: Its Origin and Development*. Oxford: Plater; San Francisco: Ignatius, 1982.

Charlton, William, et al. *The Christian Response to Industrial Capitalism*. London: Sheed and Ward, 1986.

Charvet, John "The Principle of Equality as a Substantive Principle of Society." *Political Studies* 17 (1969): 1–13.

Cliteur, P. B. "Rechtsbeginselen. Tussen natuurrecht en rechtspositivisme." *Philosophia Reformata* 49 (1984): 57–70.

Clouser, Roy. "Reason and Belief in God." *Philosophia Reformata* 68 (2003): 36–68.

———. *The Myth of Religious Neutrality: An Essay on the Hidden Role of Religious Belief in Theories*. Rev. ed. Notre Dame: University of Notre Dame Press, 2005.

———. "The Transcendental Critique Revisited and Revised." *Philosophia Reformata* 24 (2009): 21–47.

Cohen, Jean L., and Andrew Arato. *Civil Society and Political Theory.* Cambridge, MA: MIT Press, 1992.

Coker, Frederick W. *Organismic Theories of the State.* New York: Columbia University Press, 1910.

Connolly, William. *Why I Am Not a Secularist.* Minneapolis: University of Minnesota Press, 1999.

Conradie, A. L. *The Neo-Calvinistic Concept of Philosophy: A Study in the Problem of Philosophic Communication.* Natal: Natal University Press, 1960.

Cooper, Justin. "David Mitrany's Functionalist World Order." In *Political Theory and Christian Vision,* edited by Jonathan P. Chaplin and Paul Marshall, 121–141. Lanham, MD: University Press of America, 1994.

———. "The State, Transnational Relations, and Justice: A Critical Assessment of Competing Paradigms of World Word." In *Sovereignty at the Crossroads,* edited by Luis E. Lugo, 3–27. Lanham, MD: Rowman and Littlefield, 1996.

Copleston, F. C. *Aquinas.* Harmondsworth, Middlesex: Penguin, 1955.

———. *A History of Philosophy.* 9 vols. Garden City, NY: Image Books, 1962.

Daalder, Hans. "The Netherlands: Opposition in a Segmented Society." In *Political Opposition and Western Democracies,* edited by Robert A. Dahl. New Haven: Yale University Press, 1966.

Daly, Herman E., and John B. Cobb. *For the Common Good.* Boston: Beacon Press, 1994.

De Gaay Fortman, W. F., et al., eds. *Philosophy and Christianity: Philosophical Essays Dedicated to Professor Dr. Herman Dooyeweerd.* Amsterdam: North Holland, 1965.

Dengerink, J. D. *Critisch-historisch onderzoek naar de sociologische ontwikkeling van het beginsel der "souvereiniteit in eigen kring" in de 19e en 20e eeuw.* Kampen: J. H. Kok, 1948.

———. "Enkele beschouwingen over het proces van het rechtsvorming." *Rechtsgeleerd Magazijn Themis* 5 (1959): 429–460.

———. "Structuur en persoon." *Philosophia Reformata* 51 (1986): 29–44.

———. *De zin van de werkelijkheid. Een wijsgerige benadering.* Amsterdam: Vrije Universiteit Uitgeverij, 1986.

———. "De staat in de plurale samenleving." *Philosophia Reformata* 56 (1991): 132–157.

———. "In het krachtveld van het scheppingswoord. Over de modaliteiten: haar fundamentele verscheidenheid, samenhang en eenheid." *Philosophia Reformata* 59 (1994): 137–157.

D'Entrèves, A. P. *Natural Law: An Historical Survey.* New York: Harper and Row, 1951.

——. *The Notion of the State: An Introduction to Political Theory.* Oxford: Clarendon, 1967.

De Ruiter, A. C. *De grenzen van de overheidstaak in de Antirevolutionaire staatsleer.* Kampen: J. H. Kok, 1961.

Donner, A. M. "Bijdrage tot de discussie over de staatstaak." In *Rechtsgeleerde opstellen door zijn leerlingen aangeboden aan Prof. Dr. H. Dooyeweerd t.g.v. zijn 25-jarig hoogleraarschap.* Kampen: J. H. Kok, 1951.

Du Plessis, Lourens M. "Function and Role of the State." In *The Challenge of Marxist and Neo-Marxist Ideologies for Christian Scholarship,* edited by John C. Vander Stelt, 149–186. Sioux Center, IA: Dordt College, Press, 1982.

Dyson, Kenneth. *The State Tradition in Western Europe: A Study of an Idea and an Institution.* Oxford: Martin Robertson, 1980.

Eberly, Don E., ed. *The Essential Civil Society Reader: Classic Essays in the American Civil Society Debate.* Lanham, MD: Rowan and Littlefield, 2000.

Echeverria, Eduardo J. "*Fides et Ratio:* The Catholic and the Calvinist: Prospects for Rapprochement." *Philosophia Reformata* 65 (2000): 72–104.

Ehrenberg, John. *Civil Society: The Critical History of an Idea.* New York: New York University Press, 1999.

Ehrlich, Stanislaw. *Pluralism: On and Off Course.* Oxford: Pergamon, 1982.

Ehrlich, Stanislaw, and Graham Wootton, eds. *Three Faces of Pluralism: Political, Ethnic and Religious.* Farnborough: Gower, 1980.

Elbow, Matthew. *French Corporative Theory, 1789–1948: A Chapter in the History of Ideas.* New York: Columbia University Press, 1953.

Emerson, Rupert. *State and Sovereignty in Modern Germany.* New Haven: Yale University Press, 1928.

Etzioni, Amitai. *The Moral Dimension: Toward a New Economics.* New York: Free Press, 1988.

——. *New Communitarian Thinking: Persons, Virtues, Institutions, and Communities.* Charlottesville: University of Virginia Press, 1995.

——, ed. *The Essential Communitarian Reader.* Lanham, MD: Rowman and Littlefield, 1998.

Evans, P. B., et al. *Bringing the State Back In.* Cambridge: Cambridge University Press, 1985.

Faber, S. "Dooyeweerd en de rechtsgeschiedenis." In *Herman Dooyeweerd 1894–1977. Breedte en actualiteit van zijn filosofie,* ed. H. G. Geertsema et al., 77–87. Kampen: J. H. Kok, 1994.

Figgis, J. N. *Churches in the Modern State.* London: Longmans, Green, 1913.

Finnis, John. *Natural Law and Natural Rights.* Oxford: Clarendon, 1980.

Fogarty, Michael. *Christian Democracy in Western Europe, 1820–1953.* Notre Dame: University of Notre Dame Press, 1957.

Freeman, D. H. *Recent Studies in Philosophy and Theology.* Philadelphia: Presbyterian and Reformed Publishing Co., 1962.

Friedrich, C. J. "The Deification of the State." *Review of Politics* 1 (1939): 18–30.

———. *Transcendent Justice: The Religious Dimension of Constitutionalism.* Durham, NC: Duke University Press, 1964.

———, ed. *The Public Interest.* New York: Atherton, 1966.

Friesen, J. Glenn. "The Mystical Dooyeweerd: The Relation of His Thought to Franz Von Baader." *Ars Disputandi* 3 (2003). www.arsdisputandi.org/publish/articles/000088/index.html/.

———. "Dooyeweerd, Spann and the Philosophy of Totality." *Philosophia Reformata* 70 (2005): 2–22.

Fullwinder, Robert K., ed. *Civil Society, Democracy, and Civic Renewal.* Lanham, MD: Rowan and Littlefield, 1999.

Galston, William. *The Practice of Liberal Pluralism.* New York: Cambridge University Press, 2005.

Gamwell, Franklin I. *Beyond Preference: Liberal Theories of Independent Association.* Chicago: University of Chicago Press, 1984.

Gardner, E. Clinton. *Justice and Christian Ethics.* Cambridge: Cambridge University Press, 1995.

Geertsema, H. G. "Transcendentale openheid. Over het zinkarakter van de werkelijkheid in de wijsbegeerte van H. Dooyeweerd." *Philosophia Reformata* 35 (1970): 25–56, 132–155.

———. *Het menselijk karakter van ons kennen.* Amsterdam: Buijten and Schipperheijn, 1992.

———. "The Inner Reformation of Philosophy and Science and the Dialogue of Christian Faith with a Secular Culture: A Critical Assessment of Dooyeweerd's Transcendental Critique of Theoretical Thought." In *Christian Philosophy at the Close of the Twentieth Century,* edited by Sander Griffioen and Bert M. Balk, 11–28. Kampen: J. H. Kok, 1995.

———. "Which Causality? Whose Explanation?" *Philosophia Reformata* 62 (2002): 173–185.

———. "Analytical and Reformational Philosophy: Critical Reflections Regarding R. van Woudenberg's Meditation on 'Aspects' and 'Functions.'" *Philosophia Reformata* 69 (2004): 53–76.

———. "Power and Conflict in Human Relations: Tentative Reflections from a Christian Perspective." In *Philosophy Put to Work: Contemporary Issues in*

Art, Society, Politics, Science and Religion, edited by H. G. Geertsema et al., 70–99. Amsterdam Christian Studies. Amsterdam: VU University Amsterdam, 2008.

Geertsema, H. G., et al., eds. *Herman Dooyeweerd 1894–1977. Breedte en actualiteit van zijn filosofie.* Kampen: J. H. Kok, 1994.

Gellner, Ernst. "The Importance of Being Modular." In *Civil Society: Theory, History, Comparison,* edited by John A. Hall, 32–55. Cambridge: Polity, 1995.

Gerth, H. H., and C. Wright Mills, eds. *From Max Weber: Essays in Sociology.* Translated by H. H. Gerth and C. Wright Mills. New York: Oxford University Press, 1946.

Giddens, Anthony. *Central Problems in Social Theory.* London: Macmillan, 1979.

Gierke, Otto von. "The Basic Concepts of State Law and the Most Recent State-Law Theories." In *The Genossenschaft-Theory of Otto Van Gierke,* abridged and translated by John D. Lewis, 158–185. Madison: University of Wisconsin, 1932.

———. "Introduction to Volume 1 of *Das Deutsche Genossenschaftsrecht* (Berlin, 1868)." In *The Genossenschaft-Theory of Otto van Gierke,* translated by John D. Lewis, 113–118. Madison: University of Wisconsin, 1932.

———. "The Nature of Human Associations." In *The Genossenschaft-Theory of Otto Van Gierke,* edited and translated by John D. Lewis, 139–157. Madison: University of Wisconsin, 1932.

———. *Natural Law and the Theory of Society, 1500–1800.* 2 vols. Translated by Ernest Barker. Cambridge: Cambridge University Press, 1934.

———. *The Development of Political Theory.* Translated by Bernard Freyd. London: George Allen and Unwin, 1939.

———. *Associations and Law: The Classical and Early Christian Stages.* Edited and translated by George Heiman. Toronto: University of Toronto Press, 1977.

———. *Political Theories of the Middle Age.* Translated by F. W. Maitland. Cambridge: Cambridge University Press, 1987.

———. *Community in Historical Perspective.* Edited by Anthony Black. Translated by Mary Fischer. Cambridge: Cambridge University Press, 1990.

Gilby, Thomas. *Between Community and Society: A Philosophy and Theology of the State.* London: Longmans, Green, 1953.

Gilson, Étienne. *The Christian Philosophy of Thomas Aquinas.* Translated by L. K. Shook. London: Victor Gollancz, 1957.

———. *Christian Philosophy: An Introduction.* Translated by Armond Maurer. Toronto: Pontifical Institute for Mediaeval Studies, 1993.

———, ed. *The Church Speaks to the Modern World: The Social Teachings of Leo XIII.* Garden City, NY: Doubleday, 1954.

Gladdish, Kenneth. *Governing from the Centre: Politics and Policy-Making in the Netherlands.* London: Hurst and Co.; The Hague: SDU, 1991.

Glas, Gerrit. "Ego, Self and the Body: An Assessment of Dooyeweerd's Philosophical Anthropology." In *Christian Philosophy at the Close of the Twentieth Century: Assessment and Perspective,* edited by Sander Griffioen and Bert M. Balk, 67–78. Kampen: J. H. Kok, 1995.

———. "Filosofische antropologie." In *Kennis en werkelijkheid. Tweede inleiding tot een christelijke filosofie,* edited by René van Woudenberg, 86–142. Amsterdam: Buijten and Schipperheijn, 1996.

———. "Persons and Their Lives: Reformational Philosophy on Man, Ethics and Beyond." *Philosophia Reformata* 71 (2006): 31–52.

Glendon, Mary Ann. *Rights Talk: The Impoverishment of Political Discourse.* New York: Free Press, 1991.

Glenn, Charles L. *The Ambiguous Embrace: Government and Faith-Based Schools and Social Agencies.* Princeton: Princeton University Press, 2000.

Goudzwaard, Bob. *Capitalism and Progress: A Diagnosis of Western Society.* Edited and translated by Josina Van Nuis Zylstra. Toronto: Wedge; Grand Rapids: Eerdmans, 1979.

———. *Globalization and the Kingdom of God.* Grand Rapids: Baker, 2001.

Goyder, George. *The Responsible Company.* Oxford: Blackwell, 1961.

———. *The Just Enterprise.* London: André Deutsch, 1987.

Grasso, Kenneth L. "Beyond Liberalism: Human Dignity, the Free Society and the Second Vatican Council." In *Catholicism, Liberalism, and Communitarianism,* edited by Kenneth L. Grasso et al., 29–58. Lanham, MD: Rowman and Littlefield, 1995.

Griffioen, Sander. *Facing the New Corporatism.* Toronto: Christian Labour Association of Canada, 1980.

———. "De betekenis van Dooyeweerds ontwikkelingsidee." *Philosophia Reformata* 51 (1986): 83–109.

———. "Dooyeweerds programma voor de sociale wetenschap." In *Herman Dooyeweerd 1894–1977. Breedte en actualiteit van zijn filosofie,* edited by H. G. Geertsema et al., 143–171. Kampen: J. H. Kok, 1994.

———. *Moed voor cultuur. Een actuele filosofie.* Amsterdam: Buijten and Schipperheijn, 2003.

———. "Secularisme en secularisatie." *Philosophia Reformata* 73 (2008): 71–84.

Griffioen, Sander, and Bert M. Balk, eds. *Christian Philosophy at the Close of the Twentieth Century: Assessment and Perspective.* Kampen: J. H. Kok, 1995.

Griffioen, Sander, and René van Woudenberg. "Theorie van sociale gemeenschappen." In *Kennis en werkelijkheid. Tweede inleiding tot een christelijke filosofie*, edited by René van Woudenberg, 236–266. Amsterdam: Buijten and Schipperheijn, 1996.

Griffioen, Sander, and Jan Verhoogt, eds. *Norm and Context in the Social Sciences*. Lanham, MD: University Press of America, 1990.

Groen, K. "Dooyeweerd over publiekrechtelijke bedrijfsorganisatie." In *Rechtsgeleerge opstellen door zijn leerlingen aangeboden aan Prof. Dr. H. Dooyeweerd t.g.v. zijn 25-jarig hoogleraarschap*, 73–99. Kampen: J. H. Kok, 1951.

Hall, John A., ed. *Civil Society: Theory, History, Comparison*. Cambridge: Polity, 1995.

Hallowell, John H. *The Decline of Liberalism as an Ideology: With Particular Reference to German Politico-Legal Thought*. London: Kegan Paul, Trench, and Trubner, 1946.

Hanley, David. *Christian Democracy in Europe: A Comparative Perspective*. New York: Pinter, 1994.

Hart, Hendrik. *Understanding Our World: An Integral Ontology*. Lanham, MD: University Press of America, 1984.

———. "Dooyeweerd's Gegenstand Theory of Theory." In *The Legacy of Herman Dooyeweerd: Reflections on Critical Philosophy in the Christian Tradition*, edited by C. T. McIntire, 143–166. Lanham, MD: University Press of America, 1985.

———. "Creation Order in Our Philosophical Tradition: Critique and Refinement." In *An Ethos of Compassion and the Intregrity of Creation*, edited by Brian J. Walsh et al., 67–96. Lanham, MD: University Press of America, 1995.

———. "Notes on Dooyeweerd, Reason, and Order." In *Contemporary Reflections on the Philosophy of Herman Dooyeweerd*, edited by D. F. M. Strauss and M. Botting, 125–146. Lewiston, NY: Edwin Mellen Press, 2000.

Hart, Hendrik, and Kai Nielson. *Search for Community within a Withering Tradition: Conversations between a Marxian Atheist and a Calvinian Christian*. Lanham, MD: University Press of America, 1990.

Hart, Hendrik, et al., eds. *Rationality in the Calvinian Tradition*. Lanham, MD: University Press of America, 1983.

Hegel, G. W. F. *Philosophy of Right*. Translated by T. M. Knox. London: Oxford University Press, 1967.

Heiman, George. "The Sources and Significance of Hegel's Corporate Doctrine." In *Hegel's Political Philosophy*, edited by Z. A. Pelczinski, 111–135. Cambridge: Cambridge University Press, 1971.

————. "Introduction." In Otto von Gierke, *Associations and Law: The Classical and Early Christian Stages,* edited and translated by F. W. Maitland, 3–68. Toronto: University of Toronto Press, 1977.

Herbert, David. *Religion and Civil Society: Rethinking Public Religion in the Contemporary World.* London: Ashgate, 2003.

Herder, J. G. *Reflections on the Philosophy of History of Mankind.* Abridged and translated by Frank E. Manuel. Chicago: University of Chicago Press, 1968.

————. *J. G. Herder on Social and Political Culture.* Edited and translated by F. M. Barnard. Cambridge: Cambridge University Press, 1969.

Heslam, Peter. *Creating a Christian Worldview: Abraham Kuyper's Lectures on Calvinism.* Grand Rapids: Eerdmans; Carlisle: Paternoster, 1998.

Hirst, Paul. *From Statism to Pluralism: Democracy, Civil Society and Global Politics.* London: UCL Press, 1991.

————. *Associative Democracy: New Forms of Economic and Social Governance.* Amherst: University of Massachusetts Press, 1994.

————, ed. *The Pluralist Theory of the State.* London: Routledge, 1989.

Hoeven, Johan van der. "Bij de tachtigste verjaardag van Prof. Dr. Herman Dooyeweerd." *Philosophia Reformata* 39 (1974): 97–101.

————. "In Memory of Herman Dooyeweerd: Meaning, Time and Law." *Philosophia Reformata* 43 (1978): 130–144.

————. "Wetten en feiten. De 'Wijsbegeerte der Wetsidee' temidden van hedendaagse bezinning op dit thema." In *Wetenschap, wijsheid, filsoferen,* edited by P. Blokhuis et al., 92–122. Assen: Van Gorcum, 1981.

————. "Dooyeweerd en de geschiedenis van de moderne wijsbegeerte." In *Herman Dooyeweerd 1894–1977. Breedte en actualiteit van zijn filosofie,* edited by H. G. Geertsema et al., 255–274. Kampen: J. H. Kok, 1994.

————. "Portrayal of Reformational Philosophy Seems Unfair." In *An Ethos of Compassion and the Integrity of Creation,* edited by Brian J. Walsh et al., 109–114. Lanham, MD: University Press of America, 1995.

Hollander, C. den. *Christian Political Options.* The Hague: AR-Partijstichting, 1979.

Hommes, H. J. van Eikema. *De elementaire grondbegrippen der rechtswetenschap.* Deventer: Kluwer, 1971.

————. "The Function of Law and the Role of Legal Principles." *Philosophia Reformata* 39 (1974): 77–81.

————. *De samengestelde grondbegrippen der rechtswetenschap.* Zwolle: Tjeenk Willink, 1976.

————. "The Limits of the Legal Competence of the State." *Philosophia Reformata* 41 (1976): 9–23.

———. "The Material Idea of the Law-State." *Philosophia Reformata* 43 (1978): 49–60.

———. *Major Trends in the History of Legal Philosophy*. Translated by P. Brouwer and J. Kraay. Amsterdam: North Holland, 1979.

———. *Inleiding tot de wijsbegeerte van Herman Dooyeweerd*. The Hague: Martinus Nijhoff, 1982.

———. "Moderne rechtsstaat en grondrechten." *Philosophia Reformata* 47 (1982): 97–120.

Honoré, A. M. "Social Justice." In *Essays in Legal Philosophy*, edited by R. S. Summers, 61–94. Oxford: Blackwell, 1970.

Hoogland, Jan. "De uitdrukkingskracht van de transcendentale denkkritiek." *Philosophia Reformata* 59 (1994): 114–136.

Hsiao, K. C. *Political Pluralism*. London: Kegan Paul, Trench, Trubner, 1927.

Huegelin, Thomas O. *Early Modern Concepts for a Late Modern World: Althusius on Community and Federalism*. Waterloo, ON: Wilfred Laurier University Press, 1999.

Jellema, Dirk. "The Philosophy of Vollenhoven and Dooyeweerd." Part II, "Dooyeweerd and Hartmann," *Calvin Forum* (May 1954): 192–194; Part III, "A New Synthesis-Philosophy," *Calvin Forum* (October 1954): 31–33.

———. "Kuyper's Attack on Liberalism." *Review of Politics* 19 (1957): 472–485.

Jenkins, Simon. *Accountable to None: The Tory Nationalization of Britain*. Harmondsworth: Penguin, 1995.

John Paul II. *Centesimus Annus (On the Hundredth Anniversary of Rerum Novarum)*. Boston: Pauline Books and Media, 1991.

———. *Fides et Ratio*. Chicago: Pauline Books and Media, 1998.

Jordan, Grant. "The Pluralism of Pluralism: An Anti-Theory?" *Political Studies* 38 (1990): 286–301.

Kaldor, Mary. *Global Civil Society: An Answer to War*. Cambridge: Polity, 2003.

Kalsbeek, L. *Contours of a Christian Philosophy: An Introduction to Herman Dooyeweerd's Thought*. Edited by Bernard Zylstra and Josina Zylstra. Toronto: Wedge, 1975.

Kalyvas, Stathis N. *The Rise of Christian Democracy in Europe*. Ithaca: Cornell University Press, 1996.

Kariel, Henry S. "Pluralism." In *International Encyclopedia of the Social Sciences*, 12 vols., edited by David L. Sills, 164-196. Macmillan and Free Press, 1968.

Keane, John. *Global Civil Society*. Cambridge: Cambridge University Press, 2003.

———, ed. *Civil Society and the State: New European Perspectives*. London: Verso, 1988.

Kelly, John. "The Influence of Aquinas' Natural Law Theory on the Principle of 'Corporatism' in the Thought of Leo XIII and Pius XI." In *Things Old and New: Catholic Social Teaching Revisited,* edited by Frank P. McHugh and Samuel M. Natale, 104–143. Lanham, MD: University Press of America, 1993.

Kennedy, E. W. "Herman Dooyeweerd on History: An Attempt to Understand Him." *Fides et Historia* (Fall 1973): 1–21.

Kersbergen, Kees van. *Social Capitalism: A Study of Christian Democracy and the Welfare State.* New York: Routledge, 1995.

Klapwijk, Jacob. "Pluralism of Norms and Values: On the Claim and the Reception of the Universal." *Philosophia Reformata* 59 (1994): 158–192.

———. *Purpose in the Living World: Creation and Emergent Evolution.* Translated and edited by Harry Cook. Cambridge: Cambridge University Press, 2008.

Klapwijk, Jacob, et al., eds. *Bringing into Captivity Every Thought: Capita Selecta in the History of Christian Evaluations of Non-Christian Philosophy.* Lanham, MD: University Press of America, 1991.

Klink, A., ed. *Publiek gerechtigheid. Een christen-democratische visie op de rol van de overheid in de samenleving.* Houten: Bohn Stafleu Van Loghum, 1990.

Knudsen, Robert D., "The Religious Foundation of Dooyeweerd's Transcendental Method." In *Contemporary Reflections on the Philosophy of Herman Dooyeweerd,* edited by D. F. M. Strauss and M. Botting, 272–285. Lewiston, NY: Edwin Mellen Press, 2000.

Koekkoek, A. K. *Bijdrage tot een christen-democratische staatsleer.* Deventer: Kluwer, 1982.

Kooi, Cornelis van der, and Jan de Bruijn, eds. *Kuyper Reconsidered: Aspects of His Life and Work.* Amsterdam: VU Uitgeverij, 1999.

Korner, Stephen. *Kant.* Harmondsworth: Penguin, 1955.

Koyzis, David T. "Towards a Christian-Democratic Pluralism: A Comparative Study of Neothomist and Neocalvinist Political Theories." Ph.D. dissertation, University of Notre Dame, 1986.

———. *Political Visions and Illusions: A Survey and Christian Critique of Contemporary Ideologies.* Downers Grove, IL: InterVarsity Press, 2003.

Kraay, John. "Successive Conceptions in the Development of the Christian Philosophy of Herman Dooyeweerd." *Philosophia Reformata* 44 (1979): 137–149; 45 (1980): 1–40.

Kraynak, Robert. *Christian Faith and Modern Democracy.* Notre Dame: University of Notre Dame Press, 2001.

Kroef, J. van der. "Abraham Kuyper and the Rise of Neo-Calvinism in the Netherlands." *Church History* 17 (1948): 316–344.

Kselman, Thomas, and Joseph A. Buttigieg, eds. *European Christian Democracy: Historical Legacies and Comparative Perspectives.* Notre Dame: University of Notre Dame Press, 2003.

Kuiper, Roel. "Human Identity and Reformational Social Philosophy." *Philosophia Reformata* 96 (2004): 14–37.

Kuipers, Ronald A. *Critical Faith: Toward a Renewed Understanding of Religious Life and Its Public Accountability.* Amsterdam: Rodopi, 2002.

Kuipers, Ronald A., and Janet Catherina Wesselius, eds. *Philosophy as Responsibility: A Celebration of Hendrik Hart's Contribution to the Discipline.* Lanham, MD: University Press of America, 2002.

Kuyper, Abraham. *Souvereiniteit in eigen kring. Rede ter inwijding van de Vrije Universiteit.* Amsterdam: J. H. Kruyt, 1880.

———. *Antirevolutionaire staatkunde.* 2 vols. Kampen: J. H. Kok, 1916.

———. *Architectonische critiek. Fragmenten uit de sociaal-politiek geschriften van Dr. A. Kuyper.* Edited by W. F. De Gaay Fortman. Amsterdam: H. J. Paris, 1956.

———. *Lectures on Calvinism.* Grand Rapids: Eerdmans, 1961.

———. *The Problem of Poverty.* Edited by James W. Skillen. Grand Rapids: Baker Book House, 1991.

Kuypers, K. "Herdenking van Herman Dooyeweerd." *Jaarboek van de Koninklijke Nedelandse Akademie van Wetenschappen* 3 (1977): 1–8.

Lamberts, Emiel, ed. *Christian Democracy in the European Union, 1945–1995.* Leuven: Leuven University Press, 1997.

Laszlo, Erwin. *Introduction to Systems Philosophy: Toward a New Paradigm for Contemporary Thought.* New York: Harper and Row, 1972.

Leendertz, A. C. *De grond van het overheidsgezag in de Antirevolutionaire staatsleer.* Amsterdam: J. H. de Busey, 1911.

Lewis, John D. *The Genossenschaft-Theory of Otto von Gierke: A Study in Political Thought.* Madison: University of Wisconsin, 1932.

Little, David. *Religion, Order, and Law.* New York: Harper and Row, 1969.

Lovejoy, Arthur O. "The Meaning of Romanticism for the Historian of Ideas." *Journal of the History of Ideas* 2 (1941): 257–278.

Lugo, Luis E., ed. *Religion and Pluralism in Public Life: Abraham Kuyper's Legacy for the Twenty-first Century.* Grand Rapids: Eerdmans, 2000.

Lukes, Steven. *Individualism.* Oxford: Blackwell, 1973.

MacIntyre, Alasdair. *First Principles, Final Ends, and Contemporary Philosophical Issues.* Milwaukee: Marquette University Press, 1990.

MacRae, Kenneth. "The Plural Society and the Western Political Tradition." *Canadian Journal of Political Science* 12 (1979): 675–688.

Maddox, Graham. *Religion and the Rise of Democracy.* London: Routledge, 1996.

Magid, H. M. *English Political Pluralism: The Problem of Freedom and Organization.* New York: Columbia University Press, 1941.

Mandelbaum, Maurice. "Societal Facts." In *Modes of Individualism and Collectivism,* edited by J. O'Neill, 221–234. London: Heinemann, 1973.

Mannheim, Karl. "The History of the Concept of the State as an Organism: A Sociological Analysis." In *K. Mannheim: Essays on Sociology and Social Psychology,* edited by P. Kecskemeti, 165–182. London: Routledge, 1953.

Maritain, Jacques. *Christianity and Democracy.* Translated by Doris C. Anson. New York: Charles Scribner's Sons, 1944.

———. *Man and the State.* Translated by Doris C. Anson. Chicago: University of Chicago Press, 1951.

———. *Integral Humanism: Temporal and Spiritual Problems of a New Christendom.* Translated by Joseph W. Evans. Notre Dame: University of Notre Dame Press, 1973.

Marshall, Paul. "Mathematics and Politics." *Philosophia Reformata* 45 (1979): 113–136.

———. *Human Rights Theories in Christian Perspective.* Toronto: Institute for Christian Studies, 1983.

———. "Dooyeweerd's Empirical Theory of Rights." In *The Legacy of Herman Dooyeweerd: Reflections on Critical Philosophy in the Christian Tradition,* edited by C. T. McIntire, 119–142. Lanham MD: University Press of America, 1985.

———. Review of N. Wolterstorff's *Until Justice and Peace Embrace. Philosophia Reformata* 50 (1985): 89–93.

———. "Justice and Rights: Ideology and Human Rights Theories." In *Norm and Context in the Social Sciences,* edited by Sander Griffioen and Jan Verhoogt, 129–158. Lanham, MD: University Press of America, 1990.

———. "Universal Human Rights and the Role of the State." In *Sovereignty at the Crossroads,* edited by Luis E. Lugo, 153–175. Lanham, MD: Rowman and Littlefield, 1996.

Marshall, Paul, and Robert E. Vandervennen, eds. *Social Science in Christian Perspective.* Lanham, MD: University Press of America, 1988.

Marshall, Paul, et al., eds. *Stained Glass: Worldviews and Social Science.* Lanham, MD: University Press of America, 1989.

Martindale, Don. *The Nature and Types of Sociological Theory.* Boston: Houghton Mifflin, 1960.

McHugh, Frank P., and Samuel M. Natale, eds. *Things Old and New: Catholic Social Teaching Revisited*. Lanham, MD: University Press of America, 1993.

McIntire, C. T. "Dooyeweerd's Philosophy of History." In *The Legacy of Herman Dooyeweerd: Reflections on Critical Philosophy in the Christian Tradition*, edited by C. T. McIntire, 81–117. Lanham, MD: University Press of America, 1985.

————. "Herman Dooyewerd in North America." In *Reformed Theology in America*, edited by David F. Wells, 172–185. Grand Rapids: Eerdmans, 1985.

————, ed. *The Legacy of Herman Dooyeweerd: Reflections on Critical Philosophy in the Christian Tradition*. Lanham, MD: University Press of America, 1985.

Mekkes, J. P. A. *Tijd der bezinning*. Amsterdam: Buijten and Schipperheijn, 1973.

Messner, Johannes. *Social Ethics: Natural Law in the Western World*. St. Louis: B. Herder, 1965.

Mill, J. S. "Representative Government." In *J. S. Mill, Three Essays*, 145–401. Oxford: Oxford University Press, 1975.

Monsma, Stephen V., and J. Christopher Soper. *The Challenge of Pluralism: Church and State in Five Democracies*. Lanham, MD: Rowman and Littlefield, 1997.

————, eds. *Equal Treatment of Religion in a Pluralistic Society*. Grand Rapids: Eerdmans, 1998.

Moody, J. N., ed. *Church and Society: Catholic Social and Political Thought and Movements, 1789–1950*. New York: Arts Inc., 1953.

Morrall, John B. *Political Thought in Medieval Times*. London: Hutchinson University Library, 1958.

Mouffe, Chantal. *The Democratic Paradox*. New York: Verso, 2000.

Mouw, Richard, and Sander Griffioen. *Pluralisms and Horizons: An Essay in Christian Public Philosophy*. Grand Rapids: Eerdmans, 1993.

Mueller, Frank H. *The Church and the Social Question*. Washington, DC: American Enterprise Institute, 1984.

Nell-Breuning, Oswald von. *The Reorganization of the Social Economy: The Social Encyclical Developed and Explained*. Translated by Bernard Dempsey. New York: Bruce Publishing, 1936.

————. "50 Jaar 'Quadragesimo Anno.'" *Christen Democratische Verkenningen* 12 (1981): 599–606.

Newman, Jeremiah. *Foundations of Justice: A Historico-Critical Study in Thomism*. Cork: Cork University Press, 1954.

Nicholls, David. *Three Varieties of Pluralism*. London: Macmillan, 1974.

————. *The Pluralist State*. London: Macmillan, 1975.

Niebuhr, Reinhold. *Moral Man and Immoral Society.* New York: Charles Scribner's Sons, 1960.

Niemeyer, Gerhard. "Public Interest and Private Utility." In *The Public Interest,* edited by C. J. Friedrich, 1–13. New York: Atherton, 1966.

Nisbet, Robert. *The Social Philosophers.* St. Albans: Paladin, 1976.

Novak, Michael. *Catholic Social Thought and Liberal Institutions: Freedom with Justice.* 2nd ed. New Brunswick, NJ: Transaction, 1989.

———. *Is There a Third Way?* London: IEA Health and Welfare Unit, 1998.

Nozick, Robert. *Anarchy, State and Utopia.* Oxford: Blackwell, 1974.

Oakeshott, Michael. *Experience and Its Modes.* Cambridge: Cambridge University Press, 1933.

O'Donovan, Oliver. "Augustine's City of God XIX and Western Political Thought." *Dionysius* 11 (December 1987): 89–110.

———. *The Desire of the Nations: Rediscovering the Roots of Political Theology.* Cambridge: Cambridge University Press, 1996.

Olthuis, James H. *Facts, Values and Ethics.* 2nd ed. Assen: Van Gorcum, 1968.

———. "Dooyeweerd on Religion and Faith." In *The Legacy of Herman Dooyeweerd: Reflections on Critical Philosophy in the Christian Tradition,* edited by C. T. McIntire, 21–40. Lanham, MD: University Press of America, 1985.

———. "Be(com)ing: Humankind as Gift and Call." *Philosophia Reformata* 56 (1993): 153–172.

———. "Of Webs and Whirlwinds: Me, Myself and I." In *Contemporary Reflections on the Philosophy of Herman Dooyeweerd,* edited by D. F. M. Strauss and M. Botting, 31–48. Lewiston, NY: Edwin Mellen Press, 2000.

O'Neill, John, ed. *Modes of Individualism and Collectivism.* London: Heinemann, 1973.

Ouwendorp, C. "Het probleem van het universele en individuele." *Philosophia Reformata* 59 (1994): 29–57.

Ouweneel, Willem J. "Supratemporality in the Transcendental Anthropology of Herman Dooyeweerd." *Philosophia Reformata* 58 (1993): 210–220.

Pateman, Carole. *Participation and Democratic Theory.* Cambridge: Cambridge University Press, 1970.

Pelczinski, Z. A., ed. *Hegel's Political Philosophy.* Cambridge: Cambridge University Press, 1971.

Pérez-Díaz, Víctor. "The Possibility of Civil Society: Traditions, Character and Challenges." In *Civil Society: Theory, History, Comparison,* edited by John A. Hall, 80–109. Cambridge: Polity, 1995.

———, ed. *Markets and Civil Society: The European Experience in Comparative Perspective.* European Civil Society. New York: Berghahn Books, 2009.

Pius XI. *Quadragesimo Anno* (1931). Reprinted in *Two Basic Social Encyclicals.* Washington, DC: Catholic University Press, 1943.

Plant, Raymond. *Politics, Theology and History.* Cambridge: Cambridge University Press, 2001.

Plantinga, Alvin, and Nicholas Wolterstorff, eds. *Faith and Rationality.* Notre Dame: University of Notre Dame Press, 1983.

———. "Faith and Reason: Philosophers Respond to Pope John Paul II's Encyclical Letter *Fides et Ratio.*" *Books and Culture* 5, no. 4 (1999): 32.

Polanyi, Michael. *Personal Knowledge: Towards a Post-Critical Philosophy.* London: Routledge, 1962.

Popma, K. J. *Venster op de wereld.* Kampen: J. H. Kok, 1968.

Puchinger, George. "Prof. Dr. Herman Dooyeweerd (1894–1977)." In *Herman Dooyeweerd 1894–1977. Breedte en actualiteit van zijn filosofie,* edited by H. G. Geertsema et al., 11–27. Kampen: J. H. Kok, 1994.

Reiss, Hans S. *The Political Thought of the German Romantics, 1793–1815.* Translated by H. S. Reiss and P. Brown. Oxford: Blackwell, 1955.

Riessen, Hendrik van. *The Society of the Future.* Philadelphia: Presbyterian and Reformed Publishing Co., 1952.

Ritter, Gerhard. "The Origins of the Modern State." In *The Development of the Modern State,* edited by Heinz Lubasz, 13–25. New York: Macmillan, 1964.

Roberts, Christopher C. *Creation and Covenant: The Significance of Sexual Difference in the Moral Theology of Marriage.* London: T. & T. Clark, 2007.

Rommen, Heinrich. *The State in Catholic Thought: A Treatise in Political Philosophy.* St. Louis: B. Herder, 1945.

———. *The Natural Law: A Study in Legal and Social History and Philosophy.* Rev. ed. Translated by T. R. Hanley. St. Louis: B. Herder, 1947.

Rosenblum, Nancy L., ed. *Obligations of Citizenship and Demands of Faith.* Princeton: Princeton University Press, 2000.

Rosenblum, Nancy L., and Robert C. Post, eds. *Civil Society and Government.* Princeton: Princeton University Press, 2002.

Rowe, William V. "Vollenhoven's and Dooyeweerd's Appropriation of Ancient Greek Philosophy." In *In the Phrygian Mode: Neo-Calvinism, Antiquity and the Lamentations of Reformed Philosophy,* edited by Robert Sweetman, 213–229. Lanham, MD: University Press of America, 2007.

Russell, Richard A. "Philosophy and Sociology." In *A Reader in Sociology: Christian Perspectives,* edited by C. P. De Santo et al., 253–282. Scottsdale: Herald Press, 1980.

Sartori, M. "Concept Misinformation in Comparative Politics." *American Political Science Review* 64 (1970): 1033–1053.

Sassen, F. L. R. "Dutch Philosophy." *Encyclopedia of Philosophy* 5 (1967): 441–442.

Schuurman, Egbert. *Technology and the Future.* Toronto: Wedge, 1980.

———. "The Technological Culture between the Times." In *Christian Philosophy at the Close of the Twentieth Century: Assessment and Perspective,* edited by Sander Griffioen and Bert M. Balk, 185–200. Kampen: J. H. Kok, 1995.

Second Vatican Council. *Gaudium et Spes: Pastoral Constitution on the Church in the Modern World* (1965). Reprinted in *Proclaiming Justice and Peace: Documents from John XXIII to John Paul II,* edited by Michael Walsh and Brian Davies, 77–140. London: Cafod/Collins: 1984.

Seerveld, Calvin G. "Modal Aesthetics: Preliminary Questions with an Opening Hypothesis." In *Hearing and Doing: Philosophical Essays Dedicated to H. Evan Runner,* edited by J. Kraay and A. Tol, 263–294. Toronto: Wedge, 1979.

———. "Dooyeweerd's Legacy for Aesthetics: Modal Law Theory." In *The Legacy of Herman Dooyeweerd: Reflections on Critical Philosophy in the Christian Tradition,* edited by C. T. McIntire, 41–79. Lanham, MD: University Press of America, 1985.

———. "Dooyeweerd's Idea of Historical Development: Christian Respect for Cultural Diversity." *Westminster Theological Journal* 58 (1996): 41–61.

Sen, Amartya. *Development as Freedom.* Oxford: Oxford University Press, 2001.

Simon, Yves. *Philosophy of Democratic Government.* Chicago: University of Chicago Press, 1951.

Skillen, James W. "The Development of Calvinistic Political Theory in the Netherlands, with Special Reference to the Thought of Herman Dooyeweerd." Ph.D. dissertation, Duke University, 1974.

———. "The Political Theory of Johannes Althusius." *Philosophia Reformata* 39 (1974): 171–190.

———. "Herman Dooyeweerd's Contribution to the Philosophy of the Social Sciences." *Journal of American Scientific Affiliation* 31 (1979): 20–24.

———. "Towards a Comprehensive Science of Politics." *Philosophia Reformata* 53 (1988): 33–58.

———. *Recharging the American Experiment: Principled Pluralism for Genuine Civic Community.* Grand Rapids: Baker, 1994.

———. "From Covenant of Grace to Equitable Public Pluralism: The Dutch Calvinist Contribution." *Calvin Theological Journal* 31 (1996): 67–96.

———. "Politics in One World." *Philosophia Reformata* 66 (2001): 117–131.

———. *With or Against the World? America's Role among the Nations.* Lanham, MD: Rowman and Littlefield, 2005.

Skillen, James W., and Stanley W. Carlson-Thies. "Religion and Political Development in Nineteenth-Century Holland." *Publius: The Journal of Federalism* 12 (Summer 1982): 43–64.

Skillen, James W., and Rockne M. McCarthy, eds. *Political Order and the Plural Structure of Society.* Atlanta, GA: Scholars Press, 1991.

Skinner, Quentin. *The Foundations of Modern Political Thought.* 2 vols. Cambridge: Cambridge University Press, 1978.

Smith, M. J. "Pluralism, Reformed Pluralism and Neo-Pluralism: The Role of Pressure Groups in Policy-Making." *Political Studies* 38 (1990): 307–322.

Soeterman, A. "Dooyeweerd als rechtsfilosoof." In *Herman Dooyeweerd 1894–1977. Breedte en actualiteit van zijn filosofie,* edited by H. G. Geertsema et al., 28–49. Kampen: J. H. Kok, 1994.

Spykman, Gordon J. "Sphere-Sovereignty in Calvin and the Calvinist Tradition." In *Exploring the Heritage of John Calvin,* edited by D. E. Holwerda, 163–208. Grand Rapids: Baker Book House, 1976.

Stackhouse, Max. "Christianity, Civil Society and the State: A Protestant Response." In *Civil Society and Government,* edited by Nancy L. and Robert C. Post, 254–264. Princeton: Princeton University Press, 2002.

———. *God and Globalization.* Vol. 4, *Globalization and Grace.* New York: Continuum, 2007.

Stackhouse, Max, with Peter J. Paris, eds. *God and Globalization.* Vol. 1, *Religion and the Powers of the Common Life.* Princeton: Trinity Press International, 2000.

Stafleu, M. D. "On the Character of Social Communities, the State and the Public Domain." *Philosophia Reformata* 69 (2004): 125–139.

———. "The Relation Frame of Keeping Company. Reply to Andrew Basden." *Philosophia Reformata* 70 (2005): 151–164.

———. "Philosophical Ethics and the So-Called Ethical Aspect." *Philosophia Reformata* 72 (2008): 151–164.

———. "Time and History in the Philosophy of the Cosmonomic Idea." *Philosophia Reformata* 73 (2008): 154–169.

Steenkamp, P. A. J. M. *De gedachte der bedrijfsorganisatie in protestants-christelijke kring.* Kampen: J. H. Kok, 1951.

Stoker, H. G. "Die kosmiese dimensie van gebeurtenisse." *Philosophia Reformata* 29 (1964): 1–67.

Stone, Julius. "Justice not Equality." In *Justice,* edited by Eugene Kamanka and Alice Ehr-Soon Tay, 97–115. London: Edward Arnold, 1979.

Storkey, Alan. *A Christian Social Perspective.* Leicester: Inter-Varsity Press, 1979.

Strauss, D. F. M. "The Central Religious Community of Mankind in the Philosophy of the Cosmonomic Idea." *Philosophia Reformata* 37 (1972): 58–67.

———. "Philosophy and Sociology." *Philosophia Reformata* 44 (1979): 150–182.

———. "Intellectual influences upon the Reformational Philosophy of Dooyeweerd." *Philosophia Reformata* 69 (2004): 151–181.

Strauss, D. F. M., and Michelle Botting, eds. *Contemporary Reflections on the Philosophy of Herman Dooyeweerd.* Lewiston, NY: Edwin Mellen Press, 2000.

Strauss, H. J. "Nie-staatlike owerheidstaak in beskawing-samenhang." *Philosophia Reformata* 30 (1965): 198–204.

Strauss, Leo. "What Is Political Philosophy?" In *What Is Political Philosophy? and Other Studies,* 9–55. Westport, CT: Greenwood Press, 1973.

Suttorp, L. C., et al., eds. *Groen's "Ongeloof en Revolutie."* Wageningen: Zomer and Keuning, 1949.

Sweetman, Robert, ed. *In the Phrygian Mode: Neo-Calvinism, Antiquity, and the Lamentations of Reformed Philosophy.* Lanham, MD: University Press of America, 2007.

Tam, Henry. *Communitarianism: An Agenda for Politics and Citizenship.* London: Macmillan, 1998.

Tawney, R. H. *Religion and the Rise of Capitalism.* Harmondsworth: Penguin, 1926.

Taylor, Charles. *Hegel.* Cambridge: Cambridge University Press, 1975.

———. *Sources of the Self: The Making of the Modern Identity.* Cambridge, MA: Harvard University Press, 1989.

———. "Invoking Civil Society." In *Philosophical Arguments,* 204–224. Cambridge, MA: Harvard University Press, 1995.

———. *Philosophical Arguments.* Cambridge, MA: Harvard University Press, 1995.

———. *A Secular Age.* Cambridge, MA: Harvard University Press, 2007.

Telderstichting, B. M. *De publiekrechtelijke bedrijfsorganisatie in Nederland.* The Hague: Martinus Nijhoff, 1958.

Ten Napel, Hans-Martien. "The Concept of a Multicultural Democracy: A Preliminary Christian-Philosophical Appraisal." *Philosophia Reformata* 71 (2006): 145–153.

Tierney, Brian. *Religion, Law, and the Growth of Constitutional Thought, 1150–1650.* Cambridge: Cambridge University Press, 1982.

Tillich, Paul. *Love, Power and Justice: Ontological Analyses and Ethical Applications.* New York: Oxford University Press, 1954.

Tocqueville, Alexis de. *Democracy in America*. 2 vols. Edited by Philips Bradley. Translated by Henry Reeve as revised by Francis Baven. New York: Random House, 1945.

Tönnies, Ferdinand. *Community and Society*. Translated by Charles P. Loomis. East Lansing: Michigan State University Press, 1957. Originally published as *Fundamental Concepts of Sociology (Gemeinschaft und Gesellschaft)*. New York: American Book Company, 1940.

Van Creveld, Martin. *The Rise and Decline of the State*. Cambridge: Cambridge University Press, 1999.

Van Dyke, Arie J. *Groen van Prinsterer's Lectures on Unbelief and Revolution*. Toronto: Wedge, 1989.

Van Dyke, Harry. "How Kuyper Became a Christian Democrat." *Calvin Theological Journal* 3 (1998): 420–433.

Van Dyke, Vernon. "Human Rights and the Rights of Groups." *American Journal of Political Science* 18 (1974): 725–741.

———. "Collective Entities and Moral Rights: Problems in Liberal Democratic Thought." *Journal of Politics* 44 (1982): 21–40.

Van Kley, Dale K. "Dooyeweerd as Historian." In *A Christian View of History*, edited by George M. Marsden and Frank C. Roberts, 139–179. Grand Rapids: Eerdmans, 1975.

Van Til, H. R. *The Calvinistic Concept of Culture*. Philadelphia: Presbyterian and Reformed Publishing Co., 1959.

Verburgh, Marcel E. *Herman Dooyeweerd. Leven en werk van een Nederlands christen-wijsgeer*. Baarn: Ten Have, 1989.

Verkeerk, M. J., and A. Zijlstra. "Philosophical Analysis of Industrial Organizations." *Philosophia Reformata* 68 (2003): 101–122.

Vidler, Alec R. *A Century of Social Catholicism, 1820–1920*. London: SPCK, 1964.

Vincent, Andrew. *Theories of the State*. Oxford: Blackwell, 1987.

Vlot, Ad. "Cultuur- en techniekfilosofie." In *Kennis en werkelijkheid. Tweede inleiding tot een christelijke filosofie*, edited by René van Woudenberg, 203–235. Amsterdam: Buijten and Schipperheijn, 2002.

Voegelin, Eric. *The New Science of Politics*. Chicago: University of Chicago Press, 1952.

Vunderink, Ralph W. "Ground Motifs—A Modest Revision." In *Contemporary Reflections on the Philosophy of Herman Dooyeweerd*, edited by D. F. M. Strauss and M. Botting, 157–177.

Vyver, Johan van der. "The Jurisprudential Legacy of Abraham Kuyper and Leo XIII." *Markets and Morality* 5, no. 1 (2002): 211–249.

Walzer, Michael. *Spheres of Justice*. New York: Basic Books, 1984.

Warren, Mark E. *Democracy and Association*. Princeton: Princeton University Press, 2001.

Wearne, Bruce. "Deism and the Absence of Christian Sociology." *Philosophia Reformata* 68 (2003): 14–35.

Weber, Max. "Religious Rejections of the World and Their Directions." In *From Max Weber: Essays in Sociology*, edited by H. G. Gerth and C. Wright Mills. New York: Oxford University Press, 1946.

Westra, G. J. "Confessional Political Parties in the Netherlands, 1813–1946." Ph.D. dissertation, University of Michigan, 1972.

Wetenschappelijk Instituut voor het CDA. *Publieke gerechtigheid. Een christen-democratische visie op de rol van de overheid in de samenleving*. Houten: Bohn Stafleu Van Loghum, 1990.

Willey, Thomas E. *Back to Kant: The Revival of Kantianism in German Social and Historical Thought*. Detroit: Wayne State University Press, 1978.

Windmuller, J. P. *Labour Relations in the Netherlands*. Ithaca: Cornell University Press, 1969.

Wintle, Michael. *Pillars of Piety: Religion in the Netherlands in the Nineteenth Century, 1813–1901*. Hull: Hull University Press, 1987.

Witte, John, Jr. "The Development of Dooyeweerd's Concept of Rights." In *Political Theory and Christian Vision: Essays in Memory of Bernard Zylstra*, edited by Jonathan P. Chaplin and Paul Marshall, 25–55. Lanham, MD: University Press of America, 1994.

——. *The Reformation of Rights: Law, Religion and Human Rights in Early Modern Calvinism*. Cambridge: Cambridge University Press, 2007.

Woldring, H. E. S. "Het struktuurbegrip in de sociologie van H. Dooyeweerd. Een systematische en kentheoretische uiteenzetting." M.Phil. thesis, Filosofisch Instituut, Vrije Universiteit, Amsterdam, 1971.

——. "Venster op de samenleving." In *Het leven beschouwd. Facetten van het werk van Prof. Dr. K. J. Popma*, edited by Paul Koning, 220–248. Kampen: J. H. Kok; Amsterdam: Buijten and Schipperheijn, 1974.

——. "Calvinisme en sociologie. Dooyeweerd en zijn school." In *Toen en thans. De sociale wetenschappen in de jaren dertig en nu*, edited by F. Bovenkerk et al., 157–167. Baan: Ambo, 1978.

——. "Kuyper's Formal and Comprehensive Conceptions of Democracy." In *Kuyper Reconsidered: Aspects of His Life and Work*, edited by Cornelis Van der Kooi and Jan de Bruijn, 206–227. Amsterdam: VU Uitgeverij, 1999.

Woldring, H. E. S., and D. Th. Kuiper. *Reformatorische maatschappijkritiek. Ontwikkelingen op het gebied van sociale filosofie en sociologie in de kring van het Nederlandse Protestantisme van de 19e eeuw tot heden*. Kampen: J. H. Kok, 1980.

Wolfe, Alan. *Whose Keeper?: Social Science and Moral Obligation*. Berkeley: University of California Press, 1989.

Wolfe, Christopher. "Subsidiarity: The 'Other' Ground of Limited Government." In *Catholicism, Liberalism, and Communitarianism*, edited by Kenneth L. Grasso et al., 81–96. Lanham, MD: Rowman and Littlefield, 1995.

——, ed. *The Family, Civil Society, and the State*. Lanham, MD: Rowman and Littlefield, 1998.

Wolin, Sheldon. *Politics and Vision*. Boston: Little, Brown, 1960.

Wolters, Albert M. *Creation Regained: Biblical Basics for a Reformational Worldview*. Grand Rapids: Eerdmans, 1985.

——. "The Intellectual Milieu of Herman Dooyeweerd." In *The Legacy of Herman Dooyeweerd: Reflections on Critical Philosophy in the Christian Tradition*, edited by C. T. McIntire, 1–19. Lanham, MD: University Press of America, 1985.

Wolterstorff, Nicholas. *Reason within the Bounds of Religion*. Grand Rapids: Eerdmans, 1976.

——. *Until Justice and Peace Embrace*. Grand Rapids: Eerdmans, 1983.

——. "Faith and Reason: Philosophers Respond to Pope John Paul II's Encyclical Letter *Fides et Ratio*." *Books and Culture* 5, no. 4 (1999): 29.

Woods, David S. "Reconceptualizing Economics: The Contributions of Karl Polanyi." In *Political Theory and Christian Vision: Essays in Memory of Bernard Zylstra*, edited by Jonathan P. Chaplin and Paul Marshall, 247–266. Lanham, MD: University Press of America, 1994.

Woudenberg, René van. *Gelovend denken. Inleiding tot een christelijke filosofie*. Amsterdam: Buijten and Schipperheijn; Kampen: J. H. Kok, 1992.

——. "Theorie van het kennen." In *Kennis en werkelijkheid. Tweede inleiding tot een christelijke filosofie*, edited by René van Woudenberg, 21–85. Amsterdam: Buijten and Schipperheijn, 1996.

——. "'Aspects' and 'Functions' of Individual Things." *Philosophia Reformata* 68 (2003): 1–13.

——, ed. *Kennis en wekelijkheid. Tweede inleiding tot een christelijke filosofie*. Amsterdam: Buijten and Schipperheijn, 1996.

Wright, Anthony. *G. D. H. Cole and Socialist Democracy*. Oxford: Clarendon, 1979.

Young, Iris Marion. *Justice and the Politics of Difference*. Princeton: Princeton University Press, 1990.

Young, William. "Herman Dooyeweerd." In *Creative Minds in Contemporary Theology*, edited by Phillip Hughes, 270–306. Grand Rapids: Eerdmans, 1966.

Zigterman, Kent. "Dooyeweerd's Theory of Individuality Structures as an Alternative to a Substance Position, Especially That of Aristotle." M.Phil. thesis, Institute for Christian Studies, 1977.

Zuidema, S. U. "Common Grace and Christian Action in Abraham Kuyper." In *Communication and Confrontation: A Philosophical Appraisal and Critique of Modern Society and Contemporary Thought,* edited by S. U. Zuidema, 52–105. Translated by Harry Van Dyke. Toronto: Wedge, 1972.

Zuidervaart, Lambert. "The Great Turning Point: Religion and Rationality in Dooyeweerd's Transcendental Critique." *Faith and Philosophy* 21 (2004): 65–89.

———. "Good Cities or Cities of the Good? Radical Augustinianism, Societal Structures, and Normative Critique." In *Radical Orthodoxy and the Reformed Tradition: Creation, Covenant and Participation,* edited by James K. A. Smith and James H. Olthuis, 135–150. Grand Rapids: Baker Academic, 2005.

Zwart, J. "De staatsleer van Herman Dooyeweerd." *Philosophia Reformata* 45 (1980): 109–139.

———. "Overpeinzing naar aanleiding van het werk van H. J. van Eikema Hommes." *Philosophia Reformata* 50 (1985): 1–8.

———. "Rechts- en staatsfilosofie." In *Kennis en werkelijkheid. Tweede inleiding tot een christelijke filosofie,* edited by René van Woudenberg, 293–309. Amsterdam: Buijten and Schipperheijn, 1996.

Zylstra, Bernard. *From Pluralism to Collectivism: The Development of Harold Laski's Political Thought.* Assen: Van Gorcum, 1968.

———. "Voegelin on Unbelief and Revolution." In *Een staatsman ter navolging,* edited by W. F. De Gaay Fortman et al., 155–165. The Hague: Antirevolutionary Party, 1976.

INDEX

essentialism, 34, 54, 71–72, 85, 98, 107–109, 354n.48

ethical aspect, 59, 62–63, 73–74, 77, 146, 183, 188, 216, 294, 319, 343n.49, 346n.8, 379n.6, 380n.10, 408n.18

Etzioni, Amitai, 8, 403n.26, 405n.45

events, category of, 52, 55, 57, 63–66, 75, 79, 96, 340n.1, 351n.14

evolution, 61, 81, 83, 98, 316, 354n.48, 359n.81

existents, 52, 56–57, 73, 79, 90, 96–98, 160, 314, 352n.21. *See also* individuality, structures of

faith (or pistical) aspect, 56–59, 62–63, 72, 77–78, 111, 122, 173, 183, 188, 247, 247–251, 342n.19, 386n.119, 395n.113

family, 65, 93–94, 102, 117–118, 194, 242–244, 365n.69, 381n.42, 403n.35

relation to societal structures, 68, 120–121, 130–131, 135, 239, 244, 256, 273–274, 276, 281–282, 288, 290, 345n.71, 363n.58, 365n.70

relation to state, 80, 82, 100, 146, 171, 218, 228, 241, 244–246, 274, 304, 383n.71, 401n.3

structural principle of, 67, 128, 242–244

fascism, 301

Ferguson, Adam, 9–10, 324n.19

Finnis, John, 56, 341n.3

founding function, 34, 66–67, 88–89, 118–119, 127–128, 243, 274, 302, 351n.16, 361n.28

freedom, human, 34, 62, 71, 75, 86, 92, 94, 101, 136, 242, 253, 392n.51, 405n.44

Christian contribution to, 6, 10, 23

civil-legal protection of, 160, 204–206, 256, 276–278, 280, 286, 298, 404n.41

in humanistic ground motive, 43, 84, 94, 101, 230, 255, 353n.40

of individual, 94, 129, 228, 277–278, 288, 300

Free University of Amsterdam, 20–21, 24–26, 28

Friesen, J. Glenn, 331n.22

functionalism. *See* absolutization, of modal aspects

functions, modal, 34, 57–58, 66–68, 87–91, 98–100, 158, 219–220, 231, 341n.2, 346n.8, 359n.81, 366n.75, 374n.37. *See also* modal aspects

genotypes. *See* structural principles

Geertsema, H. G., 78, 217, 338n.68, 341n.2, 406n.50

Goudzwaard, Bob, 270, 275, 347n.31, 396n.127, 397n.128, 397n.143, 400n.187, 401n.6, 407n.8

Green, David, 290–291

Griffioen, Sander, 83, 92–93, 347n.22, 352n.35, 375n.48, 361n.21, 375n.48, 396n.125, 405n.43

Groen van Prinsterer, Guillaume, 369n.99

ground motives, 31, 43–45, 77, 92, 123, 151–152, 279, 311–312, 338n.61, 362n.40, 400n.1

biblical. *See* biblical ground motive

Greek, 43, 151, 336n.19, 370n.118

humanistic, 44, 82, 85, 151, 156, 255, 304, 387n.132

scholastic, 43, 336n.20

Gurvitch, George, 15

phenomenology, 26–27, 51
Philosophia Reformata, 330n.16
philosophical anthropology, 101–104,
    312, 356n.58, 370n.109, 408n.18
philosophy, nature of 50–51, 311–312,
    373n.33, 374n.34
    Christian, 39–40, 333nn.2, 3, 4, 6, 12.
    See also Calvinist philosophy
pillarization of Dutch society, 236.
    See also consociational
    democracy
pistical aspect. *See* faith (or pistical)
    aspect
Pius XI, 12. *See also Quadragesimo
    Anno;* subsidiarity, principle of
plastic horizon of human experience,
    64
Plato, 5, 52, 54, 74, 76, 96–97, 157, 166,
    275, 339n.75, 353n.44, 353n.46
pluralism, 3, 7, 13–19, 20–24, 67,
    110–111, 206, 213, 251–54,
    305–308, 324n.24, 326n.32,
    327n.43, 396n.125
    Christian, 16, 321n.2, 327nn.42, 43,
    45
    corporatist, 15
    Dooyeweerd's view of "political
    pluralism," 328n.47
    Kuyperian, 139–144. *See also* sphere
    sovereignty, societal
    liberal, 14–15
    normative institutional, 16–19
    organicist, 15
    socialist, 15
political party, 146, 173, 213–14,
    249–50
political philosophy, 156, 161
Popma, K. J., 377n.99
positivism, 36, 159–161. *See also* legal
    positivism

process of disclosure. *See* opening
    process
Protestantism, 45, 141, 147, 151, 274,
    309, 295n.109. *See also*
    Calvinism; Reformation
Proudhon, Pierre Joseph, 15
public justice, 36–37, 98–100, 181,
    184–186, 214–218, 225–241, 250,
    265–267, 290–305, 330n.13,
    376n.67, 388n.14, 390n.47,
    393n.72, 404n.40
    as political harmonization, 219–225
    as political integration, 150, 181,
    199, 201–203, 22, 237, 240–241,
    288, 291–292, 294, 299–301
    and public interest, 136, 170, 178,
    189, 207, 209–211, 226–234,
    245–246, 257, 263–264, 297–298,
    390n.47, 405n.44. *See also* state,
    as *res publica*
public-legal organization of industry
    (PBO). *See* industry, state
    regulation of
public opinion, 214–215, 251, 302,
    389n.35

Quadragesimo Anno (Pius XI), 12, 259.
    See also subsidiarity, principle of
qualifying (and leading) function, 34,
    66, 88–89, 120, 180, 184, 186,
    200–203, 230, 269, 378n.106,
    389n.35

radical type. *See* structural principles
reductionism, 56, 61, 188, 238, 316,
    343n.43, 409n.28
rechtsstaat. See constitutional
    democracy
Reformation, 6–7, 45, 274. *See also*
    Calvinism; Protestantism

JONATHAN CHAPLIN is director of the Kirby Laing Institute for
Christian Ethics, Cambridge, England.